Tithing Under The Order Of Melchizedek
Published by:
The Order of Melchizedek Leadership University
2903 W. Sunrise Dr.
Laveen, AZ 85339

Cover Design by
Workinperkins Media

The Order of Melchizedek Series Vol I

TITHING
UNDER
THE ORDER OF
MELCHIZEDEK:

The Return Of The Lost Key

By

Dr. FRANCIS MYLES

Author's Hall of Appreciation

The Lord gave the word: **great was the company**
of those that published it. Psalm 68:11

It has been said that great projects are never the work of one man, but the collective effort of a team that shares a common destiny. I want to give a heartfelt God bless you to the following brothers and sisters for making the publishing of this book a reality. May God give you a tremendous harvest for every person who will be transformed by the truths contained in this book.

1. My dear wife Carmela Real Myles
2. Morris and Blanch Hershbeger, Harrisonville, MO
3. Larry Scott, Castries, St. Lucia
4. Dr Bruce Cook
5. Gracie and Ruben Guzman
6. Kenneth and Leilani Banks
7. Isabel Hernandez
8. Breakthrough City Kingdom Embassy Church Family

DEDICATION

This book is dedicated to :

- The Kingdom of God that is advancing into every sphere of human enterprise

- To Senior Pastors of Churches who are looking for a more excellent way of exacting the tithe from their faithful followers in order to advance the Kingdom of God

- To all the Josephs and Daniels, Lydias and Esthers in the Marketplace who have been looking for a more excellent way of tithing

- To the all the faithful who have supported the church for centuries through their tithes

- To all disfranchised tithers who have ever said, "Help, my tithing is not working for me!"

- To all those who have said that "Tithing is not for New Testament believers!"

- To the faithful members of my congregation, "Royal Priesthood Fellowship Church" who have chosen to sow their lives into the apostolic vision to transform nations that God has placed on my life.

ACKNOWLEDGEMENTS

What we become in God is a sum total of the divine encounters we have had, the people we have met, the experiences that we have had and the books we have read. The saying "No man is an Island" is certainly true in the context of the authoring of this wonderful book. I want to acknowledge the impact that the following men and women of God have had on my life: Dr. Jonathan David (my father in the faith), Apostle John Eckhardt, Dr. John P. Kelly (who commissioned me as an apostle), Bishop Robert Smith (Who taught me about the One New Man), Robert Ricciardelli, Kyle and Tari Newton, Danny Seay, Prophet Richard Eberiga, Prophet Kevin Leal, Pastor Frank Rosenstein, Dr. G.E. Bradshaw and Dr Bruce Cook (my covenant brothers), Dr. Paula Price, Apostles Trevor Banks, Pam Vinnett and Cheryl Fortson. Their teachings and personal conversations with me have added to the richness of this book

While much of the material in this book is original, I have included a few quotes that have been taken from the published works of other notable Christian authors. Wherever such quotes have been used, I have given complete credit for the quote to the original author by referencing the name of the author, the name of their book, the year it was published, the name of the publisher and the exact page number where the quote is found.

TABLE OF CONTENTS

ENDORSEMENTS

There are several attacks on the Church having to do with several issues such as structure, separation of Church and state but the most vehement argument of all has to do with the issue of tithing, whether to be or not to be. Dr. Francis Myles has written a truly inspirational, revelational, insightful, biblical expose' regarding tithing. This book is a must read for all who desire the blessing of God in their life.

> — Dr. John P. Kelly, *Presiding Apostle-International Coalition of Apostles, Founder & CEO-International Christian Wealth Builders Foundation.*

Tithing Under the Order of Melchizedek: The Return of the Lost Key, is a revelation from God and it addresses one of the most misunderstood subjects in the Bible, "tithing." In this powerful book, Dr. Francis Myles continues to lead God's people to righteous living by sharing God's wisdom concerning the Order of Melchizedek. I strongly recommend this book for everyone who calls upon the Lord.

> — Dr. Robert Watkins
> *Chairman & CEO*
> *Kings & Priests International*

One of the greatest writers of Biblical truth in the history of mankind, the apostle Paul, wrote these words in Hebrews 5:10-11 in reference to Jesus Christ: *"Called of God an high priest after the order of Melchizedek. Of whom we have many things to say, and hard to be uttered, seeing ye are dull of hearing."*

It is without a doubt, time for the evolutionary clock of ministry to yield the powerful truth behind these words. Paul had many things to say about this subject because there was so much unrevealed truth about this great pattern of potential. Paul wrote only enough to make us inquisitive about this subject, but it was the "dullness" of the people's hearing that made it impossible for him to reveal what he knew about this powerful revelation. A "time-lock" in the dimension of spiritual hearing has just been opened! The "time" has now come for the unfolding of this revelation. The "key" has just been returned to us. And, since every "key" contains within its identity a pattern that further unlocks something, we can expect a great treasury of information to now come to the Church.

"Every key is a pattern" and "Every pattern is a key!" ***Tithing Under the Order of Melchizedek: The Return of the Lost Key*** will now mean the return of so many lost empowerments and technologies of the priesthood of Christ. We need clarity and understanding of those things that God has created to work for us and project us into a state of grace that cannot be denied or defeated. We cannot move into the new levels of power that God has ordained for the Church without the knowledge of how to unlock these patterns and processes. The Church will now begin to initiate brand new levels of productivity because of the proper formatting which has been revealed by this tremendous book!

We need to understand our **priestly heritage! Doubtless, it will change our strategies of living for God in this present hour!** This book is especially vital to the Body of Christ from the perspective of how it removes the **"mysteries"** of **tithing** as it applies to the priesthood ministry of Melchizedek and the present day church. There are questions in the minds of so many people...**is tithing for us today? Is there a "curse" associated with the failure to tithe? What is the proper method of tithing? Who should leaders tithe to? How will giving tithes affect my life?** All of these questions and many others are addressed in this tremendous book. **The perspective that Dr. Myles has taken is balanced, healthy and productive!**

I highly recommend this book to every leader, member, entrepreneur and believer with a covenant mentality who wishes to see the past restrictions of historical religious teaching lifted and begin to view the stellar possibilities that exist through having accountable financial relationships that mirror the original pattern of God after the Order of Melchizedek. The Body of Christ will never be the same after this!...I will never be the same after this!

— Dr. G.E. Bradshaw, *Chief Apostle*
Outpour Assemblies Network
And Global Effect Ministries Network (**GEM®**)
Dolton, Illinois

The gospel of the kingdom is laced with innumerable contextual concepts of giving and receiving. Therefore, almost every subject area in the Bible somewhat has an element of this principle. However, the subject of tithing has always been an emotional vortex and confusion for many religious believers and sects. Some say tithing is for today, but others say it is not. There is such a vast dichotomy in arguments surrounding this subject, and much of this is due because of the mishandling of scripture. In Dr. Francis Myles' book, ***Tithing Under the Order of Melchizedek: The Return of the Lost Key,*** he has mastered this tremulous, yet simple, subject by ratifying all of the misconceptions and misinterpretations of Scripture regarding tithing. I highly recommend this book. So put your seatbelt on because you are going on a much-needed journey. Your mind is going to be renewed; your theology will come in alignment with truth; but most of all, your life will be changed. There will be many "Ah..ha" moments along the way. Just breathe...stay with it…you are going to make it!

> — Dr. Shirley Clark, *Chancellor*
> *Anointed For Business Leadership Institute*
> *CEO, Clark's Consultant Group*

As I started to read ***Tithing Under the Order of Melchizedek: The Return of the Lost Key***, I became increasingly agitated because for years I had been one who was painfully manipulated by the tithe exacters. In fact, I was so burned by their teaching that to this day, after 26 years in the Lord, the "Joy of Giving" has eluded me! As agitated as I was, I read on with the hope that Dr. Myles would help me reclaim, the joy I had known as a baby Christian. I was not disappointed! Thank you Lord and thank you Dr. Myles!

> — William Sawyer
> *Vice President for Joseph Chapters*
> *Kingdom Marketplace Coalition LLC*
> *Founder and CEO, Networking In Christ*

Once again, Dr. Francis Myles brings another critical revelation truth concerning the subject of tithing to the body of Christ. ***Tithing Under the Order of Melchizedek: The Return of the Lost Key*** is a standard-setting, Bible-based, practical revelation on the subject of tithing under the Order of Melchizedek. Whenever inspiration, illumination and revelation embrace each other, a timeless truth becomes activated on earth. Reading this book will activate dormant financial blessings in your life. This is the long-awaited book on tithing; it will travel across the nations of the world as a practical wealth-building manual for the Twenty-First Century church and beyond. The manifestation of wealth transfer that has been evasive to many will become attainable as a result of the ageless answers that are revealed within the pages of this book. Now, it is with great honor and pleasure that I recommend this book to every leader in all works of life. **This is really it!**

— Dr. Richard Eberiga
President, Fortress International
Author, Speaker

The world economies are shifting and if you have read the ***Tithing Under the Order of Melchizedek,*** you know that as a Kingdom Marketplace leader we do not operate in the world system. Do I hear an "Amen"? So how do we financially operate in the most excellent way and more importantly, how do we work through Abraham's decision to tithe to Melchizedek as presented to us in Genesis 14:20? This is the lost key and we need to get this one right so that in the days to come we know we are standing on rock, not sand. In his newest book, ***Tithing Under the Order of Melchizedek: The Return of the Lost Key***, Dr. Francis Myles helped me to get clarity on the issue of tithing which gave me a fresh revelation of the mightiness of our great God."

— Willam Collins
Kingdom Entrepreneur

Kingdom Citizens, who are rightly and fully connected and submitted to Spiritual Authority, usually receive an abundance of revelations from the King, as they continue to habitually and consistently exercise their senses. However, because of a lack of balancing the revelations with experiences, they end up frustrating those who desire to put the same revelations into practice. I am thankful for the perfect counsel of the King, and appointment of one of His choice sons, in the person of

Dr. Francis Myles, whom He has given a balance and a download to communicate in such a way, that others can benefit in a more excellent way of tithing, giving and sowing. If a true leader in the Kingdom does not get his hands on this revelation, he may gain experiences, but not according to revelation knowledge, thus creating confusion.

— Pastor Aaron D. Agnew Sr.
Global Impact Prayer and Word Ministries
Fayetteville, Arkansas

It is amazing to hear fresh revelation which moves and stirs the natural man and simultaneously shakes the church. I truly believe it is time for us to start living under the Abrahamic Covenant and start enjoying the Abrahamic promises! In this remarkable book by Dr. Francis Myles, ***Tithing Under the Order of Melchizedek: The Return of the Lost Key***, he exposes many fallacies in the handling of the tithe.

God is raising up marketplace ministries that are shaking the mindset of the traditional church. Dr. Myles teaches a radical message concerning a radical God who has designed His own plan to finance His Kingdom and provide for His kings.

I must agree that tithing begins in the house of God and with its leaders. We can never be 100% with God if we are not willing to stand at least 10% with Him. This book will cause you to think you have been locked in a dark room and each page open the shutters and reveals more light. As I read it, I found myself being moved, challenged, and provoked — debating, but also submitting. If you want to grow and excel in the things of God, this is a must read. You will need to chew and digest this a bit at a time, but when something comes from God you know it is worth it.

I highly recommend this book by Dr. Francis Myles. Your library will not be complete without it. After reading it, you will be standing on the precipice of breakthrough.

— Bishop Gabriel Abdelaziz
Alphabeth Ministries
The Revival Center
Paso Robles, California

As a believer, have you ever asked, "Lord, why do I see people prosper who do not live for you?" Or, "I do all that I know and understand to do but yet I don't see the financial blessing you promised in your Word." If you've ever asked these questions and more, this book is for you.

From his life-changing book, **The Order of Melchizedek,** Dr. Myles introduced the body of Christ to a new priestly order and touched briefly on the topic of tithing so it's exciting to see a book devoted to the subject in its entirety. He has been given a special place at the feet of God where the spirit of wisdom and revelation flows through him in uncommon dimensions. In **Tithing Under the Order of Melchizedek: The Return of the Lost Key**, he will challenge what you've always believed about tithing and demonstrate a "more excellent way" that will draw you closer to God than ever before, with a solid, biblical understanding that will set you free.

Few topics are as critical to your marriage as understanding tithing; you may well reach the conclusion that some of what you've always believed was in good faith, yet in error. There are so many key points in this writing that it's impossible to choose what's most impactful. Don't just read it; ask God to speak to your heart and reveal His heart to you where tithing in concerned. Are you cursed if you don't tithe to your Church? What is the real truth about tithing? Where is the model that we are to follow as believers? This book will answer these as well as many other questions and promises to set you free from the demonic influences that torment believers. Obedience is the key and this book re-confirms this point.

— Allen Blackston
President and Co-Founder
Victorious Marriage

For many in the body of Christ, we have had the revelation of "seedtime and harvest" concerning tithes, offerings and firstfruits, and how the Father supernaturally multiples our seed, geometrically.

In Dr. Myles' new book on **Tithing Under the Order of Melchizedek: The Return of the Lost Key**, he uncovers an ancient truth and the supernatural power that is released when we tithe as Abraham did.

When Melchizedek came to Abraham, he was moved in his heart to release the first recorded tithe in the Bible. Just as Abraham did, we can now tithe into the highest order, the Order Of Melchizedek, which Jesus himself reveals he is operating under, in heaven, and release not only the harvest in our lives, but the "spirit of interception" that will supernaturally keep the enemy from stealing or destroying your harvest!

No longer does the body of Christ have to lose their inheritance, and years of work for their harvest if we employ the strategies given in this new book.

I believe this understanding given to Dr. Myles, by revelation, is the key to the release of Kingdom finances and the wealth of the wicked being given to the righteous, so the full purposes of God can be released in the earth!

— Danny Seay
Kingdom Entrepreneur

I am honored to endorse **Tithing Under the Order of Melchizedek: The Return of the Lost Key**; this book is the third in the Order of Melchizedek series by Dr. Francis Myles. These books have all touched and changed my heart as only truth is empowered to do. There have been moments of changing the core of those areas which had remained untouched for many reasons, but I have come alive with the experience of allowing myself to be the daughter of my Heavenly Father. This truth may seem obvious to others; however, for decades I had become captive to the rigors of performance; the thirst for such remained unquenched by the very thing that drove me to it. The truth is that before I am anyone - woman, sister, aunt, marketplace minister, keynote speaker - I am the daughter of a very loving Heavenly Father. The acceptance of this amazing reality has changed everything in my life.

I encourage you to allow the Father to embrace you, – all of you – as He is your answer to every question. Expect the capacity of the truth of who you are to the Father, and His desire to show you His love and move on your behalf. Reach out for His hand, as His heart is unwavering with depths of knowledge and love, and He has much to show you!

— Teri Werner
Speaker, Author,
International Life and Business Coach

Dr. Francis Myles, in this important new book, exposes the "roots and origins" of tithing and shows us "a more excellent way" of tithing under the New Testament covenant. Dr. Myles navigates with grace and skill the potential minefields associated with this emotionally-charged and controversial subject. In doing so, he brings balance, clarity and revelation to a topic that has challenged and divided the body of Christ for millennia. In an area of Christian living where "every man does what is right is his own eyes" (Judges 17:6, 21:25), Dr. Myles has provided principles, examples and historical context from Scripture that are invaluable to the modern church and all who seek to follow after Christ. I recommend this book to both ecclesiastical and marketplace leaders as a practical and theological resource, tool and guide to share with their tribes and networks.

— Dr. Bruce Cook
President & Founder, The Kingdom KEYS
Vice President, Kingdom Marketplace Coalition LLC
President, Kingdom House Publishing
President, VentureAdvisers.com, Inc.
Convener, Kingdom Economic Yearly Summit
General Partner, Kingdom Venture Partners, LP
Distributor, SoZo
Director, Glory Realm Ministries

It is my prayer that every reader of this explosive book, will embrace the truth of its message and enter into a NEW WAY OF LIVING. Dr Myles has once again provided wisdom and insight from above to empower every believer who has decided to move forward in the Kingdom. It is my desire to HONOR DR MYLES as the MAN OF GOD he is with this endorsement. I encourage everyone to add Dr. Francis Myles to their required reading lists and help break the monotony of unfruitful living. To GOD be the GLORY!

— Jess Bielby, D.D.
President of Gospel Associates Inc., and
President of Kansas Food for Life
Benton, Kansas

FOREWORD

After seeing the dire need for the Lord's people to embrace truth regarding the tithe, giving and receiving, sowing and reaping, I had plans to write a book on the subject. This however, is no longer necessary. The Lord raised up Francis Myles, a more capable servant, whom He has given the inspiration, revelation, interpretation, application and communication to benefit the body of Christ.

These are the closing days of global financial meltdown, socialistic tendencies and spiritual anemia in the body of Christ. We therefore must, with the help of this apostolic word on "Tithing under The Order of Melchizedek," graduate from the milky letter of the law, to the meaty spirit of wisdom and revelation. I believe that this word takes the Church from the failing systems of theology to the divine revelation of Kingdom "theonomics" to inherit the full blessing of Abraham.

I recommend this writing to the entire Church throughout the world as an indispensible truth to help bring us to the measure of the stature of the fullness of Christ.

— Bishop Robert E. Smith, Sr.
Total Outreach for Christ Ministries, Inc.
Little Rock, Arkansas

Dr. Francis Myles does a masterful job of bringing the whole issue of tithing out of the Old Testament and into New Testament life. Most New Testament believers are still living Old Testament lives. So often this is the result not because of the activities of our life, but the understanding and spirit from which these activities flow. As you read **Tithing Under the Order of Melchizedek: The Return of the Lost Key** allow the Holy Spirit to empower you with fresh understanding for a release of faith through the realm of tithing. Understanding grants us access into new faith realms which in turn embraces new levels of God through our acts of obedience. This book will help you in your journey in the Lord.

— Apostle Robert Henderson
Freedom Apostolic Alliance,
Robert Henderson Ministries

This book is an absolute must read, especially for any leader or believer desiring to have an impact in taking the seven secular mountains of society for the King. After reading Dr. Francis Myles' books I am convinced that the revelation is so timely and relevant for today that it has the potential of unleashing the "giant within" believers and the church today, unleashing the greatest move of God the world has ever seen! Without the revelation of the order of Melchizedek and the lost keys, it is impossible to conquer the powers that are holding systems of mankind captive. With the keys that are revealed here the unlimited power, favor, holiness and glory of God will be released on you, your ministry and the marketplace in such a powerful way that it will propel you to take the top of those mountains for His glory! Once you read this book a light bulb will go off and suddenly you will realize how to breakthrough to influence entire spheres of culture, saving souls for the kingdom of God.

Leaders will receive revelation on how to properly understand and activate the tithe under the Order of Melchizedek that will bring incredible favor from heaven and fruitfulness in every way. This book answers many of the age-old mysteries not only about the new order but about every question concerning tithing. Once you realize the immense difference in tithing under the Order of Melchizedek as opposedto tithing according to the old Levitical order of Malachi 3:10, you will not only be challenged but your worldview of life and ministry will be altered forever. Your world is about to be totally rocked by reading this book as well as the entire series!

(WARNING: This book could cause sleeplessness if reading at night as it is very addictive and can cause sudden or unexpected transformations in your ministry, marketplace, body, mind and spirit.)

— David Herzog
Motivational Speaker, Author, TV Host, Life Coach,
Nutrition Coach,
President and Co-Founder of David Herzog Ministries
Co-Host of TV Show "The Glory Zone"
www.thegloryzone.org
Author of 'Glory Invasion'
CEO of SuperHealth
(www.supernaturalhealthnow.com
CEO of David Herzog Entertainment LLC
Founder of DHE Publishing
Sedona, Arizona

PREFACE

Why did I write this book?

I wrote this book first and foremost because after nineteen years of research, the Lord gave me the permission to write the revelation that He gave me to give to the body of Christ concerning the priestly Order of Melchizedek. I wrote this book to hopefully do my part in helping **upgrade the "technology of tithing" in the global church and challenge "inaccurate patterns of tithing" which have limited our spiritual inheritance in God's Kingdom economy.**

I wrote this book because there is a cry in the heart of God for His church to "rediscover the tithe of Abraham" and become divorced from the contemporary Malachi 3:8-12 pattern of tithing. However, I did not write this book to stop people in the global church from tithing, because there is a *High Priest after the Order of Melchizedek, even our Lord Jesus Christ, who receives the endowment of tithe from His blood-washed people, who live under the New Testament.*

I wrote this book to reveal "a more excellent way of giving or exacting the tithe" –indeed, a more excellent way that will reveal the mightiness of our God and restore the "Joy of tithing" to multiplied millions in the global Church. When less than thirty percent of members of the body of Christ tithe consistently, we have to admit that something is terribly wrong with our popular methods of exacting the "tithe" from God's people. We cannot simply relegate the remaining seventy to eighty percent of inconsistent or non-tithers to simply being a group of disobedient Christians, without simultaneously questioning the spiritual technology we are employing in our Churches for exacting the tithe.

> **"To be free is not merely to cast off one's chains, but to live in a way that respects and enhances the freedom of others."**
>
> **— Nelson Mandela,**
> **former President of South Africa**

I wrote this book because I wanted to share the freedom and exceeding joy that tithing according to the pattern revealed in this book has brought to my own life and to the life of our Church. True freedom is not a gift that you can hold to yourself, because its "greatest power and expression" is found in sharing it with others. The sharing of the truths contained in this writing, has helped increase the tithing percentages of our Church as some of our non-tithing people and those who tithed inconsistently, discovered the "joy and privilege" of tithing into God's Kingdom. *All technologies, whether they are natural or spiritual, must first be tested at their point of origin, to make sure that they are both credible and functional.* I want you to know that the spiritual technology for a "New Way of Tithing in the Global Church" which is described in this book, is credible, functional and above all biblical.

I also wrote this book to give answers to the following people…

- Anybody who has ever said, **"help; my tithe is not working for me!"**

- Anybody who has ever asked the question, **"how can I tithe from an inspired heart instead of tithing from a regulated heart?"**

- Anybody who uses the **"Malachi 3:8-12 pattern of tithing!"**

- Anybody who has ever desired to know how Abraham, Isaac and Jacob **"tithed and why they tithed!"**

- Anybody who has ever asked the question, **"Is tithing for today?"**

- Anybody who has **"lost the Joy of tithing!"**

- Spiritual leaders who are looking for a manual to help them establish **"a more excellent way of tithing"** in their churches.

I also wrote this book to bring apostolic clarity to the following subjects as they relate to the priestly Order of Melchizedek:

- The priestly order of Melchizedek and why Abraham tithed into it

- The differences between the priestly Order of Aaron and the priestly order of Melchizedek

- The Power of the tithe of Abraham

- Abraham's natural and spiritual inheritance

- The spiritual benefits of the priestly Order of Melchizedek

- A more excellent way of tithing and a new way of living

- Why Malachi 3:8-12 pattern of tithing is not God's best for New Testament believers

- Why Jesus Christ is the High Priest after the Order of Melchizedek

- The prophetic future of the nation of Israel and its connection to the priestly Order of Melchizedek

- Why Satan is terrified of God's people coming under the priestly Order of Melchizedek

I know that there might be some of you who may get angry at me for attempting to divorce the global Church from the "popular Malachi 3:8-12 pattern of tithing!" I assure you that I know exactly how you feel, because there was a time I would have defended the Malachi 3:8-12 pattern of tithing with my very life; **but God has ways of "cornering us and reconfiguring our internal spirit dynamics."** I am asking that whether it's out of your own curiosity or out of the maturity of your patience, to simply allow me "my day" in the "courtroom of your mind." I know that this teaching may challenge some of your long-held views about tithing, whether you believe in tithing or not. If, after reading this book, you still do not see the validity of my arguments, then you are free to dismiss my thoughts, as the thoughts of a misinformed or misguided man. But I am beseeching you by the sure mercies of God to give this book a fair and reasonable "entrance into the courtroom of your mind." It's my heartfelt prayer that this writing will "Upgrade and shift the technology" of your understanding and practice of tithing and introduce you to a more excellent way of Kingdom living.

God's Servant
Dr. Francis Myles

CAST OF CHARACTERS

Adam

He is the first man, who was created in the image and likeness of God. He is the father of the first humans. When he disobeyed God and ate of the forbidden fruit he introduced sin and death into the human bloodline and genome.

Abraham

Abraham is the son of Terah of the land of the Chaldeans who received and obeyed the call of God to go to the land of Canaan (Present day Palestine). God made a covenant with him and gave him prophetic promises concerning his natural and spiritual descendants. He is the father of all those who walk and live by faith just like he did.

Lot

Lot was the son of Haran, Abraham's young brother who died prematurely. Abraham adopted Lot after the death of his young brother and took him with him to the Land of Promise. Lot later relocated himself away from the common habitat that he and Abraham had previously shared. He started living in the region of Sodom were he later became one of the elders of this wicked City.

Pharaoh

Pharaoh is the king of Egypt who gave Abraham a lot of material possessions in exchange for desired and expected sexual escapades with Sarah, Abraham's wife. God visited Pharaoh in a dream and rebuked him for taking Sarah, Abraham's wife. Among the possessions the king of Egypt gave to Abraham was a young Egyptian maid called Hagar, who later became the mother of Abraham's Ishmael.

Melchizedek

Melchizedek was the king of Salem and Priest of God Most high who intercepted Abraham in the valley of Chavez when he was returning from the slaughter of the Babylonian kings. Abraham was so captivated by the majestic glory and spiritual stature of this High Priest that he gave him his first tithe. Melchizedek accepted the **"tithe"** and blessed Abraham, establishing Himself as being more superior to Abraham in spiritual stature.

The King of Sodom

The king of Sodom was the principal ruler over the wicked nation called Sodom, which practiced homosexuality and every form of sexual perversion imaginable. The king of Sodom tried to buy a spiritual and political alliance with Abraham when he returned from the slaughter of the kings. Abraham refused to accept his *"demonic bribery"* and declared that he had already lifted his hands to God Most High when he gave his tithe to Melchizedek.

Isaac

Isaac was Abraham and Sarah's son of their old age who was born by divine promise. Later on, God tested Abraham by asking him to offer Isaac as a burnt offering. The offering of Isaac was a prophetic foreshadowing of the sacrificial death of our Lord Jesus Christ as the Lamb of God who takes away the sin of the world.

Abimelech

Abimelech was the king of Gerar who was almost killed by God for trying to seduce Rebekah, Isaac's wife. He later became a very reliable ally of Isaac.

Jacob

Jacob is the second-born son of Isaac and twin brother to Esau. Jacob stole Esau's birthright blessing and then escaped to Syria after he discovered that his brother wanted to kill him. On his way to Syria he camped at Bethel for the night where he met with God. It was Jacob who first introduced the concept of tithing to the house of God (local church). His grandfather Abraham introduced the concept of tithing to a man (priest), or spiritual covering.

Moses

Moses was born from the tribe of Levi at a time when Pharaoh was killing all newborn baby boys. His mother hid him in a papyrus basket, coated it with tar and pitch and placed the basket in the Nile River where Pharaoh's daughter later discovered him. Pharaoh's daughter took him and adopted him. Moses later became the spiritual father of the priestly order of Aaron, which was instituted at Mount Sinai in Arabia.

Aaron

Aaron was Moses' elder brother who served as his chief spokesman in official matters. Later on, the Lord told Moses to anoint Aaron as the first High Priest of the nation of Israel. Aaron became the first High Priest of the Levitical priesthood, which was formed after the law was *"added"* because of the transgression. He was commanded by God to collect a tithe according to the law from the rest of his brethren.

Jesus of Nazareth

Jesus of Nazareth is Mary and Joseph's son, who was conceived through the virgin birth. He was God incarnate (in human flesh), and lived among men for thirty-three and half years, and then died on the cross to pay for the sins of the whole world. He is the High Priest after the Order of Melchizedek. His eternal priesthood is administered from the heavenly sanctuary, which was not made with human hands.

Paul of Tarsus

Paul of Tarsus is the zealous Pharisee who persecuted all those who abandoned Judaism to follow the ways of Christ. He was saved by a supernatural encounter with Christ when he was knocked off his horse on his way to Damascus to persecute Christians. After his name was changed from Saul to Paul, he later wrote over half of the New Testament. Much of what has been revealed about the priestly Order of Melchizedek was revealed to and through this great apostle· of the faith.

IS TITHING FOR TODAY?

*O*ne *of the most frequently-asked questions in Christendom is a question that is related to the practice of tithing in the global Church. The question frequently asked is: "Is tithing for today?"* This seemingly innocent question arouses some of the most passionate debates among the saints, pitting those in favor of the biblical practice of tithing against those who believe that "tithing" is Modern-day extortion of gullible saints by Modern-day Pharisees. These heartfelt debates over the practice of tithing have only increased with the increase in the economic decline of many nations. These "tithing debates" in the blogosphere have also been fueled to the point of explosion by the "unrestrained and extravagant lifestyles" of many of the notable proponents of the "gospel of prosperity."

I am the senior pastor of a thriving Church in Texas (www.breakthroughcity.com), CEO of Kingdom Marketplace Coalition LLC (www.mykmcportal.com) and I am also an itinerant minister of the gospel and a serial author. My unique position in the Kingdom of God has given me a "vantage point" to preside over the question, "Is tithing for today?" I have looked into the eyes of many well-meaning Christians (Kingdom citizens is a better description) who told me how their life and personal economy changed for the better when they started tithing. I have also looked into the eyes of very sincere, God-loving children of God who have told me, "Francis, my tithe is not working for me. I have been tithing for years but the windows of heaven I was promised never opened for me." I have also looked into the eyes of those who have told me to my face that they do not believe that tithing is applicable to post-Calvary New Testament believers.

Then there are those who believe that only they are best qualified to administer their own tithes, either because they are part of a home church fellowship where there is no formal tithing structure in place, or because they have lost confidence in the stewardship mechanism or leadership of their local church. At this point, my only caution to this group of disillusioned or disenfranchised saints is that there is no Biblical precedent for tithing into oneself. Tithing from its roots and origins, when Melchizedek the King-Priest intercepted Abraham, is always connected to a legitimate and God-designated priesthood. In Abraham's case, the tithes left his hands and were given into the Order of Melchizedek. The tithes from the spoils that Abram had taken from the four kings who raided Sodom did not end up in one of his private bank accounts. I will speak more about this in Chapter Seven of this book.

A Downward Trend

Whatever side of the tithing debate you find yourself on, what is becoming increasingly clear is that there is an *unmistakable downward trend regarding the biblical practice of tithing in the global Church, and that there is great division, confusion, ignorance and controversy surrounding this important subject.* Many congregations in the global Church are reporting the lowest levels of tithing in their congregations than probably at any other time in their Church history. This serious decline in tithing is far worse in the United States and other developed nations than in most third world nations, at least on a per capita basis. What is interesting is that this global downward trend in tithing is happening at a time when there has been such a "mass proliferation" of the "prosperity message" via Christian television networks. Many pastors of small-sized churches are having to take on secular employment to help supplement their income and support their families, and some of the spouses of these pastors are also having to find secular employment in order to survive financially.

THE TITHES FROM THE SPOILS THAT ABRAM HAD TAKEN FROM THE FOUR KINGS WHO RAIDED SODOM DID NOT END UP IN ONE OF HIS PRIVATE BANK ACCOUNTS

Why the Downward Trend?

I have lived long enough to know that there is always a reason to the madness. God created us and placed us in a universe of "cause and effect." There are many causes and underlying reasons that are masked in the downward trend in tithing in the global church and we will do well to understand them. Some of the "causes" behind the decline in tithing come in the form of questions on tithing that the Church has failed to answer adequately. Some of the causes of this decline in tithing come in the form of "inaccurate doctrines on tithing" that are spreading like wildfire on the Internet and blogosphere; these have some elements of truth in them but are not based upon the *"full counsel of God"* concerning the practice of tithing in the New Testament.

By far, the biggest culprit behind the serious decline in tithing in the global Church is the "tarnished testimony and unrestrained extravagant lifestyles" of many of the notable prosperity preachers of our time. I want to go on record as saying that I believe that there is a place of true biblical prosperity that God has for His people. I believe that God desires to bless His children with both financial and material resources to advance His kingdom here on earth. Notwithstanding, I also believe that believers who come into a place of *"financial and material prosperity"* but fail to understand *"divine restraint"* are a curse to themselves and they can also bring great injury and harm to the cause of Christ. Poverty and Prosperity are two different extremes of the human condition but Jesus spent a lot of his time on earth, as recorded in the Gospels, talking about Stewardship since God is always most interested in the motives and condition of our heart. According to Scripture, the primary purpose of prosperity is not for ourselves, but for others, and for His Kingdom.

Enter the Blogosphere

The advent of the Internet, coupled with the incredible power of massive search engines such as Google and Yahoo, has accelerated the mass proliferation of "information" in today's world. While we celebrate the ability to move and amass massive blocks of information in seconds with the mere click of a mouse, this newfound freedom has also come with a serious downside. The downside to amassing and accessing massive blocks of information lies in the fact that information can be very beneficial or toxic. *The blogosphere is full of both good and spiritually toxic information, especially on the subject of tithing.*

The advent of the Internet also means that pastors can no longer think that they are the only ones who are influencing their people's attitudes towards the biblical practice of tithing. Whether pastors like it or not, many of the people in our churches are going to the Internet and "Googling" for a second opinion on much of what is being taught in the church. I have found that this is especially true when it comes to dealing with the Church's teaching on tithing. Tithing affects the wallets and purses of the people in our congregations, and assuming that some of our people are not "Googling" for a second opinion on such an important subject is a lesson in naivete on our part.

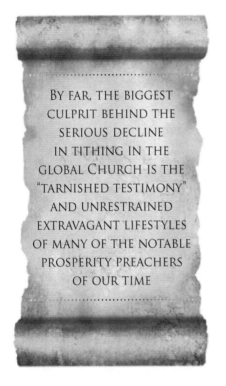

BY FAR, THE BIGGEST CULPRIT BEHIND THE SERIOUS DECLINE IN TITHING IN THE GLOBAL CHURCH IS THE "TARNISHED TESTIMONY" AND UNRESTRAINED EXTRAVAGANT LIFESTYLES OF MANY OF THE NOTABLE PROSPERITY PREACHERS OF OUR TIME

When the Lord told me to write this book, He directed me first to the Bible, and then to the Internet. The Lord challenged me to "Google" the word "Tithing" just to get a feel of what was being discussed on the blogosphere concerning this critical subject. What I discovered was both enlightening and disheartening. Some of the concerns some people on the blogosphere have on the practice of tithing in the global Church are based upon very legitimate concerns that we cannot dismiss lightly.

Some of the people who expressed their opinion on tithing on the blogosphere were outright hostile and many of them had very strong opinions against prosperity preachers. Some of the people in the blogosphere provided half-baked teachings on why they believe that tithing is an unscriptural act under the New Testament. ***Some went as far as calling tithing under the New Testament a sin.*** I quickly concluded that the blogosphere on tithing that I was on was patronized by three classes of Christians. This particular blogosphere was patronized by ***"self-appointed teachers, seekers and rebels."*** I was particularly drawn to many of the sincere seekers on the blog. Most of them were simply looking for a "more excellent way" of approaching the question and practice of tithing.

Questions and Teachings on Tithing from the Blogosphere

While I was making my divinely-orchestrated visit to the blogosphere, I was touched by a couple of the questions that were posed by some of the self-appointed teachers, seekers and rebels on the blog. I was touched by many of these questions because they unmasked many of the sentiments about tithing that are held by many of the people who patronize our churches. These questions gave me much-needed insight as to why there has been such a serious decline in tithing in the global church. I will list here some of the questions and teachings on tithing that came from the blogosphere that underscore the importance of a book on tithing such as the one you are reading now.

We will deal now with some of the questions on tithing from the blogosphere.

- Why is there no mention of tithing in Abraham's life before Genesis 14?

- Why do Church leaders use Malachi chapter three to scare believers into tithing, when it is obvious that Malachi was talking to believers who lived under the Law?

- Why do Church leaders tell us that we are cursed if we do not tithe, when the book of Galatians tells us that Christ became a Curse for us when He hung on the cross?

- Why do prosperity teachers tell us to give a tithe of our money when Abraham only gave Melchizedek a tithe of other people's stuff?

- Abraham's tithe to Melchizedek was a once-only event, so why do pastors make their church members tithe from their weekly income?

- Why do prosperity preachers (or pastors) insist that we give God his 10%, when under the New Testament God owns the entire 100%?

- Why do some prosperity teachers use Jacob's reference to tithing in Genesis 28:11-17 to endorse tithing under the New Testament, when it is clear that Jacob was bargaining with God, and bargaining with God is a sin?

So let us take a quick look now at two of the misleading teachings on tithing from the blogosphere under the titles, "Which one was justified? Tithes are 'Corban."

Which one was Justified?

Jesus taught us about two men, one of whom tithed and one of whom did not.

> *"Two men went up into the Temple to pray, one a Pharisee, and the other a tax-gatherer. The Pharisee stood, and was praying thus to himself, 'God I thank Thee that I am not like other people: swindlers, unjust, adulterers, or even like this tax gatherer. I fast twice a week; I pay tithes of all I get.' But the tax-gatherer, standing some distance away, was beating his breast, saying, 'God, be merciful to me, the sinner!' I tell you, this man went down to his house justified rather than the other; for everyone who exalts himself shall be humbled, but he who humbles himself shall be exalted."*

Luke 18:10-14

Which one was justified before God, the tither or the non-tither? (Author unkown)

In the above quote, the author of the same is attempting to use the passage of Scripture from the eighteenth chapter of the book of Luke to lead his readers in the blogosphere into believing that Jesus was using the story in this passage to demonstrate that God justifies non-tithers rather than tithers under the New Testament. Nothing could be further from the truth, but I have to give the author an *"A"* plus for having a very over- reaching imagination. To the contrary, Luke 18:10-14 is a lesson on the importance of humility and the dangers of self righteousness. The tax gatherer in the story was justified by God, not because he did not pay tithes, but because he sincerely humbled himself before God. *This passage of Scripture is a lesson on the power of humility before God and was never intended to marginalize or undermine tithing.*

Tithes are 'Corban'

> *"He was also saying to them, "You nicely set aside the commandment of God in order to keep your tradition. For Moses said, 'Honor your father and your mother'; and, 'He who speaks evil of father or mother, let him be put to death'; but you say, 'If a man says to his father, anything of mine you might have been helped by is Corban (that is to say, given to God), 'you no longer permit him to do anything for his father or his mother; thus invalidating the word of God by your tradition which you have handed down; and you do many such things as that."*

Mark 7:9-13

"If you have money your family needs, but you withhold it from them in order to pay it to the church as 'tithes,' you are doing exactly what the Pharisees did. You are saying that your money is 'Corban' and Jesus taught that by doing so you were invalidating the Word of God." **(Author unknown)**

In the above quote our unknown author from the blogosphere is now attempting to show his readers that giving tithes to the Church while our family needs money is doing the exact same thing that the Pharisees did when they placed the traditions of men above the infallible Word of God. Again nothing could be further from the truth. To the contrary, the above passage is a strong rebuke to religious leaders who compromised on applying the full counsel of the Word of God because they were taking bribes from the people. Jesus was letting the Pharisees know that tithes and offerings that were collected from the people in exchange for turning a blind eye to other important matters of the Law, were not only tainted but such actions were nullifying the power of God's Word in people's lives.

It is clear from our unknown author's interpretation of the passage of Scripture from Mark 7:9-13, that the author suffers from a spiritual disease called "humanism." ***"Since the fall of Adam and Eve, man's greatest besetting sin is the sin of "humanism."*** Humanism is a demonic ideology that places the "needs of a human being" above God's requirements. Humanism is a work of the flesh and it is rooted in "self-centeredness." When the Scriptures fall into the hands of theologians who interpret the Scriptures through the "eyes of humanism," preserving man's interest using the Scriptures takes on immediate precedence and the Scriptures suddenly lose their heavenly perspective.

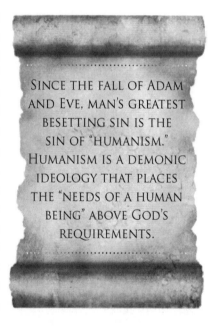

SINCE THE FALL OF ADAM AND EVE, MAN'S GREATEST BESETTING SIN IS THE SIN OF "HUMANISM." HUMANISM IS A DEMONIC IDEOLOGY THAT PLACES THE "NEEDS OF A HUMAN BEING" ABOVE GOD'S REQUIREMENTS.

If we were to take our unknown author's reasoning we would have to come to the conclusion that the prophet Elijah manipulated the widow of Zarephath in 1 Kings 17:8-15, when he challenged her to give him the first portion of her last piece of bread, when she had a son to take care of. According to the reasoning of our unknown author the widow's offering was "Corban" and invalidated the word of God, because she gave the first portion of her last piece of bread to a man of God, when her family clearly needed it. Based upon our unknown author's spiritual ideology, the portion the widow woman gave to the prophet Elijah would have been well served by saving it for her starving son. If the prophet Elijah had the same mindset that our unknown author possesses, the miracle of supernatural supply in the midst of a famine that is gloriously recorded in the said passage would never have been recorded.

What our unknown author and many of his or her followers in the blogosphere, who are against tithing fail to realize, is that man's needs are always met in all sufficiency when he or she is willing to obey God's voice and abide by His eternal principles as set forth in His Word. *Obeying an instruction from God – however ridiculous it may seem – is the quickest and surest way to meet even the most desperate of human needs.* What is more, God always chooses and delegates His authority to a man or woman of His choice. These chosen vessels (Ephesians 4:11) become God's delegated authorities in the earth, and when we heed the Word of the Lord through the mouth of these "sent ones," untold blessings can occur in our lives. Contrary to what the false prophets in the blogosphere would have us believe, submitting ourselves to God's delegated authority is not another form of "spiritual bondage." Had the widow of Zarephath not heeded the Prophet Elijah's admonition, she would have missed a great blessing from the Lord. Even though she did not see the Lord physically, God had come to her in physical form through one of His holy prophets.

Give 10% or 100% — which is which?

" *[A psalm of David.] The earth is the Lord's, and everything in it. The world and all its people belong to him.*"

Psalm 24:1

One of the favorite arguments fronted by those who would have us believe that tithing was done away with under the New Testament, goes like this: "We do not have to give our tithes to the Church under the New Testament because everything we own belongs to the Lord anyway. God does not want our ten percent; He just wants all of us. We do not need to tithe under the New Testament because we can all be led by the Holy Spirit to give freewill offerings as the need arises." Taken at face value these statements by the anti-tithing crowd seem quite reasonable and spiritual. But further investigation will quickly reveal that these "spiritual sound bites" are the same "spiritual mantras" propagated by the spiritual prophets of "humanism."

In my many years of apostolic service to the Lord, I have yet to come across anyone who opposes tithing under the New Testament who opposed the notion of giving ten percent of their income to the Church, because it hindered them from giving "more than the stipulated ten percent." I have been a pastor for a while and I have yet to come across anyone who opposes tithing who has ever told me, "Dr. Myles I am tired of being restricted to giving only ten percent of my income, when I really desire to give away 50 or 100% of my income to the kingdom of God." To the contrary, when I checked the giving records of those who are opposed to the giving of tithes, I discovered that they are usually the stingiest givers in the entire congregation. Most of them hardly give away 2% of their income to the work of the Lord, if at all.

I have come to the sobering conclusion that those who oppose tithing under the New Testament and are quick to relegate it to the Old Testament, do not do so solely out of a sincere desire to correct what they perceive as an incorrect doctrine taught by the Church. Any theological objections they have to the biblical practice of tithing are just a well designed mask to hide their real motives. Their real motives are rooted in plain old greed and self-preservation. These people have a serious love affair with their "gold" and the amount of freewill offerings that they give to the work of the Lord, compared to those who believe in tithing, clearly underscores my foregone conclusion. If they truly believed that under the New Testament God wants their 100% they would be some of the greatest givers to the work of the Lord, but sadly they are not.

Tracing the Prophetic Element in the Scriptures

"Surely the Lord God will do nothing without revealing His secret to His servants the prophets."

Amos 3:7

One of the biggest problems that many self-appointed theologians in the blogosphere and in the Church world have, that hinders their ability to properly interpret the Scriptures is not understanding the "deep and far reaching prophetic element" that weaves itself through out the scriptures. *This prophetic element in the*

Scriptures requires a "prophetic hearing ear and seeing eye" to really capture many of the hidden meanings of Scripture.

"The hearing ear, and the seeing eye, the LORD hath made even both of them."

Proverbs 20:12 (KJV)

King Solomon points out that the LORD has made provision for His children to have both a "hearing ear and a seeing eye." Why would God do such a thing? It is because God knows that much of the spiritual treasures that He has hidden in His Word for our benefit would be lost if we are not able to see "beyond the obvious meaning of a certain scriptural verse or passage." For instance the passage of Scripture below from the book of Corinthians has a deeper meaning beyond the obvious.

"...and all of them drank the same spiritual water. For they drank from the spiritual rock that traveled with them, and that rock was Christ."

1 Corinthians 10:4

In this wonderful passage of Scripture the apostle Paul is referring to the people of Israel who came out of Egypt with the prophet Moses. While the children of Israel were journeying to the promise land they passed through the Arabian Desert and at some point during their journey they experienced a serious shortage of water. When the children of Israel became thirsty they cried to the Lord and to Moses for water. God instructed the prophet Moses to strike a certain "rock" and when he did, water came out of the rock. The children of Israel drank from the rock until they were satisfied.

"I will stand before you on the rock at Mount Sinai. Strike the rock, and water will come gushing out. Then the people will able to drink. So Moses struck the rock as he was told, and water gushed out as the elders looked on."

Exodus 17:6

Looking at the above passage of Scripture at face value, it would seem that its interpretation is an "open and shut case." Moses struck the rock and God supernaturally caused the rock to release water. What else is there? But when the apostle Paul looks at this same passage of Scripture he comes up with an "interpretation" that only someone with a "hearing ear and seeing eye" can come up with. Paul tells us that the rock that Moses struck that released the water that refreshed and sustained the children of Israel in the wilderness was "Christ." In this case the "rock" is the "prophetic element", while "Christ" is the "substantiation" of this prophetic element. **Without understanding the "deep and far reaching prophetic elements" in the Scriptures, "important biblical truths" that are interconnected from the Old Testament to the New become "lost in translation."**

When I read most of the articles that were posted by those who are against tithing in the blogosphere, I quickly discovered that their erroneous assumptions were rooted in their inability to account for the "prophetic element" in the writings of Scripture. Many of them failed to perceive the "prophetic symbolism" of Abram's tithe to Melchizedek in Genesis 14. Many of them also failed to see the connection between the Old Testament priestly Order of Melchizedek and the eternal priestly ministry of our Lord Jesus Christ. They also failed to "see" the "deep and far-reaching prophetic elements in the practice of tithing." This is why they can easily relegate tithing to the Old Testament and bury this "incredible spiritual technology for breakthrough" into the coffin of something that died with the Law of Moses. **If you are truly seeking for a "more excellent way" of tithing, I believe that this book will put to rest all your previous questions on the subject of tithing.**

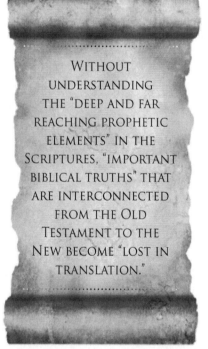

WITHOUT UNDERSTANDING THE "DEEP AND FAR REACHING PROPHETIC ELEMENTS" IN THE SCRIPTURES, "IMPORTANT BIBLICAL TRUTHS" THAT ARE INTERCONNECTED FROM THE OLD TESTAMENT TO THE NEW BECOME "LOST IN TRANSLATION."

The Order of Melchizedek

"So too Christ (the Messiah) did not exalt Himself to be made a high priest, but was appointed and exalted by Him Who said to Him, You are My Son; today I have begotten You; 6As He says also in another place, You are a Priest [appointed] forever after the order (with the rank) of Melchizedek."

Hebrews 5:5-6

Without understanding the deep and far-reaching prophetic element that weaves itself through the pages of Scripture, we will fail to recognize just how powerful Abram's meeting with Melchizedek in Genesis 14 really was. Abram's meeting with Melchizedek in the valley of Shaveh was one of the most important "God encounters" that any man could ever have. In a later chapter we will examine "all the prophetic elements" that are hidden in this life-changing meeting in Abram's life and how it affects us today. We will discover why Abram was inspired to tithe into the life and ministry of this lofty High Priest of God Most High.

Debunking Malachi 3:8-12

While I disagree with many in the blogosphere and in the Church world who believe that there is no need for tithing under the New Testament, *I also have to admit that I completely agree with many in the blogosphere who believe that Malachi 3 is an erroneous foundation for teaching tithing to New Testament believers.* I truly believe that the Church's usage of Malachi 3:8-12 as the primary foundation for tithing in the global Church is quite misleading and self-defeating. It is quite sad that some of our greatest prosperity teachers have built their whole ministry around this highly misunderstood passage from the book of Malachi. There is a "more excellent pattern of tithing" that is applicable to post-Calvary New Testament believers, that clearly transcends the dictates of Malachi 3. *If the global church does not "divorce its tithing model" from the passage in Malachi 3, the "downward trend in tithing" in the global church will only get worse.*

To help the Church divest and divorce itself from this inaccurate tithing model, I will "systematically" take you through a quick overview of the book of Malachi. *In order to do this effectively we must understand one of the most important principles of writing.* In order for any author to be effective in what he or she is trying to communicate, the author must first know his or her primary audience. Who the audience is will determine to a large extent the contextual framework of the author's work. When we attempt to separate a book that was written to a very specific audience from its intended audience, we are in essence "hijacking" the original author's primary intent. So here are two important questions that demand "surgical answers."

1. Who was the prophet Malachi's primary target audience?

2. What was his main objective for writing the book of Malachi?

To answer the first question let us examine closely the following passages of Scripture from the book of Malachi.

"A son honors his father, and a servant his master. If then I am a Father, where is My honor? And if I am a Master, where is the [reverent] fear due Me? says the Lord

of hosts to you, O priests, who despise My name. You say, How and in what way have we despised Your name? **8***When you [priests] offer blind [animals] for sacrifice, is it not evil? And when you offer the lame and the sick, is it not evil? Present such a thing [a blind or lame or sick animal] now to your governor [in payment of your taxes, and see what will happen]. Will he be pleased with you? Or will he receive you graciously? says the Lord of hosts.* **9***Now then, I [Malachi] beg [you priests], entreat God [earnestly] that He will be gracious to us. With such a gift from your hand [as a defective animal for sacrifice], will He accept it or show favor to any of you? says the Lord of hosts."*

Malachi 1:6-9

A quick and honest examination of the first chapter in Malachi quickly unmasks the prophet Malachi's primary target audience. The book of Malachi, contrary to what is taught by many prosperity teachers, was not written to rebuke the children of Israel who were robbing God of His tithes and offerings. *To the contrary, the prophet Malachi was rebuking many of the members of the Levitical priestly Order who were mishandling the Lord's tithes and offerings.*

These priests were stealing from God by sacrificing animals with blemishes to God, while keeping the best animals for themselves. This dishonorable behavior by the Levites had seriously grieved the heart of God and placed the entire priesthood in jeopardy. God even asked these wayward priests why they did not honor Him, like a son is supposed to honor his father.

"AND NOW, O you priests, this commandment is for you. **2***If you will not hear and if you will not lay it to heart to give glory to My name, says the Lord of hosts, then I will send the curse upon you, and I will curse your blessings; yes, I have already turned them to curses because you do not lay it to heart."*

Malachi 2:1-2

"For the priest's lips should guard and keep pure the knowledge [of My law], and the people should seek (inquire for and require) instruction at his mouth; for he is the messenger of the Lord of hosts."

Malachi 2:7

By the time we roll over to the second chapter of Malachi, it becomes increasingly clear that the prophet Malachi's "rod of correction" was designed to chastise members of the Levitical priesthood who were misrepresenting God. What is even more interesting is that the famous mantra of many prosperity teachers, "you will be cursed with a curse if you do not tithe" was actually referring to the "curse" that God had pronounced in Malachi 2:2. God had already promised that He would allow a curse to come upon the Levites if they did not repent from their evil deeds. If this one consideration does not debunk the Church's usage of Malachi 3 as its primary basis for its tithing model, then we have become "dull of hearing."

"But you have turned aside out of the way; you have caused many to stumble by your instruction [in the law]; you have corrupted the covenant of Levi [with Me], says the Lord of hosts. 7Even from the days of your fathers you have turned aside from My ordinances and have not kept them. Return to me, and I will return to you, says the Lord of hosts. But you say, How shall we return? 8Will a man rob or defraud God? Yet you rob and defraud Me. But you say, In what way do we rob or defraud You? [You have withheld your] tithes and offerings. 9You are cursed with the curse, for you are robbing Me, even this whole nation. 10Bring all the tithes (the whole tenth of your income) into the storehouse, that there may be food in My house, and prove Me now by it, says the Lord of hosts, if I will not open the windows of heaven for you and pour you out a blessing, that there shall not be room enough to receive it."

Malachi 3:6-10

By the time we finally get to the third chapter of Malachi, which is the Church's most favorite chapter on tithing, it is now embarrassingly clear that the prophet Malachi has not changed the object of his "harsh rebuke." Contrary to what many prosperity preachers teach, Malachi chapter three is not a "stand alone" chapter. It is not independent of the prophet Malachi's ongoing rebuke against an ailing priesthood. In Malachi 3:6 God deepens His harsh rebuke of the sinning Levites when He accuses them of stumbling many of the people of Israel and corrupting the covenant God had made with the tribe of Levi. One does not have to be a rocket scientist to figure out the obvious. Malachi chapter three in its most accurate context was not written to correct the "lack of tithing" among the laity in Israel. The passage from Malachi 3:8-12 was God's final verdict on the Levitical priests who did not repent of robbing God of His tithes and offerings.

"A priest—a descendant of Aaron—will be with the Levites as they receive these tithes. And a tenth of all that is collected as tithes will be delivered by the Levites to the Temple of our God and placed in the storerooms."

Nehemiah 10:38

Many believers in Christendom and some preachers of the gospel do not know that under the priestly Order of Aaron there were several levels or layers of tithing. Let us list these levels or layers of tithing for the sake of our study.

1. There was a tithe the general population of Israel gave to the Levites. (Numbers 18:21)

2. There was a tithe of the tithe that the Levites gave to the High Priestly Order of Aaron. (Numbers 18:25-31)

3. The people of Israel kept a tithe to pay for their annual pilgrimage to Jerusalem. (Deut 14:22-26)

4. The people paid a tithe to take care of the poor, the orphans and the widows. (Deut 14:28-29)

Once we understand these four layers of tithing under the priestly Order of Aaron, understanding the proper context of Malachi 3 becomes quite easy. When God posed the questions "Will a man rob of (from) God? And ye say wherein have we robbed you?" God quickly answered "in tithes and offerings." Who was God really talking about? Contrary to the popular teachings on this passage on tithing, God was not accusing the laity in Israel of robbing Him of His tithes and offerings. *He was accusing the "priests" (pastors or spiritual leaders of Israel) of robbing Him of tithes and offerings.*

The passage from the book of Nehemiah 10:38 completely solves the mystery of Malachi 3:8-10. The prophet Nehemiah identifies the "storehouse" that the prophet Malachi was alluding to in the third chapter of Malachi. According to the Law of Moses the Levites were instructed by Moses under divine decree to give a "tithe of the tithe" to the household of Aaron. Members of the household of Aaron were the only ones among the Levites who were appointed by God to the office of the High Priest. They lived on a "tithe" of all the "tithes" that the Levites collected from all the tribes of Israel.

During the prophet Malachi's era some of the members of the Levitical priesthood were so corrupt that they were not giving the household of Aaron their rightful portion of the tithe of the tithes. This behavior so grieved the heart of God that He sent the prophet Malachi to them with a harsh word of rebuke. When church leaders apply Malachi chapter three to lay people in the Church, they are really "overstretching the text." Those who are very zealous for Malachi 3 need to use it to rebuke pastors who do not tithe. *Speaking frankly, many pastors do not tithe and many who do tithe, tithe incorrectly.* Malachi chapter 3 is more suited to rebuking pastors who do not tithe into their spiritual covering than for rebuking lay people in the Church who do not tithe.

> *"[Earnestly] remember the law of Moses, My servant, the statutes and the ordinances which I commanded him on [Mount] Horeb [to give] to all Israel."*
>
> Malachi 4:4

We have finally reached the point where we can answer our second question. "What was the Prophet Malachi's primary objective for writing the book of Malachi?" The answer to this vital question stares us in the face when we read Malachi 4:4. The Prophet Malachi wanted the ailing Levitical priesthood to "remember the Law of Moses." *Stated simply, everything the prophet Malachi wrote in the book of Malachi was designed to help the priests who were falling short of their calling and duty to remember the Law of Moses.* Nothing could be clearer than this. So here is my challenge to you: "Are you under the Law of Moses or are you under grace?" If you believe that you are under the Law of Moses then have fun "remembering the Law of Moses." The word "remember" literally means to "put the original parts back together (reassemble)." It is clear to me that we can no longer preach the gospel of the Kingdom and live under the "dispensation of grace," while continuing to tithe according to the Law of Moses.

Money:
The lowest asset in the kingdom of God

The "undue emphasis" on money as one of the primary benefits of tithing is one of the major flaws in the teaching on tithing that is based upon the "Malachi 3:8-12 Model." Proponents of the Malachi 3:8-12 pattern of tithing are quick to inform their listeners that the primary benefit of tithing is "the supernatural acquisition of money." In consequence, the primary penalty for not tithing is the entrance of a "financial curse" in the personal economy of those who refuse to pay the Lord's tithe. This kind of undue emphasis on money as one of the primary benefits of tithing has become the source of "much frustration and debate" among many believers in the blogosphere and in the global Church.

This undue emphasis of making money the primary benefit of tithing by those who use the "Malachi 3:8-12 Tithing Model" has "frustrated and disenfranchised" many faithful tithers. Many of these faithful tithers feel like failures in life because they are still not rich. Many of them have been tithing for years and yet have experienced dismal improvement in their personal economy. This undue emphasis on money in the Malachi 3:8-12 tithing model, has also helped to produce a second group of believers in the blogosphere who are even more determined not to tithe, because the way the church teaches tithing presently does not sufficiently explain why the world is full of rich people who have never given God a tithe. Furthermore, common experience has also shown us that there are many "wealthy Christians" who attend church regularly but do not tithe and yet they seem to continue to "prosper financially." *How do we explain this seemingly contradictory phenomenon to the faithful?* Imagine telling Oprah Winfrey, Bill Gates and Donald Trump that they will be cursed with a financial curse if they do not tithe? They would laugh us to scorn and conclude that we are mentally challenged.

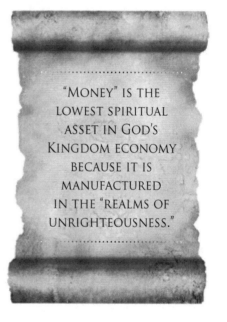

"MONEY" IS THE LOWEST SPIRITUAL ASSET IN GOD'S KINGDOM ECONOMY BECAUSE IT IS MANUFACTURED IN THE "REALMS OF UNRIGHTEOUSNESS."

"If therefore ye have not been faithful in the unrighteous mammon, who will commit to your trust true riches?"

Luke 16:11

Why are there so many wealthy people in the world who have never given God His proper endowment of tithe? The answer to this seemingly perplexing question is simple, but deeply profound in its spiritual ramification. If we let the holy book speak for itself, it becomes abundantly clear that Jesus never regarded "money" as one of the highest assets in the Kingdom of God. To the contrary, Jesus called money, "unrighteous mammon." This expression that the Lord Jesus Christ used to describe money does not mean that money by itself is "evil." **To the contrary, Jesus used this expression to indicate that "money" is the lowest spiritual asset in God's Kingdom economy because it is manufactured in the "realms of unrighteousness."** Ever since the fall of Adam and Eve, the world we live in has fallen into the zone of "unrighteousness." Money is found in abundance in this realm of "unrighteousness."

Money is so common in the "realms of unrighteousness," such that men and women can turn to their basest instincts and still have the capacity to "capture money." For example, a woman can choose to wear very seductive attire and parade herself before the eyes of lustful men. Money in exchange for sex is the multibillion-dollar industry of our times. I can assure you that within a couple of days of selling her body, this woman will probably make more money than many God-fearing people make for an entire year! A bank robber on the other hand can break into a bank and walk away with more money than many faithful tithers will ever make in an entire lifetime. How is this possible? The answer is simple. ***Money is the lowest asset in God's economy, because it is the creation of fallen man.*** *Jesus told us that "money" is not even included on the list of what Jesus called "true riches."*

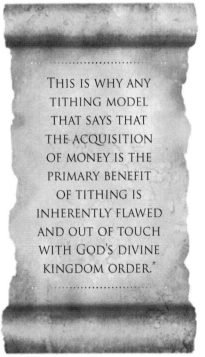

THIS IS WHY ANY TITHING MODEL THAT SAYS THAT THE ACQUISITION OF MONEY IS THE PRIMARY BENEFIT OF TITHING IS INHERENTLY FLAWED AND OUT OF TOUCH WITH GOD'S DIVINE KINGDOM ORDER."

If money is the lowest asset in God's economy, why is it that those who teach tithing according to Malachi 3:8-12, give it a place of uttermost importance? It is quite clear that money is the number one prized asset in the "Babylonian systems of human government." But in God's estimation, money comes right after we have exhausted the list of "true riches." ***This is why any tithing model that says that the acquisition of money is the primary benefit of tithing is inherently flawed and out of touch with God's divine kingdom order.*** God created the tithe to give tithers access to heaven's "true riches" and the "supernatural acquisition of money" as one of the benefits of tithing would then be a distant second. This book will show you why God waited until Abraham was very rich in gold and silver before introducing him to the powerful concept of tithing. I do not want to be misconstrued as saying that "tithing can never make a person prosper financially." ***To the contrary, I believe that tithing does invoke the grace to prosper financially upon the faithful, but money is not the primary benefit of tithing.***

Questions that demand Answers

- **Why is there no mention of tithing in Abraham's life before Genesis 14?**

"But when the right time came, God sent his Son, born of a woman, subject to the law. 5 God sent him to buy freedom for us who were slaves to the law, so that he could adopt us as his very own children."

Galatians 4:4-5

God never does anything out of its due season. **God has a perfect timing mechanism that He uses to synchronize and deploy all of His eternal purposes here on earth.** Every farmer knows that the worst mistake any farmer can make is to attempt to harvest his or her crops before they are ripe for harvest. Waiting for the right time to harvest a fruit tree does not in any way negate the importance of the fruit itself. In the same manner, God waited until He knew that the right time to introduce the "concept of tithing" to Abram had arrived.

When Abram met Melchizedek (the king-priest) in the valley of Shaveh, he had spiritually matured to the point where he could appreciate the power of the eternal truths that God was introducing to him in this glorious encounter with this lofty High Priest of God Most High. Furthermore, the prevailing circumstances on the ground had divinely lined up to further impress upon Abram's mind the awesome power of the tithe. The fact that God never told Abraham about the tithe in previous chapters does not in anyway negate the sacred importance of the divine enactment of the tithe.

- **Why do modern Church leaders use Malachi chapter three to scare or motivate believers into tithing, when it is obvious that Malachi was talking to Levitical priests who lived under the Law of Moses?**

I have already answered the above question in the previous pages of this chapter, but I will shed more light on this important question. The main reason why many Church leaders rely heavily on Malachi chapter three as their main basis for teaching or exacting the tithe is staggeringly simple. Many well-meaning spiritual leaders have not had access to a Bible-based teaching manual like the one you are reading, which can teach them how to exact the tithe under the Order of Melchizedek, instead of using the Levitical model. *Many pastors do not know that there is a more excellent way of exacting the tithe under the New Testament order of priesthood.*

"Tell me, you who want to live under the law, do you know what the law actually says?"

Galatians 4:21

Since the giving of tithes is one of the main sources of funding for the work of the ministry in most churches, pastors have to find a way to teach on the importance of tithing to their flock. Since Malachi 3 seems to present the easiest teaching on tithing, many pastors have found it an easy solution to their dilemma. In the course of writing this book, several great pastors told me: "Dr. Myles, before I heard your teaching or read your book, I had no other alternative for teaching on tithing, even though I did not like telling my flock that they were cursed if they did not tithe."

- **Why do Church leaders tell us that we are cursed if we do not tithe, when the book of Galatians tells us that Christ became a Curse for us when He hung on the cross?**

"But Christ has rescued us from the curse pronounced by the law. When he was hung on the cross, he took upon himself the curse for our wrongdoing. For it is written in the Scriptures, 'Cursed is everyone who is hung on a tree.'"

Galatians 3:13

The above passage of Scripture makes it adamantly clear that New Testament believers have been redeemed from the curse of the Law. To deny this indelible theological fact is tantamount to nullifying the finished work of Christ. Since Malachi 3:8-12 is a passage that refers to the spiritual consequences of not giving the tithe according to the Law, it follows that New Testament believers were also redeemed from this Malachi curse when Christ was hung on the cross and became a curse for us that we might inherit the blessing of Abraham.

On the other hand, I do not want to be misconstrued as suggesting that there are no spiritual consequences for not tithing under the priestly Order of Melchizedek. There are spiritual consequences for not tithing under this eternal priestly Order, which we will explore in great detail in a later chapter. *However, these spiritual consequences are deployed on a very different spiritual technology than that of imposing of a curse.* The apostle Paul is quite clear in the passage below, that under the New Testament priesthood, God does not curse His children for any reason. To the contrary, He "chastises or scourges us" when we choose to disobey His Word. *This divine chastisement and scourging is effective enough to change the heart and behavior of His dear children.* Those of God's children who are beyond the reach of this divine chastisement and scourging are already "reprobate" and have already cursed themselves by resisting the Spirit of God.

"For whom the Lord loveth he chasteneth, and scourgeth every son whom he receiveth. 7If ye endure chastening, God dealeth with you as with sons; for what son is he whom the father chasteneth not? 8But if ye be without chastisement, whereof all are partakers, then are ye bastards, and not sons."

Hebrews 12:6-8 (KJV)

- **Why do prosperity teachers tell us to give a tithe of our money when Abraham only gave Melchizedek a tithe of other people's stuff?**

I will quickly answer the above question by first saying that the one who asked this question is being rather disingenuous. How can anyone give what does not truly belong to them? It does not make sense anyway you twist this. How can you say that you gave a gift when you walked into your neighbors' yard and stole one of their bicycles and then give it to the child of another neighbor across the street? You definitely stole the bicycle, but you certainly did not give it. You can never give what you do not own. ***Giving always carries the connotation of ownership.*** It is foolish to assume that Abram gave tithes to Melchizedek from "stuff" that did not belong to him. If this were truly the case, then Abram gave Melchizedek, who was both a King and a Priest, a "mockery offering of tithes." Abram would have been judged harshly by God for mocking a priest of God Most High; to the contrary, Melchizedek blessed Abram before God.

Secondly, the question above smells of complete ignorance concerning the ancient principles of warfare. In the ancient world that Abram lived in, it was a widely-accepted tradition that "a person or a nation had the complete rights of ownership" over whatever they conquered in battle. This principle is littered throughout the pages of Scripture. *Even the Lord Jesus Himself alluded to the spiritual validity of this powerful principle of warfare.* Listen to this…

"But if I cast out devils by the Spirit of God, then the kingdom of God is come unto you. 29Or else how can one enter into a strong man's house, and spoil his goods, except he first bind the strong man? and then he will spoil his house."

Matthew 12:28-29

- **Abraham's tithe to Melchizedek was a once-only event, so why do pastors make their church members tithe from their weekly income?**

At face value the question above seems like it stands on solid footing. However, further investigation will prove otherwise. There are many once-only events in the Scriptures that establish important principles and fundamental truths that God intends to play out throughout the whole course of human history.

For instance, God only spoke once in the first chapter of Genesis, when He declared, "Let there be light!" Does this once-only event give us the right to expect the light of the Sun every day since then? Obviously the answer is yes. The Bible tells us that Jesus Christ died on the cross once-and-for-all. Does this then mean that we cannot preach about the cross of Christ and its ongoing benefits to ensuing generations? *Whenever we are dealing with the establishment of precedent, principles and fundamental doctrines, it is not the number of times the subject is mentioned in the Scriptures that matters, as much as the precedent set by the said principle.*

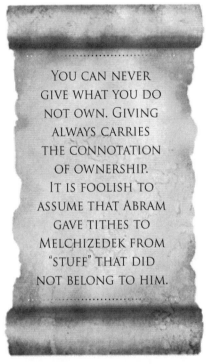

YOU CAN NEVER GIVE WHAT YOU DO NOT OWN. GIVING ALWAYS CARRIES THE CONNOTATION OF OWNERSHIP. IT IS FOOLISH TO ASSUME THAT ABRAM GAVE TITHES TO MELCHIZEDEK FROM "STUFF" THAT DID NOT BELONG TO HIM.

"Unlike those other high priests, he does not need to offer sacrifices every day. They did this for their own sins first and then for the sins of the people. But Jesus did this once for all when he offered himself as the sacrifice for the people's sins."

Hebrews 7:27

The reason why many pastors challenge the faithful in their flock to give tithes out of their weekly income, is due to the precedent that was set by Abram's initial tithe, which underscores the fact that God's eternal priesthood has legitimate right to the tithes of whatever Kingdom citizens take possession of in the marketplace. *Abram's giving of tithes was his personal acknowledgement that he owed his victory in battle to God Most High! Tithing under the Order of Melchizedek is an acknowledgement of Christ's Lordship in the believer's life. It is not a "legal requirement." It is the humble response of an "inspired heart" to the Lordship of Christ.* What Abraham did in giving the sacrifice of tithes, was no different to what pagan kings did whenever they triumphed in battle. These pagan kings were quick to credit their massive victories to their demon-gods, by giving them substantial sacrificial offerings of blood and other expensive gifts.

- **Why do some prosperity teachers use Jacob's reference to tithing in Genesis 28:11-17 to endorse tithing under the New Testament, when it is quite clear that Jacob was bargaining with God, and bargaining with God is a sin?**

Taken at face value, the question above seems to stand on solid footing. But the truth of the matter is that the answer to our blogger's question is both a "Yes and No" answer. "Yes," bargaining with God over immutable truths and principles that He has clearly revealed to us in His holy word is a sin. This is because such an attitude is a camouflage for the spirit of disobedience. "No," bargaining with God is not a sin, in situations where we are not really sure of His will; especially when our gesture of bargaining with God is made in the spirit of wanting to know God's perfect will for our lives, or when we are interceding for others. We must also not forget that the patriarchs (Abraham, Isaac and Jacob) did not have the Holy Spirit residing inside them, like He resides in the born-again spirits of New Testament believers. The Holy Spirit simply came upon them in brief intervals and then lifted His anointing after communicating His message to them. This is why the patriarchs normally asked God to give them a visible sign that would testify to the truthfulness of the divine encounter that He (God) had given them.

How many of us have dreamed dreams and have desired to know whether they were from God or not? Let us also not forget that Jacob lived during a time in human history where the people of the ancient world worshipped many demon-gods. These demon-gods would appear to the people of the ancient world in their dreams while they slept. If you were Jacob living under this type of spiritual atmosphere, wouldn't you want proof that the deity that appeared to you in your dream was actually the true and living God whom your forefathers served? The bargain Jacob made with the God who appeared to him at Bethel was quite prudent of him. Jacob knew from listening to his father Isaac that the God of Abraham was capable of doing what he had asked. *Had the God who appeared to Jacob at Bethel failed to satisfy the conditions of Jacob's bargain, Jacob would have simply concluded that He was a "false god" masquerading as the God of Abraham and Isaac.* This is why Jacob tied his tithing to the satisfaction of this bargain. Jacob wanted to make sure that he was not tithing to the "wrong God." This would explain why God was not angry with Jacob for suggesting such a bargain. To the contrary, God completely satisfied all the conditions of Jacob's bargain. The passage of Scripture below underscores this important fact.

"I am the God who appeared to you at Bethel, the place where you anointed the pillar of stone and made your vow to me. Now get ready and leave this country and return to the land of your birth."

Genesis 31:13

What is quite revealing is the fact that when God appeared to Jacob many years after appearing to him in a dream at Bethel, God reintroduces Himself as the God who met Jacob at Bethel. God also reminded Jacob of the "vow" that he had made to God at Bethel. The vow that God was referring to was the "pledge Jacob made to God concerning future tithes." Jacob had promised God that he would give him a tithe (tenth) of all that he had if God satisfied all the conditions of Jacob's bargain. God's reference to this particular "vow" that Jacob made at Bethel underscores two very important facts. *Firstly, it shows that God accepted the conditions of Jacob's bargain. Secondly, it confirms that Jacob's vow to tithe from future provisions of God was the basis for the supernatural blessing that God gave him when he was working for his uncle Laban.*

This second fact by itself should forever silence those who say that there is no "spiritual connection" between tithing and the spirit of supernatural increase. This is why using the vow Jacob made to God in Genesis 28:20 to suggest that Jacob's reference to tithing in this passage doesn't count, because it is the record of a man trying to manipulate God, is overreaching in the interpretation of this powerful passage of Scripture. Such an assumption is not only absurd but it also earmarks just how ignorant many believers are of the prevailing spiritual culture of the ancient world. It shows that we are very ignorant of how the people of the ancient world interacted with deities over their nations. Bargaining (asking for a verifiable sign) with the gods was the quickest to know the power of the said deity. This is exactly what the Prophet Elijah was doing when he challenged the people of his day by saying, "The God who answers by fire, he is the true God" (1 Kings 18).

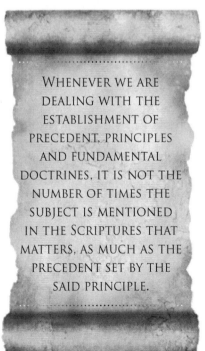

WHENEVER WE ARE DEALING WITH THE ESTABLISHMENT OF PRECEDENT, PRINCIPLES AND FUNDAMENTAL DOCTRINES, IT IS NOT THE NUMBER OF TIMES THE SUBJECT IS MENTIONED IN THE SCRIPTURES THAT MATTERS, AS MUCH AS THE PRECEDENT SET BY THE SAID PRINCIPLE.

In conclusion, I want to try to answer the question that is the genesis of this entire chapter and the basis for this entire book. *"Is tithing for today?"* *The answer is a resounding "YES!"* But I admonish you to prayerfully read this entire book before formulating your opinion, one way or the other. If you desire to discover a "more excellent way of tithing," please read on. If you are the senior pastor or bishop of a church, I pray that God will use this book to help you establish a more excellent way of tithing in your business, congregation or network of churches – *a tithing model that is completely "free of legalism," that is "driven by the prophetic streams of divine inspiration in the human heart."*

LIFE APPLICATION SECTION

Point to Ponder:

Ever since the fall of Adam and Eve, the world we live in has fallen into the zone of "unrighteousness." Money is found in abundance in this realm of "unrighteousness."

Verse to Remember:

Malachi 2:1-2 AND NOW, O you priests, this commandment is for you. 2If you will not hear and if you will not lay it to heart to give glory to My name, says the Lord of hosts, then I will send the curse upon you, and I will curse your blessings; yes, I have already turned them to curses because you do not lay it to heart.

Questions to Consider:

1. Who was the Prophet Malachi's primary target audience, when he wrote the book of Malachi?

2. Why is it erroneous to say that the giving of tithes is "Corban?"

3. What were the four levels of tithing under the Levitical priestly Order?

JOURNAL YOUR THOUGHTS

THE BOOK OF WHY

W hen I first wrote this book, this chapter was not part of the original template of my manuscript. One morning, the Holy Spirit woke me up with these words, deeply embedded in my spirit: "the book of why." I asked the Holy Spirit to explain what He was trying to tell me and the Lord said to me, "In your book on tithing, you must include a chapter called "the book of why." The Holy Spirit told me that in this chapter, he would show me why many born-again believers struggle to tithe consistently. The Lord showed me that the reason why many books lack a heartfelt and meaningful impact on the giving of God's Kingdom citizens is that they focus heavily on the "how to" more than the "question of why?"

The question of "how to" deals with the mechanisms of transport of a particular product or technology, but the question of "why" deals with the "roots and origins" of an issue at hand. After my time of prayer, I felt a deep impression in my spirit that I was to co-author this particular chapter with my dear friend Dr. Bruce Cook (founder of K.E.Y.S), who is a bona fide marketplace apostle and savvy businessman. Consequently this chapter is a hybrid of our combined thoughts and prayer on this important issue that affects the body of Christ worldwide.

The Holy Spirit promised to give us a number of "whys" that are behind the roots and origins of the struggle that the majority of the body of Christ experiences in the area of tithing. Before doing so, we will first examine the question of "why God created the tithe in the first place?'

Why Did God Create the Tithe?

Let's pause for a moment at the 30,000 foot level before resuming our microscopic analysis and reflect on why God created and established the tithe in order to gain some additional perspective. First, Tithing reflects the unselfish, generous, giving nature of our Creator and Provider. And since we are created in God's image (Gen. 1:26-28), then it is unnatural not to give. 2 Cor. 9:6 says: "Whoever sows sparingly will also reap sparingly, and whoever sows generously will also reap generously." Similarly, Prov. 22:9 says, "A generous man will himself be blessed, for he shares his food with the poor." The psychologist Abraham Maslow published his famous Hierarchy of Needs, and at the top of the list as the highest level is Self-Actualization. Imagine that! God has hard-wired us humans to search and find meaning, purpose and significance in our existence, and one of the primary forms of Self-Actualization for many people is Giving and Philanthropy. Wealthy people often seek to create a legacy or endowment to perpetuate their name or reputation or values to future generations. From a Kingdom perspective, Convergence is a much-better term than Self-Actualization. Convergence implies the intersection of gifts, callings, assignments, passions, destiny, maturity, and character, not just how much education or material possessions someone has, or how wealthy they are.

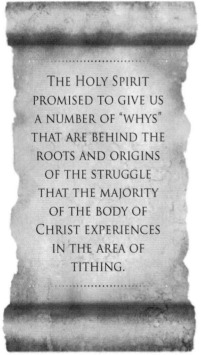

THE HOLY SPIRIT PROMISED TO GIVE US A NUMBER OF "WHYS" THAT ARE BEHIND THE ROOTS AND ORIGINS OF THE STRUGGLE THAT THE MAJORITY OF THE BODY OF CHRIST EXPERIENCES IN THE AREA OF TITHING.

The world encourages and reinforces daily in countless ways to each of us the need and desire for humans to be "self-sufficient." This inherent nature and drive of the flesh to focus on self as the center of the universe and to be the master of our own destiny is diametrically opposed to the knowledge and wisdom of God and the example and lifestyle of Jesus. Finances, intelligence, positional power, physical beauty and strength are just a few ways that humans express their "self-sufficiency." However, God is not impressed by such things. God recognizes this weakness in us and told Moses to warn the Israelites against this tendency to exalt themselves, thinking: "My power and the strength of my hands [or mind] have produced [gained} this wealth for me." Instead, they were told to "remember the Lord your God, for it is He who gives

you the ability [power] to produce [get] wealth, and so confirms his covenant..."
(Deuteronomy 8:17-18). Furthermore, Jesus told the apostle Paul on one occasion,
"My grace is sufficient for you, for my power is made perfect in weakness." (2 Cor.
12:9) After learning this lesson on the sufficiency of Christ, Paul could then write
Phil. 3:3-21.

Secondly, God does not need our tithe, but we need His protection and
provision and resources. God is omniscient, omnipotent, and omnipresent. He
owns the cattle on a thousand hills; the gold and silver belong to him. Psalm 50:12
says, "If I were hungry I would not tell you, for the world is mine, and all that is
in it." Similarly, in Job 41:11 God asks rhetorically, "Who has a claim against me
that I must pay? Everything under heaven belongs to me." So even though the
earth has been reserved for man, and we are to exercise dominion, in doing so
we are stewards, not owners, of what belongs to God. Tithing is part of our faith
journey and adventure of being a son or daughter in the Kingdom of God and
relating to Him in a personal and intimate way, and co-laboring, co-partnering,
co-creating, and co-reigning in life in Abba Father's family business. Jesus still calls
us out of the boat of comfort and complacency and bids us to walk on the water
of life with Him, fixing our eyes on Him and not our circumstances. He calls us
to become "impossibility thinkers" rather than "possibility thinkers" (Luke 1:37,
18:27) by the renewing of our minds and hearts in Christ Jesus (Rom. 12:1-2).

Third, Tithing is also a form of joy, honor and humility. Through willing
and cheerful giving (2 Corinthians 9:6-8), we honor and please God. In fact, the
Bible says that "God loves a cheerful giver." Some versions translate the word
"cheerful" as "hilarious." God wants us to be joyful in our giving; in fact, joy is
a weapon and a source of strength for us (Neh. 8:10). *"For the kingdom of God is…
righteousness, joy and peace in the Holy Spirit" (Rom. 14:17).* We should emphasize that
there is great peace that comes from tithing as well. *1 Sam 2:30 says: "Those who
honor me I will honor, but those who despise me will be disdained." Proverbs 3:9-10 says,*
"Honor the Lord with your possessions, *and with the **firstfruits** of your increase,
so your barns will be filled with plenty, and your vats will overflow with new wine."* Apostle
Robert Henderson has written several excellent books on the power and benefits
of firstfruits giving that shed additional light, but our focus here is on **tithing.** The
point is that we honor God with our giving. The Bible teaches us to give honor to
whom honor is due (Rom. 13:7)." God as the eternal Creator and Father of all
is certainly worthy of honor. Jesus also taught his disciples, *"Give to Caesar what is
Caesar's, and to God what is God's" (Matt. 22:21).* This verse clearly states that certain
things belong to God. The tithe is one of them. Since our focus is on tithing, and

not offerings, we can only mention in passing that there is also a gift or grace of liberality or generosity available to the body of Christ (Rom. 12:8). Jesus said, *"It is more blessed to give than to receive" (Acts 20:35)*. Those who are experiencing the joy of tithing, as well as other forms of giving, can attest to that.

Fourth, God is a God of increase and multiplication. Tithing is one way that God has designed for his sons and daughters to plant seeds and reap harvests. Gen. 8:22 says, "As long as the earth endures, seedtime and harvest, cold and heat, summer and winter, day and night will never cease." 2 Cor. 9:8, 10-11 adds, *"And God is able to make all grace abound to you, so that in all things at all times, having **all** that you need, you will abound in **every** good work....Now he who supplies seed to the sower and bread for food **will also supply and increase your store of seed and will enlarge the harvest of your righteousness**. You will be made rich in every way so that you can be generous on every occasion, and through us your generosity will result in thanksgiving to God."* Every good work, in every way, and on every occasion would certainly include tithing, although the context of this passage of Scripture is a collection for the needy saints in Jerusalem. God clearly wants His children and His Church to be able to sow seed and to reap a Harvest. Tithing is one type of seed, and seed helps prime the pump in the Kingdom economy, which is based on sowing and reaping rather than buying and selling. Jesus said in Luke 6:38: *"Give, and it will be given to you. A good measure, pressed down, shaken together and running over, will be poured into your lap. For with the measure you use, it will be measured to you."* Although this oft-quoted verse does not specifically mention or address tithing, it displays God's heart toward giving and sets forth cause-and-effect principles.

Fifth, God is an investor and is looking for sons and daughters who are also investors rather than slaves who are beggars or servants who are employees. God has invested heavily in humanity, which includes you and me, since the time of Adam and Eve, and continues to do so today. He is looking for a Return On Investment (R.O.I.). God is an experienced investor and invests in all economic cycles. His investments are primarily in people, and His greatest investment was His Son, Jesus. One of the reasons that some Christians, and some churches and ministries, struggle with tithing is that they have a "poverty" or "beggar" spirit and mindset. Their focus is on them and their finite resources rather than God and His infinite resources. They practice ***tipping*** rather than ***tithing***. This is dangerous since Rom. 14: 23 says: *"...everything that does not come from faith is sin."* It is beyond the scope of this writing to deal with this issue fully here, but suffice it to say this is a serious and widespread problem in the church. The apostle Paul asked this insightful question: *"He who did not spare his own Son, but gave him up for* us all—how will he not also give us **all things***?" (Rom. 8:32).* In other words, if we can trust God for our salvation, since God did not withhold even His own Son, we can trust God with the things of lesser importance. Matt. 6:31-33 tells us that God is aware of our physical needs and that if we seek Him first, *"..all these things shall be given to you as well."* Tithing is part of planting seeds in good (fertile) soil, and so we have a responsibility to discern the type of soil we are sowing into, and also a right to expect a return on our investment as well, although that is not the primary reason or motivation to tithe, as we shall see.

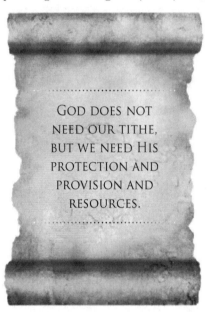

GOD DOES NOT NEED OUR TITHE, BUT WE NEED HIS PROTECTION AND PROVISION AND RESOURCES.

In closing this section, we would be remiss if we failed to mention a few well-known Christian businessmen, who are known to have given 90% of their income to advance, support and further the work of the Kingdom of God on the earth, while living on the remaining 10%. This short list for the so-called "reverse tithe" includes R.G. LeTourneau, J.C. Penney, and Stanley Tam. There are no doubt others whose giving has been in secret but whose names are written in heaven.

Why Many Christians Don't Tithe?

In a report issued Feb. 8, 2010 by The Barna Group, Ltd. it was reported:

> "One measure of American generosity that has stayed relatively consistent – despite the economic turmoil – is the practice of tithing. This is the concept embraced by many Christians of giving ten percent (or more) of one's income. Overall, 7% of all adults reported donation levels equaling at least 10% of their income. The percentage of adults who tithe has remained constant since the beginning of the decade, falling in the 5% to 7% range.
>
> Tithing levels, which could include both church and other charitable giving, were highest among **evangelicals (24% of whom give at least 10%)**, non-mainline Protestants (13%), churchgoers (11%), and non-

evangelical born again Christians (10%). Those over the age of 45 (9%) were nearly twice as likely as those under the age (5%) to tithe. Also, the study showed that income level was not correlated with tithing: just 9% of upscale adults gave at least one-tenth of their income, while 11% of the downscale set gave an equivalent proportion." (Permission granted by Barna Group Ltd. to cite this data.)

Apparently between 10% and 24% of US Christians are tithers, depending on which segment or category you belong to in the paragraph above. Probably the majority of those reading this book would fall into the largest category listed, Evangelicals, based on the definition of that term provided by Barna. That is a sobering statistic indeed and reinforces the need for this book. So despite the policies of some large Christian denominations with their annual tithe pledge commitment forms and Stewardship Committees, and the Mormon Church, which sanctions or disciplines non-tithe-paying members by barring them from being able to access or use church temples for important family ceremonies such as weddings or funerals, tithing percentages have remained about the same over the past decade in the US. Such peer pressure and negative reinforcement tactics may affect behavior in the short term, but not the long term, and have no power to change the hearts of the givers or to teach the principle of honor. Some other Christian denominations actually require their member churches to send a tithe to the national church headquarters to support a large operations staff and international outreach programs.

The Unanswered Question Of Lordship:

*"And I saw heaven opened, and behold a white horse; and he that sat upon him was called Faithful and true, and in righteousness doth he judge and make war. His eyes were as a flame of fire, and on his head were many crowns; and he had a name written, that no man knew, but he himself. And he was clothed with a vesture dipped in blood: and his name is called The Word of God. And the armies which were in heaven followed him upon white horses, clothed in fine linen, white and clean. And out of his mouth goeth a sharp sword, that with it he should smite the nations: and he shall rule them with a rod of iron: and he treadeth the winepress of the fierceness and wrath of Almighty God. And he hath on his vesture and on his thigh a name written, **KING OF KINGS, AND LORD OF LORDS.**"*

Revelation 19:11-16

The Church has begun what appears to be a *"popular"* upswing into the *"Kingdom"* mentality, lifestyle and language. But one cannot have the Kingdom *"mentality, lifestyle and language"* without the important element of *"Lordship."*

The term *"Lord"* is *"Kurios"* in Greek, meaning: *Supremacy, supreme in authority, a controller and a position of respect.* Webster defines *"Lordship"* as: *The rank or dignity of a lord; the authority or territory of a lord.* One may be a *"King"* but kings have to be strong in order to maintain dominion over their territory. *"Lordship"* is the strength of one's Kingdom attitude.

*"And **why** call ye me, Lord, Lord, and do not the things which I say?"*

Luke 6:46 (KJV)

The Holy Spirit told me that one of the primary reasons why many Kingdom citizens struggle to tithe consistently is merely a shadow of a deeper spiritual struggle. The struggle to submit to Christ as "Lord." The larger body of Christ has accepted Christ as "Savior;" but they struggle to accept him and honor as "Lord." The Body of Christ's lip-service Lordship mentality has become a raging spiritual epidemic that has weakened the global Church.

In Luke 6:46 Jesus told His apprentice apostles and his listening audience that it was redundant of them to call him "Lord" in one sentence and then refuse to do what He commanded them to do in the next. It is clear that in Jesus' mind Lordship and obedience are inseparable. You cannot have one without the other.

The Online Thesaurus dictionary defines "Lordship" as follows:

1. a person who has authority, control, or power over others; a master, chief, or ruler.

2. a person who exercises authority from property rights; an owner of land, houses, etc.

It is clear from the above definitions that the Body of Christ's struggle with the concept of Lordship of Christ has mushroomed into a cornucopia of problems, including tithing. In essence most members of the Body of Christ do not really have a tithing problem; they have a Lordship problem. Is it merely a form of Kingdom tax or a seed of honor; that we are privileged to owe to the Kingdom of God in exchange for continued prosperity within the economy of the Kingdom? It is my humble experience that believers who have matured to the point where they no longer struggle with the Lordship of Christ over their life also discovered that tithing consistently was no longer an issue in their life. They quickly come to understand the fact that fighting over 10% is redundant when the hundred percent that they own already belongs to the Lord.

*"And if any man ask you, **Why** do ye loose him? thus shall ye say unto him, Because the Lord hath need of him."*

Luke 19:31 (KJV)

I truly believe that the passage of Scripture above clearly lays down the premise for tithing for both the old and new Testaments. Jesus sent his disciples to the house of a certain man who owned a donkey. Jesus told his disciples that they would find this donkey tied to a pole in front of this man's house; He told them to loose the donkey and bring it to Jesus Christ. How could Jesus possibly lay claim to a donkey

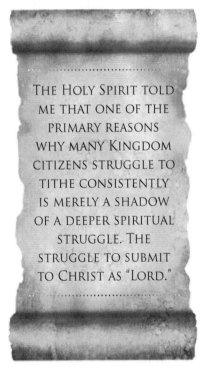

THE HOLY SPIRIT TOLD ME THAT ONE OF THE PRIMARY REASONS WHY MANY KINGDOM CITIZENS STRUGGLE TO TITHE CONSISTENTLY IS MERELY A SHADOW OF A DEEPER SPIRITUAL STRUGGLE. THE STRUGGLE TO SUBMIT TO CHRIST AS "LORD."

that belonged to another man; if he's not Lord of all? But since Jesus knew that He is Lord of all, and the creator of everything under the sun, He did not consider it robbery, when he took the donkey away from its original owner. Jesus told his disciples, that if the owner of the donkey asked them why they were taking his donkey, they were to simply say that the Lord had need of it. In Jesus' Royal mind, the declaration of his Lordship was sufficient reason for taking a donkey that belonged to another man. When we apply this principle to tithing it becomes quite clear that what we have in the body of Christ is not a tithing problem; it is a Lordship problem. Our tithe is like the donkey that we feel we own, only to discover that the Lord has need of it. Like the donkey, the Lord Jesus Christ needs our tithes to finance the advancement of His Kingdom in the earth.

Worrying About The Future:

*"And **why** take ye thought for raiment? Consider the lilies of the field, how they grow; they toil not, neither do they spin."*

Matthew 6:27-29 (KJV)

"And which of you with taking thought can add to his stature one cubit? 26If ye then be not able to do that thing which is least, why take ye thought for the rest? 27Consider the lilies how they grow: they toil not, they spin not; and yet I say unto you, that Solomon in all his glory was not arrayed like one of these."

Luke 12:25-27 (King James Version)

There are people in the body of Christ who are chronic "worriers." They worry about everything. This section of the body of Christ is one of the reasons why many members of the body of Christ struggle with tithing consistently. It is very difficult to sow tithes of honor in a spiritual atmosphere that is governed by endless worries. This section of the body of Christ is an easy prey for those who claim that tithing is an Old Testament practice which must never be imposed upon New Testament saints. These chronic "worriers" love this misguided view of tithing because it makes tithing one less thing that they have to worry about or deal with.

But the Lord Jesus Christ was adamantly clear that worrying about tomorrow and what the future holds is futile and unmasks a deep-seated disbelief in God and is His faithfulness to those who believe. Jesus also made it clear that worrying about tomorrow does not excuse us from obeying God and His word in the present. A life that is driven by worry is not God's ideal for His blood-washed children, but it does help us understand why many members of the body of Christ struggle in giving their tithes consistently.

A Fear-driven Perspective

*"And he saith unto them, **Why** are ye fearful, O ye of little faith?" Then he arose, and rebuked the winds and the sea; and there was a great calm."*

Matthew 8:25-27 (KJV)

The saying that fear is a great motivator certainly has a lot of truth to it; but it is not a complete statement. In most cases "Fear" is the great "paralyzer" of mankind. Fear can be a great motivator when it is the kind of fear that can cause us to want to obey God or walk away from doing what is evil.

But the truth of the matter is that more often than not, Fear is more of a negative paralyzing force in the lives of so many of God's people. There are far too many members of the body of Christ more governed by their fears than known by their faith. The Bible is very clear that the just shall live by faith and not by fear. But as the saying goes: It is easier said than done. A friend of mine by the name of Dr. Breakthrough defines "FEAR" as "False Evidence Appearing Real" and yet many members of the body of Christ seem to believe their fears more easily than they believe the word of God. This is "WHY" many members of the Body of Christ struggle to tithe consistently because the voice of their "FEARS" about letting "GO" of their tithe are louder than the voice of their faith or their desire to obey God.

Peter would never have become the first disciple of Christ to walk on water had he allowed his fear to choke his faith in the Christ who was bidding him to step out of the boat and walk on water. Unfortunately too many of God's people are ruled by their fears, especially their financial fears. These financial fears eventually become strongholds that choke their will or desire to honor God with their tithes. The problem with this scenario is that all fears that hinder men and women from obeying God are demonically engineered. All demonically-engineered fears are designed to rob us of the blessing that God has in store for us. I wonder what would have happened to the widow of Sidon (1 Kings 17:8-15) had she allowed her fear of lack to stop her from sowing her last piece of bread into the life and ministry of the Prophet Elijah.

Little Faith

*"Which when Jesus perceived, he said unto them, O ye of little faith, **why** reason ye among yourselves, because ye have brought no bread?"*

Matthew 16:7-9 (KJV)

Another reason why many followers of Christ struggle to give the tithe on a consistent basis is due to a spiritual disease that Jesus Christ called "Little Faith." Little Faith is faith that is easily choked and challenged by the circumstances surrounding God's people. It is the kind of faith that is barely enough to keep us saved. The only difference between followers of Christ with little faith and heathens is in the indwelling presence of the Holy Spirit. The difference pretty much ends there. Followers of Christ with "Little Faith" are controlled and governed by many of the same fleshly passions and fears that control the unsaved. It is not surprising that in a group of followers of Christ with "Little Faith," tithing consistently is quite a struggle. It takes real "faith and obedience" to tithe consistently.

The Green-eyed
Monster Called Greed

We finally get to that devious green-eyed monster called greed. This green-eyed monster is responsible for much of the systemic corruption that permeates every crevice of the marketplace. This green-eyed monster invades the souls of men and women until it bends their heart into the idolatry called "covetousness." Covetousness is the "worship or love of money" that goes beyond the natural need for money to pay for life's necessities. It is a deep-seated love of money that literally challenges God's supreme authority over the human heart. This would explain why Jesus said that you cannot serve God and mammon. Mammon is the Greek name for this devious, green-eyed monster that excites the engines of greed in the human heart.

> *"For the love of money is the root of all kinds of evil. And some people, craving money, have wandered from the true faith and pierced themselves with many sorrows."*
>
> 1 Timothy 6:10 (New Living Translation)

The corridors of human history are plastered with the blood of the innocent who became collateral damage in the quest for more money or wealth by those who were in positions of leadership over them. Kings went to war and sacrificed the lives of thousands of their royal soldiers just for the sake of increasing the royal treasury by a few more gold coins. Whenever this green-eyed monster possesses the soul of any human being, no amount of money is ever enough. There is always a governing underlying desire for more money. While this green-eyed monster rules the heart of a child of God tithing will always remain a huge struggle.

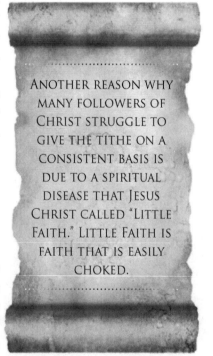

ANOTHER REASON WHY MANY FOLLOWERS OF CHRIST STRUGGLE TO GIVE THE TITHE ON A CONSISTENT BASIS IS DUE TO A SPIRITUAL DISEASE THAT JESUS CHRIST CALLED "LITTLE FAITH." LITTLE FAITH IS FAITH THAT IS EASILY CHOKED.

The Extravagant Lifestyle Of
Prosperity Preachers

> *"These people always cause trouble. Their minds are corrupt, and they have turned their backs on the truth. To them, a show of godliness is just a way to become wealthy."*
>
> Timothy 6:5 (New Living Translation)

One of the unfortunate reasons why many well-meaning people of faith have struggled to give their tithes consistently is due to the overly extravagant lifestyles of some proponents of the prosperity gospel. I want to make it very clear that I'm not against prosperity preachers and teachers and neither do I believe that there is any honor to be found in poverty. The descriptions are also clear that godliness is not about gain; it is about obedience to God.

I have witnessed the embarrassing and greed-driven extravagance of some so-called prosperity preachers. I know the Bishop in Texas of the church that had about 3000 members; his church was valued at $4.5 million but he was building himself a $7.0 million mansion to live in. Unfortunately, this Bishop never got to finish building his luxurious mansion because he was sent to prison for raping about 15 women. Many of those women were from his congregation. Stories such as this are responsible for why many well-meaning believers refuse to give their tithes. Even though I empathize with many God-fearing people who have been put off from the practice of tithing because of the extravagant and flamboyant lifestyles of some prosperity preachers, the fact remains that tithing is a sacred New Testament form of worship.

Lack Of Financial Integrity

*"And if you are untrustworthy about worldly wealth, who will trust you with the **true riches** of heaven?"*

Luke 16:11

Another reason why many God-fearing people of faith struggle to give their tithes consistently is due to the systemic lack of financial integrity that permeates the financial management systems of some congregations. I know pastors who treat their church finances as though it was their personal piggy bank. When members of their congregation pick up on this, it sends the wrong message about tithing. The truth of the matter is that the majority of church-going folk are not very wealthy. Many of them struggle to make ends meet, and as such when they tithe, they expect their monies to be treated with the greatest level of financial integrity. I really believe that the more transparent and honorable the financial management systems of a church are, the more they will attract a growing number of faithful and consistent tithers.

False Doctrines About Tithing

"Then we will no longer be immature like children. We won't be tossed and blown about by every wind of new teaching. We will not be influenced when people try to trick us with lies so clever they sound like the truth. 15 Instead, we will speak the truth in love, growing in every way more and more like Christ, who is the head of his body, the church."

Ephesians 4:14-15

I have already mentioned that when the Lord told me to write this book, he instructed me to Google the word tithing on the Internet. What I found was a mass proliferation of false doctrines on tithing. I've challenged many of these false doctrines in the first chapter of this writing. But the fact of the matter is that many of these false doctrines are responsible for why many well-meaning believers do not tithe consistently.

The Question Of Mounting Personal Debt

"Just as the rich rule the poor, so the borrower is servant to the lender."

Proverbs 22:7(New Living Translation)

Of all the reasons that we have examined thus far, the most compelling reason why many people of faith struggle to give their tithes consistently is due to mounting and overwhelming personal debt. Let's face it; the majority of the body of Christ is in dire distress when it comes to mounting personal debt. In America, for instance, the average American family is carrying $10,000 to $15,000 in credit card debt. With the high interest rates charged by many credit card companies, the average American family feels very burdened by debt. The unfortunate consequence of this mounting personal debt, is the tendency for many people of faith to treat tithing as additional debt. This attitude does little to inspire them to sow their tithes of honor.

I believe that churches that are serious about empowering the members of their congregation to deal with their mounting personal debt through biblical financial stewardship principles are going to inevitably see a rise in the tithing numbers in their congregations. How churches help the members of their congregation deal with the issue of mounting personal debt is the key to stabilizing their churches. King Solomon the richest man who has ever lived, tells us that the borrower is a slave to the lender, always.

The Question Of Obedience

"But Samuel replied, 'What is more pleasing to the Lord: your burnt offerings and sacrifices or your obedience to his voice? Listen! Obedience is better than sacrifice, and submission is better than offering the fat of rams. 23 Rebellion is as sinful as witchcraft, and stubbornness as bad as worshiping idols. So because you have rejected the command of the Lord, he has rejected you as king.'"

1 Samuel 15:22-23 (New Living Translation)

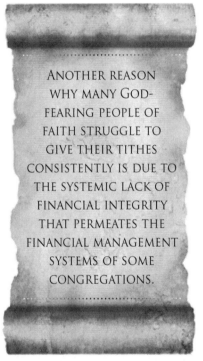

ANOTHER REASON WHY MANY GOD-FEARING PEOPLE OF FAITH STRUGGLE TO GIVE THEIR TITHES CONSISTENTLY IS DUE TO THE SYSTEMIC LACK OF FINANCIAL INTEGRITY THAT PERMEATES THE FINANCIAL MANAGEMENT SYSTEMS OF SOME CONGREGATIONS.

One of the primary reasons why many people of faith struggle with giving their tithes consistently is due to the lack of obedience to God's Word and delegated authority that is becoming an epidemic in many Congregations across the nations of the world, especially in the Western world. But the Bible is very clear that obedience is better than sacrifice.

This writing will show that tithing is an integral part of the expression of faith of Kingdom citizens, both in the Old Testament and New Testament. Paul the Apostle in the book of Hebrews (Chapter 7) makes it fairly clear that there is a priesthood in the New Testament that receives the tithes of God's people, just like there was a priesthood (Levites) that received the tithes of God's people in the Old Testament. But because the engines of disobedience are so powerful and prevalent in many of God's people, the enemy continues to rob many followers of Christ of the covenant blessings of the tithe, while simultaneously hindering the financial stability of many congregations.

Excessive Use Of
The Malachi Tithing Model

"You are under a curse, for your whole nation has been cheating me. 10 Bring all the tithes into the storehouse so there will be enough food in my Temple. If you do," says

the Lord of Heaven's Armies, "I will open the windows of heaven for you. I will pour out a blessing so great you won't have enough room to take it in! Try it! Put me to the test!"

Malachi 3:9-10 (New Living Translation)

One of the reasons why many born-again believers struggle to give their tithes consistently is due to the excessive use of the Malachi 3 tithing model by most pastors in their endeavor to exact tithes from the members of their local church. I've been told by several well-meaning, born-again believers that have been told so many times from the pulpit that they are cursed if they do not tithe, that many of them have become numb to the impact of this overused expression. Some of them told me that, "Dr Myles, why bother if I'm already cursed, because I failed to pay my tithes on several occasions in my faith walk?" But it is the serious students of the Word that have posed the most difficult challenge to the tithing question.

"Dr. Myles, why do preachers tell us that we are cursed with a curse if we do not give our tithes; when Galatians 3:13 is very clear that Jesus Christ became a curse for us on the cross? We are either cursed or the curse has been removed by Christ on the cross. So which is which?" Whenever I am asked this important theological question, my answer is always in the affirmative. Without a doubt, Christ became a curse for us on the cross so that the blessing of Abraham would come on the Gentiles. Even though tithing is important, biblical and honorable, it cannot be placed on the same level as the atoning blood of Jesus Christ. The apostle Paul is very clear in the book of Galatians that the shed blood of Jesus Christ atoned for the curse of the law. The curse described in Malachi 3:9 is part of the curse of the law.

But the real reason why most pastors rely heavily on Malachi 3 when teaching on tithing is because for many of them, Malachi 3 seems to be the best portion of Scripture, that really describes the importance of tithing to the local church. As a pastor of a thriving church myself, I know the importance of tithing to sustaining the local Ministry that most churches are involved in. But my purpose for writing this book is to show well-meaning pastors a more excellent way of exacting the tithe from New Testament believers without relying on Malachi 3.

Now we will delve into a few more excuses which are in reality demonic lies that Christians have agreed with, bought into and used repeatedly to not tithe.

1) **I can't afford it.**
   Many in the church today have a poverty mindset and spirit. They are still living as slaves rather than sons, and are lead by fear rather than faith. Many in the church are employees rather than entrepreneurs, consumers rather than producers. Many in the church live from paycheck to paycheck, barely eaking out an existence and in debt up to their eyeballs, when God desires that we have multiple streams of income (Ecc. 11:2-6).

2) **What I have to give is so small it won't make a difference.**
   God doesn't need or won't miss my little pittance. This is Shame-based thinking. *"He is that faithful in little will be ruler over much."* (Matt. 25:23) *"For if the willingness is there, the gift is acceptable according to what one has, not according to he does not have."* (2 Cor. 8:12)

3) **There is too much uncertainty in the world, politics, economy, job market, my business, my marriage, etc. to tithe.**
   I need to hoard and save for a rainy day. Again, this is Fear-based thinking and futile, fatalistic human reasoning. 2 Cor. 10:3-5 says to take captive such thoughts since they are opposed to the knowledge of Christ.

4) **Since God gave me the money I have, I should be the one to steward my tithe.** This is Pride-based thinking. Since God obviously trusts me, why should I let someone else manage my tithe? This is a "strong delusion" fueled by a spirit of control and manipulation.

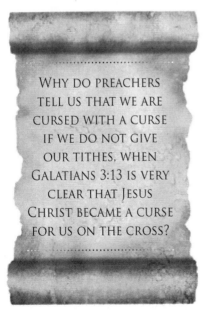

WHY DO PREACHERS TELL US THAT WE ARE CURSED WITH A CURSE IF WE DO NOT GIVE OUR TITHES, WHEN GALATIANS 3:13 IS VERY CLEAR THAT JESUS CHRIST BECAME A CURSE FOR US ON THE CROSS?

5) **The storehouse is the world, or a charity or nonprofit, not the local church.**
   Wrong. This is just another deception from Satan. More will be said on this later.

FINAL ANALYSIS

In the final analysis, this book of "WHY" only serves to show us that even though the reasons that many people of faith struggle at tithing consistently are understandable on a human level, they are nothing more than a convergence of demonic technologies that are designed to rob us of the covenantal blessings invoked by the tithe. In the final analysis, "Obedience is better than sacrifice (1 Sam 15:22)."

Interestingly enough, all of the proponents who believe that tithing is not applicable to New Testament believers have one thing in common. None of them have a burning desire to give God more than ten percent of their income, even though they believe that everything they own belongs to the Lord. And many of them have argued passionately with me that tithing is legalistic and that New Testament believers are free to give God any percentage that He wants them to give, because everything they own belongs to God 100%. What never ceases to amaze me is how God somehow seems to lead these people, collectively, to give Him and His Kingdom as little of their resources as possible. This is when I concluded that there is a diabolical conspiracy of demonic powers against the biblical practice of tithing in the body of Christ. But this book will unmask this diabolical conspiracy that is designed to rob Kingdom citizens of the benefits and privileges of tithing.

LIFE APPLICATION SECTION

Point to Ponder:

There is a diabolical conspiracy of demonic powers against the biblical practice of tithing in the body of Christ.

Verse to Remember:

"For the love of money is the root of all kinds of evil. And some people, craving money, have wandered from the true faith and pierced themselves with many sorrows."

1 Timothy 6:10

Questions to Consider:

1. Why is Greed a critical factor as to why many people of faith struggle to give their tithes consistently?

   _____
   _____
   _____
   _____

2. Why did God create or ordain the tithe?"

   _____
   _____
   _____
   _____

3. Most born again believers struggle to accept Christ's Lordship, even though they easily embrace Him as Savior, why is this so?

   _____
   _____
   _____
   _____

JOURNAL YOUR THOUGHTS

Chapter THREE

THE LOST KEY

I t is difficult to remember just how many times I have lost or misplaced my keys. I remember one occasion when I misplaced the keys to my car. I was in a hurry to get to a very important business meeting. I ran to my car so I could drive to my appointment, but when I got to the driver's door of my car I made a shocking discovery. When I dipped my hands into my pockets, the familiar feel of my fingers massaging the steel contours of my car keys was unmistakably absent, so I panicked. I was losing precious time. I began a frantic search for my lost keys. The longer the search lasted, the more anxious I became.

I searched my briefcase and then I went back into my house and ransacked it looking for my car keys. I finally found them, but I had wasted so much time in my search that my precious business meeting had come and gone. I could not do anything except beat my chest in growing frustration and deep regret. What was even more frustrating was the fact that, all the while when I was searching for my missing car keys, my car did not go anywhere. My elegant car was unmistakably present in my driveway, but I had lost the keys that I needed to drive it.

I remember another time I drove to my house after a tiring eleven-hour drive from Chicago. I was tired and hungry. All I wanted was to get into my house, eat, and take a nice hot shower and then go to sleep. The more I envisioned what would befall me once I got to my house, the faster I drove. It seemed like my car also shared my excitement. When I pulled up to the front door of my house, I switched off the ignition to my car, which came to a sudden standstill. I got out of the car and walked to the front door of my house. I inserted the key that I thought was my house key into the keyhole of my front door, when I made another frightening discovery. The key I thought was my house key was not the correct one. It looked similar to the key that opened my front door but it was not the right key. I needed a different key! So I stood there solely perplexed and on the verge of depression. I saw my vision of a breath-taking meal, hot shower and sleep suddenly dissipate. I had arrived at my house, but I could not enter. I did not have the "right key." My access into my own house had been denied.

I know that most of my readers will quickly identify with me that they too have had similar experiences. Who hasn't misplaced or lost a key at one point or another? I know people who actually lost their jobs because they lost the keys to the company safe or office. They got the pink slip because they couldn't find the key that opened the company's safe or depository that had been placed in their care. *This book is about the "return of a lost ancient key" for spiritual breakthroughs, which for the most part has been lost to a majority of the body of Christ around the world.*

The Keys of the Kingdom of Heaven

"And I will give you the keys of the Kingdom of Heaven. Whatever you forbid on earth will be forbidden in heaven, and whatever you permit on earth will be permitted in heaven."

Matthew 16:19

In the above portion of Scripture Jesus Christ told His team of apprentice apostles that He was giving them the "keys of the Kingdom of Heaven." Let us remember that Jesus did not say that He was giving them the "keys to the Kingdom of Heaven," but rather the "keys of the Kingdom of Heaven". The reason why He did not say the former is because Jesus Himself is the only "key" to the Kingdom of Heaven.

"Jesus told him, 'I am the way, the truth, and the life. No one can come to the Father except through me.'"

John 14:6

Jesus had already declared that He was both the "Key and the Door" to the Kingdom of Heaven. In other words the whole sphere of the Kingdom of Heaven never opens up to anybody until they have had a personal encounter with Jesus Christ of Nazareth. This is the message that Jesus gave to Nicodemus (John 3) when this teacher of the Law came to see Him at night. Jesus did not mince His words in telling Nicodemus that unless he was born of the Spirit he would never enter into the Kingdom of Heaven.

What Jesus gave to His apprentice apostles and to the rest of His global Church are the "keys of the Kingdom." *The keys of the Kingdom are spiritual keys that open different spiritual doors, gates, egresses, pathways or dimensions within the eternal structures of the Kingdom of Heaven.* Towards the end of His earthly messianic ministry, Jesus began to inform His apprentice apostles that He was about to return to His heavenly Father. When they heard this, they became melancholy because they felt as though He was abandoning them, which was not the case.

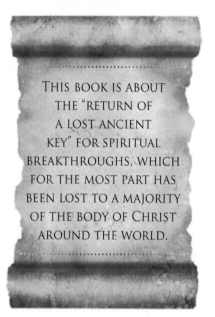

THIS BOOK IS ABOUT THE "RETURN OF A LOST ANCIENT KEY" FOR SPIRITUAL BREAKTHROUGHS, WHICH FOR THE MOST PART HAS BEEN LOST TO A MAJORITY OF THE BODY OF CHRIST AROUND THE WORLD.

A Place by His side

"Let not your heart be troubled; you believe in God, believe also in Me. In My Father's house are many mansions if it were not so, I would have told you. I go to prepare a place for you."

John 14:-1-2 (NKJV)

Most people have used the above passage of Scripture to insinuate that Jesus was talking about going to heaven to prepare spiritual mansions for God's people. As a result, many Christians spend a majority of their time here on earth basking in fairy tales about the imaginary spiritual mansions that they are going to live in when they get to heaven. The only problem with this theological approach to this passage of Scripture is simply this; the first embassy of this passage of Scripture's real meaning has little to do with Jesus preparing spiritual houses or mansions for believers. I am not suggesting that there are no actual spiritual mansions for the saints within the eternal structures of the Kingdom of Heaven.

The Kingdom of Heaven is a very real place, which has its own government, economy, citizens, armies and highly developed spiritual cities with magnificently- designed spiritual buildings that would make the best cities in America look like ghettos or forgotten wastelands. Our popular approach to this text only underscores why we need the "restoration of apostolic and prophetic technology" to the global Church so we can unlock and unmask some of the hidden meanings of Scripture. All of the Scriptures were written by prophets and apostles. Doesn't it follow therefore that in order for us to effectively unlock some of the hidden meanings of Scripture that we would need the ministries of apostles and prophets restored to the church? *All Bible doctrines are essentially apostolic and prophetic doctrines because the Bible was written by prophets and apostles.*

If we look closely at John 14:1-2, we will discover that Jesus never promised that He was going to heaven to prepare spiritual mansions for the saints. Let me paraphrase what Jesus said. "In my Father's house there are many mansions or rooms" is a statement of fact. "I go to prepare a place for you" is a statement of promise. "So that where I am so shall you be" is a statement of purpose. So the passage John 14:1-2 is a combination of three important prophetic statements – *a statement of fact, a statement of promise and a statement of purpose.*

One of these three prophetic statements had already been accomplished and the others were about to be executed. *The mansions/rooms in the Father's house that Jesus was referring to had already been prepared for us from before the foundation of the world.* What had not yet been prepared, however, was a spiritual position Jesus called "a prepared place for you." This is because Jesus Christ our eternal High Priest had not yet been crucified and His precious blood had not yet been shed for the remissions of the sins of the whole world. The blood of our faithful High Priest had not yet been presented to the Father in heaven as an eternal peace offering, between God and mankind.

> *"For he raised us from the dead along with Christ and seated us with him in the heavenly realms because we are united with Christ Jesus."*
>
> Ephesians 2:6

The passage of Scripture above is the prophetic fulfillment of John 14:1-2. The apostle Paul wrote the book of Ephesians after the death, resurrection and ascension of the Lord Jesus Christ. By the time Paul wrote the book of Ephesians, Jesus Christ our faithful High Priest had already presented the sacrifice of His own blood to His heavenly Father and secured "a place of eternal redemption" for us. In other words, by the time the apostle Paul was writing the book of Ephesians, the spiritual position called "a place prepared for you" that Jesus had promised His apprentice apostles in John 14:1-2 had already been prepared.

Spiritual Mansions in My Father's House

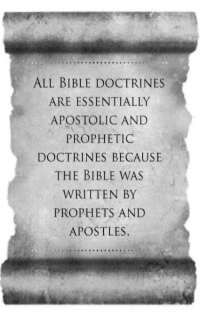

What are the many "mansions in my Father's house" that Jesus was referring to? The many mansions in my Father's house that Jesus was referring to are not exclusively spiritual residencies for the saints as some have suggested. They are both that and a whole lot more. The "many mansions or rooms" in my Father's house *are the many spiritual doors, gates, egresses, pathways or dimensions that unlock the spiritual inheritance of the "Son" (Christ) within the eternal structures of the Kingdom of Heaven.* This is why it was absolutely necessary for Jesus to take His shed blood to the Father's throne and prepare **"a special place for us."** "This place that Jesus prepared for us" is a "position of favor and intimacy by the Father's side," that gives us access to different dimensions of spiritual illumination. This spiritual light illuminates the different "keys of the Kingdom of Heaven" that Jesus gave to His church and the specific doors, pathways, gates, egresses or spiritual dimensions that these keys open within the eternal structures of the Kingdom of God. Apart from living in this place Jesus called "a place prepared for you," much of what belongs to us as the seed of Abraham, which Jesus Christ died for, will be lost in religiosity.

> *"But He said, 'You cannot see My face; for no man shall see Me, and live.' And the LORD said, "Here is a place by Me, and you shall stand on the rock."*
>
> Exodus 33:20-21 (NKJV)

God told Moses that there is "a place by me". This is the same place that Jesus was referring to, when He told his apostles "I go to prepare a place for you." As powerful and as close to God as Moses was, he did not sit in this spiritual position that Jesus called "a place prepared for you." This is because Jesus Christ was the only person who could truly offer the Father the "blood of atonement" that would forever secure this lofty position of favor, as an eternal inheritance for the seed of Abraham within the eternal structures of the Kingdom of Heaven.

Where I am so shall you be?

Finally the passage from John 14:1-2 ends with Jesus making a prophetic statement of purpose: ***"So that where I am so shall you be."*** What in God's name does this mean? This statement describes what will begin to happen once we begin to operate from the "place prepared for us by Christ on the right hand of God." When we begin to use the different keys of the Kingdom of Heaven we will quickly begin to discover the many "mansions or rooms" that these keys "open within the Father's house." For instance, when we get a revelation about the "key of healing," the "door of healing" will swing wide open. When the door of healing swings open and we step into the "mansion of healing," everything that Jesus Christ is currently doing in healing, we will also begin to do or experience here on earth. If Christ is healing the sick, we can do no less here on earth. We will become part of the heavenly orchestra here on earth.

In terms of Christ's ongoing priestly work, we will be where He is even though physically we are still living here on earth. If Jesus Christ comes knocking on the doors of our church because He wants to heal the sick among us, we will allow Him to have His way. If we refuse Him we are in effect not "where He is." If Jesus comes knocking on the doors of our church because He wishes to prophesy but we refuse to let Him prophesy through His Church, we are in effect not "where He is."

When we lose the power to live in this spiritual position of favor that Jesus called "a place prepared for you," *we will inevitably begin to become more and more anti-Christ in our spiritual dynamics. We will find ourselves calling Spirit "flesh" and flesh "Spirit" because we are not where He is.* I am in no way suggesting that churches that do not believe in prophecy or healing are the anti-Christ, by no means. However, there are many God-fearing saints who have found themselves unwilling participants in resisting the Spirit of God because He was moving in a manner that was not familiar to them. They became offended by the method God chose to reveal Himself by rather than focusing on what He was doing.

Some Kingdom citizens are like Jacob, who spent a night at Bethel (Gen 28:11) and had an encounter with God but had no idea that he was in the presence of God. When Jacob woke up from his sleep, he beat his chest in great fear and dismay when he realized that he had stationed himself by accident at the house of God. He discovered that the place where he was, was also the gateway to heaven. Most Kingdom citizens are a lot like Jacob. They are God-fearing but in most cases they have no clue as to where God is at and as such they find themselves resisting God because they do not like the package that He came in.

It's my prayer that you will rediscover "that special place of favor Jesus prepared for you" by His Father's side. This is a place of spiritual intimacy with our heavenly Father. This is the place where you and I can hear the sound of His voice and live in the favor of His presence. Finding this spiritual position Jesus called "a place prepared for you" is one of the most powerful keys to living an abundant life of favor in God's kingdom. However, this is not the "Lost Key" that this book is about. This book is an aggressive attempt to "return to you an ancient key" of immeasurable power that has been lost to many in the body of Christ.

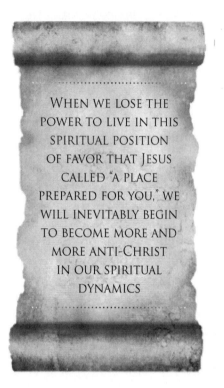

WHEN WE LOSE THE POWER TO LIVE IN THIS SPIRITUAL POSITION OF FAVOR THAT JESUS CALLED "A PLACE PREPARED FOR YOU," WE WILL INEVITABLY BEGIN TO BECOME MORE AND MORE ANTI-CHRIST IN OUR SPIRITUAL DYNAMICS

The Key of Knowledge

"What sorrow awaits you experts in religious law! For you remove the key to knowledge from the people. You don't enter the Kingdom yourselves, and you prevent others from entering."

Luke 11:52

One of the most powerful keys of the Kingdom of Heaven is what Jesus called the "Key of Knowledge." Jesus chastised the Pharisees and Sadducees who were the religious leaders of His era who were stealing the key of knowledge from the people who were under their spiritual leadership. Jesus accused these religious leaders of blocking people's entrance into the Kingdom of God. Millions of lost souls are languishing today in eternal damnation in unquenchable fires because while they were still alive, they never discovered the key of knowledge that would have enabled them to know Jesus Christ as God's chosen Messiah. The "key of knowledge" is very important to living the supernatural life. This book is an attempt to use the "key of knowledge" to restore to the Church an ancient key that will open up a "new way of living" for many people of faith.

The Key of the Apostle and Prophet

"So now you Gentiles are no longer strangers and foreigners. You are citizens along with all of God's holy people. You are members of God's family. Together, we are his house, built on the foundation of the apostles and the prophets. And the cornerstone is Christ Jesus himself."

Ephesians 2:19-20

There is a lot of buzz and controversy in the church world concerning the restoration of apostles and prophets. The subject of apostles and prophets has unleashed winds and fires of conversation, pitting those who are favorable towards this restoration against critics who are convinced that these ministries do not exist today. This is very unfortunate because there is nothing further from the truth than the suggestion that apostles and prophets are not needed in these critical times we live in. This belief only underscores how notorious the church is at misplacing or losing strategic keys of the Kingdom of Heaven that were given to it, to advance God's Kingdom agenda here on earth.

A friend of mine who runs a school of the prophets in Tulsa sent her students to do a City-wide survey to review public opinion on the subject of apostles and prophets. One of her students walked into the office of a very famous pastor and asked him to fill out the survey. When this pastor got to the section listing the fivefold ministry gifts listed in Ephesians 4:11, he circled the offices of apostle and prophet and then drew a line from the circle and pointed it to the office of the pastor. He told the student doing the survey that the offices of apostle and prophet were all rolled into the office of the pastor. This is as ridiculous as saying the offices of President and vice-President of the United States were all rolled into the office of Secretary of State. The only problem with this pastor's theology is that God forgot to tell us that he had rolled the ministries of apostles and prophets into the office of the pastor. I am sure you get the picture. In any case this pastor would have been hard pressed to find Scriptures in the Bible that would support his thesis. ***The sad truth is that the church is suffering from the lack of "apostolic and prophetic technology in many of its spiritual operations."***

Now these are the gifts Christ gave to the church: the apostles, the prophets, the evangelists, and the pastors and teachers. Their responsibility is to equip God's people to do his work and build up the church, the body of Christ. This will continue until we all come to such unity in our faith and knowledge of God's Son that we will be mature in the Lord, measuring up to the full and complete standard of Christ.

Ephesians 4:11-13

According to the above passage of Scripture, the ministry gifts of apostle, prophet, teacher, pastor and evangelist were given the same terms of lease. Christ gave all of these ministries to the church for the ***"perfecting of the saints for the work of the ministry."*** This phrase in the lease contract is the mission statement that these five fold ministry gifts were designed to fulfill. One does not have to look further than the people in our own churches to realize that there are thousands of God-loving-saints who still need to be "perfected and then released to do the work of the ministry." ***"Till we all come to the unity of the faith and of the knowledge of the Son of God"*** describes the "lease period" that God imposed on the life span of these five-fold ministry gifts. To say that apostles and prophets have passed away or to suggest that they have been rolled into the office of the pastor while admitting that the other two ministry gifts are still functional today is to tamper with a "sealed legal Kingdom document."

In the world which we live in, any attempt to alter a sealed legal document without the signature of the originator is tantamount to "document fraud" and jail houses are filled with men and women who are doing time for "document fraud." I truly believe that the spiritual consequences for practicing spiritual fraud are even more serious. But there are many reasons why the devil is terrified of the grace apostles and prophets bring to the church of the living God.

"Are we all apostles? Are we all prophets? Are we all teachers? Do we all have the power to do miracles? Do we all have the gift of healing? Do we all have the ability to speak in unknown languages? Do we all have the ability to interpret unknown languages?" Of course not!

1 Corinthians 12:29-30

I am not suggesting that every pastor out there must drop the title of pastor and become an apostle or a prophet. Neither am I suggesting that apostles and prophets are more important to the Church than the other ministerial gifts. They are just different and extremely critical to the foundation of the New Testament church. Paul the Apostle made it very clear that "everyone is not an apostle and everyone is not a prophet," but some are and those that are bring a grace to the

New Testament Church no one else can bring to the Body of Christ for the purpose of advancing the Kingdom of God. May I also suggest that some of the people we call senior pastors or bishops are actually apostles or prophets by calling? The church desperately needs the return of the "key of the apostle and prophet."

Apostolic and Prophetic Technology

"Together, we are his house, built on the foundation of the apostles and the prophets. And the cornerstone is Christ Jesus himself."

Ephesians 2:20

"This is what God in his wisdom said about you: 'I will send prophets and apostles to them, but they will kill some and persecute the others.'"

Luke 11:49

You might be wondering why I am emphasizing the fact that the Church needs the restoration of the ministries of apostles and prophets. The reasons are simple but have far-reaching spiritual implications. The Scriptures tell us that the church is built upon the foundation of apostles and prophets. This means that when it comes to the issue of **advancing the Kingdom of God here on earth, apostles and prophets are first in rank and in order of importance**; in the same way, the foundation of a house is first in rank and in order of importance when a building contractor is building a house.

Jesus made it adamantly clear that apostles and prophets were given to the Church and to the nations of the world by the "wisdom of God." **There is nothing in creation, which can outrank the wisdom of God. To deny the presence and importance of apostles and prophets to the Church is an exercise or vocation in resisting the wisdom of God.** Think about this: without apostles and prophets there would be no Bible. All the sixty-six books of the holy Bible were authored on the basis of "apostolic and prophetic" technology. Everything we know about God, angels, man and the devil was revealed to men and women who either had a prophetic or apostolic gift and ministry.

Pastors must not be afraid to recognize and welcome the ministry of true apostles and prophets. If some pastors were CEO's of Fortune 500 corporations, they would have run those corporations into financial ruin through their fear of change. Recently Microsoft, the dominant software company in the personal computer industry, has come out with a more technologically-advanced version of Windows. It's called "Windows Vista." It would be futile for corporations to refuse to upgrade their operating systems and embrace this powerful technology simply because they are afraid of change or are addicted to using the older version of Windows. *New technologies always reveal a more excellent way of doing business*. What's more, one does not have to work for Microsoft to use and benefit from their technology. In like manner, senior pastors do not have to become apostles or prophets to benefit from the usage of apostolic and prophetic technology.

> THERE IS NOTHING IN CREATION, WHICH CAN OUTRANK THE WISDOM OF GOD. TO DENY THE PRESENCE AND IMPORTANCE OF APOSTLES AND PROPHETS TO THE CHURCH IS AN EXERCISE OR VOCATION IN RESISTING THE WISDOM OF GOD.

Nevertheless, this book was not written to talk about the necessity of the "key of apostle and prophet," but to provide the pathway which will lead us to the discovery of an "ancient and most powerful key." This key is far more important than the "key of knowledge or the key of the apostle and prophet." When your eyes are opened by the Lord to see this ancient key, you will begin the process of ascendancy within your own spirit and you will come to know the power of living under the Order of Melchizedek.

The Ancient Key of the Order of Melchizedek

The Lord has taken an oath and will not break his vow: "You are a priest forever in the order of Melchizedek."

Psalm 110:4

The spirit of revelation will grab hold of you when you allow the Holy Spirit to illuminate the truths contained in the pages of this book. You will be delivered from serving God under "the spirit of law" and you will cross into the "glorious liberty" of the sons of the Kingdom. *If you have struggled with tithing, this book will bring an end to your lack of joy or victory in the area of tithing*. Once you see this "ancient Key," you will look at your "tithe" as a love letter from the very heart of God.

When you see this ancient key, you will be delivered from every generational curse that you have ever wrestled with. Have you ever been told that, "you are cursed with a curse" because you failed to pay your tithes? The discovery of this ancient key will deliver you from all church-induced "guilt trips" and also from feeling like you are cursed by God; such feelings usually are a by-product of harsh pronouncements from the pulpit. You will find yourself embracing this "new way of living." You will finally find the "power" to honor God with your tithe without any struggles whatsoever. *You will also discover the joy of tithing from an inspired heart instead of a "regulated heart."*

You might be asking, "Francis, what is the ancient Key that you are talking about"? The ancient key which I am talking about is "..............!" I am sorry but I am getting ahead of myself. I must first take you on a Bible tour before I answer your question. We will start our journey by visiting Adam, Abraham, Isaac and Jacob, the king of Sodom, Moses, Aaron, and Jesus. Our journey will end with examining the apologetic testimony of the apostle Paul about the priestly Order of Melchizedek. At the end of our short excursion, I will show you "THE ANCIENT KEY!" When you see it your life will never ever be the same again. Please read on…

LIFE APPLICATION SECTION

Point to Ponder:

One of the most powerful keys of the Kingdom of Heaven is what Jesus called the "Key to Knowledge." Jesus chastised the Pharisees and Sadducees who were the religious leaders of the day who were stealing the key to knowledge from the people who were under their spiritual leadership.

Verse to Remember:

"And I will give you the keys of the Kingdom of Heaven. Whatever you forbid on earth will be forbidden in heaven, and whatever you permit on earth will be permitted in heaven."

Matthew 16:19

Questions to Consider:

1. What are the keys of the Kingdom?

2. What did Jesus mean when He said, "I go to prepare a place for you?"

3. What are some of the functions of the keys of the Kingdom?

JOURNAL YOUR THOUGHTS

WE ARE THE SEED OF ABRAHAM

verything of God begins and manifests itself in seed form here on earth. This principle makes the "Seed" one of the most important spiritual technologies for manifesting the spiritual and natural realities of the Kingdom of God here on Earth. We must remember that the Bible tells us that we are the seed of Abraham. What in God's name does it mean to be the seed of Abraham? This is a very important question that we must answer on our journey to rediscovering the "Lost Key" which unlocks Abraham's natural and spiritual inheritance within the eternal structures of the Kingdom of Heaven.

To answer the question, "what does it mean to be the seed of Abraham?" Our spiritual trail to answering this important question will lead us through the Garden of Eden.

The Creation of Adam:
The Beginning of Human History

Then God said, "Let Us make man in Our image, according to Our likeness; let them have dominion over the fish of the sea, over the birds of the air, and over the cattle, over all[a] the earth and over every creeping thing that creeps on the earth." 27 So God created man in His own image; in the image of God He created him; male and female He created them. 28 Then God blessed them, and God said to them, "Be fruitful and multiply; fill the earth and subdue it; have dominion over the fish of the sea, over the birds of the air, and over every living thing that moves on the earth."

Gen 1:26-28 (NKJV)

When the Godhead decided to create the first man and woman, there was a divine consensus that the species called "mankind" would be created in the exact "image" and "likeness" of God. God promised Himself that these "spirit children" with an earthly body would shoulder the responsibility of extending the reach of the Kingdom of Heaven and its government here on earth. These spirit-children, male and female, whom God collectively called "Adam," were to be the exact representation of the invisible God. They were created to execute the will of God and advance His Kingdom agenda on the colonized planet called Earth.

To this end God gave them the power to...

1. Be fruitful

2. Multiply

3. Replenish the earth and subdue it

4. Have dominion

God went as far as providing the first couple with an endless supply of natural and spiritual resources by placing them inside a garden of priceless and endless abundance. This garden of abundance was called Eden. This couple lived in the favor of His presence and walked with God. To keep their tenancy in this Garden of abundance, God warned them against eating from the tree of the knowledge of good and evil. There were many fruit-bearing trees in this Garden of abundance, but none of them were as important as, the "tree of life" and the "tree of the knowledge of good and evil." Interestingly enough, God never warned Adam and Eve against eating from the "Tree of Life." This is a very important observation for us to bear in mind. Later on I will show you how the two trees in the Garden of Eden represented "two tithes and two priesthoods" and how they relate to the "Lost Key" which is the subject of this book.

The Bible tells us that in the process of time, the "serpent," which was subtler than all the creatures that were in the Garden of Eden, began to talk to Eve. This talking serpent was in actuality Satan manifesting himself as an angel of light. The serpent cast a shadow of doubt on the integrity of what God had instructed Adam and Eve not to do. The serpent told them that God was terrified of the fact that if they ate from the tree of the knowledge of good and evil they would be like God, "knowing good and evil." Nothing could have been further from the truth. When they bought into the lie, their divine light was immediately shut off. The life of God was stolen out of their spirits, which became enshrouded in death.

They also lost their "lofty position of authority" in the earthly Kingdom that God had given them. This Adamic kingdom stretched all the way to the second heaven. Everything the devil has in his power was once part of the original Adamic kingdom. Therefore it's theologically safe to say that, if the devil's spiritual headquarters is located in the second heaven (Rev 12:7), it is safe to assume that the second heaven was also part of the original genesis Kingdom that Adam was given to rule. After the fall of the first God-ordained ambassador, the devil immediately became the god of this world. Adam and Eve became his conquered subjects because they had chosen to submit

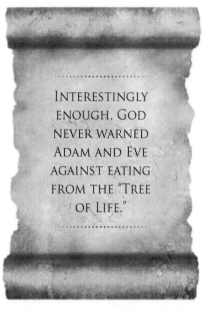

INTERESTINGLY ENOUGH, GOD NEVER WARNED ADAM AND EVE AGAINST EATING FROM THE "TREE OF LIFE."

to the devil's will. The first couple were then driven out of the governor's mansion, which was located in the Garden of abundance, and "demonic-death agencies" entered into the world and took center stage.

The Adamic Generation

"When Adam sinned, sin entered the world. Adam's sin brought death, so death spread to everyone, for everyone sinned."

Romans 5:12

After Adam fell into sin, "demonic-death agencies entered" into the human bloodline and polluted the human gene pool and set it on the pathway of death and destruction. Since Adam was the progenitor (the first father) of the entire human race, spiritual death spread to the entire human race throughout the whole course of human history. This is why every person on the planet is conceived in sin and under the penalty of spiritual death.

Every living person who has not yet surrendered his or her life to the Lordship of Jesus Christ is the "Seed of Adam." Every living person outside Christ is part of what I call the "Adamic generation." Every person who is still a part of the Adamic generation is still under the sentence of death, whether they are rich or famous. No matter how successful a person is, if they are from the seed of Adam, the "pathway of death" inside them is set towards eternal damnation unless they experience the intervention of God.

When the seed of Adam make great scientific and technological discoveries, they will eventually use their discoveries to produce death. This is because the "spiritual DNA" of the seed of Adam is set on the pathway towards death. After Adam and Eve fell into sin, God could not use them to establish a spiritual race of children who could advance the will and culture of His heavenly Kingdom here on earth. As such, God set out on a journey through the corridors of time to find a man whose "spirit of obedience" would begin to turn the entire human race from the pathway of death onto the pathway of life. God found that man in a Chaldean herdsman by the name of Abram.

The Call of Abraham

*The LORD had said to Abram, "Leave your native country, your relatives, and your father's family, and go to the land that I will show you. **2** I will make you into a great nation. I will bless you and make you famous, and you will be a blessing to others. **3** I will bless those who bless you and curse those who treat you with contempt. All the families on earth will be blessed through you."*

Genesis 12:1-3

The call of Abram the Chaldean is one of the most important prophetic callings that God ever gave to a man other than the Lord Jesus Christ. Just like Adam was the beginning of the entire human race, Abram—whose name was later changed to Abraham—became the father of a whole new race of spiritual people who are born again by the will of the Spirit. His personal journey of faith with God began to establish the spiritual foundation for the coming of Jesus Christ, the last Adam. ***Abraham's obedience to God began to "open spiritual portals for a God invasion here on earth!"***

The Covenant of Abraham

I will make a covenant with you, by which I will guarantee to give you countless descendants." At this, Abram fell face down on the ground. Then God said to him, "This is my covenant with you: I will make you the father of a multitude of nations! What's more, I am changing your name. It will no longer be Abram. Instead, you will be called Abraham, for you will be the father of many nations. I will make you extremely fruitful. Your descendants will become many nations, and kings will be among them! "I will confirm my covenant with you and your descendants after you, from generation to generation. This is the everlasting covenant: I will always be your God and the God of your descendants after you."

Genesis 17:2-7

After Abraham had consistently maintained a testimony of faith and obedience, God made a covenant with Abram and later changed his name to "Abraham." The name Abraham literally means "Abram of God Most High or father of many nations." In the covenant God made with Abraham, God told him that He was going to make him into a father of many nations. Abraham was to be the father of the nation of Israel and also the spiritual father of the New Testament royal priesthood which consists of both Jews and Gentiles who have placed their faith in Christ. God promised Abraham that even though he was well advanced in years, God was going to give him a son in his old age through his wife Sarah.

The Birth of Isaac

*"The LORD kept his word and did for Sarah exactly what he had promised. **2** She became pregnant, and she gave birth to a son for Abraham in his old age. This happened at just the time God had said it would. **3** And Abraham named their son Isaac. **4** Eight days after Isaac was born, Abraham circumcised him as God had commanded."*

Genesis 21:1-4

The miraculous birth of Isaac marked the beginning of a new era in the dealings of God with Abraham. The birth of Isaac was also marked by a spirit of acceleration in God's plan to take back His inheritance in the nations of the world, which had been lost through Adam's rebellion. Isaac was a very unique child because he was both a "sign and a type of Christ." The birth of Isaac secured Abraham's inheritance in the nation of Israel and also created a "divine portal" for the infusion of the "Messianic Seed" into the human plane. The infusion of the "Messianic

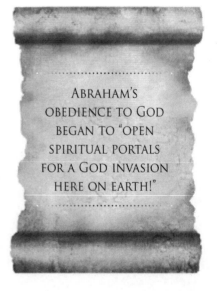

ABRAHAM'S OBEDIENCE TO GOD BEGAN TO "OPEN SPIRITUAL PORTALS FOR A GOD INVASION HERE ON EARTH!"

Seed" into the human plane was the divine means that enabled Abraham to become the father of many nations. The coming of this "Messianic Seed" would turn men from the pathway of death onto the pathway of life.

The Offering of Isaac

Some time later, God tested Abraham's faith. "Abraham!" God called. "Yes," he replied. "Here I am." "Take your son, your only son—yes, Isaac, whom you love so much—and go to the land of Moriah. Go and sacrifice him as a burnt offering on one of the mountains, which I will show you." The next morning Abraham got up early. He saddled his donkey and took two of his servants with him, along with his son, Isaac. Then he chopped wood for a fire for a burnt offering and set out for the place God had told him about. So Abraham placed the wood for the burnt offering on Isaac's shoulders, while he himself carried the fire and the knife. As the two of them walked on together, Isaac turned to Abraham and said, "Father?" "Yes, my son?" Abraham replied. "We have the fire and the wood," the boy said, "but where is the sheep for the burnt offering?" "God will provide a sheep for the burnt offering, my son," Abraham answered. And they both walked on together.

Genesis 22:1-3, 6-8

The offering of Isaac as a sacrificial seed on Mount Moriah by his father Abraham, in obedience to an instruction from God, was one of the most significant prophetic events that ever happened in Abraham's life. ***The offering of Isaac marked the fulfillment of Abraham's covenant of total obedience to God and established him as the father of many nations within the eternal structures of the Kingdom of heaven!*** The most significant thing about the offering of Isaac to God, however, is based upon the following powerful reality and consideration. When Abraham offered Isaac as a sacrificial offering of obedience to God, the only priesthood that was revealed to Abraham at the time was the "priestly Order of Melchizedek."

We know for a fact that the Lord Jesus Christ is the High Priest after the Order of Melchizedek. This means that when Abraham offered Isaac to God, he offered his only son to God under the power of this eternal priestly Order. This would explain why God was so moved by Abraham's faith and total obedience. God spoke from the heavens and swore that His covenant of blessing would never be removed from Abraham's life. Abraham's obedience in the offering of Isaac not only opened the door for the entrance of the "Messianic Seed" into the world, but it also established the priestly Order of Melchizedek as an everlasting priesthood for the "Seed of Abraham." When Abraham told his son Isaac that "God will provide Himself a lamb," Abraham's faith pulled "Christ, the Messianic Seed" into the canals of time and set Him on course towards the redemption of the whole world.

A Question I couldn't Answer?

God knows how to intervene in the course of our lives and set us on the path towards spiritual discovery and destiny. God is an expert at "troubling the waters" to force us to dig deeper into the rich mines of His Word. In 1993 I planted a church in Zambia (my native country) after resigning my job as a bookkeeper at a prestigious accounting firm.

During the course of pastoring this church, a woman whom I knew to be a very dedicated Disciple of Christ and member of my church came to me and asked me a "question I could not answer!" With all the sincerity and respect she could master, she looked me in the eyes and asked, "Pastor, why is my tithe not working for me? You know I never miss a tithe, even if I have to go hungry. But Pastor, I have seen little or no fruit come from my consistent tithing. Isn't God supposed to open the windows of heaven and pour me a blessing more than I can bear," she asked?

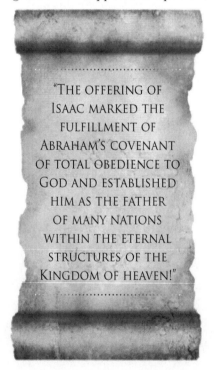

"THE OFFERING OF ISAAC MARKED THE FULFILLMENT OF ABRAHAM'S COVENANT OF TOTAL OBEDIENCE TO GOD AND ESTABLISHED HIM AS THE FATHER OF MANY NATIONS WITHIN THE ETERNAL STRUCTURES OF THE KINGDOM OF HEAVEN!"

When I looked into those very sincere eyes that were looking at me with a cry so deep and painful, I knew that some religiously-rehearsed answer would not do. Preachers are sometimes notorious for giving religiously-rehearsed answers to spiritual matters they have not diligently investigated. "My dear sister, I really do not know why your tithe is not working for you!" I answered her. She walked away dejected but thankful that I was honest in my answer. But the lack of an appropriate answer to such a fundamental question bothered me to the core of my sanctified soul. Her question kept haunting me like a hyena that has smelled an injured prey.

Little did I know that her honest question would thrust me into over fourteen years of research to answer her question. Little did I know that her question would lead me to one of the greatest spiritual discoveries of my lifetime. Little did I know that her question would be used by the Holy Spirit to lead me to the discovery of a "Lost Ancient Key" for spiritual breakthroughs, which opens up the entire priestly Order of Melchizedek and ignites the "Blessing of Abraham." While attending a prophetic conference in Tulsa, hosted by dear friends of mine, I received a prophecy that indicated that the Lord was releasing me to write the books that were inside me. While my friend was prophesying over me the Lord told me that, "I have given you the permission to release the books containing what I have shown you concerning the priestly Order of Melchizedek."

The Lord gave me tremendous peace and strong confirmations through great spiritual leaders that His time had come for me to shed light on the "Lost Key" which activates the functionality of the priestly Order of Melchizedek in the lives of God's children. God also challenged me to challenge inaccurate patterns of tithing in the body of Christ. By the grace of God I have finally answered the woman's question. I know why her tithe and that of millions of others within the body of Christ are not working for them on the level that God has always intended. I now know why only a minimal percentage of evangelicals in North America pay their tithes. Please read on…

Look to Abraham

"Listen to Me, you who follow after righteousness, You who seek the LORD: Look to the rock from which you were hewn, And to the hole of the pit from which you were dug. Look to Abraham your father, And to Sarah who bore you; For I called him alone, And blessed him and increased him."

Isaiah 51:1-2 (NKJV)

We are commanded by God Almighty to look to Abraham, our father and Sarah, who bore us according to the power of God. Unfortunately many of us have failed miserably to look to Abraham in many areas of our lives, especially in the area of tithing! Many of today's prosperity ministries are built around inaccurate patterns of tithing. These inaccurate tithing patterns have limited the Kingdom supply of the saints and limited our access into the priestly Order of Melchizedek. In order for you to appreciate the foundation my statements are based upon, I am asking that you continue this journey with me. I also want to give homage to men and women of God who teach on true biblical prosperity because they have done their best to move the church from a poverty mentality to a mentality of abundance, even though most of them promote a pattern of tithing which is not God's best for New Testament believers.

We are the Seed of Abraham

In the same way, "Abraham believed God, and God counted him as righteous because of his faith." 7 The real children of Abraham, then, are those who put their faith in God.

Galatians 3:7

Now to Abraham and his Seed were the promises made. He does not say, "And to seeds," as of many, but as of one, "And to your Seed," who is Christ.

Galatians 3:16 (NKJV)

The Bible says that we are the seed of Abraham. What does this mean? In order to answer this question we must first understand that Abraham was promised "two brands of seed." We must also understand why Christ is the ultimate and perfect Seed of Abraham. We also need to see how the two brands of seed Abraham was given on Mount Moriah unite in Christ, who is the true "Seed of Abraham."

Abraham's Two Brands of Seed

After Lot had gone, the Lord said to Abram, "Look as far as you can see in every direction—north and south, east and west. 15 I am giving all this land, as far as you can see, to you and your descendants as a permanent possession. 16 And I will give you so many descendants that, like the dust of the earth, they cannot be counted!

Genesis 13:14-16

But you promised me, 'I will surely treat you kindly, and I will multiply your descendants until they become as numerous as the sands along the seashore—too many to count.'"

Genesis 32:12

1. The "Sand Seed" of Abraham (Represents Abraham's natural descendants who are the citizens of the nation of Israel).

"I will certainly bless you. I will multiply your descendants beyond number, like the stars in the sky and the sand on the seashore. Your descendants will conquer the cities of their enemies."

Genesis 22:17

"You have given me no descendants of my own, so one of my servants will be my heir." Then the Lord said to him, "No, your servant will not be your heir, for you will have a son of your own who will be your heir." "Then the Lord took Abram outside and said to him, 'Look up into the sky and count the stars if you can. That's how many descendants you will have!' And Abram believed the Lord, and the Lord counted him as righteous because of his faith."

Genesis 15:3-6

2. The "Star Seed" of Abraham (Represents Abraham's spiritual descendants who are members of the Church of the firstborn). This group consists of every person on earth, regardless of their race (Jew or Gentile) or the color of their skin, who have accepted Jesus Christ as their personal Lord and Savior. These are the true spiritual descendants of Abraham who walk by faith and not by sight. They are the ones the apostle Paul called the "true Israel of God!"

"Neither circumcision nor uncircumcision means anything; what counts is a new creation. Peace and mercy to all who follow this rule, even to the Israel of God."

Galatians 6:15-16

The "Sand-seed" of Abraham were given Abraham's natural inheritance, which is Abraham's portion in the nations of the earth. God gave Abraham an inheritance in the nations of the earth because of his life of obedience to God. God gave Abraham's descendants according to the flesh (the Jewish nation) the land of present-day Palestine for an everlasting inheritance. This is why anybody who tries to give away the land of natural Israel to anybody is "committing spiritual fraud and trespassing on God's territory!"

However the power and influence of the nation of Israel was destined by God to extend well beyond the physical borders of modern Palestine. This is because God told Abraham that his natural descendants (the Jewish nation) would be like sand by the seashore. Interestingly enough sand is found around all the shorelines of the seven continents of the world. The sand around the shorelines of the seven continents is a "stunning prophetic proclamation to every demonic principality that Abraham has an inheritance in all the nations of the world!"

This is why no matter where you go in the world, you cannot escape the influence of Jewish technology and financial genius. In India for instance, some of the high tech companies are simply "front" corporations run and financed by Jewish businessmen. Even in the heat of Nazi tyranny, most Jewish people came out of the Holocaust with money that they had hidden in very ingenious ways. Even the maniac Hitler failed to snuff them out of the earth because Abraham's spiritual inheritance within the nations of the world, was sealed by God as an everlasting covenant.

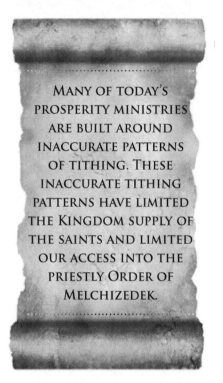

MANY OF TODAY'S PROSPERITY MINISTRIES ARE BUILT AROUND INACCURATE PATTERNS OF TITHING. THESE INACCURATE TITHING PATTERNS HAVE LIMITED THE KINGDOM SUPPLY OF THE SAINTS AND LIMITED OUR ACCESS INTO THE PRIESTLY ORDER OF MELCHIZEDEK.

Interestingly enough, sand also acts as a buffer or beachhead between the waters of the Seas and the landmass of the seven continents. All the seven continents of the world would be flooded with water if sand stops acting as a buffer or beachhead. I personally believe that the quickest way for nations to stop some of these TSUNAMIS from destroying the structure of their nations is to adopt a favorable foreign policy towards the nation of Israel. This is because "God judges the nations of the earth based upon how they treat the nation of Israel." Among all the nations of the world, Israel is the "apple of God's eye." God destroyed the nation of Egypt based upon how Pharaoh and his people treated the natural descendants of Abraham.

> *"The Lord is a warrior; Yahweh is his name! Pharaoh's chariots and army he has hurled into the sea. The finest of Pharaoh's officers are drowned in the Red Sea. The deep waters gushed over them; they sank to the bottom like a stone."*
>
> Exodus 15:3-5

Interestingly enough, the Tsunami which killed over 212,000 people in recent years happened in Indonesia and other regions that are mostly anti-Israel. This particular tsunami was the biggest tsunami in modern times, but the Bible records another catastrophic tsunami, which destroyed Pharaoh and his entire army for terrorizing the sand-seed of Abraham. Nations that have a foreign policy which is favorable towards Israel, are wise and well advised. These nations will always attract the blessing of God. This is why the blessing of God continues to rest on the United States, despite her continuous moral decline.

The "Star-seed" of Abraham who are the Church of the firstborn (Jesus Christ) were given Abraham's spiritual inheritance, which is Abraham's portion in the eternal structures of the Kingdom of heaven. This is why the Bible tells us that after Christ's ascension to the throne of His heavenly Father, Christ has made us to sit with Him in heavenly places.

"For he raised us from the dead along with Christ and seated us with him in the heavenly realms because we are united with Christ Jesus."

Ephesians 2:6

When Abraham cried to God and told Him that He had given him no "seed or offspring" and that his servant Eliezer of Damascus was going to inherit everything that God had given him, God responded quickly. He took Abraham out of his tent and told him to look towards the heavens. When Abraham lifted his head and looked at the "night sky, he saw more stars than he could count." The reason God told Abraham to look up was because stars are found in the heavens. The more Abraham looked at those stars under the anointing of the Holy Spirit, the stars suddenly began to look like spirit-children from every nation on earth. When Abraham saw in his spirit the billions of spiritual sons and daughters God was going to give him, Abraham believed God. *This belief in God's ability to give him his "star-seed descendants" was counted against him as righteousness and at that very moment Abraham became the father of many nations!*

Incidentally, stars are set as "steady points of navigation" in the heavens. When the pilgrims left the shores of Europe to come to what we now call the United States of America, their shipmasters were depending on reading the positions of certain stars in order to chart their course towards the new-found land. Those who boarded ships led by captains who did not know how to navigate by studying the patterns and positions of the stars, got lost and died at sea.

"Jesus was born in Bethlehem in Judea, during the reign of King Herod. About that time some wise men from eastern lands arrived in Jerusalem, asking, **2** *'Where is the newborn king of the Jews? We saw his star as it rose, and we have come to worship him.'"*

Matthew 2:1-2

When Christ was born in a manger in the City of Bethlehem, the Magi from the East saw His star in the sky and followed it for eight months, until it led them to Jesus. They brought Him gifts to worship Him that were worthy of a King. A "bright eastern Star" led these wise men from the East to their Lord and Savior. Our portion as Abraham's star seed is to lead men to the saving knowledge of our Lord and Savior by letting our light shine in the night seasons of people's lives.

> *"Then God said, 'Let lights appear in the sky to separate the day from the night. Let them mark off the seasons, days, and years. 15 Let these lights in the sky shine down on the earth.' And that is what happened. 16 God made two great lights— the larger one to govern the day, and the smaller one to govern the night. He also made the stars. 17 God set these lights in the sky to light the earth, 18 to govern the day and night, and to separate the light from the darkness. And God saw that it was good."*
>
> Genesis 1:14-18

God also created "stars" so they can be signs in the heavens. As Abraham's star-seed, everyone who is born again must allow the Holy Spirit to use him or her as a prophetic sign in someone's life. People ought to know that when the spiritual descendants of Abraham show up, something good is fixing to happen in their life. When Jesus stood under the Sycamore tree that Zacchaeus was resting in, He was a sign that Zacchaeus's life was fixing to change for the better. "When Jesus hung on the cross before the whole world, He was a sign that the devil was defeated and that the sins of the whole world had been paid for."

God also gave "stars" the power to determine "times and seasons." The stars of the heavens determine the clock of human calendar and natural seasons. As the star-seed of Abraham, our entrance into people's lives must set "an expiatory date on the works of the enemy" in their lives and "open up a whole new season of breakthrough" for them. ***Since we are Abraham's star-seed, we must "set nations on the calendar of God!"***

> *"Nevertheless, that time of darkness and despair will not go on forever. The land of Zebulun and Naphtali will be humbled, but there will be a time in the future when Galilee of the Gentiles, which lies along the road that runs between the Jordan and the sea, will be filled with glory. The people who walk in darkness will see a great light. For those who live in a land of deep darkness,]a light will shine."*
>
> Isaiah 9:1-2

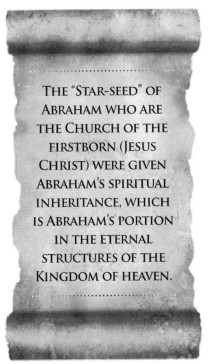

THE "STAR-SEED" OF ABRAHAM WHO ARE THE CHURCH OF THE FIRSTBORN (JESUS CHRIST) WERE GIVEN ABRAHAM'S SPIRITUAL INHERITANCE, WHICH IS ABRAHAM'S PORTION IN THE ETERNAL STRUCTURES OF THE KINGDOM OF HEAVEN.

God also gave "stars" the "power to divide the day from the night." This passage of Scripture is very rich and has far-reaching spiritual implications. The text above implies that the day is always hidden in the night. So when our friends or nations are going through their night seasons and the devil is creating havoc in their life, God will send us to separate the day of God that is trapped within their darkness. "Our light" will cause God to "break out into their night season and show them a pathway of escape and recovery!

"Let not your heart be troubled; you believe in God, believe also in Me. In My Father's house are many mansions if it were not so, I would have told you. I go to prepare a place for you."

John 14:1-2 (NKJV)

Finally, since Abraham's star-seed have been called to inherit Abraham's spiritual inheritance within the eternal structures of the Kingdom of God, *our portion of the blessing of Abraham is far greater than the portion of the blessing of Abraham that was given to natural Israel.* Abraham's spiritual inheritance consists of every spiritual blessing that is stored up in the "many mansions in My Father's house" which Jesus spoke of. Please remember that the highest and purest form of gold and silver is found in heaven. "Gold" is so abundant in the heavenly kingdom to such a degree that the "streets of heaven are all paved with gold!" All of this "gold" is part of Abraham's spiritual inheritance, which God gave to his star-seed descendants. So why are there so many of God's children who tithe consistently, yet continue to struggle financially? The answer to this perplexing question is the main reason why we need the "Return of the Lost Key."

"The twelve gates were made of pearls—each gate from a single pearl! And the main street was pure gold, as clear as glass."

Revelation 21:21

Part of the answer to this perplexing question is found in examining the incorrect tithing patterns that we have established in the global church. This is why God wants to "UPGRADE THE TECHNOLOGY OF TITHING" in the global Church. If the Body of Christ does not upgrade the spiritual technology it uses to exact the tithe; it will lose the power to take over the Seven Mountains of Babylon (the seven gates of Culture) and influence the destiny of nations. The Bible tells us that Babylon sits on seven strategic mountains and from these mountains she exercises control over the entire world.

> *"The beast you saw was once alive but isn't now. And yet he will soon come up out of the bottomless pit] and go to eternal destruction. And the people who belong to this world, whose names were not written in the Book of Life before the world was made, will be amazed at the reappearance of this beast who had died. "This calls for a mind with understanding: The seven heads of the beast represent the seven hills where the woman rules. They also represent seven kings."*
>
> Revelation 17:8-9

The seven Mountains (the seven gates of Culture), which Babylon sits on which God wants to completely infiltrate and subdue for His Kingdom are as follows:

1. The Mountain of Business

2. The Mountain of Finance

3. The Mountain of Media

4. The Mountain of Law

5. The Mountain of Sports/Celebration

6. The Mountain of Family

7. The Mountain of Church

"Everything happening in the world today can be traced back to either divine or demonic activities transpiring at one of these spiritual mountains!" Unfortunately, most of these spiritual mountains "animate" more "demonic activity and passions" than they animate the "power of the God-kind of life." This will soon change, because the LORD and His Christ have set these seven kingdoms of this world system for conquest. However, our inaccuracy in our technology of tithing has weakened our ability to raise a "prophetic company" of people who can superimpose God's Kingdom agenda over these world systems and bring them under the government of God.

Christ the Perfect and Ultimate Seed of Abraham?

"Now the promises (covenants, agreements) were decreed and made to Abraham and his Seed (his Offspring, his Heir). He [God] does not say, And to seeds (descendants, heirs), as if referring to many persons, but, And to your Seed (your Descendant, your Heir), obviously referring to one individual, Who is [none other than] Christ (the Messiah)."

Galatians 3:16 AMP

Even though the birth of Isaac marked the "beginning of the Abrahamic generation," the fullness of everything that God had intended to give to Abraham was never realized until the "birth of Jesus Christ!" Jesus Christ is both the perfect and ultimate seed of Abraham. The apostle Paul tells us that Christ is what God had on His mind when He promised Abraham that He was going to bless all the nations of the earth through his Seed. This is because Jesus Christ represents the perfect union of Abraham's natural and spiritual inheritance. "In Christ the old and new testaments come together into a perfect divine symmetry!"

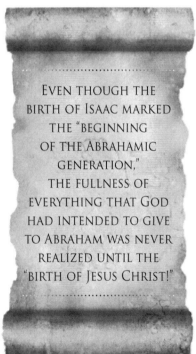

EVEN THOUGH THE BIRTH OF ISAAC MARKED THE "BEGINNING OF THE ABRAHAMIC GENERATION," THE FULLNESS OF EVERYTHING THAT GOD HAD INTENDED TO GIVE TO ABRAHAM WAS NEVER REALIZED UNTIL THE "BIRTH OF JESUS CHRIST!"

"The Good News is about his Son. In his earthly life he was born into King David's family line, and he was shown to be the Son of God when he was raised from the dead by the power of the Holy Spirit."

Romans 1:3-4

Jesus Christ is the *de facto* Seed of Abraham; He is both Abraham's Sand-seed as well as Abraham's Star-seed. Christ was born in Bethlehem of Jewish parents so He could qualify Himself as Abraham Sand-seed. The virgin birth gave Him spiritual legitimacy as the promised Jewish Messiah who would save the whole world. If Christ had been born of parents who were not of Jewish origin, He would have been a spiritual fraud to claim the title of being the Seed of Abraham. So for thirty-three years, Jesus lived and ministered to many as the Sand-seed of Abraham.

In His divine identity as the Sand-seed of Abraham, Jesus' earthly ministry was restricted to the natural boundaries of the nation of Israel. This is what He tried to tell the Canaanite woman who came to Him and begged Him to deliver her daughter who was grievously vexed by demon spirits. Jesus told her that, "I am only called to the lost house of Israel." This was not a prejudicial response on the part of Jesus; it was simply a statement of fact. As Abraham's Sand-seed, Jesus was operating within the confines of the Mosaic Law and as such His focus was to minister to the Jewish nation at that point in time. The Mosaic Law was only instituted to serve as a schoolmaster for the Jewish nation. God never ever expected Gentile nations in the Old Testament era to observe the Mosaic Law. The law was "added" to reveal the "transgression" and to act as a schoolmaster to the Jewish people until the finished work of Christ made the keeping of the Mosaic Law unnecessary.

What, then, was the purpose of the law? It was added because of transgressions until the Seed to whom the promise referred had come.

Galatians 3:19 (NIV)

This is why Jesus Christ had to die and be raised from the dead so He could also become "Abraham's Star-seed in the triumph of the resurrection!" It was only through death that Jesus became Abraham's Star-seed and the firstfruits from the dead and the Messiah of all those who are the true spiritual descendants of Abraham. The devil made a terrible miscalculation in allowing his demonic machinery to kill the Son of God through the vehicle of religion. If the devil had known that killing Jesus of Nazareth would release Him into His greatest ministry yet, the devil would never have crucified the Lord of glory. The irony of it is quite amusing. *In dying, Jesus Christ became the "promised Star-seed" of Abraham and He opened a divine portal in the heavens for Abraham to receive countless numbers of Star-seeds from across the nations of the earth.* Incidentally, the spiritual path that Jesus Christ followed in order to become Abraham's Star-seed is a "prophetic pattern for the rest of the natural descendants (the Jewish nation) of Abraham to follow." God's plan is that one day all of Abraham's natural descendants (natural Israelites) would one day find the power to become Abraham's Star-seeds when they recognize Jesus of Nazareth as the true and promised Messiah.

"Then I witnessed in heaven an event of great significance. I saw a woman clothed with the sun, with the moon beneath her feet, and a crown of twelve stars on her head. She was pregnant, and she cried out because of her labor pains and the agony

of giving birth. Then I witnessed in heaven another significant event. I saw a large red dragon with seven heads and ten horns, with seven crowns on his heads. His tail swept away one-third of the stars in the sky, and he threw them to the earth. He stood in front of the woman as she was about to give birth, ready to devour her baby as soon as it was born. She gave birth to a son who was to rule all nations with an iron rod. And her child was snatched away from the dragon and was caught up to God and to his throne."

Revelation 12:1-5

Separated by Two Distinct and Separate Priesthoods

To separate the prophetic inheritance of the two brands of seed God gave to Abraham, ***God established two separate and distinct covenants and priesthoods.*** This means that there is a priesthood that serves the Sand-seed of Abraham and another, which serves the Star-seed of Abraham. There are some similarities between the two covenants and priesthoods because they were both authored by the same God, but the similarities are minor compared to the major differences between these two priesthoods. We are well advised to discern these differences, because our future depends on it. *If we fail to discern the critical differences between these two priesthoods, we will continue in the inaccurate patterns of tithing of the past* and never fully harness or operate in the power to effectively subdue the seven mountains of Babylon for God's Kingdom.

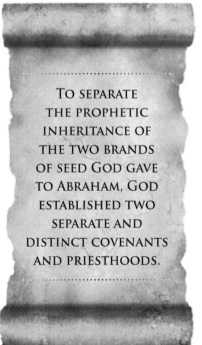

TO SEPARATE THE PROPHETIC INHERITANCE OF THE TWO BRANDS OF SEED GOD GAVE TO ABRAHAM, GOD ESTABLISHED TWO SEPARATE AND DISTINCT COVENANTS AND PRIESTHOODS.

In the first embassy, God created the "Priesthood of Aaron," who was from the tribe of Levi, to serve the "Sand-seed" of Abraham. Moses ordained and anointed him to serve in the office of the High Priest, together with his sons. God gave the Jewish nation who had come out of Egypt a "tithe according to the Law," ***which has distinctive features and functions.*** We will discuss these distinctive features and functions later on in this writing. Malachi 3:8-12 was addressed to the "Sand-seed" of Abraham who lived under the Priestly Order of Aaron, who were commanded to give tithes and offerings according to the Law. *Malachi 3:8-12 was never addressed to the "Star-seed" (the church of the firstborn) of Abraham because this tithe has very little relevance for the Star-seed of Abraham.* This will soon become obvious.

In the second embassy, God established the "Priesthood of Melchizedek" to serve the "Star-seed" of Abraham. God gave the Star-seed of Abraham a "tithe according to the Priestly Order of Melchizedek," **which also has its own distinctive features and functions.** We will fully discuss these features and functions later on. Unlike the Levitical tithe, which was based upon the Law, this tithe is based upon the "word of Oath" and draws its resources from the eternal structures of the Kingdom of God and is found in Genesis 14 and Hebrews 7. Understanding the critical differences between the priestly Order of Aaron and the priestly Order of Melchizedek will go a long way in showing us the nature of the "Lost Key" — an ancient key so powerful the devil has been terrified of you discovering this powerful key.

LIFE APPLICATION SECTION

Point to Ponder:

No matter how successful a person is, if they are of the seed of Adam the "pathway of death" inside them is already set towards eternal damnation unless they experience the intervention of God.

Verse to Remember:

"I will certainly bless you. I will multiply your descendants beyond number, like the stars in the sky and the sand on the seashore. Your descendants will conquer the cities of their enemies."

Genesis 22:17

Questions to Consider:

• Why is Jesus Christ the perfect and ultimate Seed of Abraham?

_____
_____
_____
_____

• What are the two brands of seed that Abraham was given on Mount Moriah?

_____
_____
_____
_____

• Who are the star seed of Abraham?

_____
_____
_____
_____

JOURNAL YOUR THOUGHTS

ABRAHAM MEETS MELCHIZEDEK

From the time Abraham answered the call of God to leave the land of his nativity for a land that God would show him, *he was on a collision course with one of the most powerful spiritual orders that God has ever revealed to mankind.* I have served God long enough to know that when we obey God and make choices which set us on course towards our prophetic destiny, God will become involved with the affairs of our lives.

> *The Lord had said to Abram, "Leave your native country, your relatives, and your father's family, and go to the land that I will show you. I will make you into a great nation. I will bless you and make you famous, and you will be a blessing to others. I will bless those who bless you and curse those who treat you with contempt. All the families on earth will be blessed through you."*
>
> Genesis 12:1-3

When God is involved with the affairs of our human life, the devil will also try to intercept the course of our lives to see if he can derail us from pursuing our prophetic calling. The devil knows that from the moment the "proceeding word of God" comes to us, we enter into the valley of transition until the proceeding word of the Lord concerning us has been fulfilled. *The devil knows that as a result of emotional and mental stress, financial mismanagement and human fragility, we can be forced to renegotiate our spiritual destiny when the tough gets going. Many people abort or abdicate their Kingdom assignments during periods of transition.* After God gave Abraham this powerful prophetic promise, the devil came in and set him up for a fall using the vehicle of circumstance.

> *At that time a severe famine struck the land of Canaan, forcing Abram to go down to Egypt, where he lived as a foreigner. As he was approaching the border of Egypt,*

Abram said to his wife, Sarai, "Look, you are a very beautiful woman. When the Egyptians see you, they will say, 'This is his wife. Let's kill him; then we can have her!'

Genesis 12:10-12

Without any obvious warning, demonic agencies from the second heaven began to manipulate the spiritual atmosphere and natural climate around Abraham's habitat. These "demonic powers stopped the chambers of the first heaven from pouring their rain on the land Abraham was living on!" This resulted in a serious famine, which dried up every well and any other water source around Abram. *The ensuing drought caused Abraham to panic and reconsider his position. He made a hasty decision out of his own sense of panic and insecurity and headed towards the godless nation of Egypt.* This decision would later haunt Abram for a very long time. When we know that there is a prophetic call of God upon our lives, we must make sure that "we run to God during these times of painful transition." If we fail to do so we will make hasty decisions, which will only serve to strengthen the demonic agenda against us. ***Abraham made this hasty decision because he was still immature in his relationship with God. He did not yet know the awesome power of the spiritual order that he had been called to serve under.***

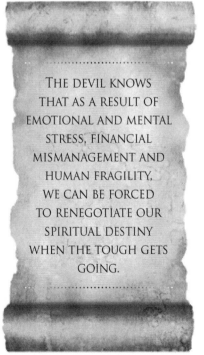

THE DEVIL KNOWS THAT AS A RESULT OF EMOTIONAL AND MENTAL STRESS, FINANCIAL MISMANAGEMENT AND HUMAN FRAGILITY, WE CAN BE FORCED TO RENEGOTIATE OUR SPIRITUAL DESTINY WHEN THE TOUGH GETS GOING.

Broken Covenants

When Abram and his household arrived at the borders of Egypt, Abram turned to his wife Sarai and had a conversation with her that would be every woman's nightmare. Instead of risking his life to protect her, Abram asked his wife to lie about the true nature of their relationship. He asked the petrified woman to tell all the inhabitants of Egypt that she was his sister instead of his wife. Abram was afraid that if the Egyptians discovered that he was the husband of such a beautiful woman, they would kill him so they could sleep with her. Sarah, being the submissive wife that she was, agreed to Abram's flawed proposal and the covenant of marriage between them was broken!

"Covenants are made and broken with words." *This is why our words are very important and carry tremendous weight in the spirit realm.* When demonic agencies saw that the spiritual borders and boundaries around Abram's marriage had been breached, these evil spirits rushed in like a pack of African hyenas to the slaughter. The princes of Pharaoh wasted no time in telling their lustful King that a beautiful Hebrew woman had just come into the land of Egypt.

> *"When the palace officials saw her, they sang her praises to Pharaoh, their king, and Sarai was taken into his palace. Then Pharaoh gave Abram many gifts because of her—sheep, goats, cattle, male and female donkeys, male and female servants, and camels. But the Lord sent terrible plagues upon Pharaoh and his household because of Sarai, Abram's wife."*

Genesis 12:15-17

Pharaoh wasted no time in bringing Sarah into his bedchamber. In exchange for anticipated sexual escapades with Sarah, Pharaoh treated Abram with great kindness because he thought that Abram was Sarah's brother. The king of Egypt gave Abram a great company of sheep, oxen, camels, male and female donkeys, plus male and female servants. ***Abram became a very rich man overnight by lying and selling out his wife!*** I am sure that Abram must have been horrified when he envisioned Pharaoh raping his beautiful wife in his bedchambers. Using Sarah as a sexual toy was definitely what the king of Egypt had in his mind when he got her into his bedroom. *God intervened and terrorized the house of Pharaoh with grievous plagues and warned Pharaoh against exploiting Sarah sexually because she was the wife of a prophet.* Pharaoh restored her back to Abram in great haste and told his servants to drive Abram and his household out of the land of Egypt.

Mixed Blessings

When Abram and Sarai left Egypt they had "more material possessions" than they had come with. The king of Egypt had given them a generous bounty before he realized that Abram had deceived him. When Pharaoh threw them out of his country, he did not take back the riches that he had given them, but the possessions that the king of Egypt gave to Abram would later prove to be more of a curse than a blessing. Among the material possessions that the king of Egypt had given to Abram and Sarai was a young Egyptian maid by the name of Hagar. The demonic trap was already set. Most people do not realize that the devil is not stupid. He knows that most people would never pick up a

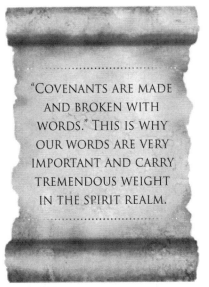

"COVENANTS ARE MADE AND BROKEN WITH WORDS." THIS IS WHY OUR WORDS ARE VERY IMPORTANT AND CARRY TREMENDOUS WEIGHT IN THE SPIRIT REALM.

venomous snake with their bare hands. *But the devil knows that if you hide the snake inside a bag filled with gold and diamonds, most people would take it in a hurry. This is why our spiritual technology for unlocking financial resources for our ministry must be accurate or we will set ourselves for a fall in our future destiny when the snakes in our moneybags begin to manifest themselves.* This is why we must rediscover this **"Lost Ancient Key"** which opens the spiritual door to a life of abundance in the Kingdom of God without any demonic encroachments.

Strife in the House

Finally Abram said to Lot, "Let's not allow this conflict to come between us or our herdsmen. After all, we are close relatives! The whole countryside is open to you. Take your choice of any section of the land you want, and we will separate. If you want the land to the left, then I'll take the land on the right. If you prefer the land on the right, then I'll go to the left." Lot took a long look at the fertile plains of the Jordan Valley in the direction of Zoar. The whole area was well watered everywhere, like the garden of the Lord or the beautiful land of Egypt. This was before the Lord destroyed Sodom and Gomorrah.

Genesis 13:8-10

Immediately after Abraham returned from the land of Egypt, there was serious strife between Abram's herdsmen and those of Lot. *"The demonic snakes that were buried in the money bags that they got from the king of Egypt were already beginning to manifest themselves in the form of strife and division in Abram's house!"* The only thing that saved the day was Abram's attitude of maturity and trust in God. The memory of God's intervening power that he and Sarah had just witnessed in the land of Egypt had left an indelible mark on his impressionable spirit. Abraham was beginning to understand the awesome power of the spiritual order that he had brought himself under when he answered the call of God.

Instead of fighting with Lot, Abram told his nephew that they needed to separate and that Lot was free to choose whatever land space he needed. Abram was going to choose whatever was left over. Lot, who was already infected by the spirit of the king of Egypt, chose the rich portion of the land next to Sodom. Sodom was the most wicked nation of the nations of the ancient world. Sodom was also the birthplace of every form of sexual perversion, including homosexuality and bestiality. Lot's carnal decision had set the stage for the pathway that would soon set Abram on a collision course with the king of Sodom and the eternal priestly Order of Melchizedek.

Abram's Greatest Embarrassment

"So Abram left Egypt and traveled north into the Negev, along with his wife and Lot and all that they owned. (Abram was very rich in livestock, silver and gold.)"

Genesis 13:1-2

During the course of writing this book, the Holy Spirit gave me a revelation that literally shook me to the core of my being. This is what the Holy Spirit told me: ***"Son, for as long as the Church thinks that Genesis 13:1-2 is the basis for Kingdom wealth, it is never going to experience real Kingdom wealth."*** This statement by the Holy Spirit shook me to the core of my being, because I have used it many times in my teachings on Kingdom prosperity. The Holy Spirit said to me, "Son, Genesis 13:1-2 is not the basis for real Kingdom wealth because Genesis 13:1-2 describes Abram's tainted wealth that He obtained by selling his wife to a demonic system." The Holy Spirit told me that "tainted wealth" can never form the basis of real Kingdom wealth. The Holy Spirit then said something to me that placed the icing on the cake. He said to me, "Many preachers in the body of Christ are doing the same thing that Abram did while he was in Egypt. They are prostituting the body of Christ for money and then calling their resulting prosperity, "real Kingdom wealth." When the Holy Spirit said this to me I had to repent, because I discovered that I was also "found wanting."

Abram replied to the king of Sodom, "I solemnly swear to the LORD, God Most High, Creator of heaven and earth that I will not take so much as a single thread or sandal thong from what belongs to you. Otherwise you might say, 'I am the one who made Abram rich."

Genesis 14:22-23

When Abram and Sarah left Egypt with an abundance of material possessions that Abram had obtained by deceiving the king of Egypt, the king of Egypt began to tell everyone who had an ear to listen that he was the one who had made Abram rich. These malicious rumors followed Abram wherever he went. It was quite embarrassing to say the least. When Abram met Melchizedek (the priest of God Most High), he got a revelation of how he could "sanctify his tainted wealth." He gave Melchizedek a tithe of all. *This divinely-inspired tithe not only destroyed the spirit of greed in Abram's life; it also became the purifying element of everything Abram owned here on earth.* Abram's tithe brought everything that he owned into divine alignment. Abram's tithe into the Order of Melchizedek "rolled away the reproach of Egypt," from his life. This is why it is important that the global Church rediscovers the Abrahamic model for tithing.

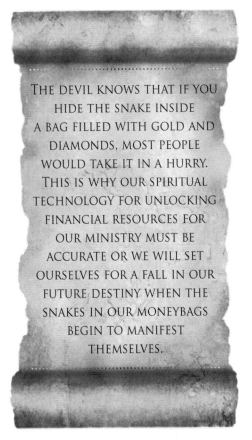

THE DEVIL KNOWS THAT IF YOU HIDE THE SNAKE INSIDE A BAG FILLED WITH GOLD AND DIAMONDS, MOST PEOPLE WOULD TAKE IT IN A HURRY. THIS IS WHY OUR SPIRITUAL TECHNOLOGY FOR UNLOCKING FINANCIAL RESOURCES FOR OUR MINISTRY MUST BE ACCURATE OR WE WILL SET OURSELVES FOR A FALL IN OUR FUTURE DESTINY WHEN THE SNAKES IN OUR MONEYBAGS BEGIN TO MANIFEST THEMSELVES.

When the king of Sodom offered Abram the gold and silver from the treasuries of Sodom, Abram knew that he could not make the same mistake twice. He knew that if he took the money, the king of Sodom was going to join the king of Egypt in declaring that he was the one who had made Abram rich. Abram's refusal of the king of Sodom's generous offer underscores the power of tithing under the Order of Melchizedek. *Finally, the Holy Spirit concluded by telling me that real Kingdom wealth in Abram's life started right after His encounter with Melchizedek, the divine king-priest in Genesis 14.*

Power to Prevail

Long after Lot moved to the wicked nation of Sodom, five powerful kings from the East came against the king of Sodom and savaged his country.

During their victorious rampage these foreign kings took men, women and children as prisoners of war. They also raped the treasuries of Sodom of most of its gold and silver. Among the prisoners of war who were taken was Lot, Abram's nephew. A man who had escaped the rampage ran to the house of Abram the Hebrew and told him that Lot had been captured by the armies of the kings from the East.

> *"The victorious invaders then plundered Sodom and Gomorrah and headed for home, taking with them all the spoils of war and the food supplies. They also captured Lot—Abram's nephew who lived in Sodom—and carried off everything he owned."*

> Genesis 14:11-12

Abram rose in haste and put on his war clothes. He put together an army of 318 men who were born and trained in his own house, and a few of his allies. With the determination of an Olympic sprinter, Abram pursued after the kings who had captured his nephew and his family. Within a period of less than twenty-four hours, Abram and his allies overtook the foreign armies and slaughtered them with his homegrown force of about 318 men! Abram rescued all of his family members and also rescued all the people of Sodom who had been taken captive. Abram also brought back all the gold and silver that these foreign kings had stolen from the treasuries of Sodom.

King of Jerusalem and Priest of God Most High

When Abram was returning from the slaughter of the foreign kings, he was intercepted by a man who was set to alter the whole course of his life. ***When Abram met this majestic man he began to realize that meeting this man was what every road in his life had been leading up to!*** Abram had by divine orchestration entered into the "moment of moments." The mystery of God was about to be revealed.

There was a majestic-divine aura and deep sense of dignity that was upon this man that Abram had never seen before. From his feet to the hair on his head, he exhibited a sense of divinity and righteousness, which was very overpowering. Abram recognized that this man was the greatest and most important man that he would ever meet here on earth.

Who was this priestly man?

There are several schools of thought concerning the identity of this mysterious High Priest who appeared to Abraham. We will quickly examine four of those schools of thought and then I will tell you what I believe is the most logical answer as to the identity of this mysterious man.

(i)   Melchizedek was the first Adam

(ii) Melchizedek was Shem, the son of Noah

(i)   Melchizedek was the priest-king of ancient Salem

(ii) Melchizedek was the pre-incarnation appearance of Christ

There are those who believe that Melchizedek was the first Adam returning in his glory. The reason they believe this is because they believe that Adam was the only man in Scripture who had "no earthly genealogy." But this belief really stands on very slippery ice, because of the following reasons:

- Even though Adam had no earthly genealogy, he nevertheless had a "spiritual genesis." The Bible clearly tells us when he was created, which means that Adam had a clear and traceable "beginning." This is in direct contrast to what the apostle Paul tells us in the seventh chapter of Hebrews about the Melchizedek, who met Abram in Genesis 14. Paul says that this particular Melchizedek was "without beginning of days or end of life." Adam's life, on the other hand, had a "beginning and a sure ending" as well.

- Secondly, Adam became a "slave to sin and its insidious powers" after he fell from grace in the Garden of Eden. This means that in his fallen sinful condition, there was simply no way Adam could be referred to as the "king of righteousness." The name Melchizedek literally means, "King of righteousness." Adam was anything but the "king of righteousness." Even before Adam and Eve fell short of God's glory, they were innocent but not righteous. They were as innocent as a newborn baby is innocent but they were not righteous. As such, there is no way Adam could be the Melchizedek that appeared to Abraham.

- Thirdly, the first Adam died without ever having broken the "sentence of death" over his own life. This in itself disqualifies him from being the "prophetic representation" of an eternal priesthood that is "driven" by the "power of an endless life." ***The Order of Melchizedek exists beyond the perimeters of death in the realms of eternity.***

There are also those who believe that Melchizedek was Shem, the son of Noah. They say that Shem was both a "king and a priest" and that he received this priesthood from his father, Noah. This belief stands on thinner ice, than those who believe that Melchizedek was the first Adam returning in his glory. Here is why.

- The Bible clearly sets out the genealogy of Noah's family in the book of Genesis, which includes Shem. This in itself clearly disqualifies Shem from being the Melchizedek who met Abraham in the valley of Shavez. Once again the apostle Paul is quite clear that this Melchizedek who met Abraham in the valley of kings "had no earthly genealogy or beginning of days." ***There is no way God would use someone whose natural genealogy could be so easily proven to "represent" an eternal priesthood that is not of this world.***

- Finally, if Melchizedek were Shem the son of Noah, it would mean that he would have had to have lived for a very long time. If this were the case it is highly probable that his appearance in the book of Genesis would have been duly noted, before and after Genesis 14. The fact that Melchizedek is not mentioned in the historical accounts of the book of Genesis except for this one meeting with Abraham further suggests that he was not Shem. Furthermore, the Bible does tell us when Shem died. Again, the apostle Paul is clear in letting us know that this Melchizedek had "no beginning of days or end of life."

Finally, there are those who believe that the Melchizedek who met Abraham when he was returning from the slaughter of the kings, was the king-priest of the ancient City of Salem. *I admit that this school of thought is much more plausible than the previous two schools of thought on the identity of this mysterious priest.* But I personally believe that this king-priest over the ancient City of Salem was not the one who commissioned Abram in Genesis 14, even though he was certainly a priest of God Most High.

THIS DIVINELY-INSPIRED TITHE NOT ONLY DESTROYED THE SPIRIT OF GREED IN ABRAM'S LIFE; IT ALSO BECAME THE PURIFYING ELEMENT OF EVERYTHING ABRAM OWNED HERE ON EARTH.

The Melchizedek priesthood in ancient Salem was merely a "shadow and forerunner" of the true heavenly Order of Melchizedek priesthood of our Lord Jesus Christ. But there are four other reasons why I believe that the Melchizedek who met Abram in the Valley of Shaveh was not the same Melchizedek who ruled the earthly City of Salem (Jerusalem).

Namely, these are:

- In the prophetic vision of King David in Psalm 110, David makes it very clear that the Order of Melchizedek is an eternal priestly ministry of Christ that has always existed in the realms of eternity before God created the world.

- Ever since the fall of Adam, every human being born of a woman is born a slave to sin, in terrible need of a savior. I just do not see how God can pattern the eternal priestly ministry of Christ after a sin-compromised earthly priesthood. The supernatural never bows to the natural. The natural can be patterned after the supernatural but never the other way round. The Melchizedek priesthood in ancient Salem was patterned after the heavenly and not the other way around.

- The Bible teaches us that all have sinned and have come short of the glory of God. If the Melchizedek who met Abraham in the valley of Shaveh was a mere mortal, I fail to see how he could possibly assume such a "lofty title" as being the "King of righteousness and Prince of peace."

- While I agree that there was a king-priest over the ancient City of Salem who represented the eternal priesthood of Christ; I do not believe that he is the one who brought Abram into covenant with God. This is because the writer of Hebrews makes it quite clear that the Melchizedek who met Abraham in Genesis 14 was "greater than Abraham." If the Melchizedek who met Abram was a "mere mortal" then it would mean that there was a man on earth who was "greater in spiritual stature" than Abraham. If this were the case then Abraham is not qualified to be the father of many nations and the spiritual father of the New Creation. This is because the "greater" is always more "honorable and more blessed" than the "lesser." Melchizedek, the king-priest of the ancient City of Salem, is therefore more "suited to be the father of many nations and the spiritual father of the New Creation" than Abraham is. If we insist that the Melchizedek who met Abram was a "mere mortal" who was stationed here on earth, we must also shift our eyes from "Abraham" and look to this "earthly Melchizedek" as being the spiritual father of the New Creation.

Finally, here is what I believe is the most probable identity of the Melchizedek who met with Abram in the king's valley. Once again, I am not suggesting that there was no king-priest by the name of Melchizedek who was king over the ancient City of Salem. My extensive study on this subject has convinced me that the Melchizedek who met Abram, was different in both glory and stature from the earthly Melchizedek, who was king of the ancient city of Salem. I personally believe that this heavenly-man, who met Abraham in the Valley of the Kings, was Christ manifesting Himself to Abraham before His virgin birth.

Maybe this is what Jesus meant when He said to the astounded Jews of His era, "Abraham saw my day!" What the Bible does tell us from examining the passage of Scripture in Genesis 14 is that this man was the "King of Salem, which is literally the City of Jerusalem." The Bible also tells us that this man was also the "King of righteousness," a term that is only befitting of Christ. The very name Melchizedek literally means, "King over the whole domain of righteousness." Who else is fully qualified to properly assume the lofty title of "King of righteousness" other than the Lord Jesus Christ?

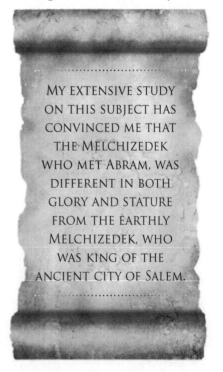

MY EXTENSIVE STUDY ON THIS SUBJECT HAS CONVINCED ME THAT THE MELCHIZEDEK WHO MET ABRAM, WAS DIFFERENT IN BOTH GLORY AND STATURE FROM THE EARTHLY MELCHIZEDEK, WHO WAS KING OF THE ANCIENT CITY OF SALEM.

The Bible also tells us that this man whom Abram met when he was returning from the slaughter of the kings was also the "Priest of God Most High". The man carried "bread and wine" which he offered to the stunned Abram. *Abram was so impressed with this awesome man that he gave Him a tenth of all the spoils*. This priestly man seemed to know everything about Abram. He even told Abram why he triumphed over such a might foreign army with only 318 men who were trained in his own house. Melchizedek informed Abram that the God of heaven and earth had sent his warring angels ahead of him into the battlefield. By the time Abram got to the camp of his enemies, their fate had already been delivered into his hands.

Heavenly bread and wine

Before Melchizedek left the scene, He blessed Abram, who was the custodian of the covenant of promise. *The fact that this man blessed Abram proves that He was more powerful and loftier than Abram.* Melchizedek also gave Abram the supernatural bread and wine that He had brought with Him from His eternal priestly order. "Bread and wine" are the eternal emblems of the priestly Order of Melchizedek. We will discuss the spiritual implications of these spiritual emblems later on. But I want to draw your attention to a very interesting declaration that Jesus made in the New Testament about Himself.

> *Jesus replied, "I am the bread of life. Whoever comes to me will never be hungry again. Whoever believes in me will never be thirsty.*
>
> John 6:35

> *And he took a cup of wine and gave thanks to God for it. He gave it to them and said, "Each of you drink from it, 28 for this is my blood, which confirms the covenant between God and his people. It is poured out as a sacrifice to forgive the sins of many.*
>
> Matthew 26:27-28

The Tithe of Abraham

> *"And blessed be God Most High, who has defeated your enemies for you." Then Abram gave Melchizedek a tenth of all the goods he had recovered.*
>
> Genesis 14:20

Abraham was so moved by this man's spiritual stature and divine royalty that he did something that was customary but not foreign to the people of the ancient world. Abraham's response to Melchizedek was ignited by his personal sense of awe and by the prevailing cultural protocol of his era. People of the ancient world never went to see a "King" without a "gift or endowment" to honor the King with. In Abraham's eyes, Melchizedek was the greatest and most glorious King that he had ever met. Out of this "deep sense of honor and personal awe," ***Abraham, the father of the faithful, gave "his first tithes into the priestly Order of Melchizedek," thereby establishing a prophetic tithing model for all his spiritual descendants.***

Abraham tithed into the royal priesthood of Melchizedek (the king-priest). Simply put, Abraham gave tithes to a "King" and not just to a "priest." Since every "King" has a "Kingdom" it is safe to assume that ***Abraham's tithes were used to support a "Kingdom." Everything that is given to a "King" becomes part of his royal estate. This means then that the "Abrahamic tithing model" is a "Kingdom-driven and Kingdom-minded tithing model." This is why it is the highest form and level of tithing mentioned in the Scriptures.*** Under the Levitical priesthood, "tithes" were given to "support the priesthood" (the clergy), whereas under the Order of Melchizedek, tithes are given to "support and sustain" the advancement of God's Kingdom here on earth. ***Since Abraham's tithes were employed to advance a "Kingdom," and Abraham is referred to as the "father of faith" and the "father of us all" (Rom. 4:1-25; Gal. 3:6-9), it is quite erroneous and misleading for us to say that there is no requirement for tithing in the New Testament, especially considering the fact that New Testament living has a greater emphasis on advancing God's Kingdom here on earth than was ever emphasized under the Old Testament.***

Furthermore, Abraham did not tithe into Melchizedek because he felt like Melchizedek could use the money. ***Abraham knew that there was nothing in his possession that could pay for the services of such a great King. Abraham's motivation for tithing and the reasons why he tithed are sadly missing in much of today's tithing practices.*** This is why it's imperative that we rediscover the "Lost Key" which activates the functionality of the priestly Order of Melchizedek in our lives.

The Lost Culture of Honor

"He lifts the poor from the dust and the needy from the garbage dump. He sets them among princes, placing them in seats of honor. For all the earth is the Lord's, and he has set the world in order."

1 Samuel 2:8

There is nothing more powerful and life-giving than the bestowment of honor upon those for whom honor is due. The primary being who deserves to be honored by all of His creation is "God." Honor is one of the most important principles of the Kingdom of God. It is the cornerstone of kingdom living; without it, kingdoms go into a state of decline. *No spiritual culture can ever be referred to as a "Kingdom culture" which does not have this "principle of honor" deeply imbedded in it.* "Honor" quickly establishes itself as a divine life-giving principle whenever it is instituted into any relationship. Marriages, governments, friendships, covenants, and business relationships flourish whenever the principle of honor is engrafted into them.

> *"Honor your father and your mother, that your days may be long upon the land which the LORD your God is giving you."*
>
> Exodus 20:12

> *"Jesus replied, And why do you break the command of God for the sake of your tradition? 4 For God said, 'Honour your father and mother' and 'Anyone who curses his father or mother must be put to death.' 5 But you say that if a man says to his father or mother, 'Whatever help you might otherwise have received from me is a gift devoted to God.'"*
>
> Matthew 15:3-5

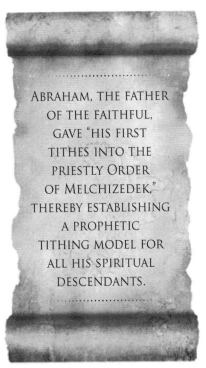

ABRAHAM, THE FATHER OF THE FAITHFUL, GAVE "HIS FIRST TITHES INTO THE PRIESTLY ORDER OF MELCHIZEDEK," THEREBY ESTABLISHING A PROPHETIC TITHING MODEL FOR ALL HIS SPIRITUAL DESCENDANTS.

In the synoptic gospels, Jesus Christ went as far as establishing the "spiritual connection" between "honor" and "material prosperity and long life." Jesus made it very clear that "children" who "honor" their "parents" are guaranteed a long and prosperous life. Children who did not honor their parents were deserving of death. Whoa! What an incredible promise from the mouth of God! It is the reason I honor my natural and spiritual parents. Unfortunately for many of us, especially those of us who live in morally-liberal nations like the United States of America, the "principle of honor" is foreign to our culture. The culture-war between Judaic-Christian values and secular liberalism has taken its toll. *We live in a nation where insulting governing authorities and undermining spiritual leaders is commonplace.* It is quite difficult to show people (including Christians) the critical importance of the "principle of honor" to the survival of any civilization.

I have been greatly saddened to see just how many Christian parents have very little control of their teenage children, because of the complete lack of honor for those in authority by many church-going teenagers. Since we have lost the culture of honor, it is quite difficult to appreciate just how powerful "tithing from an attitude of honor" really is. But I dare say that the day we "rediscover the power of the principle of honor" before God and man, is the day our lives will change dramatically for the better. The principle of honor is so powerful that it incites God to honor those who honor Him.

"Whoso keepeth the fig-tree shall eat the fruit thereof; And he that regardeth his master shall be honored."

Proverbs 27:18 (ASV)

Abraham lived in a Kingdom culture that understood the critical importance of bestowing honor on governing authorities and upon those to whom honor is due. *Abraham understood that the quickest way to unleash the "favor and blessing" of a King is to approach him from a position of heartfelt honor. The "principle of honor" was the governing principle behind Abraham's motivation for tithing into Melchizedek the King-priest.* This principle of honor is sadly missing in much of the technology of tithing in the Body of Christ. One of the main reasons why the Malachi 3:8-12 tithing model is so popular is that it "frightens Christians and Kingdom citizens into tithing." Psychologists will quickly tell you that "fear" is a great motivator. But the Bible is clear that "fear" as a motivator appeals to our lower (carnal) nature whereas "honor" appeals to our higher (spiritual) nature.

I really believe that God will use this book to restore the "principle of honor" in the Church's tithing model. Many more Kingdom citizens (including most Christians) are going to discover how to give "tithes of honor" to advance the Kingdom of God here on earth. They will quickly discover that honor is a greater motivator than fear and God will also respond by honoring them for honoring Him. What would motivate a rookie basketball or football player to use his signing-bonus money to build a magnificent home for his single mother? The answer is "honor." Honor is truly the greatest and highest motivator for giving to those in authority over us, who have served us well. Churches that are currently using the technology of tithing that is found in this book have told me that the total amount of tithing in their church has increased by over thirty percent. It did not surprise me at all. *I knew that once they established a "spiritual culture of honor" around tithing, their tithes would inevitably go up.* It is my prayer that in the near future, all tithing in the global Church will be done this way.

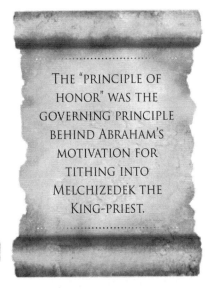

THE "PRINCIPLE OF HONOR" WAS THE GOVERNING PRINCIPLE BEHIND ABRAHAM'S MOTIVATION FOR TITHING INTO MELCHIZEDEK THE KING-PRIEST.

Seven Reasons to Give to a King

Dr. Myles Munroe in his best-selling book *Kingdom Principles*, lists seven reasons why citizens of a kingdom give to a reigning King. I have taken the liberty to quote him verbatim on these seven reasons, so that we can gain a greater understanding as to why and how Abraham tithed into Melchizedek. Please remember that Melchizedek was both the King of heavenly Jerusalem, as well as the Priest of God Most High.

1. *Royal protocol requires that a gift must be presented when visiting a king.* This is why the queen of Sheba brought such lavish gifts to King Solomon even though he was richer than she was. It was royal protocol. He would have done the same had he visited her.

2. *The gift must be fitting for the king.* Worse than approaching a king with no gift is to bring a gift unworthy of him. An inappropriate or inadequate gift amounts to an insult to the king. It shows that the giver does not properly respect the king or his authority.

3. *The gift reveals our value of "worth-ship" of the king.* The quality of what we offer the King and the attitude with which we offer it reveal much more than our words do of the value or worthiness we attach to Him.

4. *Worship demands a gift and giving is worship.* "Worth-ship" is where we get **"worship."** To worship the King means to ascribe worth or worthiness to Him. And as we have already seen, that always involves bringing Him a gift. There is no genuine worship without gift-giving. But giving is itself an act of worship and worship is always fitting for the

King. The Magi who saw his star in the east understood this, which is why they brought gifts when they came to find Him.

5. ***Giving to a king attracts his favor.*** Kings are attracted to people who give with a willing and grateful spirit. Like anyone else, a king likes to know he is loved and appreciated. The King of Heaven is the same way. The Giver is attracted to the giver and extends His favor. Gifts open doors to blessings, opportunities and prosperity.

6. ***Giving to a king acknowledges his ownership of everything.*** Remember kings are lords; they own everything in their domain. So giving to a king is simply returning to him what is already his. This is why in the Kingdom of Heaven we are always stewards and never owners.

7. ***Giving to a king is thanksgiving.*** One of the best ways to express gratitude is with a gift. Gratitude expressed is in itself a gift.

(*Kingdom Principles* by Dr. Myles Munroe, pgs. 211-213)

Saying "No" to the King of Sodom

"After Abram returned from his victory over Kedorlaomer and all his allies, the king of Sodom went out to meet him in the valley of Shaveh (that is, the King's Valley)."

Genesis 14:17

While Abram was returning from the slaughter of the kings from the East, the news of his glorious victory reached the ears of the king of Sodom. The king of Sodom got into his royal chariot almost immediately and drove to intercept Abram on his victorious return. *Abram did not know that the king of Sodom was riding ferociously towards him but the Lord did.* The "setting of the time and timing" God chose to introduce Abram to the priestly Order of Melchizedek is very significant indeed. The perfect spiritual timing of Melchizedek's appearance in Abraham's life will shed light on the awesome power of this "Lost Ancient Key." It was no coincidence that God in His infinite wisdom chose to intercept Abram's life just before the king of Sodom got to him. **God was determined to get to Abram before the devil's greatest agent did.**

The king of Sodom said to Abram, "Give back my people who were captured. But you may keep for yourself all the goods you have recovered." Abram replied to the king of Sodom, "I solemnly swear to the Lord, God Most High, Creator of heaven and earth, that I will not take so much as a single thread or sandal thong from what belongs to you. Otherwise you might say, 'I am the one who made Abram rich.'

Genesis 14: 21-23

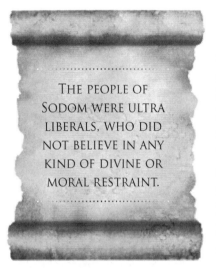

THE PEOPLE OF SODOM WERE ULTRA LIBERALS, WHO DID NOT BELIEVE IN ANY KIND OF DIVINE OR MORAL RESTRAINT.

Please remember that Sodom was the most morally-depraved country of the countries of the East. Sodom made Egypt look like it was a paradise of righteousness. Please bear in mind that the Egyptians were no saints; they were hardcore idol worshippers. They worshipped Pharaoh, frogs, the sun, lice and the river Nile just to name a few and yet the people of Sodom made the Egyptians look like saints. The people of Sodom were ultra liberals, who did not believe in any kind of divine or moral restraint.

Here is a simple glossary list of what the King of Sodom represented prophetically:

- He was the king of an ultra-liberal society who had removed every boundary of morality in the moral structure of their nation.

- He was the king of a nation that celebrated every form of sexual perversion, including homosexuality and bestiality.

- He was a king over a demonic system, which represented the mismanagement of seed, through inaccurate and unnatural sexual intercourse. The male "sperm" was designed by God to be deposited into the "woman's womb" for the purpose of reproduction and not into another man's "rectum." This diabolical practice simply destroys the seed that was designed to produce future generations.

- He was a king over a satanic system that had completely destroyed the mountain of family within the structure of his nation. Incest became a normal expression of sexuality in ancient Sodom.

- He was a king over a demonic system, which presided over ill-gained financial resources, powered by demonic technology. The people of Sodom credited their prosperity to their demon-gods.

This was the same king whose royal chariots were charging ferociously towards Abram who was headed towards the valley of Shaveh. This valley was also known as the valley of kings. Abram did not know that on that fateful day, the Valley of the Kings was going to become the "showdown stage" for the confrontation between two kings, from two different kingdoms. This divine confrontation was between the king of Sodom, who was the personification of the devil, and Melchizedek, king of Jerusalem and priest of God Most High. We will discuss in detail the prophetic implications of what the king of Sodom stands for and how the "Return of the Lost Key" will help us avoid all the encroachments of the king of Sodom.

When the king of Sodom finally got to Abram in the Valley of the Kings, he was a moment too late. The king of Jerusalem and High priest of God Most High had already intercepted Abram. Abraham had been fully introduced to the eternal priestly Order of Melchizedek. **Abraham had already partaken of the bread and wine of this heavenly priesthood and had been changed from the inside out.** There was a divine power working inside his spirit and mind like he had never known before. **When the King of Sodom tried to bribe him, he refused his luring offer.** Abraham told the King of Sodom that he had nothing in his power that he desired, even to the shoelaces of the people of Sodom that Abram had rescued. Abraham's obedience and personal encounter with the priestly Order of Melchizedek gave him the power to conquer the seductive power and influence of the king of Sodom, thus thwarting every demonic agency which was connected to the king of Sodom.

Abram had just discovered an "Ancient Key" from the Order of Melchizedek that had given him the power to resist every demonic force that was coming at him through the king of Sodom. **Abraham also received the supernatural grace to say "NO" to an offering of finances from the king of Sodom— an offer that was worth billions of dollars in today's currency.** I have seen many good ministers of the gospel who have destroyed themselves and their ministry simply because they failed to say "NO" to the king of Sodom. May God intercept us from this through the Order of Melchizedek.

LIFE APPLICATION SECTION

Point to Ponder:

When God is involved with the affairs of our human life, the devil will also hasten to intercept the course of our lives to see if he can derail us from pursuing our spiritual purpose.

Verse to Remember:

"And blessed be God Most High, who has defeated your enemies for you." Then Abram gave Melchizedek a tenth of all the goods he had recovered.

Genesis 14:20

Questions to Consider:

• How did Abraham break covenant with his wife when he went down to Egypt?

_____

_____

_____

_____

• What was Abraham's mindset when he tithed into the priestly Order of Melchizedek?

_____

_____

_____

_____

• What did Melchizedek give to Abraham in exchange for his tithes of honor?

_____

_____

_____

_____

JOURNAL YOUR THOUGHTS

Chapter Six

THE PRIESTLY ORDER OF MELCHIZEDEK

The priestly Order of Melchizedek is the highest priestly order that God ever established for His people in heaven and on earth. When Jesus Christ rose from the dead, He took the blood of the cross and presented it to His heavenly Father as a peace offering and opened a permanent pathway into the holy of holies for all eternity, for all of God's children. Jesus Christ then sat on the right hand of God, to receive His eternal mantle as the High Priest after the Order of Melchizedek. *Unfortunately many of God's children do not know much about the Order of Melchizedek.* Many Kingdom citizens do not know what is available to us through this awesome priesthood, because of inaccurate patterns of tithing which have been established in the global Church.

> *The Lord has taken an oath and will not break his vow: "You are a priest forever in the order of Melchizedek."*
>
> Psalm 110:4

In this chapter I will finally tell you "WHAT THE LOST KEY IS......" I will give you the name of this ancient key, which activates the functionality of the priestly Order of Melchizedek. However, before I do this, I want to describe with the precision of a brain surgeon what the Order of Melchizedek is all about.

The Testimony of an Apologetic Apostle

Indeed, if others have reason for confidence in their own efforts, I have even more! I was circumcised when I was eight days old. I am a pure-blooded citizen of Israel and a member of the tribe of Benjamin—a real Hebrew if there ever was one! I was a member of the Pharisees, who demand the strictest obedience to the Jewish law. I was so zealous that I harshly persecuted the church. And as for righteousness, I obeyed the law without fault.

Philippians 3:4-6

The salvation of the apostle Paul and his subsequent transition from Judaism to Christianity is one of the most important historic events in the prophetic history of the Church of the living God. No single person has contributed more to the cause of Christ and His Kingdom than Paul of Tarsus. His supernatural conversion to Christ is clearly recorded in the book of Acts and canonized in the Holy Scriptures. ***The apostle Paul through the vehicle of apostolic and prophetic technology is responsible for much of the doctrines of the Church today.*** No well-meaning New Testament believer or theologian can ignore the testimony of this Apostle and his teachings.

Of the post-Pentecost apostles of the Lord Jesus Christ, none is as qualified as the apostle Paul to teach on the priestly Order of Melchizedek and outline its supremacy over the priestly Order of Aaron. Paul was a prolific expert on Jewish laws and customs. His zeal for Judaism was unrivaled even among his peers. God could never have chosen a more qualified person to write an "apologetic discourse" in defense of the priestly Order of Melchizedek. Much of what has been revealed about the nature, power and scope of the Order of Melchizedek was revealed to this apostolic general. As such, it is from the written testimony of this great pillar of the faith where we will begin deciphering what the Order of Melchizedek is all about.

It is both a Marketplace and Priestly Ministry

The most unique aspect of the Order of Melchizedek is that unlike the Levitical priestly order, this eternal priestly order is both a marketplace and priestly ministry. This is because the High Priest (Christ) of this eternal priestly order is first and foremost a King, who does priestly work. As a King, Christ's influence extends far beyond the physical boundaries of the temple (Local Church), right into the marketplace. Every "king" owns everything that is within his kingdom. As a King-Priest, Christ has an "ongoing dual influence" over both the services of the temple and the activities of His Kingdom citizens in the marketplace.

On the other hand, the High Priest of the Levitical priestly order and his staff of priests were not permitted to engage in any form of secular business activity outside the normal activities of servicing the spiritual needs of the people of

Israel. Moses made it very clear that God did not want the Levites to be involved in any form of secular business activity. God wanted them to focus their energy on servicing the spiritual needs of the people of Israel and those of the temple. To ensure that this was the case, God gave the tithes of the remaining eleven tribes of Israel to the tribe of Levi as an everlasting inheritance.

> *"As for the tribe of Levi, your relatives, I will compensate them for their service in the Tabernacle. Instead of an allotment of land, I will give them the tithes from the entire land of Israel."*
>
> Numbers 18:21

Understanding the Order of Melchizedek will not only revolutionize how the Church exacts the tithe but it will also introduce the global Church to many creative ways of wealth creation outside the normal collection of tithes and offerings. Under the priestly Order of Melchizedek, members of the clergy do not have to depend entirely on the tithes and offerings of the people in the church to sustain the work of the ministry. Under the Order of Melchizedek the "tithes and offerings" of the people are just "one of the many streams of income" that God has made available to the New Testament Church.

Under the priestly Order of Melchizedek, senior pastors or apostolic founders of churches can be just as involved in business as they are in ministering to the spiritual needs of the people in their church. Under this eternal priestly order, spiritual leaders can lead a church while managing profitable business ventures in the marketplace. *This dual involvement in ecclesiastical and marketplace ministry increases the scope and spiritual reach of the ministries of senior leaders under the Order of Melchizedek. But I must point out the fact that the marketplace activities of an ecclesiastical minister of the gospel must never be allowed to overshadow his or her priestly functions within the local church.* Simply said, the ecclesiastical minister of the gospel must never abandon his or her primary call of God in favor of making more money in the marketplace. Whenever there is such a spiritual imbalance, the ecclesiastical five-fold minister of the gospel will begin to lose the "soul of

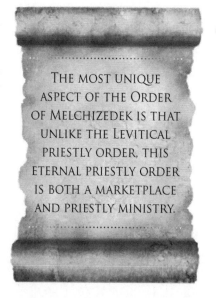

THE MOST UNIQUE ASPECT OF THE ORDER OF MELCHIZEDEK IS THAT UNLIKE THE LEVITICAL PRIESTLY ORDER, THIS ETERNAL PRIESTLY ORDER IS BOTH A MARKETPLACE AND PRIESTLY MINISTRY.

their primary prophetic calling." Ecclesiastical five-fold ministers must make sure that they never allow their success in business to overshadow God's primary call and destiny for their lives.

Under the Order of Melchizedek, senior pastors or apostolic founders of churches do not have to be limited to the people who step inside the four walls of their church. The truth of the matter is that the majority of lost souls (people) are found in the marketplace. The apostle Paul is a classic example of this powerful synergy of marketplace and priestly ministry. The apostle Paul was able to reach far more people with the gospel of the Kingdom because his apostolic ministry was never limited to the people who stepped inside the four walls of the church. Most of Paul's converts came from his interactions with the marketplace.

> *"Then Paul left Athens and went to Corinth.* **2** *There he became acquainted with a Jew named Aquila, born in Pontus, who had recently arrived from Italy with his wife, Priscilla. They had left Italy when Claudius Caesar deported all Jews from Rome.* **3** *Paul lived and worked with them, for they were tentmakers just as he was.* **4** *Each Sabbath found Paul at the synagogue, trying to convince the Jews and Greeks alike."*
>
> Acts 18:1-4

Unfortunately, many pastors in the Body of Christ are not aware that New Testament ministry is supposed to function after the Order of Melchizedek, so they are leading their churches under an "Old Testament Levitical priestly mindset." The reason I know this, is because many pastors are obsessed with tithes and offerings as the only method for raising money for the vision of their church. These pastors stress themselves into a panic, whenever they see that the tithes and offerings of the church are running low. This Levitical mindset has robbed many of these able pastors of any entrepreneurial spirit that could effectively finance their vision in the Kingdom of God. The quote below underscores just how widespread and deeply rooted this Levitical mindset really is, in much of the Body of Christ.

> "I was excited to attend my first pastoral roundtable, but that excitement turned quickly to frustration. After the laughs subsided, one pastor said, "You do not make money young man; you raise money. You have to get before your church and challenge them to give more. Teach your church to give." "Amen," the others responded.

> They went on to share with me fifty ways to handle an offering. I learned how to take an offering, receive an offering, and pull an offering. I have heard these methods echoed throughout the last twenty years.

Thus, everything I've learned from the church and in formal training about wealth-building can be summed up in two familiar words: Tithes and Offerings. That was the extent of the wealth knowledge I learned for many years." *(Rich Church Poor Church, page 20, by John Louis Muratori)*

It's an Eternal Priesthood

"...without father, without mother, without genealogy, having neither beginning of days nor end of life, but made like the Son of God, remains a priest continually."

Hebrews 7:3

"The LORD has sworn And will not relent, 'You are a priest forever According to the order of Melchizedek.'"

Psalm 110:4

The first thing that the apostle Paul and King David tell us about the priestly Order of Melchizedek is that unlike the Levitical priesthood, this priesthood is an eternal or everlasting priesthood. This powerful priestly order exists in an infinite eternal-state which can never be improved upon, because everything in this eternal realm is completely perfect. This means that there is nothing missing or broken in this spiritual order. The fact that the priestly Order of Melchizedek is eternal has far-reaching spiritual implications. It means that there is simply no end to the level and quality of spiritual representation we can expect from this glorious order, when we tithe into it.

It's built on the King's righteousness

For this Melchizedek, king of Salem, priest of the Most High God, who met Abraham returning from the slaughter of the kings and blessed him, 2 to whom also Abraham gave a tenth part of all, first being translated "king of righteousness," and then also king of Salem, meaning "king of peace,"

Hebrews 7:1-2

The second thing that the apostle Paul tells us about the priestly Order of Melchizedek is that this priesthood is built around and upon the righteousness of its High Priest. The Bible tells us that this Melchizedek was "King of righteousness." This great high priest "Melchizedek" was not only righteous but He "has dominion over the whole sphere of righteousness!" Imagine this; anything righteous that you can think or dream of, He reigns over it.

This is in huge contrast to the Levitical priesthood where the High Priests were constantly wrestling with the power of sin in their humanity. Under the Order of Melchizedek our High Priest has complete mastery over sin and He lives in complete righteousness. Righteousness in Scripture has three prongs to it. Righteousness infers, "being in right standing with God, man and the devil." If we are in right standing with God but are not in right standing with our wives or neighbors, we are not walking in the fullness of our righteousness. If we are in right standing with God and man but are in wrong standing with the devil, we are still not walking in the fullness of our righteousness. The priestly Order of Melchizedek has the power to make all Kingdom citizens completely righteous.

It Exists in an Eternal State of Peace

For this Melchizedek, king of Salem, priest of the Most High God, who met Abraham returning from the slaughter of the kings and blessed him, to whom also Abraham gave a tenth part of all, first being translated "king of righteousness," and then also king of Salem, meaning "king of peace,"

Hebrews 7:1-2

The third thing the apostle Paul shows us about this powerful priestly order is that it exists in a permanent state of peace and tranquility. This priesthood presides over the kind of supernatural peace that surpasses human comprehension. It's difficult for us to truly imagine a life without the spirit of unrest and anxiety. This is because we live in a world where there is spiritual, economic, social and political turmoil on all fronts. But when we bring ourselves under the priestly Order of Melchizedek, God will bring us into a place of supernatural rest and tranquility such as we have never experienced. The word "Peace" comes from the Hebrew

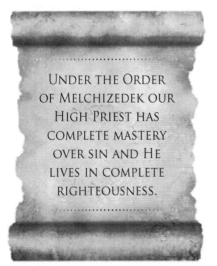

UNDER THE ORDER OF MELCHIZEDEK OUR HIGH PRIEST HAS COMPLETE MASTERY OVER SIN AND HE LIVES IN COMPLETE RIGHTEOUSNESS.

word "Shalom" which means, "nothing broken and nothing missing."

When we come into this dimension of supernatural rest and tranquility we will become the greatest demonstration of the power of God in the midst of a troubled world. For we live in a world where everyone, including the rich and the powerful, are in a constant state of unrest. People will gravitate to us wanting to know how they can drink from the same spiritual well we are drinking from. They will want to know why we have so much peace and rest in a troubled world. Since the priestly Order of Melchizedek exists in a permanent state of peace, this priestly order has the power to restore whatever is "broken or missing" in our lives.

Jesus Christ is its High Priest

So also Christ did not glorify Himself to become High Priest, but it was He who said to Him: "You are My Son, Today I have begotten You." As He also says in another place: " You are a priest forever According to the order of Melchizedek.

Hebrews 5:5-6

The fourth thing that the apostle Paul tells us about the priestly Order of Melchizedek is that in this eternal order, Jesus Christ is the presiding High Priest. In this order of priesthood, the High Priest never dies because He has an endless life and reigns over life and death. This High Priest is above the reach of death and moves in the realms of eternity. In this priestly order our High Priest is the sinless Son of God, who lived and died for our sins and then rose from the dead. What a High Priest! He is worthy of all the glory and all the honor.

Under this Priestly Order the High Priest is both a King and a Priest

For this Melchizedek, king of Salem, priest of the Most High God, who met Abraham returning from the slaughter of the kings and blessed him, to whom also Abraham gave a tenth part of all, first being translated "king of righteousness," and then also king of Salem, meaning "king of peace."

Hebrews 7:1-2

Another very fascinating aspect of the priestly Order of Melchizedek

is that in this order the High Priest is both a Priest and a King. In the priestly Order of Aaron the High Priest was simply that—a "priest" and no more. Under the Order of Aaron the High Priest had no kingly anointing and grace flowing through his life. He was operating on one spiritual cylinder, which is that of a priest. He could present the spiritual needs of the nation of Israel before God and make atonement for their sins but he had no governmental authority over the nation of Israel.

In the priestly Order of Melchizedek, the High Priest wears not only His priestly mantle but He also carries the spirit of government on His shoulders. This means that the scope of His spiritual authority and the power that He exerts over the people that are under His priesthood is infinitely greater than the power the priesthood of Aaron exerted over the nation of Israel. This means that when we bring ourselves under the priestly Order of Melchizedek, we will become shareholders in the "spirit of governmental authority" which flows from the head of our order. This is why Jesus Christ told us that under this priesthood, "whatever we bind here on earth shall be bound in heaven and whatever we loose here on earth shall be given the same license in heaven." This is what I call "packing power!"

I have taught the people in my church to go around telling each other that, "they are packing power." When we truly bring ourselves under this priestly Order of Melchizedek, we will become walking powerhouses. Wherever we go the power of God ought to explode into miraculous action. Under the Order of Melchizedek, we have no business walking in fear and defeat. Under this priestly order we truly become "Demon Busters and World Shakers!"

The High Priest of this Priestly Order has never been infected by Sin

"For such a High Priest was fitting for us, who is holy, harmless, undefiled, separate from sinners, and has become higher than the heavens; who does not need daily, as those high priests, to offer up sacrifices, first for His own sins and then for the people's, for this He did once for all when He offered up Himself."

Hebrews 7:26-27

Since the fall of Adam and Eve, men and women have been ravaged by sin and its dreadful power. When sin entered the world it unleashed death agencies into the spiritual atmosphere of the fallen Adamic kingdom, that we now call the world. ***These death agencies released by sin also corrupted the human gene pool, making every child born of a woman a prisoner of sin from the very word*** "Go." These death agencies released by sin also shortened man's life expectancy here on earth and introduced unrest in the matrix of his family relationships.

> *"Why are you so angry?" the Lord asked Cain. "Why do you look so dejected? You will be accepted if you do what is right. But if you refuse to do what is right, then watch out! Sin is crouching at the door, eager to control you. But you must subdue it and be its master." One day Cain suggested to his brother, "Let's go out into the fields." And while they were in the field, Cain attacked his brother, Abel, and killed him.*
>
> Genesis 4:6-8

The showdown between God and Cain in Genesis chapter four began with Cain's offering of disobedience, which was rejected by God for its inaccuracy. This showdown culminated in the murder of his younger brother, Abel, *showcasing just how quickly sin had invaded man's sense of right and wrong. What's worse, sin in Cain had raised its ugly head to the degree of challenging God's supreme authority over the affairs of men.* Many generations later, men and women are still trying to control the raging power of sin in their lives, to no avail. Mankind continues to search desperately for a way to curb the evil residing within. Sin has taken its terrible toll on the structure of family relationships, separating husbands from wives and children from parents. There is nothing indecent or immoral that sin will not do. The more vile and horrifying an act is, the "more" of it sin will do.

Sin has also taken its toll on the financial resources of many individuals and nations. Men and women motivated by the power of sin have stolen the life savings of others and squandered them on the altar of their personal greed. Children have had their loving parents slaughtered by thieves who broke into their house in search of money. Sin has progressively reduced mankind in every way possible, from the creature of immense dignity that he once was in the Garden of Eden, into a beast of the field. Hell is full of people serving their eternal sentence in unquenchable fires simply because they failed to find the power to break the power that sin had over their lives, while they were here on earth.

> *"But there is another power within me that is at war with my mind. This power makes me a slave to the sin that is still within me. Oh, what a miserable person I am! Who will free me from this life that is dominated by sin and death? Thank God! The answer is in Jesus Christ our Lord."*

Romans 7:23-24

The apostle Paul was no stranger to the personal struggles that he experienced trying to break the power of sin over his own life. He found that the more he tried to resist sin in the power of his own flesh, the stronger the hold of sin got on his life. As a zealous follower of Judaism at the time, he found that the more he tried to obey the righteous demands of the Mosaic Law through his sheer force of will, the more rebellious and insidious the sin nature in him became. He found himself doing the very things that he had promised himself that he would never do. Paul finally came to the sobering conclusion that the technology of sin and death had literally invaded every fiber of his being, making his body a "body of sin and death."

SIN HAS PROGRESSIVELY REDUCED MANKIND IN EVERY WAY POSSIBLE, FROM THE CREATURE OF IMMENSE DIGNITY THAT HE ONCE WAS IN THE GARDEN OF EDEN, INTO A BEAST OF THE FIELD.

As a result of his personal struggles with sin, few could appreciate the awesome power of being under a priestly order where the High Priest has complete mastery over sin and its insidious powers. **Under the priestly Order of Melchizedek the High Priest (Jesus) has never been defiled or affected by sin**. As a result, He is able to invest in us the same **supernatural grace to live above the controlling power of sin**, when we tithe into His eternal priestly order. Imagine coming into a season in your walk with the Lord where sin is no longer an issue. This is the awesome power of living under the Order of Melchizedek. This type of "prevailing grace over the sin nature" is very much available to us under this eternal priestly order.

This Order has Stewardship over all of Abraham's Spiritual Inheritance

"But Christ has rescued us from the curse pronounced by the law. When he was hung on the cross, he took upon himself the curse for our wrongdoing. For it is written in the Scriptures, 'Cursed is everyone who is hung on a tree.' [f Through Christ Jesus, God has blessed the Gentiles with the same blessing he promised to Abraham, so that we who are believers might receive the promised Holy Spirit through faith."

Galatians 3:13-14

This powerful priestly Order of Melchizedek has been given the eternal privilege of stewarding the blessing of Abraham for the purpose of Kingdom advancement. Jesus Christ, who is also the High Priest after the Order of Melchizedek, has complete stewardship over Abraham's natural and spiritual inheritance and showers it on the people who live under this powerful priestly order.

It exists in an Eternal State of life, which cannot be touched by death

"…by so much more Jesus has become a surety of a better covenant. Also there were many priests, because they were prevented by death from continuing. But He, because He continues forever, has an unchangeable priesthood."

Hebrews 7:22-24

God told Adam and Eve that if they chose to disobey Him and ate from the tree of the knowledge of good and evil they would surely die. At the time Adam and Eve could not comprehend the horrors of death because they had never seen anything die before. You can imagine the sense of horror and dismay that they must have experienced when they discovered the dead body of their son, Abel, who had been murdered by his own brother. **Death agencies had finally struck close to home and the emotional pain was almost unbearable.** There is nothing more painful to a parent than the death of their child. From henceforth generations have wrestled with the angels of death, while trying to make sense of the occasional loss of loved ones.

"Because God's children are human beings—made of flesh and blood—the Son also became flesh and blood. For only as a human being could he die, and only by dying could he break the power of the devil, who had the power of death. Only in this way could he set free all who have lived their lives as slaves to the fear of dying."

Hebrews 2:14-15

Since the first funeral, the fear of death has terrorized men and women for thousands of years. We might ask the question "what is death?" Death in its most basic form is the "cessation of life or the absence of animation." This definition also showcases the primary assignment of death agencies, which is to shut down the flow of life wherever it's flowing. If a marriage is filled with life and laughter, death agencies will begin to look for a way to bring death into the marriage. The high rate of divorce in our Modern Societies is further evidence that death agencies are working overtime to quarantine the flow of life. Death is more than a corpse lying in a casket; "it's a demonic technology which quarantines the flow of life in anything that has life in it!"

Jesus died to break the power of death that the devil had over the human race by manipulating us through our personal fear of death. Before the resurrection of Jesus Christ, death agencies continued to terrorize the world for thousands of years using man's inherent fear of death. *According to the apostle Paul, the priestly Order of Melchizedek has complete authority over the spirit of death.* The Order of Melchizedek is the custodian for the divine technology called "the Law of the Spirit of Life in Christ Jesus" which is infinitely superior to the demonic technology called "the Law of sin and death." Under the priestly Order of Aaron the High Priests kept changing because they could not serve forever by reason of death. Their ministerial assignments to the Jewish nation were always cut short by the technology of death.

When we bring ourselves under the priestly Order of Melchizedek, God will give us the power to conquer death agencies that are working against us. The priestly Order of Melchizedek cancels and quarantines the sentence of death over our lives, spiritually, emotionally and physically. Under this eternal priestly order "death itself receives a sentence of death. Death is told to die!"

How many billionaires do you know of, who would not pay astronomical amounts of money if some scientist came up with a pill which contained the "secret to the fountain of youth." A magic pill once swallowed could begin to arrest the machinery of death inside the human body and reverse the aging process. I know that if such a pill was ever invented, its originator would be a multibillionaire within hours of releasing the drug on the global market. There would be mass hysteria as the rich and famous fought their way to the front of the queue to get a piece of the pill that could allow them to live longer. Such is the power of the fear of death that exists in the inner sanctum of the human soul.

"Then, when our dying bodies have been transformed into bodies that will never die, this Scripture will be fulfilled: 'Death is swallowed up in victory. O death, where is your victory? O death, where is your sting?'"

1 Corinthians 15:54-55

What multiplied millions of people on our planet do not know is that there is a *"priestly order"* where the sentence and machinery of death at work in the human body can be restrained and reversed. The "miracle pill with the secret to the fountain of youth" has already been invented under this priestly Order of Melchizedek. It comes in the form of the "divine bread and wine," which is offered to the people who submit themselves to this powerful priestly order. This is why we have to rediscover the "Ancient Key" which activates the functionality of the Order of Melchizedek for our enjoyment.

It has no Earthly Genealogy

...to whom also Abraham gave a tenth part of all, first being translated "king of righteousness," and then also king of Salem, meaning "king of peace," without father, without mother, without genealogy, having neither beginning of days nor end of life, but made like the Son of God, remains a priest continually.

Hebrews 7:2-3

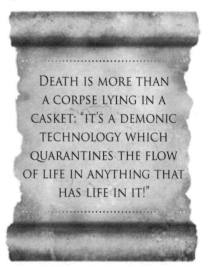

DEATH IS MORE THAN A CORPSE LYING IN A CASKET; "IT'S A DEMONIC TECHNOLOGY WHICH QUARANTINES THE FLOW OF LIFE IN ANYTHING THAT HAS LIFE IN IT!"

If you have lived long enough on our troubled planet you may have heard of the proverbial statement, "like father, like son and like mother, like daughter." You may have overheard older women look at a naughty child and comment, "Dear God, this child is just as nasty as its father." The implied meaning behind this proverbial statement is that the child and its father are cut out of the same cloth. Since the fall of Adam and Eve who are the grandparents of the entire human race, sin entered the world and corrupted the human gene pool and unleashed the poison of demonic influence in the flow of the human bloodline.

The corruption caused by sin when it entered the human gene pool, caused man's prophetic DNA which God had given him to mutate. Sin changed the inherent nature of the human genome, making it more susceptible to "demonic influences than the influence of the God-kind of life." Like a nuclear torpedo, "man's DNA" was reprogrammed to migrate towards death. Everything that a man does will at some point touch the peripherals of death. Our DNA as humans has mutated to the point that we will never be able to manifest the fullness of the God-kind of life in our DNA without requiring a supernatural blood transfusion to flush out all the death agencies that are flowing in our bloodline. This is why we need the precious blood of Jesus Christ. I feel sorry for churches that do not teach on the blood of Jesus.

"You must not bow down to them or worship them, for I, the Lord your God, am a jealous God who will not tolerate your affection for any other gods. I lay the sins of the parents upon their children; the entire family is affected—even children in the third and fourth generations of those who reject me."

Exodus 20:5

Since man's gene pool was corrupted by the entrance of sin in the human bloodline, man's DNA became the best vehicle to "transport demonic spirits and demonic tendencies" from one generation to another. Demonic agencies had hit a home run. They had guaranteed themselves "a sure transport" between the fathers and the sons. They had established a clear pathway between the mothers and their daughters. This meant that the demonic spirits that were controlling the fathers and mothers had a "sure license" through the human gene pool to continue their "tenancy in that particular family line even to the fourth generation."

Unless this "demonic license through the human genome" is revoked or restrained, the devil is going to have an upper hand in the future destinies of our sons and daughters. Unless this demonic license is canceled, the chances of our children fighting the same demons and demonic tendencies that we are fighting today is a "whopping one hundred percent." As a matter of fact, the longer demonic spirits operate within our bloodline "the stronger the demonic technology becomes" inside the chambers of our human genome.

The "demonic hills" we as parents **"fail to cross and conquer today"** will one day become "great mountains of spiritual resistance in the days of our children." This is why my heart goes out to President George W. Bush, because the troubles he experienced trying to win the peace in the Iraq War had nothing to do with the lack of genius in the commanders that he had on the ground. It had everything to do with the failure of his father, former President George H.W Bush Sr., who failed to take advantage of the silver plate opportunity he had been given in the late eighties to destroy Saddam Hussein and deliver the Iraqi people.

Years later when his son George W. Bush became president and the US and its allies went to war with Iraq, the playing fields had completely changed from a decade ago, when his father stood at the same frontiers. In the years it took for George W. Bush to get to Iraq the "demonic machinery and technology" had completely changed the "rules of engagement from the normal methods of combat to the unpredictable and suicidal tactics of zealous suicide bombers." American forces are now stuck in the Middle East without a "clear exit strategy and plan for victory." I do not blame George W. Bush; I blame his father for "failing to clear a hill in his day which later became a gigantic mountain in the days of his son."

The demonic pathway through the human genome has far-reaching spiritual implications. It means that if there have been struggles with child molestation or sexual perversion in a particular family, the genetic disposition of the descendants of this particular family will lean very heavily to the repeating of these insidious acts throughout the ensuing generations. This would explain why the history of certain families is plastered with continuous instances of divorce or the breaking away of marriages. The same demonic agencies that had broken the marriages of their parents and grandparents are now destroying theirs. These cycles of sorrow, loss and pain are repeated constantly. It's like being "trapped in the rat race."

When we consider these things and observe these endless cycles of death and destruction in the lives of people around us, we can be almost overwhelmed by it. You may find yourself asking the questions: "Is there a way out of the rut? How can I guarantee that the sins of my parents do not intercept the calendar of my life and limit my blessing?" The answer to ending these endless cycles of death, destruction and defeat is found in "rediscovering the Lost Key which activates the functionality of the power of the Order of Melchizedek over our lives."

The apostle Paul tells us that the priestly Order of Melchizedek has no "earthly genealogy, ancestry or blood line." The High Priest of the priestly Order of Melchizedek stands in a spiritual position where He has "no earthly father, mother or beginning of days." His lofty position of honor and His lack of a traceable genealogy have far-reaching spiritual implications for those who run for "cover under His eternal priestly order." Even though our Lord Jesus Christ shares in our humanity, the apostle Paul is quite clear that His priesthood is not of this world. Saint Paul makes it clear that the Levitical priestly Order operates here on earth. ***This means then that Christ's priesthood is primarily based upon His divinity and not His humanity. This is why He has a heavenly priesthood.***

"If he were here on earth, he would not even be a priest, since there already are priests who offer the gifts required by the law."

Hebrews 8:4

Since Christ's eternal priestly order is based primarily upon His divinity and not His humanity, He has no earthly genealogy that can compromise His eternal priestly order. His priesthood can never be affected by demonic influences and tendencies that have established a strong pathway through the human genome. This means that when we come under this priestly Order of Melchizedek every "Generational Curse" that has been pursuing us through our bloodline has to come to an abrupt end. What a powerful priestly order! Why would anyone in their right mind fail to give their tithes into such a powerful priesthood? Most of the ministries who teach on breaking generational curses do not have a clear-cut revelation on the Order of Melchizedek, which is why they have a limited level of success in breaking generational curses over people's lives.

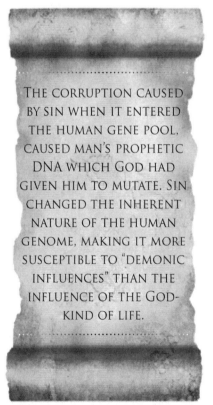

THE CORRUPTION CAUSED BY SIN WHEN IT ENTERED THE HUMAN GENE POOL, CAUSED MAN'S PROPHETIC DNA WHICH GOD HAD GIVEN HIM TO MUTATE. SIN CHANGED THE INHERENT NATURE OF THE HUMAN GENOME, MAKING IT MORE SUSCEPTIBLE TO "DEMONIC INFLUENCES" THAN THE INFLUENCE OF THE GOD-KIND OF LIFE.

God sealed this Priestly Order with an Oath

And inasmuch as He was not made priest without an oath (for they have become priests without an oath, but He with an oath by Him who said to Him: "The LORD has sworn And will not relent, 'You are a priest forever, According to the order of Melchizedek.'"

Hebrews 7:20-21

We live in a world that is constantly changing and changing the people around us as the earth rotates on its axis. In the rapid changes that are taking place around us we sometimes lose sight of vital principles which drive the engines of life. One of those vital principles, which sometimes gets lost in translation, is our ability to "trust delegated authority." Many of us have seen leadership change hands so many times that we have become weary of trusting the engines of human leadership. This is especially true in the democratic societies of the West, which normally go through a complete change of leadership every four years.

"For the law appoints as high priests men who have weakness, but the word of the oath, which came after the law, appoints the Son who has been perfected forever."

Hebrews 7:28

People may like and trust the present structure of leadership but in many cases they are not even sure that the same leaders they trust today will be available to lead them the next day. This has forced many people to have a very loose connection with delegated authority, choosing rather to become a law unto themselves. In many cases the people's loose connections with their secular leaders usually translate into "loose connections with their spiritual fathers and mothers in the house of God."

The frustrations of a constantly-changing leadership structure and climate, was one of the horrifying things that the people who lived under the priestly Order of Aaron had to deal with. The High Priests kept changing every few years as each previous High Priest died away. Even more frightening was the fact that some very good and honorable High Priests were sometimes replaced by a High priest who was corrupt and lacking in spiritual power. It would be like living in a marriage where your wife or husband is constantly changing from one day to the next. How terrifying is that?

On the other hand, the apostle Paul tells us that under the priestly Order of Melchizedek, we never have to live in fear of a sudden change in the structure and climate of leadership. The structure of leadership and the eternal position of our presiding High Priest Jesus Christ has already been "sealed by an unchangeable Oath" from the mouth of God.

"Jesus Christ is the same yesterday, today, and forever."

Hebrews 13:8

The above passage of Scripture means that under the priestly Order of Melchizedek, we can fully surrender ourselves to "our Leader Jesus Christ" while He outworks His eternal purpose in our life. This means that the priestly Order of Melchizedek creates a spiritual climate in which people can begin to have very strong spirit connections with their spiritual fathers and mothers in the Lord. The Order of Melchizedek destroys the "loose connections" between the people and their shepherds and unleashes "strong spirit connections" between those who lead and those who follow. These supernatural dimensions of "strong spirit connections and loyalty" will help us establish strong "father-son type of Churches" which have the favor to possess, faith to prevail and power to finish. Under the Order of Melchizedek we can truly build Churches that can take the City and impact the nations.

This Order is infinitely Superior to the Priestly Order of Aaron

"Now consider how great this man was, to whom even the patriarch Abraham gave a tenth of the spoils. And indeed those who are of the sons of Levi, who receive the priesthood, have a commandment to receive tithes from the people according to the law, that is, from their brethren, though they have come from the loins of Abraham; but he whose genealogy is not derived from them received tithes from Abraham and blessed him who had the promises. 7 Now beyond all contradiction the lesser is blessed by the better. Even Levi, who receives tithes, paid tithes through Abraham, so to speak, for he was still in the loins of his father when Melchizedek met him."

Hebrews 7:4-7, 9

I want you to consider the fact that Paul's epistle to the Hebrews was written to the Jews who lived in Asia Minor and it is by far the strongest and most intelligent apologetic epistle ever written by the apostle Paul. This epistle was written to convince men and women of Jewish descent who were having a tough time walking away from the dictates of the Mosaic Law in their newfound faith. These believers kept sending mixed signals, mixing the law with grace in all of their spiritual practices. We must remember that these Messianic-Jews who were converting to a "a life of faith in Christ Jesus" had spent over four thousand years of their national history under the Levitical priestly Order and changing gears to a new order of priesthood was no simple task.

This is why it was necessary for the apostle Paul to intelligently walk them through the writings of the Old and New Testaments and show them the utter superiority of the priestly Order of Melchizedek over the Levitical priesthood. Saint Paul had to show them that they were not abandoning their ancient Jewish faith in the God of Abraham, Isaac and Jacob when they brought themselves under the priestly Order of Melchizedek.

The most important argument he presented to establish the surpassing superiority of the Order of Melchizedek over the priestly Order of Aaron, is the fact that Abraham, who is the father of the Jewish nation, had himself tithed into the eternal priesthood of the Order of Melchizedek. This is significant because Abraham never ever tithed into the priestly Order of Aaron, a priesthood that was established on Mount Sinai over four hundred years after Abraham's death.

THE SEARCH FOR A PERFECT SOCIETY IS THE MOTIVATING FACTOR BEHIND THE BIRTH OF ALL WORLD RELIGIONS AND POLITICAL IDEOLOGIES THAT PLASTER OUR SOCIETY TODAY.

The apostle Paul seals his argument when he argues that "If Abraham who is the father of the Jewish nation tithed into Melchizedek, it also follows that Levi who was in the spiritual loins of Abraham when Abraham met Melchizedek also tithed into this powerful priestly Order." His argument affected these Hebrew believers in a very profound way. They were beginning to realize that the tribe of Levi whose priesthood they followed had also tithed into Melchizedek when Levi was yet in the loins of their forefather Abraham. This is why I flinch when I hear preachers teach on tithing using Malachi 3:8-12 because I know that they are training New Testament believers to access the wrong priesthood concerning their tithes and offerings.

Spiritual Perfection can only be realized through this Priestly Order

"Therefore, if perfection were through the Levitical priesthood (for under it the people received the law), what further need was there that another priest should rise according to the order of Melchizedek, and not be called according to the order of Aaron? For He testifies: 'You are a priest forever According to the order of Melchizedek.' Therefore He is also able to save to the uttermost those who come to God through Him, since He always lives to make intercession for them."

Hebrews 7:11, 25

Ever since Adam and Eve opened the portals of time to the entrance of sin, death and demons, men and women of all ages in each dispensation have been in search of a utopian society or existence where they do not have to deal with the idiosyncrasies of their own flesh life. ***The search for a perfect society is the motivating factor behind the birth of all world religions and political*** *ideologies that plaster our society today.*

The rise of Marxism, which is the philosophy created by Karl Marx which gave birth to the ideology of communism, is the result of this global pursuit for a "perfect or utopian society." As a nation the United States is rocking from the shock waves of mass legal and illegal immigration because men and women from around the world want to live in a society where they can prosper and live in peace. They are running to America to get their share of the great American dream.

> *"For on the one hand there is an annulling of the former commandment because of its weakness and unprofitableness, for the law made nothing perfect; on the other hand, there is the bringing in of a better hope, through which we draw near to."*
>
> Hebrews 7:17-19

This frantic search for a "perfect utopian" society is not a foreign experience to the human pursuit for perfection. The formation of human civilizations and the ensuing industrial and technological revolutions are all by-products of this global search for a perfect society. Every little girl dreams of growing into a beautiful woman and marrying the most amazing man on earth and living happily ever after. You can imagine the sense of emotional devastation and spiritual disillusionment some women go through once they are married, only to discover that they married the devil's first cousin.

How many times have politicians promised the masses the land of milk and honey while campaigning for the Presidency and as soon as they are elected they deliver stale bread. Why is this so? The answer is simple. Once sin and death entered the world, the "machinery of death" has been working ceaselessly and as such, whatever mankind touches or promises must one day touch the place called death.

The question that comes to mind is simply this: "Is there a sure way of creating a perfect society?" The answer is a resounding "YES"! There is a spiritual technology for creating the perfect marriage or the perfect society and it is locked up in the priestly Order of Melchizedek. The apostle Paul concludes by showing these Hebrew believers that the Levitical priesthood had no power to bring about man's greatest search, the search for a perfect society. The Order of Aaron had too many inherent flaws that made it impossible for the proper outworking of this spiritual technology. But under the priestly Order of Melchizedek, perfection in its purest form is a sure possibility. ***This is***

because this priestly order already exists in a perfect state in the realms of eternity.

This Priestly Order has its own Law

"For the priesthood being changed, of necessity there is also a change of the law. For He of whom these things are spoken belongs to another tribe, from which no man has officiated at the altar."

Hebrews 7:12-13

God has laws which govern whatever He wants to do on earth. When God established the priestly Order of Aaron, He gave Moses specific laws from the Mountain of Law (which is Mount Sinai) that were going to regulate the Levitical priesthood. These set of laws were to govern the inflow and outflow of this priesthood and the way people tithed into it. These laws were then sealed and ratified by the blood of bulls and goats.

The apostle Paul shows us that the priestly Order of Melchizedek also has its own law, which governs the outflow and inflow of this eternal priesthood. The law that the apostle Paul is talking about is the "Law of the Spirit of Life in Christ Jesus." This is the primary law, which governs the priestly Order of Melchizedek. This is why I shiver when I hear preachers and teachers of the Word tell New Testament believers that they will be "Cursed if they do not tithe" based upon Malachi 3:8-12. Nevertheless, I do understand where these honorable and sincere men and women of God are coming from because I used to say the same things.

"So now there is no condemnation for those who belong to Christ Jesus. And because you belong to him, the power of the life-giving Spirit has freed you from the power of sin that leads to death."

Romans 8:1-2

What they fail to realize is that the phrase "cursed with a curse" the prophet Malachi was referring to in this passage was a quote from the Torah. It was a "Curse" as prescribed by the Mosaic Law, which regulated the inflow and outflow of the priestly Order of Aaron. Under the Order of Aaron the law governing the priesthood made provision for the flow of both "blessings and curses" depending upon the choices the worshippers were making at the time. The reason God allowed this to happen is simple but deeply profound. The Levitical priesthood was an earthly priesthood that was quarantined in the "finite structures of time where anything is subject to change." This means that if someone got cursed for "not tithing" under the Mosaic covenant, the same Law that imposed a curse upon them could also reverse the curse within the cylinder of time if the worshippers chose to repent. *If someone got cursed by God under the eternal Order of Melchizedek, their curse could never ever be reversed no matter how much they refined their behavior after the fact. This is because everything in this royal priesthood is in an infinite state.*

I am not implying that there are no spiritual consequences for "Non-tithers" under the priestly Order of Melchizedek. There are, but these spiritual consequences are not "based upon the administration of a curse." This is because the "spirit of the Curse" does not and cannot exist in the eternal Order of Melchizedek. This priestly order is saturated with the fullness of the blessing of Abraham and that blessing has "no sorrow that can be added to it." In the global Church, we have too many Christians who are constantly being cursed and then being blessed again and so forth, based upon their inconsistencies in the area of tithing. The reason we can justify this type of scrambled theology is because we have no "clear-cut revelation concerning the priestly Order of Melchizedek and how it operates."

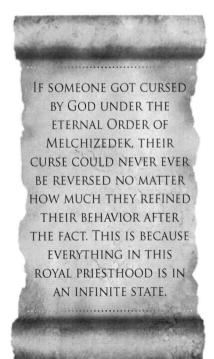

IF SOMEONE GOT CURSED BY GOD UNDER THE ETERNAL ORDER OF MELCHIZEDEK, THEIR CURSE COULD NEVER EVER BE REVERSED NO MATTER HOW MUCH THEY REFINED THEIR BEHAVIOR AFTER THE FACT. THIS IS BECAUSE EVERYTHING IN THIS ROYAL PRIESTHOOD IS IN AN INFINITE STATE.

"No longer will there be a curse upon anything. For the throne of God and of the Lamb will be there, and his servants will worship him."
Revelation 22:3

There is no "Curse" in this eternal priestly order, but the consequences for not "honoring the King of Jerusalem" with the tithe that is due Him are stiffer than those under the Levitical priesthood; however, the punishment thereof is executed on a "very different spiritual technology which has no curse in it!" I will show you how God "chastises" non-tithers under the Order of Melchizedek in a later chapter. The primary Law which governs the priestly Order of Melchizedek is the "Law of the Spirit of Life in Christ Jesus" (Romans 8:1-2) and this Law is too powerful to co-exist in the same spiritual order with the "spirit of the Curse." I just hope that you are getting excited at the prospects of living under the power of the priestly Order of Melchizedek.

The Spiritual Currency of this Priestly Order is Faith

"But without faith it is impossible to please Him, for he who comes to God must believe that He is, and that He is a rewarder of those who diligently seek Him."

Hebrews 11:6

Whether you like the Roman Catholic Church or not, it is nevertheless one of the most powerful religious institutions here on earth. This is because it is the only religious institution that I know of that has its own currency. As a novice currency trader I am very interested in how the exchange of goods and services creates currency movements across the global market. In the world we live in, you cannot buy or sell without the right currency. The currency of the United States is the Dollar, the Pound Sterling is the currency of Great Britain, the Euro Dollar is the currency of the European Union, and the Rand is the currency of South Africa, just to name a few. These different world currencies suggest that if one is to do business in a certain country, they have to convert their currency to the currency of the country they wish to do business in.

The priestly Order of Melchizedek is the richest spiritual order ever revealed to man and it has its own spiritual currency that enables all of those who desire to operate in this priestly order to buy and sell in God's Kingdom economy. This means that with this spiritual currency those who operate in the priestly Order of Melchizedek can "buy" healing, peace, prosperity, and breakthrough or "sell" (sow) their seed and believe God for a harvest. The spiritual currency of the priestly Order of Melchizedek is the "Spirit of Faith." Faith is defined as "persuasion accompanied by corresponding actions." Without the currency of "Faith" it is impossible to "please God or be rewarded" for our efforts in God's Kingdom economy.

On the other hand, the "spiritual currency for the Levitical priesthood was the letter of the Law." This means that the spiritual currency which activates the blessings of Abraham's tithing model and the spiritual currency which activates the blessings of Malachi 3:8-12 are two very different spiritual currencies. One is infinitely more powerful than the other. We will be well advised to discern this critical difference. The Bible is very clear as to the fact that, "the Law is the end of faith and faith is the end of the Law."

"For if they which are of the law be heirs, faith is made void, and the promise made of none effect."

Romans 4:14 (KJV)

Spiritual Maturity is Required to Function in this Priestly Order

"And God designated him to be a High Priest in the order of Melchizedek. There is much more we would like to say about this, but it is difficult to explain, especially since you are spiritually dull and don't seem to listen. You have been believers so long now that you ought to be teaching others. Instead, you need someone to teach you again the basic things about God's word] You are like babies who need milk and cannot eat solid food. For someone who lives on milk is still an infant and doesn't know how to do what is right. Solid food is for those who are mature, who through training have the skill to recognize the difference between right and wrong."

Hebrews 5:10-14

The question which comes to mind is simply this: "Why is it that very few believers in the global Church have a clear-cut revelation about the priestly Order of Melchizedek?" The answer to this question is simple, but has far-reaching spiritual implications. The answer to this intrinsic question is also contained in the passage of Scripture above. According to the Apostle Paul, who was given spiritual custody of the revelation concerning the priestly Order of Melchizedek; there are four reasons as to why many believers in the body of Christ have not uncovered the revelation concerning the priestly Order of Melchizedek. These reasons are listed as follows.

1. Spiritual sensitivity

   The apostle Paul lets us know that understanding and perceiving the priestly Order of Melchizedek requires an acute sense of spiritual sensitivity. This is because this priestly Order is not an earthly priestly order; it is a heavenly one. This priestly order can never be recognized; it must be revealed to the sensitive and seeking heart. Living under this priestly order requires that we command a place of intimacy with the Lord.

2. An Ear to Hear

Secondly, the apostle Paul tells us that in order to live under the priestly Order of Melchizedek we must have the ability to hear His voice and accept a more excellent way of living. If we are dull of hearing we will simply go back to doing (tithing) business as usual. We will go back to tithing according to Malachi 3:8-12. *What we will hear about this powerful spiritual Order of Melchizedek and how it impacts the technology of tithing in the body of Christ will simply disappear between our ears.*

3. Requires a change in Spiritual Diet

Thirdly, the apostle Paul tells us that in order for us to become functional members of this powerful eternal priestly order, we must be willing to change our spiritual diet. We must be willing to transition from "drinking spiritual milk to eating the solid meat of the Word of God." This is because we become what we eat. Nothing saddens me more than to observe the direction some ministers of the gospel are taking in order to attract bigger and bigger crowds. They are shifting from teaching the "deep things" of God to the "milk of God's Word." More and more pastors are abandoning their true spiritual mantles and aborting their prophetic destinies to this generation by becoming more like "secular motivational speakers" than preachers of righteous.

THE PRIESTLY ORDER OF MELCHIZEDEK IS THE RICHEST SPIRITUAL ORDER EVER REVEALED TO MAN AND IT HAS ITS OWN SPIRITUAL CURRENCY THAT ENABLES ALL OF THOSE WHO DESIRE TO OPERATE IN THIS PRIESTLY ORDER TO BUY AND SELL IN GOD'S KINGDOM ECONOMY.

What is even more depressing is the fact that the masses of people who are following these self-made "spiritual motivational gurus" will remain "spiritual desert babies" with no power to cross into their spiritual inheritance because their fathers in the faith have refused to "circumcise them" so they can begin to chew on the meat of God's holy Word. These "spiritual milk drinkers" are destined to live outside the fullness of what God has made available to His children under the Order of Melchizedek. For most of God's children, the Order of Melchizedek is available to them in their born-again spirit but only a few believers know firsthand the awesome power of this eternal priestly ministry of Christ.

4. Spiritual Training

Finally, the apostle Paul tells us that the other reason why many of God's children do not know about the priestly Order of Melchizedek is due to the lack of adequate spiritual training. **Operating under the priestly Order of Melchizedek requires skill in the way we handle the Word of righteousness.** For instance, once we are aware that we are members of the priestly Order of Melchizedek, we must be taught how to give our tithes using the tithing patterns of Genesis 14:18-20 and Hebrews 7 and not return to Malachi 3:8-12. We cannot confess that we are living under Christ's Order of Melchizedek priesthood and continue to collect our tithes and offerings from the people in our church using Malachi 3:8-12 as our prophetic backdrop. Please remember that you cannot separate the end result from the source.

Its Eternal Emblems are Bread and Wine

"And Melchizedek, the king of Salem and a priest of God Most High, brought Abram some bread and wine."

Genesis 14:18

The priestly Order of Melchizedek has its own special emblems that act as a prophetic "logo" for this divine priestly order. It does not matter what part of the world you come from; if you live in the United States you will instantly recognize the "famous yellow golden arches" as soon as you see them. When you see them you realize immediately that there is a McDonald's fast food restaurant nearby.

The eternal emblems of the priestly Order of Melchizedek are "Bread and Wine." Wherever we see the enactments of these two emblems as part of spiritual communion, they are a prophetic sign that we can all "access the priestly Order of Melchizedek." When Melchizedek appeared to Abraham and intercepted him in the Valley of the Kings, he brought with him bread and wine which he gave to Abraham. "Bread" represents "Doctrine or the Body of Christ," while 'Wine" represents "the Spirit or the blood of Jesus." These two emblems carry tremendous spiritual benefits that are unique to the priestly Order of Melchizedek. We will discuss these spiritual benefits in a later chapter.

As they were eating, Jesus took some bread and blessed it. Then he broke it in pieces and gave it to the disciples, saying, "Take this and eat it, for this is my body." And he took a cup of wine and gave thanks to God for it. He gave it to them and said, "Each of you drink from it.

Matthew 26:26-27

What is even more significant and exhilarating is that the Lord Jesus Christ whom we now know is the High Priest of the priestly Order of Melchizedek, restored the priestly Order of Melchizedek to the Jewish nation and enacted it as the only legitimate priesthood for New Testament believers at the Last Supper. During the last supper Jesus gave His apprentice apostles the same spiritual elements of "bread and wine" that Melchizedek in Genesis 14:18-20 had offered to Abraham.

Jesus was prophesying to His apprentice apostles and to every demonic principality through the enactment of the sacrament of Holy Communion, that He was the High Priest after the Order of Melchizedek. What is truly exciting about the spiritual timing of the reenactment of the priestly Order of Melchizedek by the Lord Jesus during the last supper is simply this; it happened just before He was betrayed and crucified. This means that when the Lord Jesus was betrayed, crucified and resurrected He was no longer operating under the Levitical priesthood that answers to the Mountain of Law (which is Mount Sinai in Arabia). He was operating under the priestly Order of Melchizedek, which is an infinitely higher priesthood that only answers to the heavenly Father, who is the God and King of the universe.

This is why Jesus Christ's betrayal, sufferings, crucifixion, resurrection and ultimate ascension all became infinitely more powerful and redemptive than they would have been had they occurred under the Levitical order of priesthood. This would also explain why Jesus did not defend Himself or beg for mercy from Pontius Pilate. He did not want to submit the infinitely higher Order of Melchizedek to the "infinitely lower orders" of human government. When Jesus rose from the dead, His blood of atonement could not be taken to the Mercy seat of the temple in natural Jerusalem. His atoning blood was taken to the temple of God Most High in spiritual Jerusalem, which is the mother of us all. This means that when Jesus Christ presented His own blood to His heavenly Father, He presented it under the priestly Order of Melchizedek. This would explain why the blood of Jesus Christ has tremendous redeeming power for the people who are called to live under this eternal priestly order.

This Order has its own heavenly Temple

•133•

"Here is the main point: We have a High Priest who sat down in the place of honor beside the throne of the majestic God in heaven. There he ministers in the heavenly Tabernacle, the true place of worship that was built by the Lord and not by human hands."

Hebrews 8:1-2

When Jesus rose from the dead, He took His own blood to the throne of God, which is located in spiritual Jerusalem, the holy City of God. The reason Jesus did not take His blood of atonement to the Mercy seat at the temple in natural Jerusalem is quite obvious. The temple in earthly Jerusalem was enacted to service the earthbound priesthood of Aaron. The temple in natural Jerusalem belonged to the Levitical priesthood.

Since Jesus Christ is the High Priest of the priestly Order of Melchizedek, He knew that His heavenly priesthood has its own temple located inside the walls of heavenly Jerusalem, which is the mother of us all. When Moses was instructed to build the Tabernacle in the wilderness, he was told emphatically to build it according to the pattern of the spiritual temple in heaven.

"If he were here on earth, he would not even be a priest, since there already are priests who offer the gifts required by the law. They serve in a system of worship that is only a copy, a shadow of the real one in heaven. For when Moses was getting ready to build the Tabernacle, God gave him this warning: 'Be sure that you make everything according to the pattern I have shown you here on the mountain.'"

Hebrews 8:4-5

It Services the Spiritual needs of the Star-seed of Abraham

"Here is the main point: We have a High Priest who sat down in the place of honor beside the throne of the majestic God in heaven. There he ministers in the heavenly Tabernacle, the true place of worship that was built by the Lord and not by human hands. But now Jesus, our High Priest, has been given a ministry that is far superior to the old priesthood, for he is the one who mediates for us a far better covenant with God, based on better promises."

Hebrews 8:1-2, 6

We have already made it clear that the "sand-seed" of Abraham (the Jewish

•134•

nation) were given the Levitical priestly Order to service their spiritual needs in accordance with the Mosaic Law. Aaron was the first High Priest of the Levitical priesthood. He was also Moses' elder brother and chief spokesman. The Levitical priesthood had its own set of laws and its own tithe with distinctive functions and features. Malachi 3:8-12 was addressed to the Jewish nation who lived under this priesthood.

Jesus Christ is the presiding High Priest of the eternal priestly Order of Melchizedek. This priesthood operates within the eternal structures of the Kingdom of heaven. This is the priestly order which services the spiritual needs of the "star-seed" of Abraham. Every New Testament believer is called to live and serve under this powerful priestly order. This priesthood also has its own Law and its own tithe, which has its own distinctive functions and features.

Under the Priestly Order of Melchizedek Angels Serve and Worship the High Priest

And when he brought his firstborn Son into the world, God said, "Let all of God's angels worship him." Regarding the angels, he says, "He sends his angels like the winds, his servants like flames of fire."
Hebrews 1:6-7

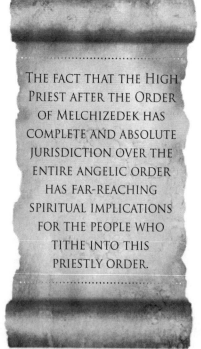

One of the most stunning aspects of the priestly Order of Melchizedek is that under this priestly order, angels were created to serve and worship the High Priest of this powerful order of priesthood. This is in striking contrast to the Levitical priestly order. Under the Levitical priesthood, the High Priest had no jurisdiction over the angelic order. Under the priestly Order of Aaron, angels worked in concert with the High Priest as he fulfilled the call of God upon his life. Under the priestly Order of Melchizedek the entire angelic agency works for the High Priest, bending to His every call and desire. What a powerful priestly order! These angels will stop at nothing to serve

THE FACT THAT THE HIGH PRIEST AFTER THE ORDER OF MELCHIZEDEK HAS COMPLETE AND ABSOLUTE JURISDICTION OVER THE ENTIRE ANGELIC ORDER HAS FAR-REACHING SPIRITUAL IMPLICATIONS FOR THE PEOPLE WHO TITHE INTO THIS PRIESTLY ORDER.

and protect the honor of the High Priest of the Order of Melchizedek. These angels have been known to kill kings of nations who do not honor this High Priest who is also "God Most High."

"Now Herod was very angry with the people of Tyre and Sidon. So they sent a delegation to make peace with him because their cities were dependent upon Herod's country for food. The delegates won the support of Blastus, Herod's personal assistant, and an appointment with Herod was granted. When the day arrived, Herod put on his royal robes, sat on his throne, and made a speech to them. The people gave him a great ovation, shouting, "It's the voice of a god, not of a man!" Instantly, an angel of the Lord struck Herod with a sickness, because he accepted the people's worship instead of giving the glory to God. So he was consumed with worms and died."

Hebrews 12:20-23

The above passage of Scripture shows us what happens to kings of nations who blatantly show disregard for the honor that is due the High Priest of the priestly Order of Melchizedek. King Herod had chosen to resist and persecute the Church of the living God. He killed James the Apostle, the brother of John and then imprisoned the apostle Peter. The spirit of the anti-Christ manifested itself through King Herod on the day that he was officiating a peace treaty with the people of Tyre and Sidon. He walked to the judgment seat with great pomp and bestowed upon himself the glory that is only reserved for God. Bewitched by his amazing charisma, the masses began to compare him to a god. In anger the angel of the Lord struck him with a sudden sickness. The angelic blow on King Herod was so powerful that he died instantly and began to decompose immediately. Worms began to ooze out of him in front of the now terrified crowd. The awesome power of the priestly Order of Melchizedek had just been displayed before the masses.

The fact that the ***High Priest after the Order of Melchizedek has complete and absolute jurisdiction over the entire angelic order has far-reaching spiritual implications for the people who tithe into this priestly order***. We have seen from what's been revealed through the progressive revelation of Scripture that angels are holy and extremely powerful beings. Miraculous things happen whenever angels show up at any location. Under the priestly Order of Melchizedek "there is no limit as to the number of angelic interventions" that the people who live under this priestly order can anticipate.

But while Peter was in prison, the church prayed very earnestly for him. The night before Peter was to be placed on trial, he was asleep, fastened with two chains between two soldiers. Others stood guard at the prison gate. Suddenly, there was a bright light in the cell, and an angel of the Lord stood before Peter. The angel struck him on the side to awaken him and said, "Quick! Get up!" And the chains fell off his wrists. Then the angel told him, "Get dressed and put on your sandals." And he did. "Now put on your coat and follow me," the angel ordered. So Peter left the cell, following the angel. But all the time he thought it was a vision. He didn't realize it was actually happening. They passed the first and second guard posts and came to the Iron Gate leading to the city, and this opened for them all by itself. So they passed through and started walking down the street, and then the angel suddenly left him. Peter finally came to his senses. "It's really true!" he said. "The Lord has sent his angel and saved me from Herod and from what the Jewish leaders[c] had planned to do to me!"

Hebrews 12:6-11

When King Herod Agrippa killed the apostle James, John's brother, and saw that it increased his political clout with some influential leaders within the Jewish community, he proceeded to imprison Peter. Peter was an apostle who lived under this priestly Order of Melchizedek. While Peter was bound up in the inner prison a supernatural light shined into his cell. The supernatural light that pierced the darkness of night in his tiny cell was that of an angel who had been sent to deliver him.

The chains of imprisonment that were around his hands and legs suddenly fell off. The angel ordered Peter to follow him. When he was following the angel, all the prison gates opened of their own accord, until Peter found himself standing outside the doors of the prison house in total freedom. Peter had just received a great deliverance from the priestly Order of Melchizedek which services the spiritual needs of the star-seed of Abraham. It is no wonder the devil wants us to limit ourselves by tithing into a lower priesthood, which does not have the same degree of spiritual power, as the "priestly Order of Melchizedek."

The Priestly Order of Melchizedek
has its own
Tithe with Distinctive Functions and Features

...to whom also Abraham gave a tenth part of all, first being translated "king of righteousness," and then also king of Salem, meaning "king of peace," without father, without mother, without genealogy, having neither beginning of days nor end of life, but

made like the Son of God, remains a priest continually.

Hebrews 7:17

The priestly Order of Melchizedek has its own "tithe" which has distinctive functions and features. In order to discover these distinctive functions and features, we will examine how Abraham tithed and why he tithed. *It's important for us to understand Abraham's mindset and his primary motivation for tithing into the Order of Melchizedek.*

"And Melchizedek, the king of Salem and a priest of God Most High, brought Abram some bread and wine. Melchizedek blessed Abram with this blessing: 'Blessed be Abram by God Most High, Creator of heaven and earth. And blessed be God Most High, who has defeated your enemies for you.' Then Abram gave Melchizedek a tenth of all the goods he had recovered."

Genesis 14:18-20

When Melchizedek intercepted Abram in the Valley of the Kings, Abraham had never met a man who had the same degree of divine aura and majestic dignity like Melchizedek. First and foremost the man was the King of Salem, which we now know to be the City of Jerusalem, which is a prophetic picture of the heavenly Jerusalem, the City of God. There was something about Melchizedek that left a lasting impression on Abraham's spirit and mind.

On top of carrying His kingly mantle with divine dignity, Melchizedek was also the Priest of God Most High. This means that Melchizedek had "spirit connections" with God on a level that Abraham could not even imagine. Besides all of this the man seemed to know everything about Abram. Struck by a deep sense of awe and uttermost respect, Abraham did something that most people who were raised in the Middle East were accustomed to. Abraham knew that he could not pay this great king and priest of God Most High, so he decided to lay at His feet a "token of his heartfelt honor for His majesty." He gave Melchizedek the "token of tithe" to honor Him and demonstrate *his heartfelt respect for the priestly order which Melchizedek represented.*

What Abraham did to honor Melchizedek was not uncommon among the people of his era. In Abraham's era there was an established tradition and protocol that we need to be aware of. No one was allowed to come before the king without bringing a "gift or endowment worthy of the King as a sign of heartfelt honor" for the king and his lofty position in the kingdom. The "honorary gift or endowment" which the people of the ancient world brought with them when they came into the presence of a king was also a "gift for the rite of passage or the right to access to the king's presence."

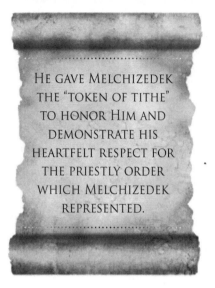

HE GAVE MELCHIZEDEK THE "TOKEN OF TITHE" TO HONOR HIM AND DEMONSTRATE HIS HEARTFELT RESPECT FOR THE PRIESTLY ORDER WHICH MELCHIZEDEK REPRESENTED.

From the spiritual setting surrounding Abraham's tithe into the priestly Order of Melchizedek, we see two very distinctive features of the "tithe of Abraham," even though this tithe has more than these two very distinctive features. In this chapter we will limit ourselves to these two. For these two features above all others separate Abraham's tithe from the "contemporary Malachi 3 tithe." These two features are as follows:

1. While the tithe under the priestly Order of Aaron was "a payment for priestly services," the tithe Abraham gave into the priestly Order of Melchizedek was given out of a "deep heartfelt expression of total honor for Melchizedek as a reigning king." Abraham knew that he could never make enough money through the course of his lifetime to pay for the services of Melchizedek, King of Salem and Priest of God Most High. This means that under the eternal priestly Order of Melchizedek, our pastors do not owe us a glossary list of priestly services in exchange for our tithe. This is because under this priestly Order the tithe is given as an expression of honor to God Most High, and is not payment for priestly services. This does not mean that pastors don't have to render priestly services to their flock, but it does mean that their flock has no right under the Order of Melchizedek to manipulate the church by withholding the Lord's tithe.

2. Secondly, Abraham gave the tithe to Melchizedek for "the rite of passage or admission into this priestly Order." Abraham wanted to become part of something infinitely greater than he was. This now leads us to the discovery of the "Lost Key" which I have been alluding to from the commencement of this book. This "Lost Key" is the best way to truly open up the whole priestly Order of Melchizedek. The rediscovery of this "Lost Key" is critical to the advancement of the Kingdom of God here on earth.

The Future of Israel is hidden in the Priestly Order of Melchizedek

"Then the angel of the Lord called again to Abraham from heaven. 'This is what the Lord says: Because you have obeyed me and have not withheld even your son, your only son, I swear by my own name that I will certainly bless you. I will multiply your descendants beyond number, like the stars in the sky and the sand on the seashore.'"

Genesis 22:17

We have already mentioned the fact that on Mount Moriah after his act of total obedience Abraham was given two brands of seed. God gave Abraham sand-seed and star-seed descendents. The sand-seed descendants of Abraham are the people of the nation of Israel. These are the descendants of Abraham according to the flesh. Their earthly genealogy can be traced back to Abraham. On the other hand the star-seed descendants of Abraham consist of every man and woman (Jew or Gentile) who has accepted Jesus Christ as his or her personal Lord and Savior. These are people who were not born again by the will of the flesh but by the will of God.

"But to all who believed him and accepted him, he gave the right to become children of God. They are reborn—not with a physical birth resulting from human passion or plan, but a birth that comes from God."

John 1:12-13

The most important thing which we must remember about the dealings of God with mankind is simply this: **God's work is always based on the "principle of continuance."** This means that God never makes covenant with the sons, but with the fathers. He then transfers His will and the spiritual accomplishments of the forefathers onto the second generation. This means that based upon this same principle of continuance or apostolic succession, the forefathers and their sons had a common spiritual call and destiny.

"The priests who collect tithes are men who die, so Melchizedek is greater than they are, because we are told that he lives on. In addition, we might even say that these Levites—the ones who collect the tithe—paid a tithe to Melchizedek when their ancestor Abraham paid a tithe to him. For although Levi wasn't born yet, the seed from which he came was in Abraham's body when Melchizedek collected the tithe from him."

Hebrews 7:8-10

In the above passage of Scripture, the apostle Paul is using the principle of continuance to show his fellow Jews that they would not be selling out on their Jewish faith if they brought themselves under the priesthood of Melchizedek. To drive this important point home, the apostle Paul proceeds to tell them that when Abraham their forefather met Melchizedek (Priest of God Most High), Levi, who is the father of the Levitical priesthood, was in the spiritual loins of Abraham during this critical time in his life. The apostle Paul proceeds to inform us that ***Levi, who was given a commandment by God to collect a tithe according to the Law, also gave a tithe to Melchizedek because Levi was still in the loins of his father Abraham*** at the time of this God-encounter.

This principle of continuance has far-reaching spiritual implications in explaining how the future of the Jewish nation is tied to the priestly Order of Melchizedek. If Paul's argument has any merit to it, it means that the spiritual call and destiny of the Jewish nation will eventually lead them into a very personal encounter with Jesus Christ who is the High Priest of God Most High after the Order of Melchizedek. This is because when Abraham met Melchizedek and submitted his life to Him, all of his natural descendants (natural Israel) were still in his spiritual loins. This means that the Jewish DNA is prophetically predisposed to recognize and acknowledge Jesus Christ as the Melchizedek of God whom their forefather Abraham met in the valley of Shaveh. When this powerful prophetic day in God arrives and the scales of spiritual blindness fall from the eyes of every living Jew, the apostle Paul tells us that at that time "all Israel shall be saved!"

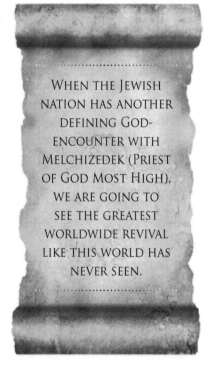

WHEN THE JEWISH NATION HAS ANOTHER DEFINING GOD-ENCOUNTER WITH MELCHIZEDEK (PRIEST OF GOD MOST HIGH), WE ARE GOING TO SEE THE GREATEST WORLDWIDE REVIVAL LIKE THIS WORLD HAS NEVER SEEN.

The prophet Zechariah seems to be very much in agreement with my deductions.

"Then I will pour out a spirit of grace and prayer on the family of David and on the people of Jerusalem. They will look on me whom they have pierced and mourn for him as for an only son. They will grieve bitterly for him as for a firstborn son who has died."

Zechariah 12:10

When the Jewish nation has another defining God-encounter with

Melchizedek (Priest of God Most High), we are going to see the greatest worldwide revival like this world has never seen. The most important facet of this great spiritual awakening is that the "sand-seed of Abraham" (the Jewish nation) will suddenly become the "star-seed of Abraham." The birth and resurrection of our Lord Jesus Christ set the spiritual pathway every Jewish person has to follow. Jesus Christ was born as the sand-seed of Abraham, but was resurrected as the star-seed of Abraham. Christ was a Jew by natural birth but He was declared the Son of God by the resurrection.

The preceding passage of Scripture from the book of Revelation strongly suggests that there is coming a day when Jewish people are going to be transformed by revelation into star-seed descendants of Abraham. When this happens, Jewish influence over the nations of the world will no longer be just earthly but also heavenly. Israel will become the woman clothed with the sun, whose head is surrounded by twelve stars. Most scholars believe that the woman with the twelve stars around her head in Revelation chapter twelve represents the twelve tribes of Israel.

> *"Then I witnessed in heaven an event of great significance. I saw a woman clothed with the sun, with the moon beneath her feet, and a crown of twelve stars on her head. She was pregnant, and she cried out because of her labor pains and the agony of giving birth."*
>
> Revelation 12:1-2

The Lost Key Revealed

We know that keys open doors, gates, egresses, portals or spiritual dimensions, depending on the type of key we have in our hands. We also know that keys are for movement. Keys can bring animation to inanimate objects.

> *"I know your works. See, I have set before you an open door, and no one can shut it; for you have a little strength, have kept My word, and have not denied My name."*
>
> Revelation 3:8

In his best-selling book *Kingdom Principles*, pages 164-168, Dr. Myles Munroe establishes the seven principles of keys. I have taken the liberty to quote him verbatim.

1. ***Keys represent access***. A key gives you instant access to everything that key opens. The secret is knowing what the key opens.

2. ***Keys represent authority.*** If you possess a key to a place, it means you have authority in that place. The key to your house means that you have authority there. The key to your car gives you authority to drive whenever you want to.

3. ***Keys represent ownership.*** Possession of a key gives you de facto ownership of whatever that key opens. Therefore, when you possess the keys of the Kingdom of heaven you have ownership of heaven on earth.

4. ***Keys represent control.*** If you possess the key to something, you control it. You control when it opens, when it closes, and who gets access to it. A key helps you control time. In other words, you decide whether to open it up at 8:00 or 10:00 or 6:00 or whenever. This gives you control over when something comes. If you need something now, you operate a key.

5. ***Keys represent authorization.*** Possession of keys means that you are authorized to act in the name and authority of the one who owns the keys. By giving us the keys of the Kingdom of Heaven, Jesus gives us the authority to influence heaven.

6. ***Keys represent power.*** Whoever gives you keys gives you power at the same time. You have control – power – over whatever you possess the keys for. If you know how to use the keys, whatever they open is at your disposal.

7. ***Keys represent freedom.*** When you have keys, you are free to go in and out. You are free to lock and unlock, to open and to close. The keys of the Kingdom give us freedom from fear and all the other limiting emotions of an earthly system.

I (Dr. Francis Myles) also want to add one more aspect of keys, which I believe will help us appreciate the power and value for the "Lost Key" which activates the functionality of the priestly Order of Melchizedek.

8. ***Keys are as valuable as what they open into.*** All keys do not open the same rooms or lead to the same treasures. Consequently a key is as valuable as the portal, egress or room it opens into. For instance, a key which opens into a bank vault full of fifty karat diamonds is much more valuable than the key which opens into an empty warehouse. If word got out that you were carrying a key which opens a bank vault filled with billions of dollars worth of precious minerals, you would immediately become the target of bounty hunters or hard-core criminals who would stop at nothing to steal the key from you. I believe this would explain why Satan and his demonic

agencies have fought so hard to disguise the "Ancient Key" which activates the functionality of the priestly Order of Melchizedek.

Finally, the answer to the question you have been asking and waiting for: "What is the Lost Key, which activates the functionality of the priestly Order of Melchizedek?" I am glad you asked me and I will tell you. Are you ready for this? Here we go... The "Lost Key" which activates the Covenant blessings of the priestly Order of Melchizedek is a **"TITHING MODEL THAT IS PATTERNED AFTER THE ORDER OF MECHIZEDEK!"** This ancient key is not just about the tithe, because tithe simply means the tenth part. The "Ancient Key" which activates the Covenant blessings of the priestly Order of Melchizedek is the **"THE ABRAHAMIC TITHING MODEL."**

The name of this powerful key means that *"the tithe we give to God must be given with the same mindset, the same spirit of faith, and heartfelt honor that compelled Abraham to give Melchizedek a tenth of all!"* Tithing under the Order of Melchizedek is an endowment bestowed by "Kingdom citizens" on the "King" (Christ) for the purpose of extending His Kingdom in the earth-realm. So it must never be done casually or with a self-serving agenda. Tithing to "get our stuff" must never become our primary motivation for tithing. Abraham did not tithe to "get," he tithed to "honor a King" and to "extend the King's Kingdom." This is why the Abrahamic tithing model is such a powerful key for releasing the power of Christ's New Testament Order of Melchizedek priesthood.

Malachi 3:8-12 is a "Levitical tithing model" which opens a much smaller doorway into the blessing of Abraham. The Malachi 3:8-12 tithing model is the "WRONG KEY" for those who want to release the power of Christ's New Testament Order of Melchizedek priesthood. I am sorry to say that for as long as we continue to employ the Malachi 3:8-12 tithing model instead of the Abrahamic tithing model stated in Genesis 14:17-22, we will never enter into the "FULLNESS" of all that God has prepared for the "STAR SEED OF ABRAHAM."

LIFE APPLICATION SECTION

Point to Ponder:

If someone got cursed from the eternal priestly Order of Melchizedek their curse could never ever be reversed no matter how much they refine their behavior after the fact, because everything in this priestly Order is in an eternal state.

Verse to Remember:

"The priests who collect tithes are men who die, so Melchizedek is greater than they are, because we are told that he lives on. In addition, we might even say that these Levites—the ones who collect the tithe—paid a tithe to Melchizedek when their ancestor Abraham paid a tithe to him. For although Levi wasn't born yet, the seed from which he came was in Abraham's body when Melchizedek collected the tithe from him."

Hebrews 7:8-10

Questions to Consider:

• Why is the priestly Order of Melchizedek the answer to man's search for a perfect or utopian society?

_____

_____

_____

_____

• Who is the High Priest of the priestly Order of Melchizedek?

_____

_____

_____

_____

• Why did Abraham tithe into the Order of Melchizedek?

_____

_____

_____

Journal Your Thoughts

HOW THE
PATRIARCHS TITHED

Whenever I am dealing with the subject of tithing five questions always come up, namely:

1. **What is my tithe?**

2. **How do I tithe?**

3. **Why should I tithe?**

4. **Where do I take my tithe?**

5. **Does every tithe go into the local church?**

These are very important questions concerning the whole process of tithing. It's critical that I answer these questions with supernatural "surgical precision." Perhaps only a few things have come under the "attack of the enemy" more than the giving of "tithes." Please take note of the fact that under the priestly Order of Melchizedek we do not "pay our tithes;" we "give our tithes." This is because there is no amount of money in this earthly economy which can "pay for the sandal straps or shoe laces" of the King of the heavenly Jerusalem, who is also the Priest of God Most High.

The Prophet John's announcement:

"…Someone is coming soon who is greater than I am—so much greater that I'm not even worthy to stoop down like a slave and untie the straps of his sandals."

Mark 1:17

The prophet John the Baptist made the above proclamation because he knew that Jesus Christ who is the King of the heavenly Jerusalem and the High Priest of God Most High, is not of this world. Christ's heavenly Kingdom is "infinitely richer" than anything we can imagine here on earth. His Kingdom also has its own "spiritual currency" which is also "infinitely higher and stronger" than the "combined buying power" of all the best worldly currencies. This is why saying that we are "paying our tithes" when we are dealing with the Order of Melchizedek is "an insult and a sure sign of dishonor." **How can a citizen in a Kingdom pay the "King" when everything he or she owns is already the property of the King?** In kingdoms the citizens do not own anything; everything they own belongs to the king. This is why "rediscovering why and how Abraham tithed" is spiritually crucial to our spiritual progress and how we approach the subject of tithing.

Look to Abraham

"Listen to Me, you who follow after righteousness, You who seek the LORD: Look to the rock from which you were hewn, And to the hole of the pit from which you were dug. 2 Look to Abraham your father, And to Sarah who bore you; For I called him alone, And blessed him and increased him."

Isaiah 51:1-2

The Bible clearly admonishes us to "look to Abraham." This means that even in the area of tithing we must look to Abraham to find "our tithing model." Henceforth in answering these five questions we will look to Abraham and his sons after him who continued to walk in the revelation that God had laid out for Abraham.

1. What is my tithe?"

"And blessed be God Most High, who has defeated your enemies for you. Then Abram gave Melchizedek a tenth of all the goods he had recovered."

Genesis 14:20

Abraham is the first person to give the "tithe" in the progressive revelation of Scripture. When Abraham was returning from the slaughter of the kings, he was intercepted by Melchizedek (the Priest of God Most High) in the valley of kings (Shaveh). The valley of kings was not too far from the country of Sodom. This divine encounter with Melchizedek moved Abraham's spirit so deeply that he was compelled by his "deep sense of awe" to give this lofty man a "gift befitting a King." Abraham gave Melchizedek "a tenth or ten percent" of "all the goods which he had recovered from the battlefield." This answers the first question, "What is my tithe?" *The tithe is the "tenth or ten percent" of everything we earn in the market place or recover from the field of battle.*

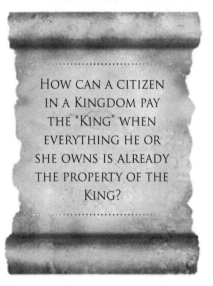

HOW CAN A CITIZEN IN A KINGDOM PAY THE "KING" WHEN EVERYTHING HE OR SHE OWNS IS ALREADY THE PROPERTY OF THE KING?

It's worth noting here that Abraham gave Melchizedek a "tithe of all the goods that he had recovered" from the battlefield, before surrendering the "rest of it" to the king of Sodom. This means that the "tithe" is taken from the "gross" and not from the "net." If you live in the United States for example, the tithe comes from your "gross salary" before "Uncle Sam" (the US government) takes its share. I personally believe that if many Kingdom citizens would tithe from the "gross and not from the net" as Abraham seemed to have done, that we would see more miracles of unexpected tax refunds and favorable tax settlements. *When we tithe from the gross I believe that we "sanctify and set apart" that part of our hard earned money that goes to the government in the form of income tax.* There are Bible teachers who believe that the "tithe" should really come out of the "net earnings" and not the "gross earnings." The basis of their argument is that the "net earnings" and not the "gross earnings" are a true reflection of what someone really earns. I personally believe in tithing off the gross earnings but I do not believe that those who tithe from their "net earnings" are necessarily wrong. The most important thing is that they also teach that the tithe is the tenth part and that it is consecrated to God.

2. "How do I tithe?"

"Consider then how great this Melchizedek was. Even Abraham, the great patriarch of Israel, recognized this by giving him a tenth of what he had taken in battle. Now the law of Moses required that the priests, who are descendants of Levi, must collect a

tithe from the rest of the people of Israel, who are also descendants of Abraham. But Melchizedek, who was not a descendant of Levi, collected a tenth from Abraham. And Melchizedek placed a blessing upon Abraham, the one who had already received the promises of God. And without question, the person who has the power to give a blessing is greater than the one who is blessed."

Hebrews 7:4-7

The second question deals with the "prevailing spiritual attitude and mindset" for tithing under the Order of Melchizedek. It's spiritually critical that we find this prevailing attitude and mindset, so that we can tithe properly. If we do not enshrine ourselves in this prevailing attitude and mindset, tithing will remain a struggle and a joyless religious activity instead of the catalyst of covenant blessings that it is. Here again, we look to Abraham who was the first "tither."

When Abraham met Melchizedek (the Priest of God Most High), he was deeply moved by this man's lofty "spiritual position as the Priest of God Most High as well as being the King of Salem." The title "King of Salem," we are told by the apostle Paul, literally means "one who is King over the whole sphere of peace" and the name "Melchizedek" means "one who is King over the domain of righteousness." In the ancient language of Aramaic the name "Melchizedek" also means "the King who makes everything right by telling the truth."

My dear friend, who else is best suited to wear these lofty titles other than our Lord Jesus Christ? The immeasurable "power and royal dignity" of this man is what moved Abraham's spirit to give Him a "tithe of all." Abraham gave this man the "tithe of all" out of a "deep sense of awe and heartfelt honor." Abraham gave the tithe to this heavenly man to honor Him. ***Abraham discerned that this man had a lofty place of honor with God, maker of heaven and earth.*** Abraham gave Melchizedek the "tithe of all" with the same "mindset" with which the nobles and citizens of the United Kingdom give "annual endowments" to the "Queen of England."

This "royal endowment" is not a "salary," because by established "royal protocol" it's well understood that "citizens in a Kingdom" cannot pay the "Crown," but they can give an "endowment of honor." ***This "royal endowment" is the visible evidence of "the heartfelt honor" that they as kingdom citizens have for the "Crown."*** When Abraham gave the "tithe of all" to Melchizedek he gave it with this same attitude and mindset. ***This means that "tithing under the Order of Melchizedek" is the "highest form of tithing" ever revealed by God to mankind.***

The governing concepts and process of tithing under the priestly Order of Melchizedek are in direct contrast to those of the Levitical priesthood where "tithing was simply payment for priestly service rendered." Since tithing under the Order of Melchizedek has nothing to do with "paying for priestly services" but the "giving of a royal endowment" to the "Crown-King," we cannot use our tithes to manipulate our spiritual leaders to give us the "priestly services" we think we deserve. *This mindset may have been acceptable under the Levitical priesthood (The Malachi Tithing Model), but it is "demonic and dishonoring" when we apply it to the Christ's Order of Melchizedek priesthood which is a Kingdom-centered tithing model.* I am not suggesting that leaders of Churches or those who provide spiritual covering should not do their best to offer priestly services to the people in their church or marketplace leaders that they give covering to. But if our spiritual leaders fall short, we have "no excuse as Kingdom citizens for withholding our tithes" in our desire to punish our spiritual leaders or the local Church. We have no legal grounds for holding the Kingdom or Church of God hostage by withholding our tithes.

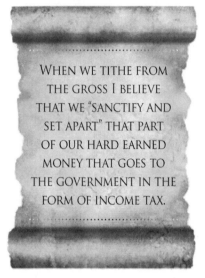

WHEN WE TITHE FROM THE GROSS I BELIEVE THAT WE "SANCTIFY AND SET APART" THAT PART OF OUR HARD EARNED MONEY THAT GOES TO THE GOVERNMENT IN THE FORM OF INCOME TAX.

3. Why should I tithe?

The third question deals with the "prevailing spiritual motivation" for tithing under the Order of Melchizedek. You would be surprised to discover just how many of God's people try to become deceptive the moment they begin to make more money. Suddenly they begin to ask questions like, "Do I really have to tithe? Why should I tithe when I am under grace? Is not tithing of the Old Testament?" If the truth was told, they are not asking these questions because they are suddenly concerned about these theological issues. The truth of the matter is that they are now asking these tithing questions because they have begun to make more money. Their "lust for money" is suddenly challenged by the church's teaching on tithing the more their wealth increases. *If the truth was told, they are looking for a way to "stop tithing" without feeling like they are sinning against God.*

In answering the question, "Why should I tithe?" We have to look to Abraham. When Abraham tithed he gave his "tenth of all" as a "royal endowment" to Melchizedek who was the Priest of God Most High, as well as King of Salem. **Dr Myles Munroe in his book Kingdom Principles says that "democratic societies" were born out of "rebellion" to Kingdom principles of governance.** Men were tired of living under the authority of abusive and sometimes corrupt "Monarchs" and so they decided to find new forms of government. Whereas we can surely empathize with the fathers of the American democratic society, who were running away from an abusive monarch in England, **one cannot help but wonder how much of the Kingdom reality we lost when we built democratic nations that are not based on a Kingdom model.**

The truth of the matter is that in a kingdom the "King owns everything that is in his kingdom, including the people." This first statement by itself should abolish all struggles about tithing because in God's Kingdom everything we own already belongs to the Lord. Giving the Lord the "tithe" that He has specially "consecrated" for the advancement of His Kingdom should be the least of our struggles. Interesting enough American Christians are some of the most zealous and faithful tax payers in the country. The American income tax is usually between 20 to 30% of one's annual income. So why is tithing such a controversial subject within the Body of Christ? I believe it is because there is a very powerful spiritual blessing attached to the tithe, that every demon in hell is terrified of. In a kingdom, citizens do not "own anything; everyone is simply a steward" of the king's property. This is why the nobles and citizens of true kingdoms were required to give "annual royal endowments" of honor to demonstrate their submission to the "Crown." These "royal endowments" were not "payment for service rendered by the king" but were "royal gifts" bestowed on the Monarch by kingdom citizens "for the continued privilege" of earning their living on the king's or crown land.

Under the Order of Melchizedek the "tithe" is a "royal endowment" from Kingdom citizens for the "continued privilege" of living and working in the King's domain. This answers our question, "Why should I tithe?" We should tithe because "everything we own" including the air we breathe and the inherent talents we possess, belongs to the King of the heavenly Jerusalem, the High Priest of God Most High. This would explain why God could legally and righteously give the land of Palestine to the Jewish nation who came out of Egypt without consulting the "inhabitants of the land of Canaan." God is the King of the universe, possessor of heaven and earth. He can give His land or riches to whomsoever He chooses. *This means then, that we should tithe for as long as we "call ourselves citizens of the Kingdom of God here on earth."*

Kingdom citizens must always give Jesus Christ his "befitting royal endowment" of tithe. It is my personal conviction that continued failure to do so will eventually result in the King of kings *"removing his seal of approval"* from our lives. King Jesus may also *"remove us from our position of stewardship in His Kingdom."* This is not to say that the lack of tithing can result in someone losing their salvation. Our salvation is based upon the finished work of Christ and not on our efforts. *But our stewardship position in heaven's Kingdom economy is based upon our faithfulness to the established principles of the Kingdom.*

> *Let a man so account of us, as of the ministers of Christ, and stewards of the mysteries of God. Moreover it is required in stewards, that a man be found faithful.*
>
> *1 Corinthians 4:1-2 (KJV)*

Under the Levitical priesthood, non-tithers were cursed with a "curse" but under the Order of Melchizedek non-tithers risk losing the "King's seal of approval!" Under the Order of Melchizedek if we do not tithe, God will not place a "financial curse" on our life because He has already blessed us with all spiritual blessings in heavenly places (Ephesians 1:3). But our failure to tithe will begin to "mortgage or undermine" the "quality and level of divine favor" that God desires to flow towards us. Somebody said, "one day of favor can cancel many years of struggle and poverty in a person's life!" If this is the case, why in heaven's

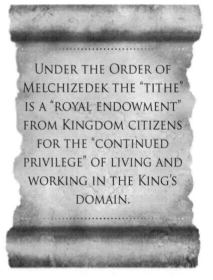

UNDER THE ORDER OF MELCHIZEDEK THE "TITHE" IS A "ROYAL ENDOWMENT" FROM KINGDOM CITIZENS FOR THE "CONTINUED PRIVILEGE" OF LIVING AND WORKING IN THE KING'S DOMAIN.

name would anyone want to risk the favor of God over their lives for simply withholding the tithe that is due Him? Please remember that the condition for personal salvation (faith in the finished work of Christ) is different from the condition that God requires from His people in order to establish us as stewards of His Kingdom economy. This condition is "faithfulness" to the timeless principles of His Kingdom that are clearly laid out in His word. This last condition is what Jesus Christ was trying to impress upon us when he taught on the parable of the talents.

4. Where do I give my tithe?

This question deals with the *"prevailing spiritual flow"* that the tithe takes under the priestly Order of Melchizedek or what I call the "Genesis 14:18-20" pattern of tithing. Under the priestly Order of Melchizedek, the spiritual flow of the giving of the tithe is a "two stream" approach. This two-stream approach answers the question of where and to whom you give your tithe.

Before diving into this very critical question, I must first acknowledge the wide diversity in how churches around the world view this critical topic. It is not my desire to divide the Body of Christ over this matter but rather to share my core convictions and the reasons behind them. I do this with utmost humility. I will not be offended if you disagree with me. I only humbly request that if you do disagree with me that you would do so not out of your predetermined conclusions on this subject without giving my arguments the scriptural investigation that they deserve. I have observed that too many times "Tithing" is either defended or opposed more by emotion and preconceived ideas than by spiritual precedence and biblical facts.

Those who may not be able to receive the structure or logistics of what I am about to share, I ask that you instead imbibe the principles behind what I share and implement those principles in a way that best fits your context and convictions. Please do not throw the baby out with the bathwater. I am also asking fellow leaders within the global Church not to set up legalistic top down structures to force any believer to do anything contrary to their free will or conscience. The New Testament never gives spiritual leaders the authority to force Kingdom citizens to violate their conscience. The principles undergirding where a person tithes are grounded in the foundations of tithing out of honor, tithing to the source of bread and wine, and tithing to the source of blessing.

With that as a background, my personal conviction is that the two streams the tithe should flow into are as follows…

(a). The first stream is the giving of the tithe to the "Local Church."

(b). The second stream is the giving of the tithe to a "Man of God or Spiritual Covering."

The first stream of tithing addresses the question of "how church members or spiritual sons and daughters in the house (local church) ought to tithe." I cannot tell you just how many times well-meaning Christians have walked up to me and said to me, "Brother Myles, God told me to give my tithe to an orphanage or the Red Cross." Nothing could be further from the truth. There is nothing wrong with giving your offerings to such charitable organizations, but the tithe almost always goes to your local church if you belong to one. This is because God has already placed you under the "spiritual covering" of the "greater one" (your senior pastor), who is anointed by God to "feed you, with heavenly bread and wine." When Jacob was fleeing from Esau he came to a place called "Bethel," which literally means "the assembled house of God." He spent the night there and slept on one of the stones of that place. While he was sleeping he had a life-changing encounter with God in a dream. In this dream Jacob saw an open heaven and a ladder, which stretched from the earth to the third heaven. Angels were ascending and descending on this ladder.

"Then Jacob awoke from his sleep and said,—Surely the LORD is in this place, and I wasn't even aware of it! But he was also afraid and said,—What an awesome place this is! It is none other than the house of God, the very gateway to heaven! The next morning Jacob got up very early. He took the stone he had rested his head against, and he set it upright as a memorial pillar. Then he poured olive oil over it. He named that place Bethel (which means—house of God), although the name of the nearby village was Luz. Then Jacob made this vow: —If God will indeed be with me and protect me on this journey, and if he will provide me with food and clothing, and if I return safely to my father's home, then the LORD will certainly be my God. And this memorial pillar I have set up will become a place for worshiping God, and I will present to God a tenth of everything he gives me."

Genesis 28:16-22

When Jacob woke up the following morning, he was deeply moved by what he had seen and heard in his dream. He realized that the place where he was standing was none other than the "house of God." The "house of God" is a prophetic picture of the local Church. Once Jacob realized that the place on which he was standing was the "house of God" and the "Gate of heaven," he made a "covenant of tithe" with the God of this place. At this particular time in Jacob's life, Jacob had not yet become a "father of his own house." He was still part of "his father's house." This is a very important observation, because Jacob's "covenant of tithe" with the "house of God" is the same covenant God expects all church members to make with Him. **This means that "if you are not the senior pastor/minister of your own Church," your tithes (in most cases) belong to the house of God or the local Church you attend regularly**. This also means that giving your tithe to a "missionary you simply feel sorry for or the Red Cross" is tantamount to "breaking your covenant of tithe with God and the

Local church that you attend." This inaccurate behavior pattern will not draw the Covenantal blessings of God upon your life, but will only serve to repel them. But there are special and rare cases of tithing where the tithes do not necessarily go to the local church. We will discuss these special cases later on. For the most part, those who attend a church of choice on a regular basis, should strive to give their tithes of honor at the church were they are currently planted.

Abraham shall command his sons

"And the LORD said, —Shall I hide from Abraham what I am doing, since Abraham shall surely become a great and mighty nation, and all the nations of the earth shall be blessed in him? For I have known him, in order that he may command his children and his household after him, that they keep the way of the LORD, to do righteousness and justice, that the LORD may bring to Abraham what He has spoken to him."

Genesis 18:17-19

As we head towards the conclusion of this chapter, we will now attempt to answer the question, *"how did the Patriarchs tithe?"* When the Bible talks of the Patriarchs, it is usually referring to Abraham, Isaac, Jacob and his twelve sons. In the seventh chapter of the book of Hebrews, the apostle Paul makes it very clear that when Abraham met Melchizedek (the Priest of God Most High) and gave Him "tithes of all," the Levitical priesthood did not even exist.

"And yet Melchizedek, who was not a descendant of Levi, collected a tithe from Abraham. And Melchizedek bestowed a blessing upon Abraham, the one who had already received the promises of God. And without question, the person who has the power to give a blessing is greater than the one who is blessed. The priests who collect tithes are men who die, so Melchizedek is greater than they are, because we are told that he lives on. In addition, we might even say that these Levites—the ones who collect the tithe—paid a tithe to Melchizedek when their ancestor Abraham paid a tithe to him. For although Levi wasn't born yet, the seed from which he came was in Abraham's body when Melchizedek collected the tithe from him."

Hebrews 7:6-10

Paul the Apostle makes it very clear that the priestly Order of Melchizedek preceded the priestly Order of Aaron. He even goes further to show us that even the tribe of Levi who were commanded by the Law to collect tithes from their brethren also "tithed into the priestly Order of Melchizedek." When Abraham

•156•

tithed into Melchizedek, it was about four hundred and thirty years before the giving of the Law to Moses on Mount Sinai. This obvious truth has far-reaching spiritual implications.

One question quickly comes to mind: "If the Patriarchs did not know about the Levitical priesthood, what priestly Order did they tithe into, if and when they tithed?" The answer is dazzling, but obvious. All of the Patriarchs, *if and when they tithed*, tithed into the priestly Order of Melchizedek. How did they know that they needed to tithe into this powerful priestly Order, *if and when they tithed?* The answer is simple. Abraham told them about his life-changing encounter with Melchizedek and about the priesthood which this heavenly man presides over.

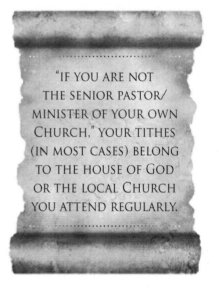

"IF YOU ARE NOT THE SENIOR PASTOR/ MINISTER OF YOUR OWN CHURCH," YOUR TITHES (IN MOST CASES) BELONG TO THE HOUSE OF GOD OR THE LOCAL CHURCH YOU ATTEND REGULARLY.

When God was about to destroy the land of Sodom and Gomorrah for its great wickedness, this is the testimony that God gave concerning Abraham's leadership abilities. "For I know that Abraham will surely command his sons after him to follow after My ways." What a powerful testimony about a man's life coming from the mouth of God! Abraham was not a "weak, spineless leader" who lacked the courage to instruct his children to obey God. Abraham was a great leader who knew very well how to "impart" the spiritual things that God had revealed to him, to his sons. The most logical conclusion therefore, is that all the Patriarchs tithed into the priestly Order of Melchizedek, if and when they did tithe. If and when they tithed, they did not give a "tithe according to Malachi 3:8-12;" most likely they gave their "tithes into the Order of Melchizedek." I am using the expression, "if and when they tithed" because the Bible does not specifically confirm or disaffirm the practice of tithing in Isaac's life. But the fact that his son Jacob knew about tithing is strong circumstantial evidence that Isaac also practiced tithing in one form or other. Imagine this: Joseph, the first global finance minister and businessman extraordinaire, identified himself with the priestly Order of Melchizedek. When we consider the massive financial and political power that Joseph came into, we will begin to catch a glimpse of the power of "identifying ourselves with the priestly Order of Melchizedek."

The Second Stream of Tithing

The second stream or embassy of tithing addresses the question of how "some marketplace leaders, itinerant ministers or a senior pastor" of a church ought to tithe. This first stream of tithing is "dual directional." In this second stream the tithe is "tithed up and across!" When it is "tithed up" the tithe goes to a man or woman of God, whom the senior pastor, itinerant minister or marketplace leader regards as a God-ordained spiritual father or covering. This is the person from whom the senior pastor, itinerant minister or marketplace leader receives his or her primary "bread and wine" for continued personal spiritual development and accountability.

When the tithe is "tithed across," it goes to a "God-ordained group of peer-level senior ministers" whom the senior pastor, itinerant minister or marketplace leader has chosen to be spiritually accountable to. This group of God-ordained peer level senior ministers will then represent the "Order of Melchizedek" to the senior pastor, itinerant minister or marketplace leader. *The lack of functional spiritual accountability to a "spiritual covering" by many senior pastors, itinerant ministers or marketplace leaders has brought great damage to the image of the global church.* The Church's public image got tarnished when some of these senior pastors, itinerant ministers or marketplace leaders fell into sexual sin, spousal abuse or were caught stealing money from their churches, ministries or businesses.

This is why rediscovering the power of the priestly Order of Melchizedek is so important to the global Church. *Only the priestly Order of Melchizedek can effectively "heal the lack of functional spiritual accountability" which exists among so many senior pastors, itinerant ministers and marketplace leaders.* From my observation over many years, I believe the greatest culprits of "inaccurate tithing patterns" are apostolic leaders or senior pastors of churches. As a senior pastor of a thriving church, I have also been guilty of "cheating" on my personal tithing patterns. What am I referring to? I am referring to the practice of senior pastors "giving their entire tithe" to their own local Church. I really believe that this practice is spiritually flawed. I really believe that every senior pastor or minister needs a pastor/spiritual father or a group of peer-level ministers whom he or she can submit his or her life to. All of us are a scandal waiting to happen when left to ourselves. This accountability group can never be a group of "Yes men or women" who lack the power to bring down the rod of correction in our lives. What we call our spiritual covering must be able to bring us under the knife of God's correction or we are wasting our tithes tithing into a spiritual covering that simply rubber stamps our spiritual arrogance and deceptive tendencies. Our spiritual covering must have "teeth to it." If our spouses cannot call our so-called "spiritual covering" and get help when we are misrepresenting God, then our so-called spiritual covering is NOT operating under the Order of Melchizedek. Melchizedek, the eternal King-Priest, did not intercept Abram to rubber stamp Abram's deceptive behavior in the Marketplace. *On the contrary, He came to circumcise him with the sword of God's Word and never apologized for it.* When Melchizedek left, Abram was a changed man. This life-transforming spiritual covering is "worth" tithing into.

This "pastor/spiritual father or accountability group" will then represent "the Order of Melchizedek" to the senior pastor/minister who has submitted his or her life to the same. I highly recommend that Senior pastors/ministers "give all or a reasonable portion" of their personal tithe to the "pastor/spiritual father or accountability group" who are laboring to keep them in the straight and narrow path. The remaining portion of their personal tithe can then be sown in their local church, if they are not comfortable giving it all to their spiritual covering. But I believe the "more excellent way" is for senior pastors/ministers to sow "their entire personal tithe" into the life and ministry of their spiritual father/covering or into the ministries of their "peer-level accountability group." I believe that God has given me scriptural evidence for what I am proposing.

"For this man (Jesus) was counted worthy of more glory than Moses, inasmuch as he who hath builded the house hath more honour than the house. 4For every house is builded by some man; but he that built all things is God."
Hebrews 3:3-4 (KJV, adapted by author)

"But Melchizedek, who was not a descendant of Levi, collected a tenth from Abraham. And Melchizedek placed a blessing upon Abraham, the one who had already received the promises of God. 7 And without question, the person who has the power to give a blessing is greater than the one who is blessed."
Hebrews 7:6-7

The above passages of Scripture are the reason I believe that the practice of senior pastors/ministers tithing into their own local Church is an "inaccurate pattern of tithing." The apostle Paul compares the great prophet Moses to our Lord Jesus Christ and comes to the staggering conclusion that our Lord Jesus Christ was and is immeasurably more glorious than Moses. I am sure that everyone reading this book would agree with Paul's summation. But the apostle Paul goes a step further in his desire to prove and quench any doubts as to the

THE LACK OF FUNCTIONAL SPIRITUAL ACCOUNTABILITY TO A "SPIRITUAL COVERING" BY MANY SENIOR PASTORS, ITINERANT MINISTER OR MARKETPLACE LEADERS HAS BROUGHT GREAT DAMAGE TO THE IMAGE OF THE GLOBAL CHURCH.

superiority of Christ over the great prophet, Moses. Please remember that the book of Hebrews was an apologetic book written to convince Jewish believers that they were making the right choice in choosing Jesus Christ over Moses.

Paul goes on to say that the "difference in glory and honor" between Jesus Christ and Moses, is similar to the one that exists between the "builder of the house" and the "house itself." This verse shows us one of the "most neglected apostolic principles" that God uses in building His Kingdom here on earth. When God is building His Kingdom He places "more glory and honor" on the "builder of the house" (the senior pastor/set man) than on the "house" (congregation) itself. When people drive through a very expensive neighborhood to look at expensive and breath-taking, multimillion dollar homes, they know intuitively that the person who built the gorgeous and expensive home has more splendor than the house itself. This is why people often inquire as to who owns and lives in a beautiful house that they deeply admire. *Denominations that do not esteem the senior pastors of their Churches while placing undue emphasis on the congregation, are guilty of violating one of the most "important principles for Kingdom building."* I have been saddened many times by over-zealous elders and deacons who place "more honor" on the congregation than they have placed on their senior pastor. They forget the fact that their senior pastor is the man or woman that God is using to build the local Church.

The apostle Paul goes on further and points to the "marked difference in glory and honor" between Melchizedek and Abraham. In so doing the apostle Paul underscores another very important "apostolic principle" God uses in building His Kingdom here on earth. Paul argues that since Melchizedek is the one who blessed Abraham, he was "greater in stature" than Abraham. Paul then identifies the spiritual principle behind his conclusion. In the "spiritual realm" the "lesser or subordinate" is "blessed by the greater or senior minister." This spiritual principle is even more so true for those of us who live under the Order of Melchizedek.

This "apostolic Kingdom-building principle" of the "lesser being blessed by the greater" is especially true when one is considering how the tithe is disbursed. When Paul was teaching on this principle of the "lesser being blessed by the greater," he was employing this principle in the context of Abraham's encounter with Melchizedek. Paul was using this principle to explain what happened to Abraham when he tithed into Melchizedek. The "lesser one (Abraham) received a covenantal blessing from the greater one (Melchizedek)." The spiritual implication is staggering but obvious. The spiritual implication is simply this: the "tithe" always travels in the "direction of the greater" and never flows from the "greater" to the "lesser." The "greater" can either be one individual or a group of peer-level leaders whom the senior pastor/minister submits his or her life to.

Million-Dollar Questions

Here are two million-dollar questions that every senior pastor or minister must answer honestly. *"If the builder of the house has more glory and honor than the house and the lesser is blessed by the greater," how would you justify tithing into your own Church?"* How can you as the senior pastor/minister "tithe down, instead of tithing up or across" and still expect the "covenantal blessing of tithing" to flow towards your life? When we as senior pastors tithe into the Church that we are leading, one way or the other, we still end up controlling how our tithe is spent because we have oversight over the money that comes into our Church. *We can easily find a way to make our tithe benefit us personally.* I truly believe that when many senior pastors/ministers are delivered from these "inaccurate patterns of tithing," there will be an "explosion of tithing" in the global Church. This is because true Spirit-led revival or reformation always begins with the head (leadership). I rest my case.

These inaccurate patterns of tithing among senior pastors/ministers would also explain why God has not given us the grace to lead everyone in our churches into a lifestyle of complete obedience to God in the area of tithing. *How can God give us this power when we are actively cheating on our personal tithe?* As senior pastors/ministers giving our entire personal tithe to our own churches is like "taking money from one of our pockets and then putting it into the other pocket." This is what many senior pastors call tithing. The problem behind this practice is simply this: "One way or the other the tithe money we give to our own church always ends up under our control!" How would we feel if our people also began to tithe into themselves? Selah.

"And blessed be God Most High, who has defeated your enemies for you. Then Abram gave Melchizedek a tenth of all the goods he had recovered."

Genesis 14:20

When Abraham gave his first tithe, he gave it to "honor a man who was a Priest of God Most High." Abraham recognized the fact that this man had been raised by God to "intercept his life with the blessing of God." ***Abraham's first tithe was tithed into a man of God who had the "spiritual stature" to move Abraham into his spiritual destiny. This man, Melchizedek, became Abraham's "Storehouse."*** This man, Melchizedek who was a Priest of God Most High gave Abram, "heavenly Bread and Wine." "Bread" represents "spiritual nourishment or the doctrine of the Kingdom of God," while "Wine" represents the "Spirit of the Kingdom of God and it also represents the anointing for service!" Apostolic leaders, Bishops or senior pastors of Churches must "discern the man or men who represent the Order of Melchizedek" to them, so they can give their personal tithe or a portion of it into this "man or group of men." Part of my personal tithe for instance, goes to my spiritual father, who is my "primary input for the spiritual nourishment" I am receiving from the Lord. The remaining portion of it is "tithed into a group of peer-level senior ministers" whom I am spiritually accountable to. My personal tithes never go into my church's bank account.

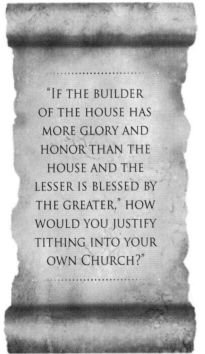

"IF THE BUILDER OF THE HOUSE HAS MORE GLORY AND HONOR THAN THE HOUSE AND THE LESSER IS BLESSED BY THE GREATER," HOW WOULD YOU JUSTIFY TITHING INTO YOUR OWN CHURCH?"

Nevertheless, I am not suggesting that if the senior pastor/minister has a "para-church ministry" that they should take the tithes of their independent ministry organization and tithe it into their spiritual fathers or spiritual covering. In most cases a para-church ministry always falls under the covering of the local Church that the senior minister pastors; as such, any tithes from a para-church ministry organization must be tithed into the senior pastor/minister's own church, unless they choose differently. *My bone of contention is with "how senior pastors/ministers dispose of their personal tithe from income which is due to them personally."* I truly believe that if we follow Abraham's example, we will multiply the blessing of God over our life and ministry. As senior pastors/ministers we are quick at telling our congregations "to bring their tithes to the storehouse (local church) where they are being fed the meat of God's Word!" If this statement is true of the people we shepherd, why is it not true of us? I rest my case.

5. Does every tithe go into my local church?

"Then Melchizedek king of Salem also brought out bread and wine, he was the priest of God most high and He blessed him and said, Blessed be Abram of God most high, possessor of heaven and earth who has delivered your enemies into your hand and he gave him a tithe of all."

Genesis 14:18-20 (KJV)

This final question – Does every tithe go into my local Church? – is a very intricate question that must be handled with surgical precision and forensic aptitude. Several years back had I been asked the same question, my answer would have been an emphatic, "Yes!" I would have said, "Yes, every tithe always goes into the local church." Like most pastors, I would have defended my answer to this final question with my life. But God has since proved me wrong both by revelation and by personal experience.

The Holy Spirit showed me that there are **special cases** in which the tithe does not go to the local church of the person attending the same. ***But even though these cases do not violate the principles of tithing under the Order of Melchizedek, they are the EXCEPTION and not the rule.*** These special cases affect and apply to only a small section of the body of Christ. The tithes of the majority of the body of Christ generally belong to the local church that they attend on a regular basis. This is because the local Church is the primary embassy that God has appointed to advance the Kingdom in the community or City that the church (local congregation) is based in.

Before I explain these special cases of tithing, I need to lay a foundation for what I'm about to say. Tithing under the Order of Melchizedek is always predicated on who is the primary channel that God is using to feed us the heavenly bread and the wine that is helping us to enter into our prophetic destiny in God. This principle establishes who has the right to the tithe in our life. This primary channel has to be a constant prophetic voice into our lives and not just a "one night stand" prophetic or apostolic voice so to speak. *In most cases, the person who has the right to the tithes is usually the senior pastor of the local church that we attend on a regular basis, since he or she is the primary source of the bread of deliverance and the wine of revelation for the local church (congregation). Just to be clear, I am NOT suggesting that all the tithes of the members of a local congregation be given to the senior pastor personally, but to the local church that he or she pastors..*

But over the years, God has introduced me to members of that small section of the body of Christ, who did not feel comfortable tithing into the local church that they were attending, because they felt that the pastor of the church that they were attending was not the primary channel of the heavenly bread and the wine that they were living on in their march towards destiny. They had no problem giving their offerings to their pastor; they just struggled with giving their tithes to a pastor who did not represent the Order of Melchizedek to them. At first I thought this was arrogance and spiritual immaturity on the part of this special class of Kingdom citizens who found themselves in this type of situation in churches across the world.

For awhile, I dismissed this special class of Kingdom citizens as a bunch of arrogant and rebellious saints. But God pulled the carpet from under me when He put me in a situation where I became part of that small section of the body of Christ, that did not feel comfortable giving tithes into the local church that I attended at the time. This small section of the body of Christ usually includes many itinerant ministers, and some marketplace leaders. In 2001, I moved to Oklahoma City after I got married. I started attending a church that I had helped to grow while I was still living in Chicago. The pastor of the church was a dear friend of mine, but he was definitely not my spiritual father or covering even though attending his church while I lived in the city was the most logical choice for me. It was both fun and convenient. I sowed a lot of offerings into my friend's church, but I continued to give my tithe to my spiritual father, who was the primary channel of the heavenly bread and wine that I needed to move forward into my destiny. To my friend's credit, he respected my desire to remain honorable in my relationship to the man or men that God had raised to represent the Order of Melchizedek in my life.

While I was in my friend's church, I served as a spiritual advisor to his board of elders, but I never became an elder in his church. This is because it would have been out of order for me to be an elder in a church that I did not feel comfortable tithing into. No one should ever be an elder in a church that they do not feel comfortable tithing into. But I was very generous in the offerings that I gave into my friend's church. *But like I said at the beginning of this section, this special class of Kingdom citizens is the EXCEPTION and not the rule.* I know that there some pastors of churches who will be very annoyed or irritated with me for mentioning such an exception. *But the reality is this;* ***it is better for people to tithe by revelation than by compulsion. Revelation always wins over compulsion.*** If scaring the saints with the curse of Malachi 3 had been very successful in improving the levels of tithing in the global Church, the Holy Spirit would never have summoned me to write a book like the one that you are reading!

Let me simulate a real life scenario that happens often to help cement the fact that there are special cases where the tithe does not necessarily go into the local church of the person giving the tithe. While John Doe was living in Florida, Pastor Jesse became John Doe's pastor and spiritual father. Pastor Jesse really worked very hard on discipling John Doe and turning his business around. While living in Florida, John Doe attended Pastor Jesse's church and never missed a service. John Doe was so grateful to God that he had a caring and loving spiritual father like Pastor Jesse.

IT IS BETTER FOR PEOPLE TO TITHE BY REVELATION THAN BY COMPULSION. REVELATION ALWAYS WINS OVER COMPULSION.

But one day John Doe's business moved him to New York, where he began to attend New York Fellowship Church (fictional name) pastored by Jim Ducker. Even though John Doe enjoys his new church in New York, his highest loyalty is still attached to Pastor Jesse, whom he regards as his spiritual father. John Doe's deep sense of loyalty and honor compels him to send his tithes to Pastor Jesse's church even though he now regularly attends Pastor Jim Ducker's church. Those who are very dogmatic about the fact that the tithe always goes into the local church that a person attends would judge John Doe's actions very harshly and call him rebellious. But how can John Doe deny the fact that the primary source of the heavenly bread and wine that is changing his life is coming from his relationship with Pastor Jesse even though he now lives in New York where he attends Pastor Jim Ducker's church.

Under the Order of Melchizedek, John Doe's tithing pattern is completely acceptable, provided that Pastor Jesse and John Doe maintain a healthy and ongoing vibrant spiritual father-son relationship. *But like I said at the beginning, this scenario is the EXCEPTION and not the rule.* For the most part (about 95% of the time) the tithe of God's people belongs to the local church that they attend. As a general disclaimer, *this section is not meant or intended to give license to anyone to tithe wherever they feel like it; only those who are spiritually immature and unstable may come up with such an erroneous conclusion.*

My sheep hear my voice, and I know them, and they follow me.

John 10:27 (KJV)

Pastors who are afraid that this section on the special cases of tithing might cause their people to give their tithes to their favorite Televangelist, author or teacher need to heed Christ's admonition in John 10:27. Jesus Christ, the great shepherd of the sheep, gave us three key qualities of a true shepherd or pastor. These three qualities represent the "honor" that God has placed upon every true shepherd who truly loves and cares for the sheep.

(i). Jesus said the Sheep always listen to the voice of the shepherd.

(ii). The true shepherd has a very real and meaningful relationship with the sheep, and know his sheep intimately.

(iii). Sheep will naturally follow the voice and leadership of the shepherd.

The point I am driving at is this: any true shepherd or pastor never has to worry about his or her sheep following the voice of a stranger. Consequently, sheep will not give tithes that belong to the house of the Shepherd to another. Senior pastors (of whom I am one) need to learn to trust the Holy Spirit, who is the one Jesus Christ commissioned to assign His sheep (His people) to the shepherd or pastor of His choice. Gone should be the days when pastors fight over church members. Fighting over church members is another form of idolatry because it exalts human power over God's power. The apostle Paul made it very clear that it is God who gives the increase, not our intimidation or manipulation.

This book is NOT written to steer people away from tithing to their local church, by no means. I am a pastor over a local church in McKinney, Texas and I would never write a book that would undermine the critical importance of tithing into the local church. Rather, *this book is meant to resuscitate the dying engines of tithing in the Body of Christ by restoring all proper, Biblical channels of tithing, including channels that religious tradition may consider controversial.* Far from being controversial, I am only trying to be very practical and realistic. When Kingdom citizens realize that they are NOT being coerced into tithing, but are simply being reintroduced to a more excellent way of tithing, the numbers of committed tithers within the Body of Christ will rise exponentially.

Here is a second scenario. I have met several dear children of God who have given up on the organized church for a season, because they were hurt deeply by church leadership. Many of these people have told me that they would rather watch Christian television on Sunday morning than drive to any church. While I disagree with their solution of choice, I do empathize with their emotional and spiritual disillusionment with many of the flaws of the institutional church and with certain leaders. God wants His people to learn how to live and function effectively with the rest of the Body of Christ, and the local church is the best place for this important spiritual exercise. But my acknowledgement of the dilemma that many of these Kingdom citizens find themselves in does not solve their tithing dilemma. Since they are not part of a local church, how do they get to participate in the technology of tithing?

My answer to these believers, while they are in this season, is that they need to send their tithes to a Televangelist, author or preacher of the gospel whom they feel supernaturally drawn to, who is also feeding their spirit with that heavenly bread and wine. It is better for Kingdom citizens to be tithing into a ministry that propagates the gospel of the Kingdom than to throw their tithes at secular charitable organizations like the Red Cross (I know of disfranchised believers who are doing this). By sending their tithes to the Televangelist, author or preacher that they have identified as the primary channel of that precious heavenly bread and wine, they can still participate in the covenant blessings of the tithe, while they are waiting on God to heal them from the offenses that they picked up in the organized church. But I strongly caution these Kingdom believers not to allow themselves to dwell in this valley of indecision for too long. God created us for community. God wants us to be part of a community of shared values and interests. Being part of a stable and caring local church is God's best option for planting us in a Kingdom community with people of like precious faith and growing us into the image of His Son Jesus.

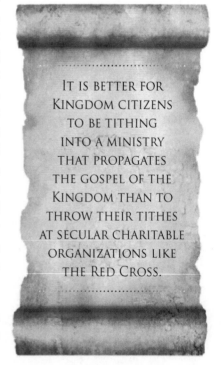

IT IS BETTER FOR KINGDOM CITIZENS TO BE TITHING INTO A MINISTRY THAT PROPAGATES THE GOSPEL OF THE KINGDOM THAN TO THROW THEIR TITHES AT SECULAR CHARITABLE ORGANIZATIONS LIKE THE RED CROSS.

Here is a third scenario. There are a growing number of internet and house churches that are mushrooming all over the world. The internet or house church movement is not a movement that the organized church can simply ignore or wish away. The truth of the matter is that there are tens of millions of born-again believers who belong to an internet or house church and have no desire to join the ranks of the organized church. But since most houses churches have no paid staff or full-time ministers, how do members of these house fellowships disburse their tithes?

Once again, every member of the Body of Christ is under the Order of Melchizedek whether they know it or not. Under the Order of Melchizedek, the Holy Spirit always raises a man or a group of persons who are ordained to represent this eternal priestly Order in the life of the believer. This person or persons must be the primary channel of that precious heavenly bread and wine that God will be using to sustain us in our advancement towards our God-given destiny. Once a believer who attends a house church fellowship identifies such a person or persons, they need to start tithing into the ministry or ministries of the same to activate the covenantal blessings of the tithe. There is absolutely no New Testament believer who is excused from tithing, because under the New Testament, tithes are used to fuel and finance the advancement of the Kingdom of God. *How can we say we love God's Kingdom on one hand and then refuse to give tithes of honor that are used to finance the gospel of the Kingdom?*

While many of those who attend house churches are very genuine in their motivations, there is also a growing number of spiritual dissidents who join house church fellowships simply to avoid the giving of tithes. To this group I can only say that any person who is determined to avoid the giving of tithes will NEVER know the incredible privilege of living under Christ's Order of Melchizedek priesthood. This is because without Abraham's encounter with the Order of Melchizedek (Genesis 14), the whole practice of tithing would have been nonexistent. It is the eternal Order of Melchizedek (Christ's eternal priestly ministry) that introduced humanity (Abram) to the technology of tithing in order to advance the Kingdom of God here on earth. I am just glad that God has never gone out of His way to avoid giving us all the incredible benefits of salvation like some of His people do in their endeavor to avoid the giving of tithes to the Kingdom of God. Only the judgment seat of Christ will reveal the deep ramifications of their error and greed.

Here is a fourth scenario: Since Abraham's tithes were given to a King who has a Kingdom, we can conclude that one of the primary motivations and purpose of tithing under the Order of Melchizedek is to advance the Kingdom of God in the earth. I know of cases where very mature Christians believed the Holy Spirit directed them to send their tithes to an apostolic church-planting missionary organization that is dedicated to taking the gospel of the Kingdom to unreached people groups and to help the persecuted church in foreign nations. One such case involved a very faithful and stable Christian couple that I knew and I also saw the fruits of righteousness that their act of obedience produced on the mission field. But this same couple were the first to admit that as a general rule they tithed faithfully and consistently into their local church. But in those special moments when the Holy Spirit directed them to temporarily shift the direction of their tithes into these "sold out to the Kingdom" missionary organizations, they believed they had license from God to do this. Who was I to argue with their steadfast conviction, especially since I knew that they were not flaky believers? But my prayerful contemplation has led me to a personal conviction that these types of special tithing cases do exist. It is a shame that sometimes the global church is so self-serving, so self-focused and so self-resource-consuming that it neglects heaven's highest agenda which is the finishing of the Great Commission. This is quite pitiful.

Many of these Christ-centered apostolic missionary organizations live off the offerings of God's people and when there is a recession, they are normally the first ones to be cut and neglected. Are these Christ-centered church planting missionary organizations that are risking it all to advance God's Kingdom among unreached people groups and persecuted regions of the world of lesser value in God's Kingdom than the local church? Some of these Christ-centered apostolic missionary organizations are feeding hundreds of thousands around the world with that precious heavenly bread and wine through ongoing Bible courses. *But I need to reemphasize that these special cases of tithing are the EXCEPTION and not the RULE!*

Finally, there is an erroneous misconception that I need to correct before concluding this section. There are those who believe that they can take their tithes and give them to a charitable organization such as the Red Cross or an orphanage or a community food bank in order to help the poor. This is a gross miscalculation on their part. It is perfectly fine for them to use their offerings and give it to the Red Cross or an orphanage or food bank if they so desire, *but tithes are governed by a very different spiritual technology.* The right to receive the tithe under the Order of Melchizedek is always connected to the person or persons that God is using to give us the bread of deliverance and the wine of revelation in order to advance the Kingdom of God in and through us. The

Red Cross or an orphanage cannot do this for us. The tithe must always be given into the life or ministry of the person or persons that God has made responsible for feeding us with His heavenly bread and wine for our life. Since the senior pastor of the local church is usually the primary feeder of the bread and the wine in his or her congregation, their church is more often than not the best soil to tithe into, except in those very rare cases that we have already alluded to. Giving our tithes to philanthropy is an exercise in futility and simply belies our ignorance of the power and sacredness of the tithe under the Order of Melchizedek.

LIFE APPLICATION SECTION

Point to Ponder:

Under the priestly Order of Melchizedek the giving of tithes is not payment for priestly services rendered but the giving of a royal endowment to the King of kings by his kingdom citizens.

Verse to Remember:

"'And blessed be God Most High, who has defeated your enemies for you.' Then Abram gave Melchizedek a tenth of all the goods he had recovered."

Genesis 14:20

Questions to Consider:

* What is the tithe?

_____

_____

_____

* Why should I tithe?

_____

_____

_____

* Where do I give my tithe?"

_____

_____

_____

_____

Journal Your Thoughts

THE KING OF SODOM

Please bear in mind that Sodom was the most morally bankrupt nation among the countries of the East, during Abraham's era. The people of Sodom and Gomorrah made Egypt look like it was a paradise of righteousness. The Egyptians were hard-core idol worshippers. They worshipped Pharaoh, frogs, the sun, lice, and the river Nile just to name a few and yet the people of Sodom made the Egyptians look morally conservative. *The people of Sodom were ultra spiritual and social liberals, who did not believe in heeding any kind of divine restraint.*

This reminds me of some of today's churches who have been taken over by the doctrine of demons. Most of these doctrines of demons come in the form of a message of "greasy grace" which refuses to condemn sin in the Church for fear of losing people who have not yet made up their minds to sell-out to Christ. In this chapter we will take an introspective look at the king and people of Sodom to unmask what they represent prophetically, and how this ties itself to the power of rediscovering the Order of Melchizedek and the Abrahamic tithing model.

Here is a simple glossary list of what the king of Sodom represents prophetically:

- He was the king of an ultra-liberal society who had removed every boundary of morality in the structure of their nation.

- He was the king of a nation that celebrated every form of sexual perversion, including homosexuality and bestiality.

- He represented the diabolical mismanagement of seed, through inaccurate and perverted sexual intercourse. This diabolical mismanagement of seed causes future apostles, prophets, pastors, presidents and so forth to die in the rectum. This was never the plan of God.

- He completely destroyed the mountain of family within the structure of his nation. This would explain why Lot's daughters did not see anything wrong with having sex with their own father.

- He represented ill-gained financial resources, which were gained by using demonic technology.

- The king of Sodom was a prophetic picture of "the spirit of the Anti-Christ." The spirit of the anti-Christ is the spirit which stands opposed to anything righteous and Christ-like.

- The king of Sodom was so devoted to operating in spiritual darkness, that he became the personification of the spirit of Satan here on earth.

- The king of Sodom is a prophetic representation of the spirit of Babylon which is the principal spirit behind the systems of this world.

The Country of Sodom

THE PEOPLE OF
SODOM WERE ULTRA
SPIRITUAL AND
SOCIAL LIBERALS,
WHO DID NOT
BELIEVE IN HEEDING
TO ANY KIND OF
DIVINE RESTRAINT.

So the Lord told Abraham, "I have heard a great outcry from Sodom and Gomorrah, because their sin is so flagrant. I am going down to see if their actions are as wicked as I have heard. If not, I want to know."

Genesis 18:20-21

The country of Sodom was so obnoxiously wicked that God decided to come down from heaven to check it out for Himself. The flagrant nature of the sin and sexual perversity in this wicked country had reached the ears of God. The people of Sodom under the guidance of the king of Sodom had transformed the country of Sodom into a "hell house." The country of Sodom had become a "little satanic empire" here on earth. It had become the base of operations for fallen angels and every foul spirit. Every sexual sin you can think of, including homosexuality and bestiality, were practiced freely in this wicked City.

According to *Roget's Thesaurus*, "Bestiality" by definition means "sexual relations between a person and an animal or sodomy." The very name Sodom tells us just how depraved and sexually perverse this ancient City really was. Some of the people of Sodom were having sex with animals and the king of Sodom did not see anything wrong with these practices. It's not surprising that God came down to see this wicked country just like He had come down to see the building of the tower of Babel.

> *But before they retired for the night, all the men of Sodom, young and old, came from all over the city and surrounded the house. They shouted to Lot, "Where are the men who came to spend the night with you? Bring them out to us so we can have sex with them!" So Lot stepped outside to talk to them, shutting the door behind him. "Please, my brothers," he begged, "don't do such a wicked thing. Look, I have two virgin daughters. Let me bring them out to you, and you can do with them as you wish. But please, leave these men alone, for they are my guests and are under my protection."*
>
> Genesis 19:4-8

Interestingly enough, what we call the gay lifestyle today, originated from this ancient City, which God judged by "burning it to the ground with fire and brimstone" for being horrendously wicked. The sin of homosexuality was one of the sins of sexual perversion for which God judged this country for. What amazes me is how some so-called Bible-believing churches who use the Bible as their final authority in matters of doctrine, waver on this subject. Below is a quote from the editorial page of *Charisma* magazine of the February issue of 2007, written by J. Lee Grady, which underscores how **the seductive and corrupting power of the king of Sodom is creeping into the lifestream of the global church.**

"A while later Jay Bakker let the world know what he really believes. He told *Radar* magazine: "This sounds so churchy, but I felt like God spoke to my heart and said (homosexuality) is not a sin"....So I am blowing the whistle. This is an official apostasy alert. In case you haven't noticed, Jay is not the only voice in the blogosphere claiming that God has changed His mind about homosexuality. The Episcopal Church voted to ordain a gay bishop in 2003. Many gay affirming churches are sprouting up in Middle America – including some that claim to be Pentecostal. In fact, the founder of the largest gay denomination in the country, Troy Perry, was raised in the Church of God of Prophecy.

"What Troy Perry, Jay Bakker and the Episcopalians are offering America is a new religion that guarantees no hell and requires no holiness. It's a limp, spineless Christianity that cannot confront sin for fear of being" judgmental." It is an impotent gospel which tells people who wrestle with homosexuality that they might as well indulge. It welcomes everyone with a polite "come as you are" mantra, but in the end is incapable of breaking the power of addiction or sexual dysfunction. It uses politically-correct, feel-good words such as "tolerance," "acceptance" and "grace," terms that sound hip and sexy in today's permissive culture. It is a golden calf, shiny and seductive, forged by those whose goal is to invent a new morality. This "gay-affirming gospel" is a toxic heresy that must be addressed boldly from our pulpits in 2007. I pray that there is enough moral backbone left in the church to face this challenge." (Golden Calf Religion article, by J. Lee Grady published in *Charisma Magazine*)

I normally never add such long quotes in any of my books, but this quote is far too important to quote out of context. This article shows us how the seductive power of the king of Sodom is trying to redefine the fundamental tenets of the gospel of our Lord Jesus Christ. This quote from our dear brother Lee Grady also underscores why we need to "rediscover the Abrahamic tithing model which is based upon the priestly Order of Melchizedek."

The priestly Order of Melchizedek is the only spiritual order available to the people of our planet which has the spiritual power to "intercept the seductive and corrupting power of the king of Sodom" from "polluting the drinking water" of the Church of the living God. It is the only spiritual order

THE SEDUCTIVE AND CORRUPTING POWER OF THE KING OF SODOM IS CREEPING INTO THE LIFE STREAM OF THE GLOBAL CHURCH.

which has the power to deliver every man and woman who is struggling with the sin of homosexuality, which originates from the ancient City of Sodom. The divine interception of Abram by Melchizedek just before the king of Sodom intercepted him has far-reaching spiritual implications for the future of the global church. *Hidden in this historical encounter between Abram and Melchizedek are divine strategies for "closing demonic portals" which release spiritual and sexual perversion into a generation.*

Don't go down to Egypt

At that time a severe famine struck the land of Canaan, forcing Abram to go down to Egypt, where he lived as a foreigner. As he was approaching the border of Egypt, Abram said to his wife, Sarai, "Look, you are a very beautiful woman. When the Egyptians see you, they will say, 'This is his wife. Let's kill him; then we can have her!'

Gen 12:10-12

One of the critical dangers we are most likely to face on our journey towards our God-given destiny is the danger of aborting our prophetic destiny during periods of painful transition. When the devil saw that Abram and Sarai were passionately moving forward in the direction of the God-given destiny, he began to manipulate the weather and managed to create an artificial drought around Abraham's natural habitat. We must not forget that the first heaven which is responsible for controlling natural times and seasons here on earth is in a "fallen state." This means that this part of the heavens can be "easily manipulated by demonic powers."

This is why it's dangerous for God's people to make spiritual decisions based upon what's happening in their natural environment. Please remember that there are two major spiritual technologies at work in the earth realm, "the Law of the Spirit of Life in Christ Jesus" and "the Law of sin and death." **The former is a divine technology while the latter is a demonic technology which "drives the machinery of death" here on earth.** The biggest difference between these two spiritual technologies is simply this: God's technology works from our "spirit within to bring God's life to everything on the outside," whereas the demonic technology works from "the outside in, killing everything on the inside." When we make decisions based upon what we are seeing on the outside we may be walking into demonic entrapment. This is exactly what happened to Abram. He saw the wells of water that he needed to sustain his livestock drying up and he panicked. In his panic he made a hasty decision to move to Egypt which placed him on the pathway of death and destruction.

When Abram got to the borders of Egypt he broke his marriage covenant with his wife, Sarah and brought her into a covenant of lies, simply to protect himself. In Egypt his dear wife was almost raped by the king of Egypt who wanted to sleep with her with unrestrained lust. In exchange for sexual encounters with Sarah, Pharaoh (the king of Egypt) gave Abram and his nephew Lot an abundance of male and female servants, livestock, gold and silver from the treasuries of Egypt.

Had Abram known that that this "tainted deal" with the king of Egypt had set him on a "collision course with the king of Sodom," he would never have taken this demonic deal. Had God not intervened, Sarah would have been raped by the king of Egypt and Abram would have been killed by Pharaoh once he discovered that Abraham had deceived him. When Abram and Sarah were given an eviction notice to leave the land of Egypt, they left with a lot of money and material possessions that they had taken from the treasuries of Egypt. *Unfortunately, their ill-gained wealth had come at a terrible price*, which would soon begin to manifest itself in their future destiny.

Lot moves to Sodom

Finally Abram said to Lot, "Let's not allow this conflict to come between us or our herdsmen. After all, we are close relatives! The whole countryside is open to you. Take your choice of any section of the land you want, and we will separate. If you want the land to the left, then I'll take the land on the right. If you prefer the land on the right, then I'll go to the left." Lot took a long look at the fertile plains of the Jordan Valley in the direction of Zoar. The whole area was well watered everywhere, like the garden of the Lord or the beautiful land of Egypt. (This was before the Lord destroyed Sodom and Gomorrah.)

Genesis 13:8-10

Abram's decision to move to Egypt during this time of famine had muddied the waters in his relationship with his nephew, Lot. Whenever we disobey God in our decision-making process, the spiritual consequences of our spiritual inaccuracy almost always manifest themselves in the arena of our closest relationships. This was certainly the case between Abram and Lot. After they returned from Egypt, loaded with an abundance of resources that they had taken from the treasuries of Egypt, there was "serious strife and division" which broke out between Abram's herdsmen and Lot's herdsmen. The presence of spirits of strife and division in our closest relationships is always a sign that demonic agencies are swimming in the "spiritual wells" we are drinking from.

The strife between Abram and Lot became so hostile that Abram decided to call for a truce. Abram told Lot that there was no need for them to fight for the land because they were family. Even though he was the senior, Abram gave Lot the power of first choice concerning the land which was before them. Abram told Lot that he would take whatever was left behind. *(Coincidentally, when we come into a place of spiritual stature we can do more with the "leftovers"*

than most people can do with a whole pie). The powerful divine intervention of God in the land of Egypt which had delivered his wife Sarah from Pharaoh's bedchamber and spared his own life had left an indelible mark on Abram's spirit. He was beginning to grasp the awesome power of the God he had chosen to serve. This is why he refused to fight with Lot over the issue of land.

"Lot took a long look at the fertile plains of the Jordan Valley in the direction of Zoar. The whole area was well watered everywhere, like the garden of the Lord or the beautiful land of Egypt. (This was before the Lord destroyed Sodom and Gomorrah.)"

Genesis 13:8-10

Lot, who did not know how to make spiritual decisions from his spirit, looked at the evidence presented to him by his natural eyes and decided to pitch his tent near the wicked country of Sodom. The plains surrounding the Cities of Sodom and Gomorrah at that time were very fertile and richly supplied with water. Lot figured that he had hit a jackpot. From the outside it would appear as if "Lot" had made a great decision but the decision was a disastrous one. Lot did not know that the path towards Sodom which he had chosen was on a collision course with God's divine judgment of fire and brimstone.

If Lot had known that his decision to settle near Sodom, would one day cause him to lose everything that he had worked for all his life, he would have been terrified. Had he known that his decision to settle in the plains of Sodom would one day transform his dear wife into a pillar of salt and influence his two daughters to commit incest, he would have been horrified. His decision to move to Sodom brought him under the power of the king of Sodom. Unfortunately, Lot did not have the "spiritual fortitude to resist the powerful demonic influence of the king of Sodom."

Lot's carnal decision to live near Sodom unknowingly placed Abram on a collision course with the seductive and corruptive power of the king of Sodom. "Lot" was the "small fish" set as the spiritual bait to draw in "Abram the big fish." The devil knew that the covenant of God to bless all the nations was with Abraham and not with Lot. It was Abraham the devil wanted; Lot

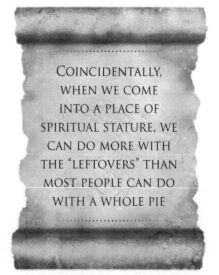

COINCIDENTALLY, WHEN WE COME INTO A PLACE OF SPIRITUAL STATURE, WE CAN DO MORE WITH THE "LEFTOVERS" THAN MOST PEOPLE CAN DO WITH A WHOLE PIE

was simply collateral damage. The devil knew that Abraham loved his nephew deeply and would not hesitate to come to his rescue.

Fighting on the losing side

"As it happened, the valley of the Dead Sea was filled with tar pits. And as the army of the kings of Sodom and Gomorrah fled, some fell into the tar pits, while the rest escaped into the mountains. The victorious invaders then plundered Sodom and Gomorrah and headed for home, taking with them all the spoils of war and the food supplies. They also captured Lot—Abram's nephew who lived in Sodom—and carried off everything he owned. But one of Lot's men escaped and reported everything to Abram the Hebrew, who was living near the oak grove belonging to Mamre the Amorite. Mamre and his relatives, Eshcol and Aner, were Abram's allies."

Genesis 14:10-13

We have already shown you what the king of Sodom represents in a prophetic sense. ***Everything he stands for is anti-Christ and anti-Kingdom.*** When Lot and his family moved their residence into the country of Sodom, they did not know that the divine judgment of this wicked City had already been set in stone in the corridors of eternity. The judgment of fire and brimstone (which is actually the Lake of fire manifesting itself before the end of the age) was on a collision course with the king of Sodom and all his people. Lot had placed himself on the pathway of death and destruction.

When we identify ourselves with the king of Sodom and not with the King of Jerusalem, we are setting ourselves up for death and destruction in the near future. It grieves me deeply to see just how many pastors are "watering down the gospel" message in order to attract larger crowds. These carnal decisions are unknowingly setting up these pastors to align themselves and their ministries with the spirit of the king of Sodom. For most of them their true ministry in the Kingdom of God will be destroyed by the enemy. This is exactly what happened to Lot and his family. ***Driven by an "unhealthy desire to prosper at all costs," some pastors have placed themselves in very compromising positions.*** Many are finding themselves fighting on the same side as the king of Sodom.

When we align ourselves with the king of Sodom and begin to eat from the same plate that this diabolical spirit is feeding from, we shall also suffer the consequences. The king of Sodom was already "quarantined for death and destruction by divine decree." As for Lot, his close ties with the king of Sodom made him become a partaker of this wicked king's judgment. Lot went into Sodom as a wealthy righteous man, but he came out of Sodom as a "financially bankrupt and backslidden" preacher of righteousness. Please do not fight on the same side as the king of Sodom in your desire to be famous or have a mega ministry which appeals to the masses. I believe that God can give us such a great reputation and ministry without becoming allies with the king of Sodom. I am not opposed to anybody having a mega church or ministry, but we must make sure that the "spiritual technology we are using to grow our reputation or ministry is not borrowed from Sodom!"

Divine Interception

"After Abram returned from his victory over Kedorlaomer and all his allies, the king of Sodom went out to meet him in the valley of Shaveh (that is, the King's Valley). And Melchizedek, the king of Salem and a priest of God Most High, brought Abram some bread and wine. Melchizedek blessed Abram with this blessing: 'Blessed be Abram by God Most High, Creator of heaven and earth. And blessed be God Most High, who has defeated your enemies for you.' Then Abram gave Melchizedek a tenth of all the goods he had recovered."

Genesis 14:17-20

We are living in very dangerous times where we are constantly seeing the security and sovereignty of nations threatened by international terrorism. For many of us who live in the United States, we will never forget the horrors of September 11th, 2001, which brought the portals of terror right to our doorsteps. The rise of rogue nations such as North Korea and Iran who are determined to build nuclear weapons, while simultaneously promising the world that they would wipe out Israel from the face of the earth, has not helped to ease our fears.

The growing threat of international terrorism posed by the rapid rise of "radical Islamists" and the rise of rogue nations such as Iran, has forced world powers like the United States of America, Great Britain, Russia and China to invest heavily in "nuclear missile interception technology." This technology specializes in enhancing the ability of nations to intercept nuclear missiles or warheads that might be launched against the countries of the West by some fanatical terrorists. This technology gives nations such as the United States of America, the military power to defuse a nuclear missile or warhead in mid-air, rendering it useless as to its original objective.

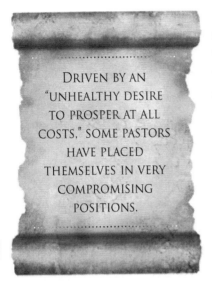

DRIVEN BY AN "UNHEALTHY DESIRE TO PROSPER AT ALL COSTS," SOME PASTORS HAVE PLACED THEMSELVES IN VERY COMPROMISING POSITIONS.

I want you to know that thousands of years before the powers of the West thought of developing this powerful technology, God had this spiritual technology functioning perfectly in the priestly Order of Melchizedek. To help you appreciate the intercepting power of the priestly Order of Melchizedek, I have taken the liberty to give you clear-cut definitions of the word "intercept" from Roget's Dictionary.

To **"intercept"** means:

✳ To take, seize, or halt (someone or something on the way from one place to another); cut off from an intended destination: to intercept a messenger.

✳ To see or overhear (a message, transmission, etc., meant for another).

✳ To stop or check (passage, travel, etc.): to intercept the traitor's escape.

✳ To take possession of (a ball or puck) during an attempted pass by an opposing team.

✳ To stop or interrupt the course, progress, or transmission of.

✳ To destroy or disperse (enemy aircraft or a missile or missiles) in the air on the way to a target.

✳ To stop the natural course of (light, water, etc.).

✳ To intersect.

✳ To prevent or cut off the operation or effect of.

✳ To cut off from access, sight, etc.

I hope that you are as excited as I am at the "far-reaching spiritual implications" of what it means to be intercepted by God before we are hit by a "demonic nuclear missile." Abram had just had a resounding victory over the kings from the East who had invaded Sodom and kidnapped Lot and his family. News of his resounding victory quickly reached the ears of the king of Sodom. The king of Sodom quickly informed the keeper of his royal chariots to mount his horses because they were about to go on a trip to intercept Abram on his return from the slaughter of the kings. The king of Sodom put on his royal garments and fumed himself in the oils and fragrances of Sodom which were also offered in worship to his demon gods. With the smell of hell oozing from his body, the king of Sodom drove his chariots like a mad car-driver racing to the finish line. **He was in a demonic hurry to intercept Abram, but he was too late...**

Moments before the king of Sodom and his diplomatic entourage from the land of Sodom arrived, Melchizedek, the High Priest of God Most High intercepted Abram. This Melchizedek is the man that many scholars believe was a pre-incarnation manifestation of Christ. This priestly man, who was a prophetic representation of the eternal priesthood of our Lord Jesus Christ, intercepted Abram just before the king of Sodom got to him. This divine encounter between Abram and Melchizedek was so powerful and life changing that Abram did something that he had never done before. *"Abram gave this Priest of God Most High, his first tithe..."*

Abram gave Melchizedek his tithe out of his heartfelt desire to "honor this lofty man's high office" and also because Abram wanted to "have an ordination into this eternal priestly order." Abram had no idea as to the far-reaching spiritual ramifications of the tithe that he gave to Melchizedek. Abram had no idea just how this one act of faith would shift things in the realm of the spirit. Abram did not know that **his tithe into this eternal priestly order would save him and his seed from the seductive and corrupting power of the king of Sodom.** He did not yet realize that had he not established a "covenant of tithe with the King of Jerusalem," he would have "lost the spiritual battle with the king of Sodom." By establishing a covenant of tithe, Abram defused the combined power of every demonic agency which was represented by the king of Sodom in the spirit realm."

Melchizedek (the king-priest) gave Abram, "heavenly bread and wine" in exchange for his tithe. This heavenly bread and wine completely reconfigured Abraham's internal spirit dynamics. This heavenly bread and wine gave Abraham a "new spiritual position with the power to prevail," a position that Abram would soon need to win one of his greatest spiritual battles yet.

Don't do Business with the King of Sodom

After Abram returned from his victory over Kedorlaomer and all his allies, the king of Sodom went out to meet him in the valley of Shaveh (that is, the King's Valley). The king of Sodom said to Abram, "Give back my people who were captured. But you may keep for yourself all the goods you have recovered." Abram replied to the king of Sodom, "I solemnly swear to the Lord, God Most High, Creator of heaven and earth that I will not take so much as a single thread or sandal thong from what belongs to you. Otherwise you might say, 'I am the one who made Abram rich.'

Genesis 14:17,21-23

Moments after Melchizedek's departure, the chariots of the king of Sodom screeched to a noisome halt, shooting speckles of dust into the thin air. The king of Sodom dismounted and in royal pomp walked over to Abram. The king of Sodom had heard of Abram but he had never met him in person until now. The king of Sodom gave Abraham a hideous smile and proceeded to make a deal with him. Had the king of Sodom succeeded in manipulating Abraham into signing this "demonic contract" that the king of Sodom was passing off as a great business proposal, God would have had to look for another man to do what He had called Abraham to do. This is how serious this confrontation was to Abram's future destiny and God's purpose for his life.

The king of Sodom told Abraham to give him his people back. But he told Abraham that he could keep "the money" which the foreign invaders had stolen from the treasuries of Sodom. If Abraham had been like some ministers I know, he would have taken the "bounty from the treasuries of Sodom" and televised

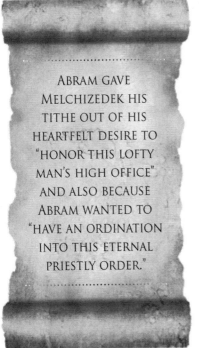

ABRAM GAVE MELCHIZEDEK HIS TITHE OUT OF HIS HEARTFELT DESIRE TO "HONOR THIS LOFTY MAN'S HIGH OFFICE" AND ALSO BECAUSE ABRAM WANTED TO "HAVE AN ORDINATION INTO THIS ETERNAL PRIESTLY ORDER."

it as testimony of a great "financial miracle." Fortunately, Abraham had just been touched by the priestly Order of Melchizedek and with the eyes of his "awakened spirit" he saw all the "poisonous snakes" that were hidden in the money bags that the king of Sodom was offering him. Had Abram taken the money from the treasuries of Sodom, he would have opened a spiritual portal for every demonic agency from the abyss which were operating in the life of the king of Sodom.

Instead of taking the money the king of Sodom offered him, Abram emphatically and publicly told the king of Sodom that his answer was a resounding, heartfelt, "NO!" Abram told the king of Sodom that there was nothing that he owned in all of Sodom which Abram desired for himself or his ministry. Abraham then proceeded to tell the king of Sodom the two main reasons why he had turned down his offer.

The first reason revealed the source of Abraham's power:

> *Abram replied to the king of Sodom, "I solemnly swear to the Lord, God Most High, Creator of heaven and earth,* **23** *that I will not take so much as a single thread or sandal thong from what belongs to you.*

Genesis 14:22

The foremost reason why Abraham refused the offer of money from the hands of the king of Sodom was because he had just established a covenant of tithe with God through Melchizedek who was the Priest of God Most High. His divine encounter with Melchizedek had shown him that God was his source for everything he needed to fulfill the prophetic call upon his life. This awesome encounter with the High Priest of the priestly Order of Melchizedek had "completely shut down the wells of greed inside the chambers of Abraham's sanctified soul." The glittering gold and silver from the treasuries of Sodom suddenly lost their lustrous appeal.

The second reason revealed the hidden demonic agenda behind the offer of the king of Sodom.

> *Otherwise you might say, 'I am the one who made Abram rich.'*

Genesis 14:22

The second reason Abraham refused the financial offer from the hands of the king of Sodom is because he knew by experience that when you take money from the devil there will always be hell to pay in the near future! Abraham had made a similar mistake a couple of years earlier when he had stretched out his hands to receive gold and silver from the hands of the king of Egypt. ***From that day forward Abraham was haunted by constant rumors that the king of Egypt was boasting and telling people that he was the one who had made Abram rich.*** These stories caused Abraham tremendous personal pain and embarrassment. The king of Sodom was now offering him the same deal, but Abram discerned that the financial offer of the king of Sodom was much more sinister and spiritually poisonous than that of the king of Egypt. The "bread and wine" which he had received from the eternal priestly Order of Melchizedek had "blessed him with a keen sense of spiritual awareness and discernment!"

Snakes in Money Bags

When the palace officials saw her, they sang her praises to Pharaoh, their king, and Sarai was taken into his palace. Then Pharaoh gave Abram many gifts because of her—sheep, goats, cattle, male and female donkeys, male and female servants, and camels. But the Lord sent terrible plagues upon Pharaoh and his household because of Sarai, Abram's wife. So Pharaoh summoned Abram and accused him sharply. "What have you done to me?" he demanded. "Why didn't you tell me she was your wife? Why did you say, 'She is my sister,' and allow me to take her as my wife? Now then, here is your wife. Take her and get out of here!"

Genesis 12:15-19

Abraham's ability to turn down the generous offer of the king of Sodom has far-reaching spiritual ramifications for the seed of Abraham. According to the principle of apostolic succession, we were all in the spiritual loins of Abraham when he said "NO" to the King of Sodom and rose above the seductive power of the gold and silver of this world. This means that if we rediscover Abraham's tithing model and our connection through it to the priestly Order of Melchizedek, the "seductive power of Mammon will be broken over our lives!" However, this will not happen until we see how our tithe connects us to the eternal priestly Order of Melchizedek.

Perhaps nothing has destroyed more good ministries than the seductive and corrupting power of money and sex. The corridors of human history are canvassed with the tragic stories of great men and women of God who used to have great earth-shaking ministries. But some of these great servants of God and their ministries were destroyed because they failed to say, "NO" to the king of Sodom. At the peak of their ministry and national notoriety, the chariots of the king of Sodom (the devil) stopped at their doorsteps and the king of Sodom made them an offer they failed to refuse. Since they failed to say "NO" to the king of Sodom, the scandalous fall of their great ministries now plagues us all. What's even more tragic is that some of the great ministries of our time that have great public appeal have already fallen to the power of the king of Sodom. They have become contaminated by the demonic Sodomic system. Even though everything on the outside looks appealing to the naked eye, the process of spiritual decline in their lives and ministries has already started. Only God and the devil know that they are carrying snakes in their money bags. "The machinery of death is already at work in their glamorous ministries."

Nothing can open demonic portals into our life and ministry for the king of Sodom to travel on like "inaccurate patterns of unlocking financial resources for our ministry." We must remember that just because something works does not mean it is right. We can manipulate the saints for money and make them give us whatever we want. But this demonic behavior in us will only set us up for death and destruction in our future destiny.

Abraham and Lot became very wealthy almost overnight when Abram lied and told Pharaoh that Sarah was his sister instead of his wife. The king of Egypt with a mouth dripping with undisguised sexual lust for Sarah gave Abram and Lot an abundance of gold, silver, and livestock, plus male and female servants. ***Abram's lie worked in his favor for a season, before it turned on him. He got blessed by cheating a king and manipulating his wife into lying against her own conscience.***

PERHAPS NOTHING HAS DESTROYED MORE GOOD MINISTRIES THAN THE SEDUCTIVE AND CORRUPTING POWER OF MONEY AND SEX.

Abram left Egypt with the bounty he had made by lying to Pharaoh and placing his wife in a very compromising situation. Abraham thought he got away with it. Nothing could have been further from the truth. What Abraham did not realize is that "resources" that are gained from using "demonic technology always come filled with snakes." These demonically-engineered snakes are preprogrammed by the enemy to strike and inject us with their poison at a strategic time in our future destiny when we are the most vulnerable. This usually happens at a time when the devil can cause the most damage to the cause of Christ. One of the snakes that was in the money bags that the king of Egypt gave to Abram was a young Egyptian maid by the name of "Hagar." The devil had "set her up as his trump card.' She was a ticking time bomb in Abraham's future destiny. When she finally exploded in Abraham and Sarah's lives, she produced an "Ishmael" in Abraham's bloodline. ***The consequences of this mistake in Abraham's life are still being felt and played out on the global scene thousands of years later.***

The Tithe of Abraham

It is absolutely essential that there be a serious and thorough upgrade in the spiritual technology that the global Church employs to exact the tithe. ***The global Church must rediscover Abraham's tithing model***. This Abrahamic tithing model (which is found in Genesis 14:7-22 and Hebrews 7) must be injected into the spiritual operations of the global Church. The contemporary Malachi 3:8-12 tithing model is "NOT THE RIGHT KEY FOR ADVANCING THE KINGDOM!" The Malachi 3:8-12 tithing model opens into the "WRONG DOOR!" This "Levitical tithe" does not have the power to release the type of interception that we need to avoid all the demonic entrapments that have been set against us (Kingdom citizens) by the king of Sodom (the devil).

This does not mean that God will not bless members of the global Church who use this Levitical tithing model. God in His mercy has blessed many in the Church who tithe according to Malachi 3:8-12, but the blessing is limited at best. I believe this is why the majority of people in the body of Christ who have been tithing faithfully for years have not seen dramatic changes in their spiritual lives and in their personal economy. *It seems to me that the greatest beneficiaries of the prosperity message in its current form are those who teach it, and who also have a national or international media platform to exact massive offerings for themselves from the masses.* But God wants us to transition to a superior "Kingdom-minded" tithing model that will usher many in the Church into the dimension of shared prosperity.

The Abrahamic tithing model which is found in the fourteenth chapter of Genesis is the only technology of tithing which will release the power we need inside our spirits to completely overcome the seductive power of the king of Sodom. Abraham's tithe is the tithe that is based upon and patterned after the priestly Order of Melchizedek. This is the "ONLY TITHING MODEL WHICH UNLOCKS THE BLESSINGS OF THE PRIESTLY ORDER OF MELCHIZEDEK!" When we start tithing as Abraham did, we are truly "looking to Abraham" who is the father of us all.

LIFE APPLICATION SECTION

Point to Ponder:

The priestly Order of Melchizedek is the only spiritual Order available to the people of our planet which has the spiritual power to intercept the seductive and corrupting power of the King of Sodom from polluting the drinking water of the Church of the living God.

Verse to Remember:

"Otherwise you might say, 'I am the one who made Abram rich.'"

Genesis 14:22

Questions to Consider:

•   What does the king of Sodom represent prophetically?

_____

_____

_____

_____

_____

•   How did Abraham's tithe into Melchizedek protect him from the seductive power of the king of Sodom?

_____

_____

_____

_____

JOURNAL YOUR THOUGHTS

Chapter
NINE

THE PRIESTLY
ORDER OF AARON

A while back my wife and I were guests in the beautiful home of one of my dear friends who pastors a thriving and governing Church in Tulsa, Oklahoma. This dear friend of mine is a well known national and international prophetess. We were sitting around her coffee table in her gorgeous kitchen, talking about things pertaining to the Kingdom of God.

Suddenly the presence of the Lord came upon her and she gave me that "prophetic bulls-eye look," which seemed to be saying, "Francis, God wants to talk to you." She started to prophesy into my life. Here is a part of what she told me through the Spirit of God. "God has called you to teach the body of Christ, roots and origins. Many people in the body of Christ do not like roots and origins, but you do," says the Lord. "God is going to use you to show the body of Christ that if the roots and origins of something they are doing are satanic, they cannot make them godly no matter what they do to them!"

Roots and Origins

When I left her house, what she had prophesied over me was ringing in my spirit like a fire alarm which had been set off by the presence of a consuming fire. All I kept hearing in my spirit were the words, "You have been called to teach the body of Christ roots and origins." Suddenly God was all over me, like a mother chicken hovers over her chicks. He started conversing with me. God began to show me things in my past that I had gone through, both the good and the bad. God showed me how everything that I had gone through was skillfully designed to bring me to a place were I could experientially and conceptually understand the type of call that God had placed upon my life. The prophecy I had just received brought into focus what has always been there in my life, but was somehow hidden from me.

God spoke to my spirit and said, "Son, I have surely called you to teach the body of Christ on the roots and origins of divine and demonic technologies and how they work!" As the light of God's glory exploded in my spirit, I started to see some of my past experiences in a new light. I was amazed to see the handwriting of God even in some very painful experiences that I had gone through. I will now share with you one of those experiences. I am hoping my story will shed light on the subject of roots and origins and how they affect us in the realm of the spirit.

In October 2002, my wife and I flew to Malaysia to attend a school of ministry hosted by Dr Jonathan David. During this school of ministry, Dr Jonathan David summoned my wife and I in front of one hundred pastors who had gathered from all over the world. He then started prophesying over us. The heart of the prophetic word was simply this; "God was calling us to start a Church in the United States!"

When we flew back to the United States, we began planning our Church launch. We were living in Oklahoma City at the time. Around this time a woman from Chicago who had attended one of my revival services there, called me. She asked me when I was going to start a church in Chicago. I knew from how well attended my Chicago conferences had been in the past that I had a decent following in the City of Chicago. So I took the call from this woman as a prophetic sign from God to start a church in Chicago.

> "GOD IS GOING TO USE YOU TO SHOW THE BODY OF CHRIST THAT IF THE ROOTS AND ORIGINS OF SOMETHING THEY ARE DOING ARE SATANIC, THEY CANNOT MAKE THEM GODLY NO MATTER WHAT THEY DO TO THEM!"

As soon as I announced to my wife that we were moving to Chicago, there was a strange uneasiness which crept into my spirit. Unfortunately, I ignored the uneasiness that was building inside my spirit and explained it away as simply the fear of moving across state lines. I wish this is all it was. Trust me, I have since learned my lesson never to ignore the prompting of the Holy Spirit.

When we arrived in Chicago, things started to go wrong almost immediately. First and foremost, the house we moved into was shrouded in a bitter legal controversy.

The self-professing Christian real estate agent who had found us this house conveniently forgot to tell us that the house we were moving into was already in foreclosure proceedings.

Secondly, the church plant was not growing as fast I had anticipated. What's more, the businesswoman who had called us in Oklahoma asking us to start a church in Chicago, only attended one of our church services, then disappeared. The church offerings were terribly low, so I was forced to attack our savings in order to support us and a church that I had started in the power of the flesh. Within a couple of months we had exhausted our savings and things were getting really desperate. The increased spiritual tension, coupled with the ensuing financial crisis, caused my wife and I to start arguing a lot. Our home was a not a home of peace during that short but painful excursion to Chicago.

In the midst of all of this spiritual turmoil, the same uneasiness I had felt before we left Oklahoma City only grew stronger. This mounting spiritual uneasiness robbed me of the little bit of joy I got out of the dismal successes we were experiencing in the growth of the new church plant. In my spirit I kept hearing God say things like, "You are not supposed to be here. This is not the place I have called you to. No matter what you do here My blessing on your life will be limited at best!"

In my desperation I made a call to Malaysia to talk with Dr. Jonathan David, who I highly respect as a true prophet of God and father in the faith. I told him that I knew that I was asking him in reverse, but I wanted him to pray and see if I was supposed to be in Chicago. He agreed to pray about my predicament and told me to call him back within two weeks.

During those two weeks I must have prayed and repented a gazillion times for having missed God. I was desperate. I was begging God to reconsider and bless what I was doing in Chicago. I negotiated with God desperately and asked Him to remember just how sincere my heart was in my service to Him. But my efforts to move on God to change His mind fell on deaf ears because my predicament had nothing to do with how pure and sincere my heart was before God. Instead it had everything to do with the "spiritual roots and origins" of the church I was asking Him to bless.

When the two weeks were up, I called Dr. Jonathan David and asked him to tell me what God had revealed to him. He proceeded to tell me that God had told him that "if I stayed in Chicago I would be able to build the church, but I would always struggle." He went on to tell me that while he was praying for me, he saw a vision of a throne of glory rising out of the state of Texas and the Lord told him that the church which He had called me to build for Him was in Texas and not Chicago! God told him that if I moved to Texas, He would give me a great church and a spiritual base from which my ministry would have a lasting impact on the whole of the United States. When I got off the phone with him, I knew I had a huge decision to make. The church I was pastoring in Chicago had now grown to around thirty-forty members.

It did not take me very much time to make my decision. God allowed the devil to overplay his hand to show me the dangerous position I was in, in the realm of the spirit. On a rainy and icy day, I decided to drive to a suburb called Calumet City to visit some pastor friends of mine. I stopped at the traffic light waiting for it to turn green. When it did, I quickly made my turn and what I saw heading towards me at full speed completely horrified me. Coming in my lane at a very high speed was a huge emergency ambulance truck, headed right for my small Mitsubishi Gallant!

If I have ever smelled death in my life, I truly smelled it that day. Out of sheer panic and chemical reflex, I swerved to the right to get out of harm's way and collided head-on with a stationary car which was waiting for the traffic light to turn green on that side of the road. The big emergency ambulance truck missed my small car by inches. My small car was a wreck, but I came out alive, without any scratches. I was terrified. The Spirit of God spoke to my heart and said, "If you do not leave Chicago, you will surely die here!"

I called my wife and told her that we were moving from Chicago. I told her that I was going to close the church we had started. She was very relieved. The Sunday following my near fatal accident, I humbly stood before our church members and asked for their forgiveness for misleading them by thinking that I could be their spiritual shepherd outside the perfect will of God. I told them that I had founded the church on a spirit of rebellion to the inner witness of the Holy Spirit, who had tried to warn me not to leave Oklahoma City.

I told them that no matter how sincere I was or they were in our service to God, God was not going to place His full blessing on our church because its "true spiritual roots and origins were based upon a spirit of rebellion to God's authority!" I begged them to forgive me and to release me from the responsibility of being their pastor. They did this with tears of regret. The people wept bitterly because they truly loved my wife and me. Seeing their tears of regret just made me more determined to get back into God's perfect will for my life, so they could also get back into theirs. ***This painful experience taught me the seriousness of "spiritual roots and origins" in the realms of the spirit.***

Lord, can Ishmael become Isaac?

Then Abraham bowed down to the ground, but he laughed to himself in disbelief. "How could I become a father at the age of 100?" he thought. "And how can Sarah have a baby when she is ninety years old?" So Abraham said to God, "May Ishmael live under your special blessing!" But God replied, "No—Sarah, your wife, will give birth to a son for you. You will name him Isaac, and I will confirm my covenant with him and his descendants as an everlasting covenant.

Genesis 17:17-19

We see this powerful prophetic principle concerning spiritual roots and origins, played out in a most revealing way in the life of Abraham, the father of faith. God had made a covenant promise to Abraham that he would give him a son who would be born through his wife, Sarah. When God gave this prophetic promise to Abraham and Sarah it was much easier for them to believe it because they were both relatively young.

Unfortunately, months of waiting turned into many years of waiting. Along the way Sarah herself gave up the hope of becoming a mother in her old age, so she came up with what looked like a brilliant idea, but was in actuality the "kiss of death." Sarah decided to help God fulfill His word of promise. She informed Abraham that she wanted him to sleep with her Egyptian maid Hagar so that the child that she gave birth to would be Sarah's.

I imagine that Sarah did not have a difficult time selling her new idea to her aging husband. How often does an old married man get the complete permission of his wife to sleep with a beautiful eighteen year old woman? Abraham was probably in Hagar's tent long before Sarah could have second thoughts. From the outside, Sarah's idea was brilliant, except for the fact that she and Abraham had not only walked into a demonic trap but they had just made a monumental error that would haunt them for the rest of their lives.

So Abram had sexual relations with Hagar, and she became pregnant. But when Hagar knew she was pregnant, she began to treat her mistress, Sarai, with contempt. 5 *Then Sarai said to Abram, "This is all your fault! I put my servant into your arms, but now that she's pregnant she treats me with contempt. The Lord will show who's wrong—you or me!"*

Genesis 16:4-5

Like a rattlesnake which has been forced into a corner, Sarah's brilliant plan quickly backfired and struck at the very core of her marriage with Abraham. The son who was born through her Egyptian maid whom she had thought would bring her great joy, only brought sorrow and death into her life. The ensuing spiritual tension created serious marital problems and infighting between Abraham and Sarah.

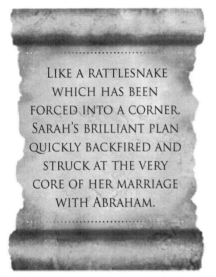

LIKE A RATTLESNAKE WHICH HAS BEEN FORCED INTO A CORNER, SARAH'S BRILLIANT PLAN QUICKLY BACKFIRED AND STRUCK AT THE VERY CORE OF HER MARRIAGE WITH ABRAHAM.

Sarah wondered why her sincere and well-thought-out plan to help God, turned out so terribly. The answer is found in understanding spiritual roots and origins. If something has its roots and origins in a satanic power play, there is little we can do to it, to change the true nature of what the thing is really about. Hagar's son, Ishmael, was born out of a spirit of "self-will and rebellion to God's authority." There was no way this child could bring the "fullness of joy and laughter" which God had promised would come with the birth of Isaac. The spiritual roots and origins of Abraham's Ishmael went all the way back to the ten gods of Egypt, not to mention the devil himself who was the principal spirit behind Egyptian idolatry.

When the appointed time came for God's Isaac to be born, Abraham had a difficult time releasing his faith because he was so enamored with the child that he had produced by his own power. Abraham actually interceded for Ishmael before God and asked God to use him in the place of Isaac. God would not hear of it. It was not because God did not respect Abraham's prayer request. God refused to hear of it because Abraham did not know the spiritual ramifications of what he was asking for. ***He did not know that when something is built on "demonic technology," its root system is rooted in hellish operations.*** No matter what God did to Ishmael, Ishmael would have remained at best half divine and half devilish. Ishmael was a mixed blessing at best.

This is precisely why I have serious issues with the popular Malachi 3:8-12 pattern of tithing, **because I know that it originates out of the Mountain of Law and its spiritual roots are steeped in legalism.** The Malachi 3:8-12 pattern of tithing describes a **Levitical tithe which was paid according to the law.** This means that "no matter how we try to spiritualize and decorate the Malachi tithing model to make it applicable to New Testament believers, its true spiritual roots and origins will always lead us back to the Mountain of Law."

Once we head back to the Mountain of Law, the fruit this mountain produces which is "legalism" will inevitably creep into our internal motivation for the giving of the tithe. Before we know it we will start basing our relationship with a loving God on the basis of whether we gave our tithes or not. The works of the Law will quickly crush and snuff out the precious embers of the flames of grace inside our heart. Just look at how well-meaning men and women of God curse God's people from the pulpit whenever they start talking about the giving of tithes and offerings.

> *"All praise to God, the Father of our Lord Jesus Christ, who has blessed us with every spiritual blessing in the heavenly realms because we are united with Christ. 4 Even before he made the world, God loved us and chose us in Christ to be holy and without fault in his eyes."*
>
> Ephesians 1:3-4

My skin crawls whenever I hear highly anointed men and women of God pronounce "curses" on their people from the pulpit. With unfeigned passion they tell their terrified people that they are "cursed" if they do not pay their tithes. Without a doubt the basis for their harsh pronouncements is Malachi 3:8-12. **It's no wonder there is so little joy in tithing in the global Church.** What's worse, we fail to discern the true spiritual condition of New Testament believers and just how perfect and complete the finished work of Christ really is. The apostle Paul reminds us in Heb. 9:15-28 that without the death of the testator and the shedding of blood, a "new testament" or "covenant" is void and cannot take effect. Since Christ fulfilled these conditions, a more excellent covenant or testament went into effect for humanity upon the death of Christ. Under the new covenant, the curse of the Law was truly canceled when Christ was crucified on the cross.

What is even more baffling to me is that according to Malachi 3:8-12, God clearly said that the priests were cursed with a curse by robbing Him of "tithes and offerings." **Why is it that those who enforce the Malachi 3:8-12 tithing model only say that someone is "cursed" if they withhold their tithe, but not their** *offerings?* This looks like selective amnesia interpretation of the Scriptures and a clear violation of the message of Malachi 3:8-12. Under the Levitical priesthood, there were specific offerings which the people of Israel had to give to the priesthood. If they withheld certain prescribed offerings, a curse would come upon them, in the same way that it did when they withheld their tithes.

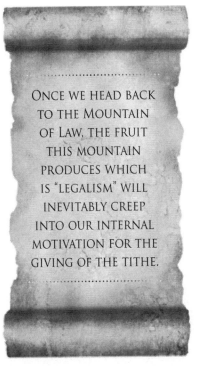

ONCE WE HEAD BACK TO THE MOUNTAIN OF LAW, THE FRUIT THIS MOUNTAIN PRODUCES WHICH IS "LEGALISM" WILL INEVITABLY CREEP INTO OUR INTERNAL MOTIVATION FOR THE GIVING OF THE TITHE.

In Ephesians 1:3-4 the apostle Paul makes it adamantly clear that "God the Father of our Lord Jesus Christ, has already (past tense) blessed us (not cursed us) with every spiritual blessing in the heavenly realms." So why do we tell our people that they are cursed, because they did not pay their tithes? Either the Father of our Lord Jesus Christ has already blessed every New Testament believer or we are still cursed. Which is it? I challenge the church of Jesus Christ to "choose you this day" which divine Order God wants us to live under in the area of tithing. I know that we are trying to motivate our people to give their tithes as they should, but the spiritual technology we are using is actually counterproductive and dangerous. There is a more excellent way of motivating the saints to give God His proper endowment of tithe. This is why this book has been written and placed in your hands by the Holy Spirit.

I have discovered that one of the quickest and most effective ways to test spiritual technologies is to apply them to our natural family. Imagine what would happen if parents are constantly telling their children that if they do not do their homework, they will place them under a curse? If parents keep saying this to their children, what kind of spiritual dynamics do you think they will create inside the spirits of their children? They will create fear, insecurity, resentment, behavior modification and legalism. The children will end up with a driving ambition to earn their parents' love, as well as their acceptance and approval. Their children would also have serious emotional problems that would require them to spend months in specialized therapy with talk show host, Dr Phil. (Just a joke, but you get the point!)

I am sure that if you love your children, you may be horrified by the picture I just painted. But why do well-meaning pastors do this to God's children? The answer is simply this: the Malachi 3:8-12 tithing model will always lead us back to the Mountain of Law, which **breeds religious legalism and practices**. Just take a closer look at people who use the Malachi 3:8-12 tithing model. **These believers vacillate between being blessed in one moment to being cursed in the next moment, as easily as one changes clothes**. When they tithe they say they are blessed. When they miss a tithe they think they are cursed. But as soon as they start tithing again they are blessed again. This is spiritual confusion and double-mindedness and a complete denial of the finished work of Christ. I am not suggesting that there are no spiritual consequences for not tithing under the priestly Order of Melchizedek. I am only saying that the punishment for not tithing is not the superimposition of a curse over the lives of God's children.

Understanding the Laws of Faith

I know that there are those who will be quick to point out that the Church has experienced great spiritual and financial blessings under the Malachi 3:8-12 tithing model. They will quickly respond by saying, "If the Malachi 3:8-12 tithing model is not for New Testament believers, why has God blessed the Church under this pattern of tithing?" This question is a very valid question which needs to be answered with surgical precision. The answer to this question is based upon a dichotomy of reasons.

IT'S DANGEROUS TO DEPEND ENTIRELY ON THE EVIDENCE OF MATERIAL BLESSINGS TO DETERMINE DIVINE APPROVAL.

1. The first reason has to do with the Mercy of God.

2. The second reason has to do with how the Law of Faith works.

There is something called the mercy of God, which in many cases causes God to overlook our faults and bless us in spite of ourselves. We know without a shadow of doubt that it was not God's perfect will for Abraham to sire a child through Hagar, his Egyptian maid. The sexual union between Abraham and Hagar which resulted in the birth of Ishmael was definitely outside the parameters of God's revealed will to both Abraham and Sarah. When God's appointed time for the birth of Isaac came, Abraham had lost his personal excitement for the birth of Isaac. Instead of giving God his resounding "amen," Abraham begged God to allow Ishmael to take the place of Isaac, the son of promise. God refused to alter His revealed will, but God did something very extraordinary and worth noting.

> *Then Abraham bowed down to the ground, but he laughed to himself in disbelief. "How could I become a father at the age of 100?" he thought. "And how can Sarah have a baby when she is ninety years old?" So Abraham said to God, "May Ishmael live under your special blessing!" But God replied, "No—Sarah, your wife, will give birth to a son for you. You will name him Isaac, and I will confirm my covenant with him and his descendants as an everlasting covenant. As for Ishmael, I will bless him also, just as you have asked. I will make him extremely fruitful and multiply his descendants. He will become the father of twelve princes, and I will make him a great nation. But my covenant will be confirmed with Isaac, who will be born to you and Sarah about this time next year."*
>
> Genesis 17:17-21

Even though the birth of Ishmael was clearly outside the will of God, God's mercy proclaimed a limited blessing upon Ishmael and his descendants. The blessing God placed on Ishmael was not God's way of endorsing what Abraham had done. God was simply demonstrating the riches of His mercy towards Abraham. ***This is why it's dangerous to depend entirely on the evidence of material blessings to determine divine approval.*** In some cases the flow of divine blessings in our lives has very little to do with our spiritual accuracy, but are mere evidences of God's mercy towards His children. To this very day the blessing of prosperity which God conferred upon Abraham's Ishmael can be seen remarkably on the Arabic nations who are the true descendants of Ishmael. Most Arabic nations are blessed with great deposits of oil, but they are also breeding grounds for international terrorism.

The second reason why God has blessed the global Church so mightily under the Malachi 3:8-12 pattern of tithing has to do with understanding one of the basic laws of faith. This basic law of faith is simply this, "everything we do in the Kingdom of God will be done to us according to our faith." This is because faith is the spiritual currency of the Kingdom. Jesus used this expression several times in the synoptic gospels to show us that this law of faith can operate even in the midst of spiritual inaccuracy. This is why faith must work alongside the Spirit of revelation. This is because faith by its very nature is largely dependent upon knowledge.

Then Jesus said to the centurion, "Go your way; and as you have believed, so let it be done for you." And his servant was healed that same hour.

Matthew 8:13

Let us examine the supernatural healings of three people in Scripture – the healing of the woman with the issue of blood, the healing of Jairus' daughter, and the healing of the Roman centurion's servant. The woman with the issue of blood got healed when she said to herself that she was going to get healed the minute she touched the hem of His garment. The only problem with the method she chose to exact her healing from God was simply this: it put her in a place where she had to fight her way through the massive crowd to get to Jesus. This was no small task for a woman whose strength and body had been ravaged by years of continuous bleeding. But when she finally touched the hem of His garment, she got healed. God responded to her according to her faith.

She had heard about Jesus, so she came up behind him through the crowd and touched his robe. **28** *For she thought to herself, "If I can just touch his robe, I will be healed."*

Mark 5:27-28

Jairus, the ruler of the Synagogue, on the other hand, exacted the healing he needed for his daughter in a very different way. He told Jesus that he believed that if Jesus traveled to his house his daughter would be healed. Only God knows how long it took for Jesus to walk all the way to Jairus' house. Maybe it took him a couple of hours of walking. When Jesus finally arrived, He was able to raise Jairus' daughter from the dead. God performed this miracle according to Jairus' faith.

Then a leader of the local synagogue, whose name was Jairus, arrived. When he saw Jesus, he fell at his feet, pleading fervently with him. "My little daughter is dying," he said. "Please come and lay your hands on her; heal her so she can live."

Mark 5:22-23

The most astounding healing took place when Jesus healed the Roman centurion's servant. Jesus received word through the leaders of a Jewish synagogue that there was a Roman centurion, who was a great supporter of Israel, whose beloved servant was severely sick. When Jesus headed towards the house of this Roman Centurion, the centurion sent some of his servants to deliver a message which quickly became music to Jesus' ears. The Roman centurion informed Jesus that he understood how authority worked since he was a high-ranking officer in the Roman army. He told Jesus not to come to his house but to "simply speak the word" and his dying servant would be healed.

Jesus quickly commented that He had never seen such great faith in the whole of Israel. Apparently the Roman Centurion had discovered a "more excellent way" of exacting healing from God. If Jairus and the woman with the issue of blood had known about this "more excellent way of exacting healing" they would have spared themselves all the drama that they went through before they got their healing. Jesus then spoke the word, and at that very instant the Roman Centurion's servant was healed. *God performed this miracle in accordance with the Roman centurion's faith.*

This book was not written to imply that the Malachi 3:8-12 tithing model has done nothing for the Church, but to simply suggest "a more excellent way of exacting the tithe from post-Calvary New Testament believers." So here is my question: "If God has blessed the global Church under an inaccurate Malachi 3:8-12 tithing model, what kind of Covenantal blessings await the Church that rediscovers the Abrahamic tithing model which is connected to Christ's eternal Order of Melchizedek priesthood?" I leave you to do the math and I rest my case.

When Jesus returned to Capernaum, a Roman officer came and pleaded with him, 6 "Lord, my young servant lies in bed, paralyzed and in terrible pain."7 Jesus said, "I will come and heal him."8 But the officer said, "Lord, I am not worthy to have you come into my home. Just say the word from where you are, and my servant will be healed.

Matthew 8:5-8

Three Generational Mantles

One of the truths which will help us have a clear-cut understanding of the priestly Order of Aaron (the Levitical priesthood) is to understand the three spiritual mantles or spiritual operations which were made available to the people who lived under the Mosaic Covenant of Law. There are three spiritual mantles which serviced the people who lived under the Old Testament. These spiritual mantles are:

1. The Kingly Mantle

2. The Prophetic Mantle

3. The Priestly Mantle

Under the Old Testament the operation of the "kingly and the priestly mantles" was taken out of the eternal structures of the Kingdom of heaven and was placed inside the "time driven" structures of the Mountain of Law. *This means that under the Mosaic dispensation, the flow of the kingly and priestly mantles was executed in accordance with the Mosaic Covenant of Law.* Under the Old Testament the kingly and priestly mantles could never function above the regulations of the Mountain of Law. Under the Mosaic Covenant of Law the Levites (the priesthood) were responsible for teaching the nation of Israel the Law of God, but it was the Kings of Israel who had the power to enforce it. Under the Mosaic Covenant dispensation, Jewish kings could never make laws because the laws that governed the nation of Israel were already established by God under the Mosaic Covenant of Law.

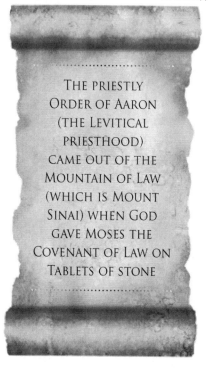

THE PRIESTLY ORDER OF AARON (THE LEVITICAL PRIESTHOOD) CAME OUT OF THE MOUNTAIN OF LAW (WHICH IS MOUNT SINAI) WHEN GOD GAVE MOSES THE COVENANT OF LAW ON TABLETS OF STONE

What is worth noting here is that God never ever placed the prophetic mantle under the Mountain of Law! God kept the operations of the prophetic mantle separate from the operations and restrictive time-driven structures of the Mountain of Law. This does not mean that Old Testament prophets were personally above the Law of Moses; it simply means that their "prophetic mantles" could easily "transcend" the restrictive dictates of the Mountain of Law. Even in the Old Testament the operation of the prophet's mantle was based upon the eternal structures of the Kingdom of Heaven. *This is why prophets were very important to the people of Israel, because their prophetic grace transcended the restrictive nature of the Mountain of Law.* This is why much of what is written in the prophetic books of the Old Testament has a lot of relevance for New Testament believers.

The point I am trying to drive to is simply this: "other than the prophetic mantle, the operation of the kingly and priestly mantles was based upon the Mountain of Law." **This simply means that tithing under the Levitical priesthood is and was always in accordance with the Law.** This means that no matter what we say or do, we cannot change the spiritual roots and origins of the Malachi 3:8-12 tithing model. The Mosaic spirit which governs this Levitical tithe will always lead us back to the Mountain of Law. This would explain why the Malachi 3:8-12 tithing model easily lends itself to "legalism."

The Priestly Order of Aaron

"Call for your brother, Aaron, and his sons, Nadab, Abihu, Eleazar, and Ithamar. Set them apart from the rest of the people of Israel so they may minister to me and be my priests."

Exodus 28:1

There are only two priestly orders which God ever gave to mankind – the priestly Order of Aaron and the priestly Order of Melchizedek. For this reason both of these priesthoods are very important to God's revealed will for His people. The priestly Order of Aaron (the Levitical priesthood) came out of the Mountain of Law (which is Mount Sinai) when God gave Moses the Covenant of Law on Tablets of stone. We will now go over a summarized overview of the spiritual characteristics of the Levitical priesthood.

1. The Levitical priestly Order was based upon the Mountain of Law.

"So if the priesthood of Levi, on which the law was based, could have achieved the perfection God intended, why did God need to establish a different priesthood, with a priest in the order of Melchizedek instead of the order of Levi and Aaron?"

Hebrews 7:11

2. The Levitical priestly Order derived all its High Priests from the sons of Aaron.

"Now take Aaron your brother, and his sons with him, from among the children of Israel, that he may minister to Me as priest, Aaron and Aaron's sons: Nadab, Abihu, Elemazar, and Ithamar."

Exodus 28:1 (NKJV)

3. The Levitical priestly Order was commanded to collect tithes from their brethren in accordance with the Law.

"Now the law of Moses required that the priests, who are descendants of Levi, must collect a tithe from the rest of the people of Israel, who are also descendants of Abraham."

Hebrews 7:5

4. The tithing under the Levitical priestly Order was simply payment for priestly services rendered to the people.

"As for the tribe of Levi, your relatives, I will compensate them for their service in the Tabernacle. Instead of an allotment of land, I will give them the tithes from the entire land of Israel."

Numbers 18:21

5 Under the Levitical priestly Order, the priesthood was only chosen from the tribe of Levi.

"So if the priesthood of Levi, on which the law was based, could have achieved the perfection God intended, why did God need to establish a different priesthood, with a priest in the order of Melchizedek instead of the order of Levi and Aaron."

Hebrews 7:11

6. Under the Levitical priestly Order, the priests were responsible for teaching the Jewish nation how to abide by the Mosaic Law.

"The words of a priest's lips should preserve knowledge of God, and people should go to him for instruction, for the priest is the messenger of the Lord of Heaven's Armies. **8** *But you priests have left God's paths. Your instructions have caused many to stumble into sin. You have corrupted the covenant I made with the Levites," says the Lord of Heaven's Armies."*

Malachi 2:7-8

7. Under the Levitical priestly Order the priests had no ownership of land.

And the Lord said to Aaron, "You priests will receive no allotment of land or share of property among the people of Israel. I am your share and your allotment."

Numbers 18:20

8. Under the Levitical priestly Order, the High Priest could only come into the holy of holies once a year.

"But only the high priest ever entered the Most Holy Place, and only once a year. And he always offered blood for his own sins and for the sins the people had committed in ignorance."

Hebrews 9:7

9. Under the Levitical priestly Order, a curse as prescribed by the Mosaic Law was placed upon those who withheld their tithes and offerings.

"Should people cheat God? Yet you have cheated me! "But you ask, 'What do you mean? When did we ever cheat you?' "You have cheated me of the tithes and offerings due to me. You are under a curse, for your whole nation has been cheating me.'

Malachi 3:8-9

10. The Levitical priestly Order was ordained by God to minister to the Jewish nation who lived under the Mosaic Covenant of Law.

"Fasten the two stones on the shoulder-pieces of the ephod as a reminder that Aaron represents the people of Israel. Aaron will carry these names on his shoulders as a constant reminder whenever he goes before the Lord."

Exodus 28:12

11. The spiritual jurisdiction of the Levitical priestly Order did not extend beyond the natural borders of Israel. This is why Jews who were in captivity had to pray facing the direction of the City of Jerusalem in order to get their prayers answered.

"But when Daniel learned that the law had been signed, he went home and knelt down as usual in his upstairs room, with its windows open toward Jerusalem. He prayed three times a day, just as he had always done, giving thanks to his God."

Daniel 6:10

12. The Levitical priestly Order was responsible for offering gifts and sacrifices to God for the remissions of the sins of the Jewish nation.

"When these things were all in place, the priests regularly entered the first room[c] as they performed their religious duties. 7 But only the high priest ever entered the Most Holy Place, and only once a year. And he always offered blood for his own sins and for the sins the people had committed in ignorance."

Hebrews 9:6-7

13. Under Levitical priestly Order, the High Priest had to offer gifts and sacrifices for his own sins.

"He is the kind of high priest we need because he is holy and blameless, unstained by sin. He has been set apart from sinners and has been given the highest place of honor in heaven.] 27 Unlike those other high priests, he does not need to offer sacrifices every day. They did this for their own sins first and then for the sins of the people."

Hebrews 7:26-27

14. The Levitical priestly Order was designed to be a transitional priestly Order, until the arrival of the priestly Order of Melchizedek through our Lord Jesus Christ.

"But now Jesus, our High Priest, has been given a ministry that is far superior to the old priesthood, for he is the one who mediates for us a far better covenant with God, based on better promises. If the first covenant had been faultless, there would have been no need for a second covenant to replace it."

Hebrews 8:6-7

15. The Levitical priestly Order was constantly harassed by the spirit of death.

"There were many priests under the old system, for death prevented them from remaining in office. But because Jesus lives forever, his priesthood lasts forever."

Hebrews 7:23

16. The Levitical priestly Order is an earthly priesthood, which ministers outside the eternal structures of the Kingdom of heaven.

"If he were here on earth, he would not even be a priest, since there already are priests who offer the gifts required by the law. They serve in a system of worship that is only a copy, a shadow of the real one in heaven."

Hebrews 8:4-5

17. The Levitical priestly Order was constantly held hostage by the personal and inherent weaknesses of its High Priests.

"The law appointed high priests who were limited by human weakness. But after the law was given, God appointed his Son with an oath, and his Son has been made the perfect High Priest forever."

Hebrews 7:28

18. The Levitical priestly Order was harassed constantly by generational spirits and curses, because it was based on an earthly ancestry.

"Every high priest is a man chosen to represent other people in their dealings with God. He presents their gifts to God and offers sacrifices for their sins. And he is able to deal gently with ignorant and wayward people because he himself is subject to the same weaknesses. That is why he must offer sacrifices for his own sins as well as theirs."

Hebrews 5:1-3

19. Under the Levitical priestly Order, only the priests from the tribe of Levi could come near the presence of God.

"From now on, no Israelites except priests or Levites may approach the Tabernacle. If they come too near, they will be judged guilty and will die."

Numbers 18:22

20. According to the Malachi 3:8-12 pattern of tithing, there are at least six major benefits of tithing into the Levitical priestly Order.

Bring all the tithes into the storehouse, That there may be food in My house, And try Me now in this, "Says the LORD of hosts, " If I will not open for you the windows of heaven And pour out for you such blessing That there will not be room enough to receive it." And I will rebuke the devourer for your sakes, So that he will not destroy the fruit of your ground, Nor shall the vine fail to bear fruit for you in the field," Says the LORD of hosts; And all nations will call you blessed, For you will be a delightful land," Says the LORD of hosts.

Malachi 3:10-12 (NKJV)

Spiritual Benefits of Tithing into the Levitical Priesthood

1. The Opening of the Windows of heaven
2. A Poured Out Blessing with not enough room to receive it
3. The Rebuking of the Devourer by God for the people's sake
4. Preservation of the Fruits of the ground
5. Protection from untimely harvest
6. Nations shall call you blessed

There were Two Trees

And out of the ground the LORD God made every tree grow that is pleasant to the sight and good for food. The tree of life was also in the midst of the garden, and the tree of the knowledge of good and evil.

Genesis 2:9

The Old Testament is full of important prophetic patterns. Whenever these prophetic patterns are illuminated by the Holy Spirit, they reveal spiritual pathways to important spiritual truths. The Scriptures give us a very detailed account of the creation and the beginning of human and animal life as we know it. We are told in the Genesis account that God planted a Garden in Eden, where He placed the man whom He had created.

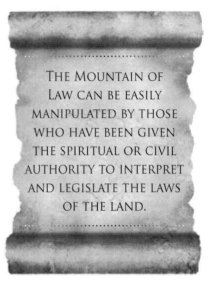

THE MOUNTAIN OF LAW CAN BE EASILY MANIPULATED BY THOSE WHO HAVE BEEN GIVEN THE SPIRITUAL OR CIVIL AUTHORITY TO INTERPRET AND LEGISLATE THE LAWS OF THE LAND.

This divine garden was a garden of tremendous beauty and untold abundance. The most unique thing about this garden is that God planted two spiritual trees on the center of the garden. *The two trees were the tree of life and the tree of the knowledge of good and evil*. These two trees have powerful prophetic symbolic representations. These two trees allude to the Old and New Testaments. These two trees speak of the first and last Adam. Most importantly, these two trees serve as a prophetic picture of the only two priesthoods that God ever gave to mankind. The tree of life which speaks of Christ correlates with the eternal priestly Order of Melchizedek, whereas the tree of the knowledge of good and evil speaks of the Mountain of Law and correlates with the earthly priestly Order of Aaron.

The tree of the knowledge of good and evil is the Mountain of Law. The Mountain of Law is the foundation of right and wrong, justice and injustice, good and evil. This is why the Ten Commandments which Moses wrote under divine inspiration are based upon the Mountain of Law. The Mountain of Law also controls the flow of blessings and curses within the earthly structure. *The Mountain of Law is the basis for determining rewards and punishment within the earthly realm.* The Mountain of Law is also the foundation of the judicial systems of most Law-abiding nations. The Mountain of Law can be easily manipulated by those who have been given the spiritual or civil authority to interpret and legislate the laws of the land.

It was never God's will for Adam and Eve to eat of the fruit that originated from the Mountain of Law. God told them very plainly that eating from the tree of the knowledge of good and evil, would only result in introducing them to the machinery of death. This is because the Mountain of Law always stirs man's individual sense of reasoning, placing him in a position where he (and not God) has to decide what is good and what is evil. *This in itself is death, because spiritual death is simply separation from God in any area of our lives.*

God never ever intended for man to eat from the tree of the knowledge of good and evil, but from the tree of Life. Have you ever wondered why God never warned Adam and Eve against eating from the tree of Life? The answer is simply this: the tree of Life represented the incorruptible Life of Christ and God never stops people from partaking of the Life of His dear Son. If Adam and Eve had eaten of the tree of Life instead of the forbidden tree, their entire system of reasoning would have taken on the complete nature of Christ. God would have been the focal point of their reasoning, instead of self. So here are two million-dollar questions: "Why did God base His covenant with Israel on the basis of the Mountain of Law? Why would God base the Levitical priesthood on the foundation of the Mountain of Law?"

"I have discovered this principle of life—that when I want to do what is right, I inevitably do what is wrong. I love God's law with all my heart. But there is another power[b] within me that is at war with my mind. This power makes me a slave to the sin that is still within me."

Romans 7:21-23

The answer to the first question is simply this: God wanted to show the children of Israel and all the inhabitants of the earth how utterly depraved and self-absorbed mankind has become. God had to show the children of Israel just how much they needed a Savior who could save them from themselves and from the righteous demands of the Law of Moses. Inherently they knew that the Law of God was good and that its righteous demands were also honorable. But they also discovered that their fallen nature was set against obeying God's holy law even when their minds agreed with it.

Before God gave the nation of Israel the Covenant of Law they had no idea just how widespread the sin nature in them had become. This is why the Bible says that before the giving of the Law there was no sin. This statement does not in anyway mean that there was no sin at work in the earth before the giving of the Mosaic Law. But before the Law was given, there was nothing that we could measure ourselves against to see whether or not we were in compliance with God's Law. It was a state of lawlessness summarized by "each man did what was right in his own eyes."

"The old system under the law of Moses was only a shadow, a dim preview of the good things to come, not the good things themselves. The sacrifices under that system were repeated again and again, year after year, but they were never able to provide

perfect cleansing for those who came to worship. If they could have provided perfect cleansing, the sacrifices would have stopped, for the worshipers would have been purified once for all time, and their feelings of guilt would have disappeared."

Hebrews 10:1-2

The answer to the second question builds upon the answer to the first. The reason God built the priestly Order of Aaron on the basis of the Mountain of Law was to demonstrate to the children of Israel that there was no way that they could be redeemed from the power of sin and death by following the works of the law. After innumerable blood sacrifices the people who lived under the Levitical priesthood began to discover that their many sacrifices did little to ease their guilt-ridden conscience. This constant struggle with the machinery of sin in their lives began to breed a sense of spiritual despair and desperation among the people, which in turn made the people look forward to the coming of a future Messiah who would save them from sin.

There were Two Women and Two Sons

"Tell me, you who want to live under the law, do you know what the law actually says? The Scriptures say that Abraham had two sons, one from his slave wife and one from his freeborn wife. The son of the slave wife was born in a human attempt to bring about the fulfillment of God's promise. But the son of the freeborn wife was born as God's own fulfillment of his promise. These two women serve as an illustration of God's two covenants. The first woman, Hagar, represents Mount Sinai where people received the law that enslaved them. And now Jerusalem is just like Mount Sinai in Arabia, because she and her children live in slavery to the law. But the other woman, Sarah, represents the heavenly Jerusalem. She is the free woman, and she is our mother."

Galatians 4:21-26

The apostle Paul also tells us that Abraham's two sons are of great consequence in the progressive revelation of God to His people. Saint Paul tells us that Abraham's two sons, Ishmael and Isaac, represent two priesthoods and two separate and distinct covenants of God with man. The great apostle to the Church tells us that Ishmael who came out of Hagar represents the Covenant of Law which God gave to Moses on Mount Sinai. The apostle Paul also tells us that this covenant from Mount Sinai is serviced by an earthly priesthood which operates out of the temple in natural Jerusalem. We know that this priesthood is the Levitical priesthood.

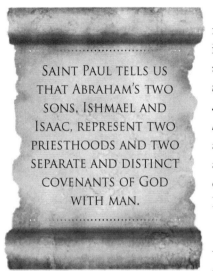

SAINT PAUL TELLS US THAT ABRAHAM'S TWO SONS, ISHMAEL AND ISAAC, REPRESENT TWO PRIESTHOODS AND TWO SEPARATE AND DISTINCT COVENANTS OF GOD WITH MAN.

The apostle Paul also tells us that natural Jerusalem (including everything in it) is in bondage with her children. *So why in God's name would we want to tithe into a priesthood which Paul says is in a season of bondage with her children?* This is exactly what we are doing when we teach people to tithe according to Malachi 3:8-12, which describes a tithe in accordance with the Law.

On the other hand, Paul the Apostle tells us that Abraham's second son, Isaac represents the New Testament Covenant of Grace and spiritual Jerusalem which is the mother of us all. We know from the Scriptures that the priestly Order of Melchizedek is a heavenly priesthood which operates from within the eternal structures of spiritual Jerusalem. This is the priesthood that we need to be tithing into. This Abrahamic tithing model is going to bring us into great spiritual freedom even as spiritual Jerusalem is free.

How the Mosaic Generation Tithed

"So I want to remind you, though you already know these things, that Jesus first rescued the nation of Israel from Egypt, but later he destroyed those who did not remain faithful."

Jude 1:5

When we use the phrase "the Mosaic generation," we are referring to the generation of Israelites who came out of Egypt with Moses up to the generation of Israelites who saw the birth and crucifixion of Jesus Christ. Before concluding this chapter we will now look at how the Mosaic generation tithed.

1. They paid a tithe according to the Law.

"Now the law of Moses required that the priests, who are descendants of Levi, must collect a tithe from the rest of the people of Israel, who are also descendants of Abraham."

Hebrews 7:5

Please remember that the Levitical priesthood was based upon the Mountain of Law. This means that even the paying and practice of tithing was done in accordance with the Mosaic Covenant of Law. Under the Levitical priesthood, paying one's tithes was as expected and as required as the paying of taxes. Paying taxes in America is the law of the land and it is strictly enforced. Failure to pay one's taxes can have disastrous consequences. This is what the paying of tithes was like under the priestly Order of Aaron.

2.   Their tithe was payment for priestly services rendered.

"As for the tribe of Levi, your relatives, I will compensate them for their service in the Tabernacle. Instead of an allotment of land, I will give them the tithes from the entire land of Israel."

Numbers 18:21

Under the Levitical priesthood, the "concept of giving tithes did not really exist." The tithe was not "given;" it was "paid out." The difference here is critical, inviting further investigation. "Giving" always involves the concept of "freewill and also invokes the involvement of our highest nature," while "paying" always involves the concept of "meeting one's financial obligations." Here is an example to illustrate my point.

My gas company is a company based out of Houston, Texas called "Reliant Energy." Every month this company is responsible for providing the energy I need to run my house. At the end of the month they send me a bill for the services that they have rendered. The fact of the matter is that I have no emotional obligation to them, but I definitely have a financial obligation to them. They have provided a service, whose benefits I enjoyed for a whole month and now it is my time to pay for services rendered. Failure to do so would result in my gas being turned off. What's more, failure to pay a legitimate bill over time is tantamount to stealing, and can potentially harm your credit rating.

Tithing under the Mosaic generation was no different from the above illustration. Tithing under the Levitical priesthood was strictly payment for priestly services that the tribes of Israel were receiving from the priesthood. Members of the tribe of Levi who were also the priests of Israel were not allowed by divine decree to own their own land. God gave them no inheritance of land. Their life occupation was to serve in the office of a priest all the days of their lives.

To ensure that the priests and their families did not starve to death or live in poverty, God gave them the tithes of the tribes of Israel. The tithes of the

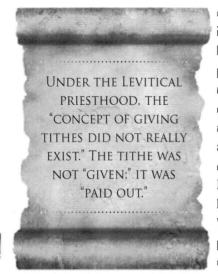

UNDER THE LEVITICAL PRIESTHOOD, THE "CONCEPT OF GIVING TITHES DID NOT REALLY EXIST." THE TITHE WAS NOT "GIVEN;" IT WAS "PAID OUT."

children of Israel became the spiritual inheritance of the tribe of Levi. These tithes became the rightful wages of the Levitical priesthood. *This is why tithing under the Levitical priesthood was "paid out" and not "given out." The people had no choice but to pay it. Failure to do so was tantamount to "stealing or robbing a bank."* This is exactly what the Prophet Malachi is alluding to in Malachi 3:8, when he asks the question, "Will a man rob God?" Withholding tithes under the Levitical priesthood was like evading the paying of one's taxes. In the United States of America people have been thrown into prison for tax evasion. This is because the US government considers tax evasion another form of robbing the government. In America, tax evasion is a felony offense.

On the other hand, since the tithe was payment for priestly services, the people of Israel who tithed into the Levitical priesthood had a legal right to expect the priests to provide them with the stipulated priestly services. If the priests failed to perform their priestly assignments to the people, they automatically forfeited their rights to the tithes of the people. This is the prevailing context of the book of Malachi.

Under the priestly Order of Melchizedek, the tithe is "given as a royal endowment of honor." It is never ever "paid out." This is because the High Priest after the Order of Melchizedek (Jesus Christ) is both God and King, and as such He can never be under the payroll of His own Kingdom citizens. To even imply the "paying of tithes" is an insult under this divine royal priestly Order. This means that under the Order of Melchizedek, our pastors do not have to give us priestly services in order to earn our tithes.

Under the priestly Order of Melchizedek, our tithes already belong to our faithful High Priest who is both God and King of the Universe. As God and King, Christ does not need to perform for us in order to earn our tithe, because everything we have and use to acquire resources belongs to Him, anyway. But out of our own "free will" we can choose to "give Him" the royal endowment of tithe as faithful stewards in His Kingdom.

Under the priestly Order of Melchizedek, the priestly services that our High Priest provides for His Kingdom citizens through His earthly under-shepherds (senior pastors, bishops and apostolic leaders) are secondary to the fact that He is worthy of all our praise and adoration. This also means that under the priestly Order of Melchizedek, we cannot withhold our tithes from the Church where God has planted us, even when we feel like the senior pastor is not giving us sufficient priestly services. *The demonic mindset which causes people to withhold their tithes originates from the Church's usage of Malachi 3:8-12 as our New Testament model of tithing.* This inaccuracy in our technology of tithing must come to an end.

Nevertheless, I do not want to be misconstrued that I am supporting the spiritual neglect of the sheep by senior leaders of Churches. This is a far cry from what I am suggesting. It is very important for senior church leaders to do their best to feed the flock that God has placed in their care. And depending on the size of the organization, wise leaders will delegate or assign some portion of this "pastoral" work to faithful men, just as Moses did when he appointed the seventy elders. But I do want to be clear that New Testament believers do not have the right or spiritual grounds under

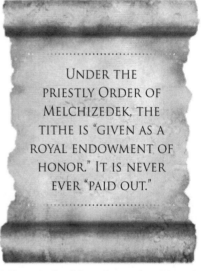

UNDER THE PRIESTLY ORDER OF MELCHIZEDEK, THE TITHE IS "GIVEN AS A ROYAL ENDOWMENT OF HONOR." IT IS NEVER EVER "PAID OUT."

the priestly Order of Melchizedek for withholding their tithes from the Church of God because they are offended with the senior pastor.

3. A Curse as prescribed by the Mosaic Law came upon non-tithers.

"You are under a curse, for your whole nation has been cheating me."

Malachi 3:9

The prophet Malachi asks a very important question: "Will a man rob God?" He then proceeds to tell the Jewish people who lived under the Mosaic Covenant of Law just how they had robbed God. Malachi told them that they had robbed God by withholding the tithes and offerings that they were required by the Law to pay to the Levites and the household of Aaron in exchange for the priestly services that they were receiving. The sentence for withholding these tithes and offerings was the superimposition of a curse upon their lives. The Prophet Haggai describes in great detail how this curse worked itself out.

> *"Then the Lord sent this message through the prophet Haggai: "Why are you living in luxurious houses while my house lies in ruins? This is what the Lord of Heaven's Armies says: Look at what's happening to you! You have planted much but harvest little. You eat but are not satisfied. You drink but are still thirsty. You put on clothes but cannot keep warm. Your wages disappear as though you were putting them in pockets filled with holes!"*

Haggai 1:3-6

Here is the billion-dollar question: "Who cursed these non-tithers and why did they get cursed?" The answer is simple but deeply profound. These non-tithers were not cursed by God but by the Mountain of Law that the whole Levitical priesthood was founded on. **Had God cursed them, the curse would have remained unbreakable, because everything God decrees in eternity becomes eternal.** These non-tithers were cursed by the same Mosaic Law which guaranteed them the blessings of God if they obeyed its righteous requirements. This means that: if they were cursed for not obeying the righteous demands of the Law in the area of tithes and offerings, they could also break the curse imposed by the Law by simply coming back into a place of obedience to the same Law. The reason why such a "curse" was imposed upon non-tithing Israelites is due to the fact that the Mountain of Law is the basis for blessings and curses within the "cylinder of time." The Mountain of Law makes allowances for the release of both good and evil, blessings and curses, life and death, from the same spiritual stream. God in His infinite wisdom placed the Mountain of Law within the cylinder of time. *"Time" therefore is the greatest custodian of whatever issues out of the Mountain of Law. This is why when the Law puts a person in prison, they are said to be "doing time."*

The time span for the flow of "generational blessings" was set to span a thousand generations, whereas the life span of "generational curses" were set to run up to the fourth generation. This is very important for us to understand. God quarantined the power of whatever issues out of the Mountain of Law within the cylinder of time to ensure that there is always "a way of escape" for those who find themselves on the wrong side of the Law. This means then that whatever curse falls upon us within the cylinder of time can be also reversed "in time" by the power of God when we make the right choices." Time therefore is the most important spiritual factor that controls whatever comes out of the Mountain of Law.

"Then the angel showed me a river with the water of life, clear as crystal, flowing from the throne of God and of the Lamb. 2 It flowed down the center of the main street. On each side of the river grew a tree of life, bearing twelve crops of fruit, with a fresh crop each month. The leaves were used for medicine to heal the nations. 3 No longer will there be a curse upon anything. For the throne of God and of the Lamb will be there, and his servants will worship him."

Rev 22:1-3

On the other hand, the priestly Order of Melchizedek operates from within the "eternal structures of the Kingdom of Heaven." This eternal priesthood operates out of the same eternal structure where we find the "throne of God and of the Lamb." *According to the Apostle John, "no curse" can exist in a spiritual structure which contains both the throne of God and of the Lamb.* This is why New Testament pastors cannot threaten New Testament believers who live under the priestly Order of Melchizedek with a "curse" if they fail to give their tithes and offerings.

Please remember that the priestly Order of Melchizedek operates out of the "Tree of Life," which has "no curse in it." This does not mean that there are no spiritual consequences for not tithing under the priestly Order of Melchizedek. Under Christ's Order of Melchizedek priesthood, "non-tithers" are "Chastised" and not "Cursed." Under the New Testament, God uses the instrument of "divine chastisement" to discipline or correct the rebellious among His blood-washed children. Under the priestly Order of Melchizedek, non-tithers are "chastised" with a "diminishing capacity for manifesting the favor of God." When our spiritual capacity for manifesting the favor of God becomes diminished, it is quite difficult to get the spiritual breakthroughs we need in "reasonable time frames." Spiritual breakthroughs that should come relatively easy in our life suddenly become subject to serious warfare in the spiritual realm, because our ability to manifest the favor of God is constantly diminishing. If we continue to dishonor God by refusing to give Him His proper endowment of tithe, God will eventually stop giving us the "bread and wine" of revelation. This means that the flow of God's divine revelation and the anointing of His precious Holy Spirit will also begin to diminish. This is because under the priestly Order of Melchizedek, the Holy Spirit is given to those who obey the Priest of God Most High and the King of kings (even our Lord Jesus Christ).

"And we are His witnesses to these things, and so also is the Holy Spirit whom God has given to those who obey Him."

Acts 5:32

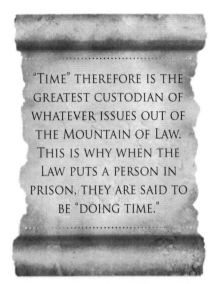

4. They brought their tithes to the Storehouse.

"Bring all the tithes into the storehouse so there will be enough food in my Temple. If you do," says the Lord of Heaven's Armies, *"I will open the windows of heaven for you. I will pour out a blessing so great you won't have enough room to take it in! Try it! Put me to the test!"*

Malachi 3:10

Under the Mosaic generation the people who were serviced by the Levitical priesthood were also instructed to bring their tithes and offerings to the Storehouse, which was the temple of God in Jerusalem. God promised to open the windows of heaven for them and pour out a blessing for them if they brought their tithes and offerings to His house. The bringing of tithes and offerings to the storehouse (local Church) is one of the similarities between the Levitical priesthood and the priestly Order of Melchizedek. Under both priestly orders, one of the sacred places that God has sanctified to receive the tithes of God's people, is the storehouse (local Church).

LIFE APPLICATION SECTION

Point to Ponder:

According to the apostle John, "no curse" can exist in an eternal structure which has both the throne of God and of the Lamb. This is why as pastors we cannot threaten New Testament believers who live and tithe into the priestly Order of Melchizedek with a curse if they do not tithe.

Verse to Remember:

"So if the priesthood of Levi, on which the law was based, could have achieved the perfection God intended, why did God need to establish a different priesthood, with a priest in the order of Melchizedek instead of the order of Levi and Aaron?"

Hebrews 7:11

Questions to Consider:

• Who was the first High Priest of the Levitical priesthood?

_____

_____

_____

_____

_____

• Why was the tithe a payment for priestly services under the priestly Order of Aaron?

_____

_____

_____

_____

Journal Your Thoughts

THE POWER OF
THE TITHE

O ne of the major differences between the Levitical priestly
Order and the priestly Order of Melchizedek is that the
"power of the tithe" under each of these priesthoods is
significantly different. Comparing the power of the tithe under these
two priestly orders is like **comparing the power of a grenade to
the power of a nuclear bomb.** If you were to drop a grenade in a
crowded market you might kill and injure a handful of people and cause
a little bit of structural damage. On the other hand if we were to drop
a nuclear bomb the resulting loss of lives and the ensuing structural
damage would be catastrophic.

I know that this illustration might be too graphic for some people
but I am trying to illustrate the astronomical difference between
the **power of the tithe** under the priestly order of Aaron and the
priestly order of Melchizedek. There are **seven major factors** which
determine the power of the tithe that we will examine closely in
this chapter.

The Nature of the High Priest

The first spiritual factor which affects the power of the tithe is the
"spiritual nature of the High Priest who presides over the priesthood"
that we are tithing into. Consider for instance that Eli's tenure as the
High Priest over the nation of Israel released spiritual darkness and
apathy in the nation because of his spiritual passivity. When Samuel
was about twelve years old the Word of the Lord came to him. The
first book of Samuel describes in great detail the spiritual prevailing
atmosphere at the time with this expression: "the visions of God were

rare in those days." When the presiding priesthood is corrupt and weak in its spiritual dynamics, the "proceeding Word of God becomes rare and the light of God's word does not shine brightly."

"Meanwhile, the boy Samuel served the Lord by assisting Eli. Now in those days messages from the Lord were very rare, and visions were quite uncommon. 2 One night Eli, who was almost blind by now, had gone to bed. 3 The lamp of God had not yet gone out, and Samuel was sleeping in the Tabernacle near the Ark of God."

1 Samuel 3:1-2

COMPARING THE POWER OF THE TITHE UNDER THESE TWO PRIESTLY ORDERS IS LIKE COMPARING THE POWER OF A GRENADE TO THE POWER OF A NUCLEAR BOMB.

Every priesthood draws its life and anointing from the spiritual stature of its High Priest. This is why Eli's failure to father and discipline his sons, Hophni and Phinehas, short-circuited the flow and move of God in the priesthood of Eli. God failed to do mighty things through the priesthood of Eli, because his "passivity as a natural father" to his sons had seriously compromised the spiritual integrity of his priesthood. The priesthood lost its spiritual potency and became set on the pathway of death. Under Eli's watch the ungodly Philistines "captured the Ark of God!" When Eli heard of this he fell from his chair, broke his neck and died.

Aaron, the first High Priest of the nation of Israel, was also subject to "demonic influences and human manipulation." When the people of Israel saw that Moses was taking too long in returning to them from his time with God, they "pressured Aaron to make them a golden calf which they could worship in the place of God!" Aaron succumbed to the constant pressure from the people and made them a diabolical golden calf that they started worshipping. This diabolical action by Aaron, who was the presiding High Priest at the time, *opened the door for spiritual invasion by demon-powers and compromised the power and integrity of the priesthood.*

"All the people took the gold rings from their ears and brought them to Aaron. Then Aaron took the gold, melted it down, and molded it into the shape of a calf. When the people saw it, they exclaimed, 'O Israel, these are the gods who brought you out of the land of Egypt!'"

Exodus 32:3-4

Under the priestly Order of Melchizedek, our High Priest is both "perfect man and perfect God." Jesus Christ was so much man that He got hungry and also got tired. He was so much God that He spoke to a man who had been dead for four days and raised him from the dead. His spiritual nature is one of complete and uninterrupted righteousness. The high priest of the priestly Order of Melchizedek has never been stained by personal sin. He lives in a place of mastery over the machinery of sin and death. He is the very essence of the anointing. He is the "Christ" which literally means, "the anointed One and His anointing." No other High Priest has ever worn this title.

Even though all the High Priests under the Levitical priesthood were anointed by God, none of them was "saturated with the presence and anointing of the Holy Spirit" like Jesus was. The testimony of the Prophet John the Baptist concerning the High Priest (Jesus Christ) of the priestly Order of Melchizedek is simply this; *"...to **Him has been given the Spirit without measure"*** (**John 2**). We can't even fathom the unlimited measure of spiritual power which the High Priest of the priestly Order of Melchizedek brings to bear upon the ***"tithe of those who tithe into His eternal priestly Order."*** The "Malachi 3:8-12 tithing model" connects our tithe to the "limited anointing and spiritual stature" of the earth-bound Levitical priesthood. When we employ the Malachi tithing model we are short- circuiting and limiting our own spiritual blessings.

> *"The law appointed high priests who were limited by human weakness. But after the law was given, God appointed his Son with an oath, and his Son has been made the perfect High Priest forever."*
>
> Hebrews 7:28

The Spiritual Rank of the High Priest

The second critical factor which seriously affects the power of the tithe between the Levitical priesthood and the priestly Order of Melchizedek is "the spiritual rank of the presiding High Priest." Everything in the Kingdom of God and in the kingdom of darkness is based upon spiritual ranking. The spiritual rank a person occupies within the eternal structures of the Kingdom of Heaven will greatly influence how demon-powers and circumstances respond to the sound of their voice of command. Let's consider for a moment the role which spiritual ranking played in the humiliation of the seven sons of Sceva who were overpowered by a demon-possessed man.

A group of Jews was traveling from town to town casting out evil spirits. They tried to use the name of the Lord Jesus in their incantation, saying, "I command you in the name of Jesus, whom Paul preaches, to come out!" Seven sons of Sceva, a leading priest, were doing this. But one time when they tried it, the evil spirit replied, "I know Jesus, and I know Paul, but who are you?" Then the man with the evil spirit leaped on them, overpowered them, and attacked them with such violence that they fled from the house, naked and battered.

Acts 19:13-16

The seven sons of Sceva observed the apostle Paul casting out demons and sought to imitate him. They thought that Paul's spiritual power and authority over demonic spirits was derived from a spiritual formula. So they copied Paul's method for casting out demons and tried to duplicate this spiritual technology with disastrous consequences. They went into the house of a demon-possessed man and began the process of casting out the evil spirits that were residing in him. Here is what they said to the demon-powers: "We charge you to come out of this man in the name of Jesus Christ whom Paul preaches about!"

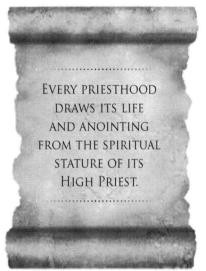

EVERY PRIESTHOOD DRAWS ITS LIFE AND ANOINTING FROM THE SPIRITUAL STATURE OF ITS HIGH PRIEST.

At the sound of their voice of command the demon-possessed man responded by saying, "Jesus we know and Paul we know, but who are you?" The demonic spirits inside this man knew that the sons of Sceva had no spiritual rank of authority in the realm of the spirit. What followed spread like wildfire throughout the City of Ephesus and brought the whole City under the fear of the Lord. The demon-possessed man rose and overpowered the seven sons of Sceva and beat them naked. They ran into the City streets naked and bleeding profusely.

But to the Son he says, "Your throne, O God, endures forever and ever. You rule with a scepter of justice."

Hebrews 1:8

The "spiritual rank" of the High Priest of the priestly Order of Melchizedek is one of the "loftiest spiritual ranks ever held by a man."

First and foremost under the priestly Order of Melchizedek, our High Priest is God Most High. The High Priest of the New Testament Order of Melchizedek priesthood is as "divine and as eternal as God the Father." He (Christ) has no beginning of days or end of life. Everything in creation was created by Him and through Him. This in itself places Him in a spiritual rank which no other man could ever attain to. We know for a fact that the High Priests of the Levitical priesthood were "mere mortals chosen from among men." They had a spiritual rank that was based upon the office of the high priest which God gave them under the Mosaic Covenant.

"Therefore, God elevated him to the place of highest honor and gave him the name above all other names, that at the name of Jesus every knee should bow, in heaven and on earth and under the earth."

Philippians 2:9-10

Secondly, as a man the High Priest of the priestly Order of Melchizedek also occupies the "loftiest spiritual position the heavenly Father has ever given to a man!" The apostle Paul shows us from the above passage of Scripture how Jesus earned this lofty position. Saint Paul tells us that Jesus' life of total obedience to God, even to the point of sacrificing His own life by embracing the shameful death of the cross "earned Him this lofty position of authority." The apostle Paul tells us that because of His life of explicit obedience to God, that God gave Him (Jesus) a name that is above every other name.

This name has "complete authority in heaven, on earth and in the underworld!" The usage of the word "name" in this passage literally means "title." When a heavyweight boxer defeats every opponent in his division he is given the title of world heavyweight boxing champion. This new title describes the fact that, the said boxer holds the loftiest rank in the whole world of boxing. Jesus completely defeated sin, the devil and death and as such God gave Him the loftiest title ever given to a man and then set Him on the right hand of the throne of God.

This is why tithing into the priestly Order of Melchizedek is so very powerful. ***The lofty spiritual rank of its High Priest "multiplies the spiritual power backing our tithe,"*** compared to tithing into the Levitical priesthood. When we tithe as Abraham tithed we "increase the power of our tithe exponentially!" This would explain why the devil would love to see the global Church continue to employ the Malachi 3:8-12 tithing model.

The Spiritual Authority of the High Priest

Jesus came and told his disciples, "I have been given all authority in heaven and on earth. Therefore, go and make disciples of all the nations, baptizing them in the name of the Father and the Son and the Holy Spirit. Teach these new disciples to obey all the commands I have given you. And be sure of this: I am with you always, even to the end of the age."

Matthew 28:18-20

THE "SPIRITUAL RANK" OF THE HIGH PRIEST OF THE PRIESTLY ORDER OF MELCHIZEDEK IS ONE OF THE "LOFTIEST SPIRITUAL RANKS EVER HELD BY A MAN."

The third spiritual factor which affects the power of the tithe between the Levitical priesthood and the priestly Order of Melchizedek is the "spiritual authority of the High Priest." Let us examine the level of spiritual authority that God invested in the High Priests of the Levitical priesthood and then compare their level of spiritual authority to that of the High Priest of the priestly Order of Melchizedek. The High Priest of the Levitical priesthood had a very "limited scope of spiritual authority." First and foremost their spiritual authority was limited to "governing the daily affairs of the temple and meeting the spiritual needs of the Jewish nation." The high priest under the Levitical priesthood had dismal spiritual authority over the kings and prophets of Israel, who were given a different anointing and function within the nation of Israel.

"Therefore, God elevated him to the place of highest honor and gave him the name above all other names, that at the name of Jesus every knee should bow, in heaven and on earth and under the earth."

Philippians 2:9-10

On the other hand the High Priest of the priestly Order of Melchizedek has an *"unlimited scope of spiritual authority." His spiritual authority is deep and far-reaching.* When Jesus rose from the dead, He told His apprentice apostles that they could go into the entire world in the power of His name, because He had been given "all authority in heaven and on earth!" The apostle Paul also tells us that Jesus Christ, the High Priest of the priestly Order of Melchizedek, was given a "name higher than any other name." This name yields tremendous spiritual authority in the spirit world. The Bible says that at the mention of this name, "every knee in heaven, on earth and in the underworld has to bow and confess" that Jesus Christ is Lord. What an authority!

It is safe to assume that when we tithe into the priestly Order of Melchizedek, the "highest form of spiritual authority known to man and angels is superimposed over our tithes." The unlimited scope of authority of the High priest of the priestly Order of Melchizedek gives our tithe the spiritual authority and power to release whatever belongs to us, whether those things are being held up in heaven or on earth. The tithe also gains the power to release whatever is being held up by demonic forces from the underworld. Since the spiritual authority of the High Priest of the priestly Order of Melchizedek extends to every known spiritual and natural border, our tithe also takes on this power. This means that tithing into the priestly Order of Melchizedek can open up entire nations for Kingdom advancement.

The Spiritual Scope of the Tithe

"Here is the main point: We have a High Priest who sat down in the place of honor beside the throne of the majestic God in heaven. There he ministers in the heavenly Tabernacle, the true place of worship that was built by the Lord and not by human hands."

Hebrews 8:1-2

The fourth spiritual factor which affects the power of the tithe between the Levitical priesthood and the priestly Order of Melchizedek is the "spiritual scope of the tithe." When we talk about the spiritual scope of the tithe we are talking about the size of the spiritual territory the tithe covers. The spiritual scope of the tithe is tied to the spiritual scope of the priesthood it serves. We know that the Levitical priesthood was an earthly priesthood based upon the shadow of things to come and that its spiritual reach did not extend beyond the borders of the Jewish nation.

This is why the Levitical tithe could only open the "windows of heaven" because it serviced an earthly priesthood which was "operating from the outside of the true sanctuary which is in heaven." The Malachi 3:8-12 tithing model is limited to opening the windows of heaven, but it has "no power to open the doors of heaven." To open the doors of heaven would require that one possesses the "keys of the kingdom of heaven," which this priesthood did not have access to.

"Bring all the tithes into the storehouse so there will be enough food in my Temple. If you do," *says the Lord of Heaven's Armies, "I will open the windows of heaven for you. I will pour out* *a blessing so great you won't have enough room to take it in! Try it! Put me to the test!"*

Malachi 3:10

On the other hand the "spiritual scope" of the tithe that is based upon *the Abrahamic tithing model is "vast and far-reaching."* This is because this Abrahamic tithing model serves a priesthood which "operates from the inside of the heavenly temple." This is why this tithing model can open the doors of the kingdom of Heaven, because the tithers (New Covenant believers) have been given the "keys of the kingdom of Heaven." This is why it saddens me when I hear well-meaning teachers of the gospel tell New Testament believers that when they tithe, God will open the windows of heaven. *"Please remember that if* *we are being fed through windows, then we are still living and operating* *from the outside of the Father's house!"*

"And I will give you the keys of the Kingdom of Heaven. Whatever you forbid on earth will *be forbidden in heaven, and whatever you permit on earth will be permitted in heaven."*

Matthew 16:19

The Ministry of the High Priest

"But now Jesus, our High Priest, has been given a ministry that is far superior to the *old priesthood, for he is the one who mediates for us a far better covenant with God,* *based on better promises."*

Hebrews 8:6

The fifth spiritual factor which differentiates the power of the tithe *between the Levitical priesthood and the priestly Order of Melchizedek* *is "the spiritual ministry" of the High Priest.* The apostle Paul tells us that Christ's superiority over the High Priests of the Levitical priesthood is also based upon the fact that Jesus has a more "excellent ministry than they did" which is "established upon a superior covenant."

The apostle Paul calls this excellent ministry the "ministry of the Spirit," whereas the ministry of the High Priests of the Levitical priesthood was the "ministry of the letter." In the entire Old Testament, you will not find any High Priest under the Levitical priesthood who had a ministry of "raising the dead, casting out devils and healing the sick." Yet we see the High Priest of the priestly

Order of Melchizedek, even our Lord Jesus Christ, operating in "all these dimensions of the Spirit." This means that when we tithe into the priestly Order of Melchizedek, our tithe "literally activates God's resurrection and healing power over our lives."

The Covenant the Priesthood stands on

"But now Jesus, our High Priest, has been given a ministry that is far superior to the old priesthood, for he is the one who mediates for us a far better covenant with God, based on better promises."

Hebrews 8:6

THE MALACHI 3:8-12 TITHING MODEL IS LIMITED TO OPENING THE WINDOWS OF HEAVEN, BUT IT HAS "NO POWER TO OPEN THE DOORS OF HEAVEN."

The sixth spiritual factor which determines the power of the tithe is the "covenant that the priesthood stands on." Please remember that there is "no tithing model" that is not attached to a "priesthood." Tithing is always tied to a priesthood. The apostle Paul tells us that the priestly Order of Melchizedek of which our Lord Jesus is the presiding High Priest is superior to the Levitical priesthood because it is "established on a more excellent covenant with God!" This covenant comes packaged with "excellent promises" for the people who live under this royal priesthood.

This is why tithing into the priestly Order of Melchizedek can activate the manifestation of precious promises of God from His holy Word. There are many of God's people who are "nursing unfulfilled personal prophecies." I truly believe that when we begin to tithe into the priestly Order of Melchizedek, God will "supernaturally quicken the fulfillment" of prophetic promises which He has given us in the past.

The Functions and Features of the Tithe

The final spiritual factor which determines the power of the tithe under these two priestly orders is the ***"distinctive functions and features"*** of the tithe.

These distinctive functions and features allude to the power that God has invested in the tithe. We will now quickly examine these distinctive features and functions.

1. The "tithe" under the Levitical priesthood was a payment for priestly services rendered, whereas under the priestly Order of Melchizedek, the "tithe" is given as a royal endowment to honor the "King" (Christ) and extend His "Kingdom" here on earth.

2. Under the priestly Order of Melchizedek, the "tithe" is given to express heartfelt honor for His Majesty King Jesus, our eternal High Priest, whereas under the Levitical priesthood, the "tithe" was given out of a sense of legal obligation.

3. The "tithe" under the Levitical priesthood was a "transitional tithe" which was designed to service the Jewish nation until the installation of Christ's New Testament Order of Melchizedek, and until they come to acknowledge that Jesus Christ is the promised Messiah.

4. Under the priestly Order of Melchizedek, the "tithes" of Kingdom citizens are used to support and sustain the advancement of the Kingdom of God here on earth, whereas under the Levitical priestly order the "tithes" of the Jewish nation were used primarily to support and sustain the priesthood.

5. Under the Levitical priesthood, non-tithers were punished by a "Curse" as prescribed by the Law of Moses.

6. Under the priestly Order of Melchizedek, non-tithers are chastised with a diminished capacity for manifesting the FAVOR of God! Instead of cursing the non-tithers, God simply diminishes or removes His level of approval on their lives.

LIFE APPLICATION SECTION

Point to Ponder:

Under the priestly order of Melchizedek, non-tithers are punished by a diminished capacity for manifesting the supernatural FAVOR of God in their life.

Verse to Remember:

"But now Jesus, our High Priest, has been given a ministry that is far superior to the old priesthood, for he is the one who mediates for us a far better covenant with God, based on better promises."

Hebrews 8:6

Questions to Consider:

*   How does the fact that the priestly Order of Melchizedek is established on a better covenant affect the power of tithe?

_____

_____

_____

_____

_____

*   What are the other spiritual factors that affect the power of the tithe?

_____

_____

_____

_____

_____

Journal Your Thoughts

SIMILARITIES AND DIFFERENCES

*T*here are significant and discernable differences between the tithing model that is based upon the Order of Melchizedek and the Levitical tithing model. These differences are a result of the fact that the two priesthoods are significantly different, in their spiritual nature and spiritual expression. But there are also some similarities between these two priestly orders. We will thoroughly examine these critical differences and similarities in this section of our study. We will offer complete Scriptural proof for these differences and similarities.

1. The Abrahamic tithing model is for a people of faith who live under the New Testament Covenant of Grace, whereas the Malachi tithing model is for people who live under the Mosaic Covenant of Law.

"In the same way, 'Abraham believed God, and God counted him as righteous because of his faith.' The real children of Abraham, then, are those who put their faith in God. This is what I am trying to say: The agreement God made with Abraham could not be canceled 430 years later when God gave the law to Moses. God would be breaking his promise. For if the inheritance could be received by keeping the law, then it would not be the result of accepting God's promise. But God graciously gave it to Abraham as a promise."

Galatians 3:6-7,17-18

"Now the law of Moses required that the priests, who are descendants of Levi, must collect a tithe from the rest of the people of Israel, who are also descendants of Abraham. So if the priesthood of Levi, on which the law was based, could have achieved the perfection God intended, why did God need to

establish a different priesthood, with a priest in the order of Melchizedek instead of the order of Levi and Aaron?"

Hebrews 7:5, 11

The Abrahamic tithing model is the tithing model that is based upon the priestly Order of Melchizedek; it was designed to service New Testament believers who live by faith just like Abraham did. The Scriptures make it quite clear that God's Covenant of Grace with Abraham was established 430 years before God gave Moses the Covenant of Law. This means that God's Covenant of Grace with Abraham can never be nullified by the Mosaic Law which came later. The Bible lets us know that the tithe of Abraham which he tithed into Melchizedek in Genesis 14:20, is *infinitely more powerful than the Levitical tithe* (which is the contemporary Malachi 3:8-12 tithe) which is based upon the Mountain of Law.

In some of his epistles the apostle Paul gave a stern warning to Jewish believers who were attempting to mix "the Covenant of Law with the Covenant of Grace." Paul warned them of the spiritual dangers of such misguided practices. Paul told them that the "prophetic inheritance of Abraham" was not founded on the "Covenant of Law," but on a "supernatural faith promise." Paul warns that we stand in danger of forfeiting our portion of Abraham's prophetic inheritance if we think we can access it by submitting ourselves to the Levitical priestly Order, which was built upon the Mountain of Law. This is exactly what we are doing when we collect our tithes and offerings on the basis of Malachi 3:8-12. We must use Genesis 14:18-20 and Hebrews 7 as the prophetic backdrop for collecting tithes and offerings in our churches.

2. The Abrahamic tithing model is based on a spiritual relationship of sonship with God, whereas the Malachi tithing model is based upon a legal contract that God made with the Jewish nation to reveal the transgression.

"Tell me, you who want to live under the law, do you know what the law actually says? The Scriptures say that Abraham had two sons, one from his slave wife and one from his freeborn wife. The son of the slave wife was born in a human attempt to bring about the fulfillment of God's promise. But the son of the freeborn wife was born as God's own fulfillment of his promise. These two women serve as an illustration of God's two covenants. The first woman, Hagar, represents Mount Sinai where people received the law that enslaved them. And now Jerusalem is just like Mount Sinai in Arabia,] because she and her children live in slavery to the law. But the other woman, Sarah, represents the heavenly Jerusalem. She is the free woman, and she is our mother."

Galatians 4:21-26

The apostle Paul makes it quite clear that those who lived under the Mosaic Covenant of Law, even though they were the natural descendants of Abraham, had for the most part a contractual relationship with God. This would explain why **they were constantly striving to attain a righteousness that was based upon the works of the Law.** Unfortunately the "more they tried to please God by the works of the Law the more they became imprisoned by it." The Law only served to demonstrate to the children of Israel that it was impossible to please God by keeping the works of the Law.

On the other hand, those of us who "walk by faith and not by sight" are the true children of Abraham. We who are justified by faith and not by the works of the Law are the true citizens of the heavenly Jerusalem which is the mother of us all. I have already shown you that the priestly Order of Melchizedek operates out of the holy City, spiritual Jerusalem. This is the spiritual City that the apostle Paul compares to Sarah and calls the mother of us all.

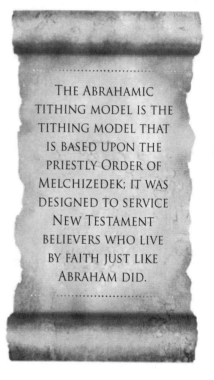

THE ABRAHAMIC TITHING MODEL IS THE TITHING MODEL THAT IS BASED UPON THE PRIESTLY ORDER OF MELCHIZEDEK; IT WAS DESIGNED TO SERVICE NEW TESTAMENT BELIEVERS WHO LIVE BY FAITH JUST LIKE ABRAHAM DID.

3. The Abrahamic tithing model is of a higher heavenly order while the Malachi tithing model is of a lower spiritual and earthly order.

"Here is the main point: We have a High Priest who sat down in the place of honor beside the throne of the majestic God in heaven. There he ministers in the heavenly Tabernacle, the true place of worship that was built by the Lord and not by human hands. And since every high priest is required to offer gifts and sacrifices, our High Priest must make an offering, too. If he were here on earth, he would not even be a priest, since there already are priests who offer the gifts required by the law. They serve in a system of worship that is only a copy, a shadow of the real one in heaven. For when Moses was getting ready to build the Tabernacle, God gave him this warning: "Be sure that you make everything according to the pattern I have shown you here on the mountain."

Hebrews 8:1-5

The prolific writer of the book of Hebrews tells us very clearly that we have a High Priest after the Order of Melchizedek, even our Lord Jesus Christ who is seated in the heavenly Tabernacle, which is the true sanctuary of worship that was built by the hands of God. The apostle Paul proceeds to tell us that, had Jesus Christ been on earth He would not be a High Priest because there is already an "earthly priesthood here on earth which operates from God's temple in natural Jerusalem." The Levitical temple was later destroyed by the Roman army, a sure visible prophetic sign that the resurrection of Jesus Christ had precipitated a change in the priesthood.

By this one statement the great apostle makes it adamantly clear that the priestly Order of Melchizedek is a heavenly priesthood while the Levitical or priestly Order of Aaron is an earthly priesthood. It follows therefore that the tithing model that is based upon the priestly Order of Melchizedek (which describes the tithe of Abraham) *is of a higher spiritual order whereas the popular contemporary Malachi 3:8-12 tithing model is of a lower spiritual and earthly order.* This does not mean that the "Malachi 3:8-12 tithing model" is not spiritual. It is just of a lower spiritual order. We know that the Law is spiritual, but Paul says that it was seriously compromised by the sinful nature of the people it was meant to serve, who had no inherent power to live by all of its righteous requirements. *This is why it's critical that we upgrade the technology of tithing in our churches from the Malachi 3:8-12 tithing model to the Genesis 14:18-20 tithing model.* The vast majority of churches need to establish a more excellent way of tithing.

4. Under the priestly Order of Melchizedek, tithers are fed with heavenly bread and wine, whereas tithers under the Levitical priesthood (Malachi tithing model) are fed with the fruits of the ground.

And Melchizedek, the king of Salem and a priest of God Most High, brought Abram some bread and wine. Melchizedek blessed Abram with this blessing: "Blessed be Abram by God Most High, Creator of heaven and earth. And blessed be God Most High, who has defeated your enemies for you." Then Abram gave Melchizedek a tenth of all the goods he had recovered.

Genesis 14:18-20

"Should people cheat God? Yet you have cheated me! "But you ask, 'What do you mean? When did we ever cheat you? "You have cheated me of the tithes and offerings due to me. You are under a curse, for your whole nation has been cheating me. Bring all the tithes into the storehouse so there will be enough food in my Temple. If you do,"

says the Lord of Heaven's Armies, "I will open the windows of heaven for you. I will pour out a blessing so great you won't have enough room to take it in! Try it! Put me to the test! Your crops will be abundant, for I will guard them from insects and disease. Your grapes will not fall from the vine before they are ripe," says the Lord of Heaven's Armies. "Then all nations will call you blessed, for your land will be such a delight," says the Lord of Heaven's Armies.

Malachi 3:8-12

I have already shown you from the Scriptures that the priestly Order of Melchizedek is a heavenly priesthood, while the Levitical priestly Order is an earthly priesthood. This critical difference has far-reaching spiritual ramifications for those who tithe into these two priestly orders. I want to be very clear that when I state that the Levitical priestly Order was an earthly priesthood, I am not suggesting that there was nothing spiritual about the Levitical priesthood. Everything which starts with God is spiritual. But the Bible is quite clear that the entire Levitical priesthood was a "shadow or an earthly copy" of spiritual elements within the eternal structure of the heavenly temple, which was made without human hands. Moses, the spiritual father of the Levitical priesthood, was also admonished by God to build the earthly Tabernacle according to the pattern of the heavenly one.

For I pass on to you what I received from the Lord himself. On the night when he was betrayed, the Lord Jesus took some bread and gave thanks to God for it. Then he broke it in pieces and said, "This is my body, which is given for you.] Do this to remember me." In the same way, he took the cup of wine after supper, saying, "This cup is the new covenant between God and his people—an agreement confirmed with my blood. Do this to remember me as often as you drink it." For every time you eat this bread and drink this cup, you are announcing the Lord's death until he comes again.

1 Corinthians 11:23-26

Under the priestly Order of Melchizedek, tithers such as Abraham are given "heavenly bread and wine" in exchange for their tithe. On the other hand, tithers under the Levitical priestly Order were given the "fruits of the ground" in exchange for their tithe. This is because the prophetic inheritance of the "sand-seed of Abraham" is earth-bound, while the prophetic inheritance of the "star-seed of Abraham" (those of us who are born again) is heaven-bound. Please remember that the "star-seed" of Abraham includes everyone who is born of the Spirit, both Jews and Gentiles.

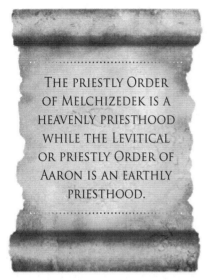

THE PRIESTLY ORDER OF MELCHIZEDEK IS A HEAVENLY PRIESTHOOD WHILE THE LEVITICAL OR PRIESTLY ORDER OF AARON IS AN EARTHLY PRIESTHOOD.

"Bread and wine" are the spiritual emblems of the priestly Order of Melchizedek. It is not surprising then that our Lord Jesus Christ, who is also the High Priest of the priestly Order of Melchizedek, initiated the celebration of these two spiritual emblems through the sacrament of Holy Communion. Every time we use these two spiritual elements in the celebration of Holy Communion, we are "proclaiming the fact that we are now under the priestly Order of Melchizedek." Unfortunately, during the weekly time of giving our tithes and offerings, many churches quickly distance themselves from this powerful eternal priestly Order and revert back to the Levitical priesthood, because of the global church's obsession with Malachi 3:8-12.

5. Under the priestly Order of Melchizedek, tithers have been given the power to rebuke the devourer (the devil) for themselves, whereas tithers under the Levitical priesthood did not have the spiritual stature to rebuke the devourer (the devil) for themselves.

Bring all the tithes into the storehouse, That there may be food in My house, And try Me now in this," Says the LORD of hosts, " If I will not open for you the windows of heaven, And pour out for you such blessing That there will not be room enough to receive it. " And I will rebuke the devourer for your sakes, So that he will not destroy the fruit of your ground, Nor shall the vine fail to bear fruit for you in the field," Says the LORD of hosts;

Malachi 3:10-11

Then Melchizedek king of Salem brought out bread and wine; he was the priest of God Most High. And he blessed him and said: "Blessed be Abram of God Most High, Possessor of heaven and earth; And blessed be God Most High, Who has delivered your enemies into your hand." And he gave him a tithe of all.

Genesis 14:18-20 (NKJV)

When the seventy-two disciples returned, they joyfully reported to him, "Lord, even the demons obey us when we use your name!" "Yes," he told them, "I saw Satan fall from heaven like lightning! Look, I have given you authority over all the power of the enemy and you can walk among snakes and scorpions and crush them. Nothing will injure you. But don't rejoice because evil spirits obey you; rejoice because your names are registered in heaven."

Luke 10:17-19

Perhaps one of the most significant differences between the priestly Order of Melchizedek and the Levitical priesthood is found in the degree of "spiritual authority" that God has invested in the tithers. Under the Levitical priesthood the majority of tithers did not have the "inherent spiritual authority or stature" to rebuke the devil for themselves. This is because under the Old Testament only the "king, prophet and priest" were filled with the Holy Spirit and anointed for service. This would explain the proper context of Malachi 3:11, which says *"I will rebuke the devourer for your sakes, So that he will not destroy the fruit of your ground, nor shall the vine fail to bear fruit for you in the field,"* *Says the LORD of hosts.*

This expression by God suggests that tithers under the Levitical priesthood had no "spiritual jurisdictional authority" over demonic spirits. This is why I cringe when I hear well-meaning teachers of the Gospel quote Malachi 3:11 and *superimpose its promise over New Testament believers who belong to a higher and more powerful New Testament order of priesthood.* If we intend to sit and wait on God to rebuke the devourer on our behalf we will be waiting for a very long time. In the meantime, demons will continue to create havoc in our midst. Under the New Testament order of priesthood, Jesus gave us the authority to rebuke the devourer (the devil) for ourselves using the authority vested in His name. Believing and proposing anything to the contrary is to "rob ourselves of the awesome benefits of the finished work of Christ!"

Jesus cut him short. "Be quiet! Come out of the man," he ordered. At that, the demon threw the man to the floor as the crowd watched; then it came out of him without hurting him further. Amazed, the people exclaimed, "What authority and power this man's words possess! Even evil spirits obey him, and they flee at his command!" The news about Jesus spread through every village in the entire region.

Luke 4:35-36

When the people of Jesus' day saw the casting out of demons by a Jewish rabbi they were very astonished. They were amazed at the degree of spiritual power and authority which was flowing through His words. They were amazed

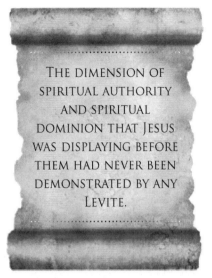

THE DIMENSION OF SPIRITUAL AUTHORITY AND SPIRITUAL DOMINION THAT JESUS WAS DISPLAYING BEFORE THEM HAD NEVER BEEN DEMONSTRATED BY ANY LEVITE.

when they saw that even demons were obeying His every command. The dimension of spiritual authority and spiritual dominion that Jesus was displaying before them had never been demonstrated by any Levite. Through His miraculous ministry Jesus was establishing a different priestly order.

Jesus transferred this same dimension of spiritual authority to His apprentice apostles. These men ultimately became the first apostles under the New Testament priestly Order of Melchizedek. They also began to "rebuke the devourer (the devil)" for themselves and to their complete surprise they discovered that "under this new spiritual order of priesthood" that Jesus was establishing, "demonic spirits were also subject to them through His name." They discovered that they were operating in a "spiritual technology" which was infinitely more powerful than the promise of Malachi 3:11.

These apprentice apostles quickly discovered that under this New Testament Order of Melchizedek priesthood, they did not have to wait on God to "rebuke the devourer" on their behalf. They discovered that the Spirit of Christ had come to "reside inside their regenerated spirits." As such they could rebuke the devourer (the devil) for themselves through the "power of God that was residing inside their spirits." When Melchizedek met Abraham, this Priest of God Most High was quick to point out to Abraham "why he had won the fight with his enemies so quickly, with such a limited number of soldiers."

This is what Melchizedek told Abraham…"Blessed be Abram of God Most High, Possessor of heaven and earth; And blessed be God Most High, who has delivered your enemies into your hand." Under the priestly Order of Melchizedek, God delivers our enemies (the devil) into our hands. This means that we get to tell the devil to "stay" or "get lost." Under the Levitical priesthood, God "worked for them," but under the priestly Order of Melchizedek, God "works in and through us." Said simply, Christ is in "us" and we are "in" Christ.

6. Under the priestly Order of Melchizedek, tithers are given the keys of the Kingdom of Heaven, whereas tithers under the Levitical priesthood were told to "seek and knock."

"And I also say to you that you are Peter, and on this rock I will build My church, and the gates of Hades shall not prevail against it. And I will give you the keys of the kingdom of heaven, and whatever you bind on earth will be bound in heaven, and whatever you loose on earth will be loosed in heaven."

Matthew 16:18-19

"Ask, and it will be given to you; seek, and you will find; knock, and it will be opened to you. For everyone who asks receives, and he who seeks finds, and to him who knocks it will be opened."

Matthew 7:7-8

"When these things were all in place, the priests regularly entered the first room as they performed their religious duties. But only the high priest ever entered the Most Holy Place, and only once a year. And he always offered blood for his own sins and for the sins the people had committed in ignorance. By these regulations the Holy Spirit revealed that the entrance to the Most Holy Place was not freely open as long as the Tabernacle and the system it represented were still in use."

Hebrews 9:6-9

Perhaps one of the most misunderstood scriptural passages in the Bible is Matthew 7:7-8. I have heard very well-meaning teachers and preachers of the gospel use this passage to teach New Testament believers the importance of "persistency in prayer." While their sincere efforts are to be applauded, their application of this passage to describe New Testament believers who live under the New Testament Order of Melchizedek priesthood is fundamentally flawed. *Their misapplication of this passage of Scripture lies in their failure to discern the critical differences between the priestly Order of Melchizedek and the Levitical priesthood.* This is the same reason why many members of the Body of Christ use Malachi 3:8-12 as their spiritual model for tithing.

The apostle Paul, who wrote over two-thirds of the New Testament, tells us that the Levitical priesthood was an earthly priesthood. It was a shadow of the heavenly tabernacle and priesthood. Paul shows us that the Levitical priesthood functions outside the perimeters of the true Tabernacle of God, which is located in spiritual Jerusalem in heavenly places. **Saint Paul tells us that the presence of the veil between the holy place and the holy of holies was a "prophetic sign" that the "pathway into God's holy presence" had not yet been fully secured for the people who lived and tithed into the Levitical priesthood.**

The Levites and the other eleven tribes of Israel who were under their priestly jurisdiction were operating from the "outside" of the true Tabernacle of God, which is in heaven. This would explain why Jesus Christ encouraged them to "ask, seek and knock" because eventually the "Door (Jesus)" would be opened unto them, and their days of serving an earthly priesthood which ministers from the outside of the true tabernacle of God would come to an end. They would then be given access to the New Testament priestly Order of Melchizedek which ministers from the "inside continually." *Matthew 7:7-8 was addressed to the Jewish nation, who lived under the Mosaic Covenant of Law, and who were looking for the appearance of the promised Messiah.*

SAINT PAUL TELLS US THAT THE PRESENCE OF THE VEIL BETWEEN THE HOLY PLACE AND THE HOLY OF HOLIES WAS A "PROPHETIC SIGN" THAT THE "PATHWAY INTO GOD'S HOLY PRESENCE" HAD NOT YET BEEN FULLY SECURED FOR THE PEOPLE WHO LIVED AND TITHED INTO THE LEVITICAL PRIESTHOOD.

On the other hand, Matthew 16:18-19 was not addressed to the Jewish nation who lived under the Levitical priesthood. It was addressed to New Testament believers who are members of the New Creation royal priesthood, with Jesus Christ as our chief Apostle and High Priest. Kingdom citizens who live under this new order of priesthood were given "the keys of the Kingdom of Heaven" and were then "made to sit in heavenly places in Christ Jesus."

"For he raised us from the dead along with Christ and seated us with him in the heavenly realms because we are united with Christ Jesus."
Ephesians 2:6

The Scriptures are very clear that we are under a "New Order" of priesthood which allows us to minister from "within the holy of holies continually." Would it not be regrettable and even comical if you found one of your children knocking profusely on the front door to your house, while the keys to every door in your house are dangling from his or her belt? *Knocking is only appropriate for visitors and strangers who do not have the keys to our house. Once a person gives us keys to their house, "their action of giving us the keys to their residence changes the technology of access."* By their freewill action of giving us the keys to their residence, they inevitably deliver us from the "old technology of having to knock in order to enter." This is why the rediscovery of the "Lost Key" which is the "Abrahamic tithing model which is based upon the priestly Order of Melchizedek" is so critical. This ancient key (tithing model) will bring us into the "spiritual awareness" of what it means to be part of this powerful eternal priestly Order of Melchizedek. This new spiritual outlook will bring reformation to some of our inaccurate doctrines in the global Church.

7. The Abrahamic tithing model is the tithing model of "Kingdom citizens," whereas the Malachi/Levitical tithing model is the tithing model that God designed for the Old Testament Jewish nation.

"And indeed those who are of the sons of Levi, who receive the priesthood, have a commandment to receive tithes from the people according to the law, that is, from their brethren, though they have come from the loins of Abraham; Now beyond all contradiction the lesser is blessed by the better. Here mortal men receive tithes, but there he receives them, of whom it is witnessed that he lives."

Hebrews 7:5,7-8

We have already mentioned the fact that the Levitical priesthood was given to the nation of Israel as a "transitional priesthood," until the "time of the Messiah!" God's purpose has always been to re-introduce the Jewish nation to the priestly Order of Melchizedek just like He introduced it to their forefather, Abraham. Many of the spiritual practices under the Levitical priesthood were meant to pass away after Christ's death and resurrection. Paul the Apostle is very clear as to the fact that the Levitical tithing model was designed to service the Jewish nation and no one else. This is especially true when you consider the fact that this "tithing model was based upon the Mountain of Law, which excluded every one who was not part of the commonwealth of Israel."

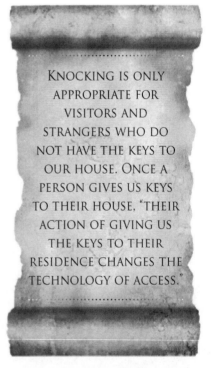

KNOCKING IS ONLY APPROPRIATE FOR VISITORS AND STRANGERS WHO DO NOT HAVE THE KEYS TO OUR HOUSE. ONCE A PERSON GIVES US KEYS TO THEIR HOUSE, "THEIR ACTION OF GIVING US THE KEYS TO THEIR RESIDENCE CHANGES THE TECHNOLOGY OF ACCESS."

On the other hand, Abraham's tithe into the Order of Melchizedek transcends the restrictions of the Mosaic Covenant of Law because it was established 430 years before the giving of the Law on Mount Sinai. We have already proven beyond a shadow of doubt that the priesthood of Melchizedek is an eternal and heavenly priesthood. We can therefore conclude that Abraham's tithing model is the ideal tithing model for Kingdom citizens, while the Malachi 3:8-12 tithing model is a tithing model that was designed for the Jewish nation. The Abrahamic tithing model was designed to service all those who believe in the "gospel of the Kingdom"—first the Jew, then the Gentile.

8. Under the priestly Order of Melchizedek, tithers tithe for love and honor, whereas under the Levitical priesthood, tithers tithed in exchange for priestly services rendered.

"And blessed be God Most High, who has defeated your enemies for you." Then Abram gave Melchizedek a tenth of all the goods he had recovered.

Genesis 14:20

And the Lord said to Aaron, "You priests will receive no allotment of land or share of property among the people of Israel. I am your share and your allotment. As for the tribe of Levi, your relatives, I will compensate them for their service in the Tabernacle. Instead of an allotment of land, I will give them the tithes from the entire land of Israel.

Numbers 18:20-21

We have already mentioned the fact that under the priestly Order of Melchizedek the High Priest is both a "King and Priest." Most importantly, the High Priest under the priestly Order of Melchizedek is also "God Most High." I have already shown you that as a "King," our High Priest (Christ Jesus) commands the preferential treatment and honor which is due to any sovereign King. *Royal protocol demands that those who approach a King must come bearing "gifts to honor" the King with. These gifts of honor are designed to celebrate the "glory and worthiness" of the King.*

These "gifts of honor" are "not payments for the king's services." Any suggestion that these gifts of honor are payment for the king's services would be a great insult to any true king. *Kings can never be on the "payroll" of their kingdom citizens because they "own everything that is within their kingdom."* As "God Most High," the High Priest of the priestly Order of Melchizedek (Jesus Christ) commands a "loftier place of honor" than any earthly king. When Abraham "tithed into Melchizedek, he was armed with this understanding." *This means that the primary motivation behind the Abrahamic tithing model is diametrically different from that of the popular and often-quoted Malachi 3:8-12 tithing model.*

On the other hand, the "primary motivation" for tithing under the Levitical priesthood had very little to do with the "bestowing of honor on a King." Under the Levitical priestly Order, the tithe in its simplest form was simply "payment for priestly services rendered." God did not permit Moses to allocate the possession of land to the priestly tribe of Levi; God wanted the Levites to focus their complete energy on representing the spiritual needs of the Jewish nation before Him. Members of the tribe of Levi were not allowed to own their own businesses since their first business was attending to the matters of the temple.

ROYAL PROTOCOL DEMANDS THAT THOSE WHO APPROACH A KING MUST COME BEARING "GIFTS TO HONOR" THE KING WITH.

To ensure that these priestly men and their families did not starve to death, God gave them the "tithes of the rest of the tribes of Israel" as "payment for their priestly services." God did not want the priesthood to be tempted to pursue secular employment and abandon the work of the temple. This is why the passage from "Malachi 3:8-12" was a stern rebuke from God against the Levites and some of the people of Israel who were "stealing from God by withholding their tithes and offerings." Tithing under the Levitical priesthood was no different than dining at a good restaurant and then refusing to pay for the meal. This act would be called "stealing from the owner of the restaurant." This is the contextual application of Malachi 3:8-12.

The primary motivation for the Malachi 3:8-12 pattern of tithing is "payment for priestly services." This would explain why New Testament believers who use Malachi 3:8-12 as a tithing model have an "inherent expectation of service" from their pastors when they "pay" their tithes. This would explain why some Christians get very angry and vindictive when they feel that their pastors are not giving them sufficient pastoral care. God help the pastor who fails to visit them in person when they are sick. *Many of these Christians choose to hold the local Church hostage by withholding their tithes.*

The first station of their outraged will is evidenced in the "withholding of their tithes" from their local Church. Many of these Christians conclude that their senior pastor forfeited his or her ability to command their "tithe" when he or she failed to provide the necessary priestly services that they felt they were entitled to. If the senior pastor does not play to their tune, they leave the church immediately. They leave the Church and start searching for a new Church where they can find a pastor who is willing to work very hard at earning their tithe. *Many good churches have been destroyed by this "demonic mentality and culture" because our "tithing model as we have taught it, is fundamentally flawed."*

Under the priestly Order of Melchizedek, the "giving of tithe" has nothing to do with "paying for priestly services rendered." Under this eternal priestly Order, God expects us to "give our tithes" whether we get the necessary priestly services from our pastors or not. Under this divine priestly Order, we cannot exercise the option of withholding our tithes in an effort to punish the "senior pastor or hold the local Church hostage." *Tithing under the priestly Order of Melchizedek is not "payment for services rendered, but a royal endowment" bestowed on His majesty by His "Kingdom citizens" for the "continued privilege" of working on the "King's land."* When the Church comes into this "prevailing Kingdom mentality" of tithing, we will see the "Day of God" break-out on the global Church.

9. Under the priestly Order of Melchizedek, the tithe was sealed by the blood of Jesus Christ, while under the Levitical priesthood, the tithe was sealed by the blood of animals.

"So Christ has now become the High Priest over all the good things that have come. He has entered that greater, more perfect Tabernacle in heaven, which was not made by human hands and is not part of this created world. 12 With his own blood—not the blood of goats and calves—he entered the Most Holy Place once for all time and secured our redemption forever."

Hebrews 9:11-12

Without a shadow of doubt, one of the most powerful differences between the priestly Order of Melchizedek and the Levitical priesthood is the "spiritual value and power" of the blood that was used to seal these two divine priestly Orders. Everything in the Levitical priesthood was "sealed and powered" by the blood of "sacrificial animals." This means that even the "tithe of Malachi 3" was sealed and powered by the blood of the same sacrificial animals.

On the other hand, under the priestly Order of Melchizedek, all the articles of the true Tabernacle of God in heaven were "sealed and powered" by the "precious blood of the Son of God." This important fact has far-reaching spiritual ramifications for those who tithe into the priestly Order of Melchizedek. This means that the "tithe that is based upon the priestly Order of Melchizedek" was sealed and is now "continuously powered by the blood of Jesus Christ." WOW! We have already discussed the far-reaching spiritual ramifications of this "awesome factor" in the chapter on the "Power of the tithe."

THE PRIMARY MOTIVATION FOR THE MALACHI 3:8-12 PATTERN OF TITHING IS "PAYMENT FOR PRIESTLY SERVICES."

10. Under the Levitical priesthood the High Priest was chosen from among sinful men to represent men before God.

"He is the kind of high priest we need because he is holy and blameless, unstained by sin. He has been set apart from sinners and has been given the highest place of honor in heaven. Unlike those other high priests, he does not need to offer sacrifices every day. They did this for their own sins first and then for the sins of the people."

Hebrews 7:26

Another very fascinating critical difference between the priestly Order of Melchizedek and the Levitical priesthood is found in the "spiritual nature and stature of the High Priest." Under the Levitical priesthood the High Priest was chosen from the "company of sinful men," who were continuously struggling with the sin nature. This means that under the priestly Order of Aaron the High Priests were for the most part "victims of the sin nature," which in most cases "compromised the spiritual integrity of their priestly ministry." Since they were partakers of the sin nature, the High Priests under the Levitical priesthood were easily manipulated by demonic powers. Some of them used their High office to "exact personal gain and pleasure."

Under the priestly Order of Melchizedek, the High Priest who is the Lord Jesus Christ, has never been stained by "personal sin and never will be." The only time that Christ ever touched sin was when it pleased His heavenly Father to make Him a "sacrificial lamb for the sins of the whole world." His ongoing priestly ministry is carried out on the platform of the "highest level of spiritual integrity" possible. *Under this priestly Order of Melchizedek, we never have to worry that our High Priest might "mess up or abuse His spiritual power."* This is why we need to come under this divine order of priesthood by "changing how we tithe." The High Priest of the priestly Order of Melchizedek has complete "mastery over the law of sin and death." He is also willing to give this power over sin to the people who live under His eternal priesthood.

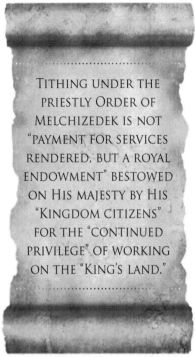

TITHING UNDER THE PRIESTLY ORDER OF MELCHIZEDEK IS NOT "PAYMENT FOR SERVICES RENDERED, BUT A ROYAL ENDOWMENT" BESTOWED ON HIS MAJESTY BY HIS "KINGDOM CITIZENS" FOR THE "CONTINUED PRIVILEGE" OF WORKING ON THE "KING'S LAND."

11.   Under the priestly Order of Aaron the focus of the priesthood was to represent man's interest before God.

"Every high priest is a man chosen to represent other people in their dealings with God. He presents their gifts to God and offers sacrifices for their sins. And he is able to deal gently with ignorant and wayward people because he himself is subject to the same weaknesses. That is why he must offer sacrifices for his own sins as well as theirs."

Hebrews 5:1-3

Another interesting difference between the Levitical priesthood and the Order of Melchizedek is found in the "focus of ministry." Under the priestly Order of Aaron, the High Priest was chosen from among sinful men for the express purpose of "representing the spiritual needs of the people before God." This means that the spiritual engines of this entire priesthood were driven by the "desire to represent men's interests" before God. **Man's interests took a predominant role in this priesthood.** *We will soon see that under the priestly Order of Melchizedek,* **God's interests take precedence over man's interests.**

12. Under the priestly Order of Melchizedek, the High Priest is chosen from the Eternal structure of the Godhead.

Regarding the angels, he says, "He sends his angels like the winds, his servants like flames of fire." But to the Son he says, "Your throne, O God, endures forever and ever. You rule with a scepter of justice.

Hebrews 1:7-8

That is why Christ did not honor himself by assuming he could become High Priest. No, he was chosen by God, who said to him, "You are my Son. Today I have become your Father. And in another passage God said to him, "You are a priest forever in the order of Melchizedek."

Hebrews 5:5-6

Of the many critical differences between the Levitical priesthood and the priestly Order of Melchizedek, perhaps there is nothing as important as what we are about to say. Under the priestly *Order of Melchizedek the High Priest was chosen from the "eternal structure of the Godhead," whereas under the Levitical system the High Priest was chosen from among men.* Under the priestly Order of Melchizedek our High Priest is more than a man; He is first and foremost "God Most High, the possessor of heaven and earth." What a lofty title our High Priest has! This means that the High Priest of this powerful priestly Order of Melchizedek possess the same characteristics of deity as God the Father. This is also the testimony of the Nicene faith creed.

13. Under the priestly Order of Melchizedek the focus of the priesthood is to represent God's interest before men.

"Even though Jesus was God's Son, he learned obedience from the things he suffered. In this way, God qualified him as a perfect High Priest, and he became the source of eternal salvation for all those who obey him. And God designated him to be a High Priest in the order of Melchizedek."

Hebrews 5:8-10

"For it is not possible for the blood of bulls and goats to take away sins. That is why, when Christ came into the world, he said to God, "You did not want animal sacrifices or sin offerings. But you have given me a body to offer. You were not pleased with burnt offerings or other offerings for sin. Then I said, 'Look, I have come to do your will, O God— as is written about me in the Scriptures.'"

Hebrews 10:4-7

We have already seen that under the Levitical priesthood, "representing man's interest" before God took precedence over representing **God's interests before His Kingdom citizens.** *This is because the Levitical priests had the same struggles with sin that the people had, so they had a vested interest in wanting God to meet the spiritual needs of the people.* On the other hand under the priestly Order of Melchizedek, the High Priest was chosen from the eternal structures of the Godhead. The High Priest of the priestly Order of Melchizedek lives in the very throne room of God. *He has complete access to the presence of the heavenly Father at all times.*

Since the High Priest of this eternal priestly Order is also "God Most High," *the spiritual focus of His priesthood is to "represent God's interests before men."* He works through the Holy Spirit, who resides inside the regenerated spirits of His Kingdom citizens to bring about the "will of God" in the earth. Under the priestly Order of Melchizedek, the High Priest is under "divine mandate" to squash every form of "selfish interest or human agenda" which is opposed to "God's original plans and purposes." The High Priest of this powerful priestly Order is under divine mandate to "cultivate and steward" God's inheritance in the saints.

14. Under the priestly Order of Aaron the tithe had no power to break the sentence of death, whereas under the priestly Order of Melchizedek the tithe has the inherent power to break the Cycle of death.

"Jesus became a priest, not by meeting the physical requirement of belonging to the tribe of Levi, but by the power of a life that cannot be destroyed. There were many priests under the old system, for death prevented them from remaining in office. But because Jesus lives forever, his priesthood lasts forever. Therefore he is able, once and forever, to save those who come to God through him. He lives forever to intercede with God on their behalf."

Hebrews 7:16,23-25

Perhaps there is nothing which scares most people like the "fear of death." Perhaps this would explain why the fear of death is one of the devil's favorite weapons. Under the Levitical priestly Order, the priesthood was constantly being harassed by the "angel of death." The Levitical priesthood that the Old Testament Jewish nation tithed into did not have the power to overcome and overturn the "technology of death."

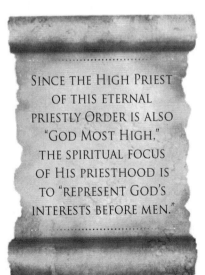

SINCE THE HIGH PRIEST OF THIS ETERNAL PRIESTLY ORDER IS ALSO "GOD MOST HIGH," THE SPIRITUAL FOCUS OF HIS PRIESTHOOD IS TO "REPRESENT GOD'S INTERESTS BEFORE MEN."

On the other hand, the High Priest of the priestly Order of Melchizedek is God Most High, who has no beginning of days or end of life. *He has already conquered death and has complete mastery over it.* This means that the Abrahamic tithing model which is based upon the priestly Order of Melchizedek has the capacity to empower tithers in the process of "breaking and reversing death cycles." This is one of the critical differences between these two priestly orders. This critical difference unmasks the awesome power of the priestly Order of Melchizedek and why we need to tithe into it.

15. The Levitical priesthood was rigged with inconsistencies because of the differing levels of integrity between the different High Priests, whereas under the priestly Order of Melchizedek, the spiritual integrity of the priesthood is as solid as a rock.

"He is the kind of high priest we need because he is holy and blameless, unstained by sin. He has been set apart from sinners and has been given the highest place of honor in heaven. Unlike those other high priests, he does not need to offer sacrifices every day. They did this for their own sins first and then for the sins of the people. But Jesus did this once for all when he offered himself as the sacrifice for the people's sins. The law appointed high priests who were limited by human weakness."

Hebrews 7:26-28

There are fewer things in life that are more important than "personal and corporate integrity." Great ministries, businesses and even nations have fallen from grace due to the lack of moral integrity. Roget's thesaurus defines "Integrity" as "adherence to moral and ethical principles; soundness of moral character." **When people do not discern integrity in leadership, this breeds a sense of "mistrust and insecurity" within the ranks.** If this "breach is not repaired" it may eventually lead the people into "open rebellion or anarchy." On the other hand, when people can discern the force of integrity in their leaders, it "unleashes waves of loyalty and commitment" within the ranks.

The issue of spiritual integrity is one of the most important differences between the priestly Order of Melchizedek and the Levitical priesthood. Under the Levitical priesthood the High Priests were chosen from among sinful men who were already compromised by "inherent genetic weaknesses in certain areas of their lives." Some High Priests were "financially corrupt" and took bribes in exchange for priestly services and perverted justice. Some had systemic "sexual-sin issues," like the two sons of the High Priest Eli, Hophni and Phinehas (1 Sam 2:12-16). These inherent weaknesses in the priesthood created serious and ongoing "trust issues" between the people and the Levitical priesthood. At certain times the people got a "rare treat" whenever a High Priest emerged whose "spiritual integrity and moral fortitude helped restore the people's confidence in the priesthood, like Samuel for instance."

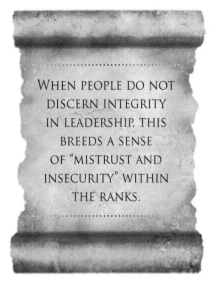

WHEN PEOPLE DO NOT DISCERN INTEGRITY IN LEADERSHIP, THIS BREEDS A SENSE OF "MISTRUST AND INSECURITY" WITHIN THE RANKS.

Under the priestly Order of Melchizedek we never ever have to worry about the "spiritual integrity" of our High Priest. The High Priest of our priestly Order is God Most High, and He is "holy, blameless, sinless and separate from sinners." Even if His "subordinate priests" (leaders of local churches) falter in their personal integrity, we do not have to hold the house of God hostage by withholding our tithes. Our tithe is a "royal endowment" that we have the privilege of bestowing on the King of kings and Priest of God Most High.

According to the "principle of authority," the purity and life stream of any organization is derived from its "head." As the head of the Church, Jesus Christ our faithful High Priest stands uncorrupted and undefiled. This is why under the priestly Order of Melchizedek there is "no reason why anybody should ever withhold their tithe." Doing so only activates the "the law of sin and death" in our lives and unmasks the fact that we do not really know the true nature of this eternal priestly Order of Melchizedek.

16. Under the Levitical priesthood, the spiritual scope of the priesthood did not extend beyond the natural borders of the nation of Israel, whereas under the priestly Order of Melchizedek, the spiritual scope of the priesthood is infinite and far reaching.

A Gentile woman who lived there came to him, pleading, "Have mercy on me, O Lord, Son of David! For my daughter is possessed by a demon that torments her severely." But Jesus gave her no reply, not even a word. Then his disciples urged him to send her away. "Tell her to go away," they said. "She is bothering us with all her begging." Then Jesus said to the woman, "I was sent only to help God's lost sheep—the people of Israel."
Matthew 15:22-24

Jesus came and told his disciples, "I have been given all authority in heaven and on earth. Therefore, go and make disciples of all the nations, baptizing them in the name of the Father and the Son and the Holy Spirit. Teach these new disciples to obey all the commands I have given you. And be sure of this: I am with you always, even to the end of the age."
Matthew 28:18-20

We have already seen from the Scriptures that the Levitical tithing model is a tithing model that was prescribed by the Mosaic Law. The Levites were instructed to collect tithes from their brethren as payment for priestly services. *Please remember that God never designed the Levitical priesthood to service people who were born outside the commonwealth of Israel.* Moses, the Law giver, never ever intended to have the Mosaic Covenant of Law imposed on Gentile nations who were not part of the commonwealth of Israel. Even the great ministry of our Lord Jesus Christ was limited to the "lost house of Israel" while He was here on earth because Jesus was also operating under the Mosaic Covenant of Law.

But when Jesus rose from the dead after conquering sin and death on the cross, He announced to His apprentice apostles that the "spiritual reach" of His New Testament priestly order would reach the ends of the earth. What we call the "Great Commission" is simply Christ's official announcement that we have "crossed over" from the Levitical order of priesthood, which was limited to the Jewish nation, to the New Creation royal priesthood. The New Creation royal priesthood (Order of Melchizedek) has no limitations in the scope of its spiritual reach. This is why "tithing into the Order of Melchizedek will cause nations to open up for Kingdom advancement."

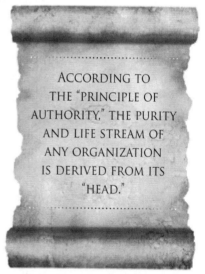

ACCORDING TO THE "PRINCIPLE OF AUTHORITY," THE PURITY AND LIFE STREAM OF ANY ORGANIZATION IS DERIVED FROM ITS "HEAD."

17. Under the priestly Order of Aaron, the High Priest offered annual gifts and sacrifices from the people to appease the wrath of God, whereas under the priestly Order of Melchizedek, the High Priest offered the ultimate sacrifice of Himself to God and appeased God's wrath forever.

"The old system under the law of Moses was only a shadow, a dim preview of the good things to come, not the good things themselves. The sacrifices under that system were repeated again and again, year after year, but they were never able to provide perfect cleansing for those who came to worship. If they could have provided perfect cleansing, the sacrifices would have stopped, for the worshipers would have been purified once for all time, and their feelings of guilt would have disappeared. But instead, those sacrifices actually reminded them of their sins year after year."

Hebrews 10:1-3

First, Christ said, "You did not want animal sacrifices or sin offerings or burnt offerings or other offerings for sin, nor were you pleased with them" (though they are required by the law of Moses). Then he said, "Look, I have come to do your will." He cancels the first covenant in order to put the second into effect. For God's will was for us to be made holy by the sacrifice of the body of Jesus Christ, once for all time.

Hebrews 10:8-10

Another equally important difference between the Levitical priesthood and the priestly Order of Melchizedek is found in the "spiritual value of the sacrificial offerings which were employed to appease God's righteous anger against sin." From the beginning of time God has made it quite clear that "His holiness can never co-exist with sin." When Adam and Eve allowed sin to touch their innocent spirits, God was forced to separate Himself from them. God also expelled them from Eden, the "Garden of inheritance." Ever since this catastrophic fall from grace there has been a cry in the human heart: redemption from the power of sin. Men and women of all ages want to have uninterrupted communion with God, but sin has proved to be too powerful an obstacle.

TITHING INTO THE PRIESTLY ORDER OF MELCHIZEDEK WILL GIVE US THE "POWER TO PREVAIL OVER PERSONAL SIN."

Under the Levitical priesthood the Levites sacrificed animals year after year in order to gain some level of access to God's presence and secure forgiveness for their sins and those of the people. Unfortunately, the blood of bulls and goats could only "cover sin from the eyes of God" but failed to stop the "engines of sin" from operating inside the worshippers. Under the priestly Order of Melchizedek our High Priest, Jesus Christ was able to completely satisfy the "righteous demands of God's law" by the offering of His own life and the shedding of His blood. *This is why tithing into the priestly Order of Melchizedek will give us the "power to prevail over personal sin."*

18. Under both priesthoods the High Priest was called by God.

And no one can become a high priest simply because he wants such an honor. He must be called by God for this work, just as Aaron was. That is why Christ did not honor himself by assuming he could become High Priest. No, he was chosen by God, who said to him, "You are my Son. Today I have become your Father." And in another passage God said to him, "You are a priest forever in the order of Melchizedek."

Hebrews 5:4-6

We have finally come to one of the most important similarities between the Levitical priesthood and the priestly Order of Melchizedek. It is very important for us to understand this similarity. It is the very thing that gives "spiritual legitimacy" to both of these priestly orders. Under both of these priestly orders, the High Priests could not appoint themselves; *they had to have a "bona fide call of God" upon their lives to serve in this lofty office.*

The apostle Paul tells us that only God can confer upon a man's life the "honor" that comes with the office of the High Priest. To stand in this office without a clear divine call of God, is an exercise in the worst kind of "spiritual fraud." In the Levitical priesthood, only Aaron and his sons could serve in the office of the High Priest. God had called and anointed them as a family to stand in this lofty office, until the time of reformation.

Under the priestly Order of Melchizedek, Jesus Christ is the only High Priest who will ever wear the mantle of this lofty office. God ordained Jesus Christ to this high priestly office, with an "oath." This is why when we tithe into this eternal priestly order, we are tithing into a divine priestly order that God Himself has "sealed with an unbreakable oath." How can our tithe fail to work for us? Oh, I forgot; we are still tithing according to Malachi 3:8-12! This might explain why many faithful tithers in the church fail to see noticeable spiritual breakthroughs as a result of their tithing.

19. Under the Levitical priesthood, the High Priest entered the holy of holies once a year, whereas under the priestly Order of Melchizedek, the High Priest has permanent residency in the holy of holies.

"When these things were all in place, the priests regularly entered the first room as they performed their religious duties. But only the high priest ever entered the Most Holy Place, and only once a year. And he always offered blood for his own sins and for the sins the people had committed in ignorance."

Hebrews 9:6-7

"Here is the main point: We have a High Priest who sat down in the place of honor beside the throne of the majestic God in heaven. There he ministers in the heavenly Tabernacle, the true place of worship that was built by the Lord and not by human hands."

Hebrews 8:1-2

If someone walked up to you and asked you this question: "Which group do you want to belong to—the group that lives inside the White House or the group that gets to visit the White House once a year?" I am sure your answer would be a resounding, "I want to belong to the one which lives inside the White House." It would not take a rocket scientist to figure out why. Those who live in the White House have "unlimited access to the White House and the President who lives there," while those who get to visit "once a year" have "limited and restricted access" to the White House.

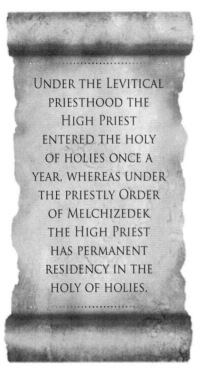

UNDER THE LEVITICAL PRIESTHOOD THE HIGH PRIEST ENTERED THE HOLY OF HOLIES ONCE A YEAR, WHEREAS UNDER THE PRIESTLY ORDER OF MELCHIZEDEK THE HIGH PRIEST HAS PERMANENT RESIDENCY IN THE HOLY OF HOLIES.

Under the Levitical priesthood, once a year the High Priest was given access to the holy of holies. He got to see the Shekinah glory of God only once in an entire year. The rest of the year "access" to the dwelling place of God's presence was completely "forbidden." Anybody who tried to "access" this lofty place was killed instantly. *Under the priestly Order of Melchizedek, we have a High Priest who has "unlimited access" to God's presence in the holy of holies, in the true Tabernacle of God which is in heaven.* Our High Priest (Jesus Christ) lives with God every second of eternity. This is why "miraculous things happen for believers who tithe into this priestly Order of Melchizedek." ***Our tithes of honor act like a "point of contact" with this powerful eternal priestly order,*** which gives us the same level of "unlimited access" to the presence of God as our High Priest enjoys.

This is why I "cringe in fear" when I hear sincere men and women of God tell New Testament believers (who live under the priestly Order of Melchizedek) to "tithe according to Malachi and then believe God to open the windows of heaven." My dear friend, "if we are being fed through windows, it means that the door to the Father's house is still locked and we are still operating from the outside." This belief system is a complete contradiction of Paul's apostolic teachings.

The belief that God will open the "windows of heaven" when we tithe goes against all the "apostolic teachings" of all the apostles of the Lord Jesus Christ who wrote the New Testament. For all the apostles agree that "New Testament post-Calvary followers of Christ are no longer operating from the outside-in like the Mosaic Generation. Saint Paul tells us that we have been "brought inside" our Father's house by His only begotten Son (Jesus Christ). Paul tells us in the book of Ephesians that Christ has made us (His Church) to sit with Him in heavenly places. Please explain to me how we can be fed through windows, if we are already inside the house? I truly believe that there is "no doctrine which is more inaccurate than the Church's teaching on tithing." This is why it's infinitely crucial that we rediscover the "Lost Key," which is the "Abrahamic tithing model which is based upon the priestly Order of Melchizedek." The Malachi 3:8-12 pattern of tithing is "keeping us on the outside of our heavenly Father's house," when Christ paid a hefty price to bring us in. The Genesis 14:17-20 Abrahamic tithing model will "bring us in and keep us inside the eternal structures of the Kingdom."

21. Under the Levitical priesthood, assimilation into the priestly order happened automatically after the day of circumcision, whereas under the priestly Order of Melchizedek, assimilation into the priesthood does not happen until there has been a personal Encounter with the High Priest (Jesus Christ).

"If there are foreigners living among you who want to celebrate the Lord's Passover, let all their males be circumcised. Only then may they celebrate the Passover with you like any native-born Israelite. But no uncircumcised male may ever eat the Passover meal."

Exodus 12:48

Jesus replied, "I assure you, no one can enter the Kingdom of God without being born of water and the Spirit. Humans can reproduce only human life, but the Holy Spirit gives birth to spiritual life."

John 3:5-6

Another equally important difference between the Levitical priesthood and the priestly Order of Melchizedek is found in how the people who lived under these priesthoods were admitted into the priestly order itself. Under the Levitical priesthood, the proof that someone had become a member of the priesthood was determined by the physical act of "circumcision." This is because the Levitical priesthood was an earthly priesthood and required only a "physical sign" to demonstrate a person's commitment to the priestly order.

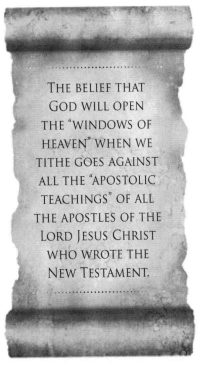

THE BELIEF THAT GOD WILL OPEN THE "WINDOWS OF HEAVEN" WHEN WE TITHE GOES AGAINST ALL THE "APOSTOLIC TEACHINGS" OF ALL THE APOSTLES OF THE LORD JESUS CHRIST WHO WROTE THE NEW TESTAMENT.

On the other hand, under the priestly Order of Melchizedek, entrance into this powerful eternal priestly order requires a more "invasive and life-changing spiritual sign" before a person is admitted into this order of priesthood. According to Jesus Christ who is the High Priest of the Order of Melchizedek, membership in this divine priestly order requires "a spiritual rebirth" which brings about a "true circumcision of the heart" and not just the flesh. *This spiritual birth is "initiated by a personal encounter" with Jesus Christ who is the High Priest of God Most High.* Jesus told Nicodemus, who lived under the Levitical priesthood, that "unless he was born again" he couldn't enter into the "Kingdom of God." This is why tithing into this priestly Order of Melchizedek is so powerful. It "opens our spiritual eyes, so we can understand God's divine Kingdom order and how we can bring nations under this powerful eternal priesthood."

22. Under the Levitical priesthood, the priesthood was easily compromised by demonic influences that were passed down through the genealogy of the High Priest, whereas under the priestly Order of Melchizedek, the priesthood can never be compromised by demonic influences because our High Priest (Christ) has no earthly genealogy or beginning of days.

"He is the kind of high priest we need because he is holy and blameless, unstained by sin. He has been set apart from sinners and has been given the highest place of honor in heaven. Unlike those other high priests, he does not need to offer sacrifices every day. They did this for their own sins first and then for the sins of the people. But Jesus did this once for all when he offered himself as the sacrifice for the people's sins. The law appointed high priests who were limited by human weakness."
Hebrews 7:26-28

This Melchizedek was king of the city of Salem and also a priest of God Most High. When Abraham was returning home after winning a great battle against the kings, Melchizedek met him and blessed him. 2 Then Abraham took a tenth of all he had captured in battle and gave it to Melchizedek. The name Melchizedek means "king of justice," and king of Salem means "king of peace." **3** *There is no record of his father or mother or any of his ancestors—no beginning or end to his life. He remains a priest forever, resembling the Son of God.*

Hebrews 7:1-3

There is a lot of talk today about the ministry of "breaking generational curses." Ministries are rising all around us who claim to have the power to break generational curses over entire families. While I deeply applaud the efforts of all of those who have a sincere desire to see God's people delivered from the "power of demonic influences," which have been passed down to them generationally, I have serious reservations about the spiritual technology most of these deliverance ministries are employing to do this. Many of these deliverance ministers have experienced some level of success in this arena. But I believe that there is a more excellent way of breaking generational curses. My personal contention with many deliverance ministers who "teach on breaking generational curses" is that many of them have no "clear-cut revelation concerning the priestly Order of Melchizedek" and do not know the profound effect that understanding the Order of Melchizedek will bring to bear on their ability to permanently break generational curses.

The apostle Paul tells us that the priestly Order of Melchizedek "has no earthly ancestry or genealogy." **The High Priest of this eternal priestly order in His divine nature as Christ has "no earthly father or mother" or any such earthly genealogy.** Even though our Lord Jesus Christ was born through the virgin birth, the fact of the matter is that He (Christ) has always existed in the realms of eternity before anything was ever created. It doesn't take a rocket scientist to figure out the fact that "generational curses can only come upon us through our father's or mother's bloodline." *This being said, it follows then that the most "powerful" method for delivering Kingdom citizens from the power of generational curses is "introducing them to the priestly Order of Melchizedek and showing them how tithing into this priestly order destroys the yoke of generational curses."* This is because the priestly Order of Melchizedek is the only divine priestly order known to mankind which "exists beyond the reach of any generational curse." When deliverance ministers discover this "spiritual technology for breaking generational curses," they will see more people set free from the power of the evil one than ever before.

23. Under the Levitical priesthood the High Priest stood in the office of a priest and as such the priesthood was only serviced by a priestly anointing, whereas under the Order of Melchizedek our High Priest is

both a King and a Priest. As a result, New Creation royal priesthood is serviced by a kingly, prophetic and priestly anointing.

"And these are the garments which they shall make: a breastplate, an ephod, a robe, a skillfully woven tunic, a turban, and a sash. So they shall make holy garments for Aaron your brother and his sons, that he may minister to Me as priest."

Exodus 28:4

This Melchizedek was king of the city of Salem and also a priest of God Most High. When Abraham was returning home after winning a great battle against the kings, Melchizedek met him and blessed him. Then Abraham took a tenth of all he had captured in battle and gave it to Melchizedek. The name Melchizedek means "king of justice," and king of Salem means "king of peace." There is no record of his father or mother or any of his ancestors—no beginning or end to his life. He remains a priest forever, resembling the Son of God.

Hebrews 7:1-3

Under the Levitical priesthood the "primary anointing" which was driving the spiritual engines of this earthly priesthood was the "priestly anointing." This means that the Levitical priesthood functioned on one spiritual cylinder. The priestly anointing has the following effects on the people it touches. "It gives them a desire to commune with God, pray, fast, worship and repent from their sins."

On the other hand, the priestly Order of Melchizedek is serviced by "three powerful anointings or operations of the Spirit" instead of one. The priestly Order of Melchizedek is driven by these three spiritual cylinders: the "kingly, prophetic and priestly" anointings. The "kingly anointing" causes people to become "very governmental, territorial and militant in their spirit dynamics," whereas the "prophetic anointing" causes "people to be much more spontaneous, insightful and sensitive to the voice of God." We have already mentioned what the priestly anointing does.

THE MOST "POWERFUL" METHOD FOR DELIVERING KINGDOM CITIZENS FROM THE POWER OF GENERATIONAL CURSES IS "INTRODUCING THEM TO THE PRIESTLY ORDER OF MELCHIZEDEK AND SHOWING THEM HOW TITHING INTO THIS PRIESTLY ORDER DESTROYS THE YOKE OF GENERATIONAL CURSES."

You do not have to be a NASA astronaut or rocket scientist to figure out what will happen when you "combine all the spiritual effects of these three anointings and package them into one spiritual dosage" and then inject this spiritual dosage into the life stream of the global Church. What a dynamic and territorial church we will end up with! It will certainly be a "Church without blemishes or wrinkles." It will be a glorious Church, the Church of the firstborn.

Although the ministerial offices of "king, prophet and priest" were also operational under the commonwealth of Israel, they "functioned as separate spiritual cylinders." There were times when the kings of Israel killed priests, and there were times when the priests conspired with the people to kill the prophets of God. Before Jesus Christ arrived on the scene, no man had ever managed to "successfully harness these three anointings under one spiritual mantle" in perfect spiritual symmetry. Jesus Christ, the High Priest of the priestly Order of Melchizedek, managed to do this. This is why I cannot overemphasize the power of the "Genesis 14:17-20 Abrahamic tithing model." We must now teach the people of God to begin to tithe into the priestly Order of Melchizedek armed with this information.

24. Under both priesthoods the tithe belongs to the storehouse, which is the local Church.

"Bring this tithe to the designated place of worship—the place the Lord your God chooses for his name to be honored—and eat it there in his presence. This applies to your tithes of grain, new wine, olive oil, and the firstborn males of your flocks and herds. Doing this will teach you always to fear the Lord your God."

Deuteronomy 14:23

Then Jacob awoke from his sleep and said, "Surely the Lord is in this place, and I wasn't even aware of it!" But he was also afraid and said, "What an awesome place this is! It is none other than the house of God, the very gateway to heaven!" The next morning Jacob got up very early. He took the stone he had rested his head against, and he set it upright as a memorial pillar. Then he poured olive oil over it. He named that place Bethel (which means "house of God"), although the name of the nearby village was Luz. Then Jacob made this vow: "If God will indeed be with me and protect me on this journey, and if he will provide me with food and clothing, and if I return safely to my father's home, then the Lord will certainly be my God. And this memorial pillar I have set up will become a place for worshiping God, and I will present to God a tenth of everything he gives me."

Genesis 28:16-22

LIFE APPLICATION SECTION

Point to Ponder:

The most accurate and powerful method for delivering people from the power of generational curses is "introducing them to the priestly Order of Melchizedek and showing them how tithing into this priestly Order shuts down the flow of generational curses".

Verse to Remember:

Then Jacob awoke from his sleep and said, "Surely the LORD is in this place, and I wasn't even aware of it!" But he was also afraid and said, "What an awesome place this is! It is none other than the house of God, the very gateway to heaven!"

Genesis 28:16-17

Questions to Consider:

- What is one of the similarities between the priestly Order of Aaron and the priestly Order of Melchizedek?

_____

_____

_____

_____

_____

- What are some of the main differences between these two priestly Orders?"

_____

_____

_____

_____

_____

JOURNAL YOUR THOUGHTS

Chapter
TWELVE

BENEFITS OF THE ABRAHAMIC TITHING MODEL

Without a shadow of doubt there are some very powerful spiritual benefits which will begin to flow our way when we shift from the Malachi 3:8-12 tithing model to the Genesis 14:18-20 Abrahamic tithing model.** The spiritual benefits of tithing into the priestly Order of Melchizedek are infinitely greater than the spiritual benefits of tithing into the Levitical priesthood. For the sake of our study we will quickly list the spiritual benefits of tithing into the Levitical priesthood and then contrast them with the spiritual benefits of tithing into the priestly Order of Melchizedek.

Benefits of the Malachi 3:8-12 Tithing Model

"Will a man rob God? Yet you have robbed Me! But you say, 'In what way have we robbed You?' In tithes and offerings. You are cursed with a curse, For you have robbed Me, Even this whole nation. Bring all the tithes into the storehouse, That there may be food in My house, And try Me now in this," "Says the LORD of hosts, "If I will not open for you the windows of heaven And pour out for you such blessing That there will not be room enough to receive it."And I will rebuke the devourer for your sakes, So that he will not destroy the fruit of your ground, Nor shall the vine fail to bear fruit for you in the field," "Says the LORD of hosts; And all nations will call you blessed, For you will be a delightful land," "Says the LORD of hosts.

Malachi 3:8-12

Here is a simple summary of the benefits of tithing into the Levitical priesthood based upon the above passage of Scripture from the book of Malachi.

1. Open windows of heaven

2. A poured out blessing beyond our capacity to receive

3. God rebukes the devourer on our behalf

4. A harvest of the fruits of the ground

5. Nations will call us blessed

The Windows of Heaven
versus the Doors of Heaven

One of the spiritual benefits promised to tithers who employ the Malachi 3:8-12 tithing model is that *"God will open the windows of heaven and pour out a blessing"* onto their life. The only challenge that I have with this promise is simply this: "if the blessing is being poured out of the windows of heaven," it means that the recipients of the blessing in question are "operating from the outside" of the eternal structures of the Kingdom of Heaven. It is tragic when New Testament believers come to believe that "they are operating from the outside of the Kingdom of Heaven." *This belief goes against everything that the Lord Jesus Christ and His apostles taught us about post-Calvary New Testament living.*

Jesus replied, "I tell you the truth, unless you are born again, you cannot see the Kingdom of God." "What do you mean?" exclaimed Nicodemus. "How can an old man go back into his mother's womb and be born again?" Jesus replied, "I assure you, no one can enter the Kingdom of God without being born of water and the Spirit.

John 3:3-5

When Nicodemus, a notable teacher of the Law, came to Jesus in the night hours, an interesting conversation broke out between these two spiritual leaders. Nicodemus wanted to know the secret behind Jesus' spiritual power. Jesus responded by telling Nicodemus that even though he was a teacher of the Law and lived under the Levitical priesthood he couldn't enter the Kingdom of God, until he was born of the Spirit. I am not a rocket scientist but it sounds to me like Jesus was telling Nicodemus that he was "operating from outside of the spiritual order that Jesus Christ was a part of." Jesus told him explicitly that he had to be "born again" to "enter into the Kingdom of God." So here is the million-dollar question: *"If being born again brings us into the Kingdom of God, why do we tithe as though we are still on the outside looking in?"* I rest my case.

That is what the Scriptures mean when they say, "No eye has seen, no ear has heard, and no mind has imagined what God has prepared for those who love him."

1 Corinthians 2:9

We are no longer strangers and outsiders to the house of God the Father. Jesus already told us that He had given us the "keys of the Kingdom of Heaven" and if this is the case then we need to be asking God to open the "doors of the Kingdom of Heaven" instead of waiting on God to open the "windows of heaven."

Access to a "No Limit Blessing"

Bring all the tithes into the storehouse, That there may be food in My house, And try Me now in this, "Says the LORD of hosts, "If I will not open for you the windows of heaven And pour out for you such blessing That there will not be room enough to receive it.

Malachi 3:10

One of the promises for tithing, which was bequeathed upon the people who tithed into the Levitical priesthood, was "a poured out blessing that the tithers did not have room enough to receive." Right away you can see that something is seriously wrong with this picture of promise. What we thought was a "great blessing" was actually a "limited blessing" compared to the fullness of what God has prepared for the New Testament Church. Anytime you are the "recipient of a blessing" beyond your "capacity" to receive, you have a real problem on your hands. Why would God pour out a blessing for His people that they

IT IS TRAGIC WHEN NEW TESTAMENT BELIEVERS COME TO BELIEVE THAT "THEY ARE OPERATING FROM THE OUTSIDE OF THE KINGDOM OF HEAVEN."

did not have "enough room to receive" in its fullness? This is a very legitimate question; I am glad you asked me, so I will answer you.

"Now I say that the heir, as long as he is a child, does not differ at all from a slave, though he is master of all, is under guardians and stewards until the time appointed by the father. Even so we, when we were children, were in bondage under the elements of the world. But when the fullness of the time had come, God sent forth His Son, born of a woman, born under the law, to redeem those who were under the law, that we might receive the adoption as sons."

Galatians 4:1-5

The above passage of Scripture contains the answer to this perplexing question. Under the Mosaic Covenant of Law, everything was merely a "shadow" of things to come. In other words God never revealed anything in its "fullness" in the Old Testament. Based upon the teachings of the apostle Paul everything that happened under the Old Testament Covenant of Law was but a "shadow" of "things to come." This means that whatever God did under the Mosaic Covenant Dispensation, He was working towards its "fullest expression in Christ." The apostle Paul tells us that when Jesus was born of the virgin birth, the period called the "fullness of time was initiated." *This means that since the virgin birth of Jesus Christ, God wants to deal with all of His people from a "position of fullness" and not from a position of "types and shadows."* Under the Levitical priesthood, tithers were given a "poured blessing" that was beyond their capacity to receive, simply because God had not yet established a "spiritual structure in the Old Testament" that could contain the "fullness of the blessing of Abraham."

When Jesus said "it is finished" when He was on the cross, the Old Testament transitional period of "types and shadows" came to a sudden end. Jesus Christ's death on the cross marked the beginning of the day of "fullness" for everything God had prepared for the Seed of Abraham from before the foundation of the world. This means that when we give a "tithe that is based upon the priestly Order of Melchizedek," our tithe has the power to infinitely "increase our spiritual capacity to receive the fullness of the blessing of Abraham," which God wants to confer upon us as His dear children.

"But as it is written: Eye has not seen, nor ear heard, nor have entered into the heart of man the things which God has prepared for those who love Him."

I Corinthians 2:9-10

The Place called Jehovah Jireh

When they arrived at the place where God had told him to go, Abraham built an altar and arranged the wood on it. Then he tied his son, Isaac, and laid him on the altar on top of the wood. And Abraham picked up the knife to kill his son as a sacrifice. At that moment the angel of the Lord called to him from heaven, "Abraham! Abraham!" "Yes," Abraham replied. "Here I am!" "Don't lay a hand on the boy!" the angel said. "Do not hurt him in any way, for now I know that you truly fear God. You have not withheld from me even your son, your only son." Then Abraham looked up and saw a ram caught by its horns in a thicket. So he took the ram and sacrificed it as a burnt offering in place of his son. Abraham named the place Yahweh-Yireh (which means "the Lord will provide"). To this day, people still use that name as a proverb: "On the mountain of the Lord it will be provided."

Genesis 22:9-14

When we begin to view everything which transpired in Abraham's life from the perspective of the priestly Order of Melchizedek, starting from the time Abram was introduced to Melchizedek (Genesis 14), to the day he died, we will discover many amazing benefits of tithing into this eternal priestly order. I believe that Abraham continued to tithe in one form or the other into the Order of Melchizedek, because he passed on the "concept of tithing" to his grandson Jacob (Genesis 28:11-16). One way or the other Abraham managed to pass on the "concept of tithing to his entire family-line."

Besides his life-changing meeting with Melchizedek the Priest of God Most High, the most significant spiritual event which took place in Abraham's life happened in the last embassy of his life here on earth. After waiting for what may have seemed like a "lifetime," Abraham's wife, Sarah, gave birth to their first and only son. To say that Abraham and Sarah were very emotionally attached to their son Isaac is an understatement. Notwithstanding, God asked Abraham to sacrifice his only son, Isaac on Mount Moriah. As difficult as it must have been, Abraham obeyed the voice of God and took his only son, Isaac to Mount Moriah. *When they got to the top of the Mountain, Abraham bound his son Isaac and placed him on the altar to sacrifice him to God.*

We know from what the Scriptures teach us that you cannot "offer tithes or sacrifices to a deity" without going through "the deity's designated priesthood." These three spiritual elements – "tithes, sacrifices and priesthoods" – are inseparably connected. You can never have one without the other. Here is the billion dollar question? ***"When Abraham offered his son Isaac as a sacrifice to God on Mount Moriah, what priesthood was he associating his sacrifice with?"*** The answer is simple but deeply profound. It was the eternal priestly Order of Melchizedek. It was the only spiritual priesthood that was clearly revealed to Abraham, at the time. *Just* *before Abraham struck his son with the death blow, God had a change of heart.* He called Abram's name from out of the heavens and showed him a ram that was caught in the thicket, right behind him.

> *Then the angel of the Lord called again to Abraham from heaven. "This is what the Lord says: Because you have obeyed me and have not withheld even your son, your only son, I swear by my own name that I will certainly bless you. I will multiply your descendants beyond number, like the stars in the sky and the sand on the seashore. Your descendants will conquer the cities of their enemies. And through your descendants all the nations of the earth will be blessed—all because you have obeyed me."*
>
> Genesis 22:15-18

Abraham called the name of the place that God had brought him to "Jehovah Jireh." *"Jehovah Jireh"* means, "the Lord shall provide at His Mountain." It is important to take note of the fact that the name "Jehovah Jireh" is not necessarily the name of God. **It is the name of a "place in the spirit realm" that Abraham discovered when he obeyed God in the offering of his son, Isaac.** This spiritual place was and still is a place of total provision. God has decorated it with an "unlimited supply of spiritual and material resources" for advancing His Kingdom here on earth. Abraham through his obedience had discovered a place of total provision under the Order of Melchizedek. *May God help us to find this place of total provision when we choose to live that place of total obedience to His revealed Will for our life.*

SINCE THE VIRGIN BIRTH OF JESUS CHRIST, GOD WANTS TO DEAL WITH ALL OF HIS PEOPLE FROM A "POSITION OF FULLNESS" AND NOT FROM A POSITION OF "TYPES AND SHADOWS."

This means that when we tithe into the priestly Order of Melchizedek, we are actually "opening up a spiritual pathway" which can lead us into a "place of abundant spiritual and financial resources!" I truly believe that tithing into the priestly Order of Melchizedek will "inject us with the same spirit of total obedience" to God which was manifested in Abraham's life. *This place of total obedience to God gave Abraham the grace to "offer his only son, Isaac" to God as a living sacrifice.* God was so deeply moved by this one act of obedience in Abraham's life that He sealed the blessing of Abraham with an "unchangeable Oath."

Access to An infinitely greater Contingency of Angels

"No, you have come to Mount Zion, to the city of the living God, the heavenly Jerusalem, and to countless thousands of angels in a joyful gathering. You have come to the assembly of God's firstborn children, whose names are written in heaven. You have come to God himself, who is the judge over all things. You have come to the spirits of the righteous ones in heaven who have now been made perfect."

Hebrews 12:22-23

We have already established the fact that God never did or revealed anything in its "fullness" under the Old Testament Covenant of Law, because it was built upon the "shadow or copy" of heavenly things. We know for a fact that the "substance of something" has more weight and presence than the "shadow of it." One of the most powerful blessings that God ever gave to His people in both the Old and New Testament is the powerful ministry of His holy angels. In both Testaments we see the pages of Scripture sauced with "angelic interventions" in the affairs of men.

"The LORD has established His throne in heaven, And His kingdom rules over all. Bless the LORD, you His angels, Who excel in strength, who do His word, Heeding the voice of His word."

Psalm 103:19-20 (NKJV)

The above passage of Scripture shows us how God exerts His almighty influence over the affairs of nations. **God exerts His "kingdom rule" over the affairs of nations through the powerful ministry of His holy angels.** This prophetic passage from the book of Psalms also gives us three very unique characteristics of these holy angels, which are:

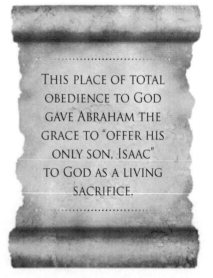

THIS PLACE OF TOTAL OBEDIENCE TO GOD GAVE ABRAHAM THE GRACE TO "OFFER HIS ONLY SON, ISAAC" TO GOD AS A LIVING SACRIFICE.

1. Angels excel in strength. To excel at something means "to be extremely good at." Angels are extremely good at being strong in spirit and in power.

2. Angels are the "heavenly agents" responsible for "executing God's will." They also demonstrate the power of His Word here on earth. This means that nothing of God happens here on earth without the involvement of angelic agencies.

3. Angels are "summoned into divine activity" by God's people "giving voice" to God's written Word.

The apostle Paul tells us that there was an angelic agency which was assigned to the Levitical priesthood and to all the people of Israel who lived under the Mosaic Covenant. This angelic agency was assigned to bring about "miraculous answers" to the prayers of God's people who lived under the Mosaic Covenant of Law; as well as execute divine judgment against those who failed to honor God's Law. Unfortunately this angelic agency could never "operate in its fullness" because Jesus Christ had not yet died to redeem the world from sin and introduce a "new spiritual world order." When Jesus Christ came into the world, the prophetic era the Scriptures call the "fullness of time" was initiated. Now we can experience everything of God in its fullness.

"But ye are come unto mount Sion, and unto the city of the living God, the heavenly Jerusalem, and to an innumerable company of angels."

Hebrews 12:23 (NKJV)

The apostle Paul tells us that the priestly Order of Melchizedek which operates out of the temple of God in spiritual Jerusalem **has an infinite supply of angels.** The angelic agency which services tithers under the priestly Order of Melchizedek is a "gazillion times" more powerful than the "limited operations" of the angelic agency which serviced tithers under the Levitical priesthood. This is why tithing into the priestly Order of Melchizedek "will provoke the greatest intervention of angels" in our lives than we have ever seen. This is why believing God for "miraculous provisions and answers to prayer" must become the easiest thing for us to do, who live under the New Testament Order of Melchizedek priesthood.

GOD EXERTS HIS "KINGDOM RULE" OVER THE AFFAIRS OF NATIONS THROUGH THE POWERFUL MINISTRY OF HIS HOLY ANGELS

This is why I believe that those of us who tithe into the priestly Order of Melchizedek have the "power to transform and influence entire nations" for the Kingdom of God. This is because our efforts to advance the Kingdom of God are "undergirded by the largest and most powerful contingency of angels." God is very interested in influencing the lives of individuals, but His highest desire is to impact entire nations. We must realize that as tithers into the priestly Order of Melchizedek, the King of the heavenly Jerusalem wants to use us to "impact and influence entire nations." We must never forget that our God is the "God of the nations."

Intercepts the Seductive Power of the King of Sodom

"And the king of Sodom said unto Abram, Give me the persons, and take the goods to thyself. And Abram said to the king of Sodom, I have lifted up my hand unto Jehovah, God Most High, possessor of heaven and earth, that I will not take a thread nor a shoe-latchet nor aught that is thine, lest thou shouldest say, I have made Abram rich."

Genesis 14:21-23

I am tired of seeing too many good ministries get destroyed during the peak season of their usefulness to the Kingdom of God. The demise of these powerful ministers of the gospel usually occurs at a strategic time when the devil knows that the fall from grace of these great "spiritual icons" will cause great harm to the cause of Christ. Bishop T.D Jakes once said that one of the spiritual dangers to ministers of the gospel is what he called spiritual "PMS." "PMS" stands for "Power, Money and Sex."

This "PMS" problem identifies three areas that accelerate the "process of spiritual decay and decline" in the lives of God's people if these areas are not handled in the spirit of integrity. The reason so many good people and ministries get destroyed in these three areas is largely due to the fact that these three areas of human endeavor are for the most part "under the governing influence of the king of Sodom," a territorial demonic entity which is the "mother of spiritual perversion and open rebellion to God's authority." We need to be aware that there is a very strong "machinery of death" which is behind the global lust for "Power, Money and Sex."

One of the first spiritual benefits that Abraham received from tithing into the priestly Order of Melchizedek was *"divine interception" from being influenced or controlled by the "demonic and seductive power" of the king of Sodom.* The king of Sodom got to Abram just after the departure of Melchizedek. This ungodly king offered Abraham what he thought was the deal of a lifetime. *He offered Abraham all the gold and silver from the treasuries of Sodom.* Had the king of Sodom offered Abraham the same deal a couple years earlier, Abram would have probably taken the "bait." Fortunately, the tithe that he had sown into the priestly Order of Melchizedek had given Abram the "supernatural grace" to resist the demonic offer of gold and silver from the hands of the king of Sodom. Moments after giving his first tithe to Melchizedek, Abraham solved all his past "PMS" problems. He found the power to say "NO" to the corruptive influence of "Power, Money and Sex."

Ministers of the gospel are in great need of this same divine power. When we start tithing into the priestly Order of Melchizedek based upon the prophetic model established by Abraham in Genesis 14:18-20 and Hebrews chapter 7, *we are going to see God intercept many "demonic nuclear missiles" that were headed our way.* This divine interception from the seductive power of the king of Sodom is desperately needed in the Church today. If God does not supernaturally intercept many of our business people, some of them are going to fall prey to the demonic Sodomic system. Some of these marketplace ministers will end up making financial deals with the king of Sodom and literally destroy themselves and their families. We need God Almighty to "intercept" the train of the king of Sodom, before it destroys us. *Tithing under the Order of Melchizedek precipitates both the "climate and conditions" necessary for God to initiate the "Technology of Divine Interception."* The release of the Spirit of Divine Interception is one of the primary benefits of tithing under the Order of Melchizedek.

I AM TIRED OF SEEING TOO MANY GOOD MINISTRIES GET DESTROYED DURING THE PEAK SEASON OF THEIR USEFULNESS TO THE KINGDOM OF GOD

Supernatural Access to Bread and Wine

"Then Melchizedek king of Salem brought out bread and wine; "

Genesis 14:18 (NKJ)

The above passage of Scripture tells us that there was a divine covenant exchange that took place between Abram and Melchizedek, the King-Priest. Melchizedek gave Abram "bread and wine" and Abram gave Him "tithes of honor." Let us examine the prophetic implications of the sacred bread and wine that Melchizedek's priesthood made available to Abram.

In the Bible there are seven prophetic representations of bread. We have listed here these seven prophetic dimensions of the sacred bread that Melchizedek gave to Abram. By simply examining the seven prophetic representations of the sacred bread that this king-priest gave to Abram, we will quickly come to terms with the critical importance of this "sacred bread of the Order of Melchizedek" and why tithing into such an eternal order is so powerful.

Bread in the Bible symbolizes the following seven prophetic dimensions:

1. The doctrine of the Kingdom of God

Jesus also used this illustration: "The Kingdom of Heaven is like the yeast a woman used in making bread. Even though she put only a little yeast in three measures of flour, it permeated every part of the dough."

Matthew 13:33

2. The Life or Body of Christ

As they were eating, Jesus took some **bread** *and blessed it. Then he broke it in pieces and gave it to the disciples, saying, "Take this and eat it, for this is my body."*

Matthew 26:26

Jesus replied, "I am the bread of life. Whoever comes to me will never be hungry again. Whoever believes in me will never be thirsty."

John 6:35

3. Deliverance from Demonic Oppression

And behold, a woman of Canaan came from that region and cried out to Him, saying, "Have mercy on me, O Lord, Son of David! My daughter is severely demon-possessed." 23 But He answered her not a word. And His disciples came and urged Him, saying, "Send her away, for she cries out after us." 24 But He answered and said, "I was not sent except to the lost sheep of the house of Israel." 25 Then she came and worshiped Him, saying, "Lord, help me!" 26 But He answered and said, "It is *not good to take the children's bread and throw it to the little dogs." **27** And she said, "Yes, Lord, yet even the little dogs eat the crumbs which fall from their masters' table."*

Matthew 15:22-27 NKJV

4. God's Manifested Presence

*"Place the **Bread** of the Presence on the table to remain before me at all times."*

Exodus 25:30

5. The Word of God

*During that time the devil came and said to him, "If you are the Son of God, tell these stones to become loaves of bread." **4** But Jesus told him, "No! The Scriptures say, 'People do not live by bread alone, but by every word that comes from the mouth of God.'"*

Matthew 4:3-4

6. Spiritual Nourishment or Spiritual Prosperity

*So He said to them, "When you pray, say: Our Father in heaven, Hallowed be Your name. Your kingdom come. Your will be done. On earth as it is in heaven. **3** Give us day by day our daily bread."*

Luke 11:2-3

But Jesus told him, "No! The Scriptures say, 'People do not live by bread alone, but by every word that comes from the mouth of God.'"

Matthew 4:4

7. Natural Nourishment or Material Prosperity

"In the sweat of your face you shall eat bread Till you return to the ground, For out of it you were taken; For dust you are, And to dust you shall return."

Genesis 3:19 NKJV

"...and the seven years of famine began to come, as Joseph had said. The famine was in all lands, but in all the land of Egypt there was bread."

Genesis 41:54 NKJV

The Sacred Wine

"And Melchizedek, the king of Salem and a priest of God Most High, brought Abram some bread and wine."

Genesis 14:18

The second vital spiritual element that Melchizedek's priesthood gave to Abram when this King-Priest intercepted him in the Valley of the Kings was the "sacred Wine." Understanding the prophetic symbolism of this sacred wine will usher us into a whole new dimension of life-giving revelation. These symbolisms will further underscore why the Order of Melchizedek is such a rich soil to tithe into. I am not insinuating that tithing is the only way to access these priceless blessings, but it is clear that the "tithes" that Abram gave to Melchizedek was how he ratified this incredible covenant exchange that Melchizedek's priesthood had initiated in Abram's life. Based upon the prophetic writings of the holy writ, "Wine" symbolizes the following:

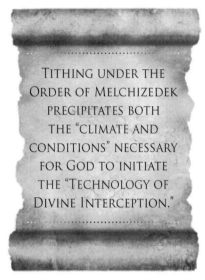

TITHING UNDER THE ORDER OF MELCHIZEDEK PRECIPITATES BOTH THE "CLIMATE AND CONDITIONS" NECESSARY FOR GOD TO INITIATE THE "TECHNOLOGY OF DIVINE INTERCEPTION."

1. The Spirit of the Kingdom of God

"And do not get drunk with wine, for that is debauchery; but ever be filled and stimulated with the [Holy] Spirit. **19***Speak out to one another in psalms and hymns and spiritual songs, offering praise with voices [and instruments] and making melody with all your heart to the Lord,* **20***At all times and for everything giving thanks in the name of our Lord Jesus Christ to God the Father."*

Ephesians 5:18-20 AMP

"But if I am casting out demons by the Spirit of God, then the Kingdom of God has arrived among you."

Matthew 12:28

2. Spiritual Intoxication

"He ties his foal to a grapevine, the colt of his donkey to a choice vine. He washes his clothes in wine, his robes in the blood of grapes. **12** *His eyes are darker than wine, and his teeth are whiter than milk."*

Genesis 49:11-12

So they were all amazed and perplexed, saying to one another, "Whatever could this mean?" **13** *Others mocking said, "They are full of new wine."* **14** *But Peter, standing up with the eleven, raised his voice and said to them, "Men of Judea and all who* *dwell in Jerusalem, let this be known to you, and heed my words.* **15** *For these are not drunk, as you suppose, since it is only the third hour of the day.*

Acts 2:12-14 NKJV

3. The Blood of Jesus

And he took a cup of wine and gave thanks to God for it. He gave it to them and said, "Each of you drink from it, **28** *for this is my blood, which confirms the covenant[a] between God and his people. It is poured out as a sacrifice to forgive the sins of many."*

Matthew 26:27-28

4. The Anointing of the Holy Spirit

"Then the LORD awaked as one out of sleep, and like a mighty man that shouteth by reason of wine."

Psalm 78:65

"These people are not drunk, as some of you are assuming. Nine o'clock in the morning is much too early for that. **16** *No, what you see was predicted long ago by the prophet Joel:* **17** *'In the last days,' God says, 'I will pour out my Spirit upon all people. Your sons and daughters will prophesy. Your young men will see visions, and your old men will dream dreams.'"*

Acts 2:15-17

5. The Joy of the Lord

"And wine that maketh glad the heart of man, and oil to make his face to shine, and bread which strengtheneth man's heart.."

Psalm 104:15 KJV

"Go thy way, eat thy bread with joy, and drink thy wine with a merry heart; for God now accepteth thy works."

Ecclesiastes 9:7 KJV

6. The Generational Blessing

Isaac said to Esau, "I have made Jacob your master and have declared that all his brothers will be his servants. I have guaranteed him an abundance of grain and wine— what is left for me to give you, my son?"

Genesis 27:37

Now there was a man named Naboth, from Jezreel, who owned a vineyard in Jezreel beside the palace of King Ahab of Samaria. 2 One day Ahab said to Naboth, "Since your vineyard is so convenient to my palace, I would like to buy it to use as a vegetable garden. I will give you a better vineyard in exchange, or if you prefer, I will pay you for it." 3 But Naboth replied, "The Lord forbid that I should give you the inheritance that was passed down by my ancestors."

1 Kings 21:1-3

The Blessing of a Powerful Name

The above passages of Scripture strongly suggest that "names" play a critical role in determining the nature of a thing and how it ultimately functions. Before Isaac was born God called out his name. Before King Josiah was born, God called out his name and announced his revivalist destiny. Before the birth of the prophet John the Baptist the angel Gabriel appeared to his father Zachariah and gave him explicit instructions to name his firstborn son, John.

The angel Gabriel appears one final time in the New Testament to announce the birth of the world's promised Messiah (Jesus). When the angel Gabriel appeared to Joseph in a dream, he told him to call the child who was going to be born out of Mary's womb, Jesus! The name "Jesus" means "Savior." These incidences clearly showcase the utter importance of names in the spirit realm. An incorrect name can give birth to an inaccurate expression of a person or an entity's intended purpose.

"And out of the ground the LORD God formed every beast of the field, and every fowl of the air; and brought them unto Adam to see what he would call them: and whatsoever Adam called every living creature, that was the name thereof."

Genesis 2:19 KJV

I am afraid that many members of the Body of Christ do not really respect the "technology of names" as much as God does. But the truth of the matter is that this ancient spiritual technology is the method that God uses to determine the capacity, function and nature of a thing. God imparted this "technology of names" to Adam. The Bible says that God brought all the animals on earth to Adam to see what he would "call or name them." The Bible tells us that whatever "name" Adam gave to any animal, the new "name" completely enshrined that particular animals' "purpose, potential and nature."

The "technology of names" also shows us that whoever names a person, a product or an organization has inherent power over what they name. Before Abram was intercepted by Melchizedek's eternal royal priesthood, he was known simply as "Abram." The name "Abram" means the "exalted father." Immediately after encountering the power of Melchizedek's priesthood, Abram's name was changed to "Abraham" which means "father of many nations." Abram went through a radical "change of heart." *He discovered that internally he had gone through a holy and radical spiritual reconfiguration. God had surgically removed the heart of an "exalted father" and replaced It with the heart of a "father of many nations."* His new heart mirrored the heart of a true and selfless spiritual father. The self-absorbed, self-serving and self-centered heart of an exalted father had been supernaturally annihilated! He knew that things would never be as they once were. Tithing under the Order of Melchizedek empowers born-again believers to reinforce their "New Creation" identity in Christ. This is why tithing under the Order of Melchizedek is so powerful.

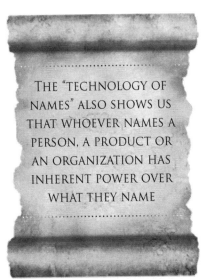

THE "TECHNOLOGY OF NAMES" ALSO SHOWS US THAT WHOEVER NAMES A PERSON, A PRODUCT OR AN ORGANIZATION HAS INHERENT POWER OVER WHAT THEY NAME

Power over the Engines of Greed

When Abram got to the borders of Egypt during a time of deep economic recession, he broke the covenant of marriage with his wife and brought her into a covenant of lies, in order to protect himself and save his business. In Egypt his dear wife was almost raped by the king of Egypt who wanted to sleep with her with unfeigned lust. In exchange for exploiting Sarah sexually, Abram and his nephew Lot were given an abundance of male and female servants. The king of Egypt also gave him plenty of livestock, gold and silver from the treasuries of Egypt.

Had Abram known that that this *"tainted deal"* with the king of Egypt had set him on a *"collision course with the king of Sodom,"* he would have never sabotaged himself, like he did. Had God not intervened, Sarah would have been raped by the king of Egypt and Abram would have been killed by Pharaoh once he discovered that Abram had actually deceived him. This is why being of the Order of Melchizedek is so important. This kingly-priesthood of our Lord Jesus Christ can really preserve our families, if we truly submit ourselves to it. Instead of being killed, Abram and Sarah were given an eviction notice to leave the land of Egypt. Abram and Lot left with a lot of money and material possessions from the treasuries of Egypt. **Unfortunately, their ill-gained wealth had come at a terrible price.**

> *After Abram returned from his victory over Kedorlaomer and all his allies, the king of Sodom went out to meet him in the valley of Shaveh (that is, the King's Valley). The king of Sodom said to Abram, "Give back my people who were captured. But you may keep for yourself all the goods you have recovered." Abram replied to the king of Sodom, "I solemnly swear to the Lord, God Most High, Creator of heaven and earth that I will not take so much as a single thread or sandal thong from what belongs to you. Otherwise you might say, 'I am the one who made Abram rich.'*

Genesis 14:17,21-23

When the king of Sodom got in front of Abram, he gave him a financial proposal that he was convinced Abram would find irresistible. Instead of taking the money the king of Sodom had offered him, Abram emphatically and publicly told the king of Sodom that his answer was a resounding heartfelt, *"NO!"* Abram told the king of Sodom that there was nothing that he owned in all of Sodom which Abram desired for himself or his ministry. Truly, the power of the tithe that Abram had tithed into Melchizedek's priesthood had "shut down the engines of greed" in his sanctified soul. Tithing under the Order of Melchizedek has the power to "annihilate the engines of greed in the lives of Kingdom citizens." This is why the Church needs to rediscover the Abrahamic tithing model.

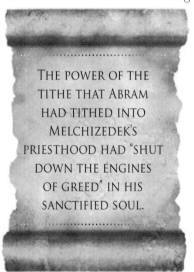

THE POWER OF THE TITHE THAT ABRAM HAD TITHED INTO MELCHIZEDEK'S PRIESTHOOD HAD "SHUT DOWN THE ENGINES OF GREED" IN HIS SANCTIFIED SOUL.

Gives us the Power to Prevail

> *Then Melchizedek king of Salem brought out bread and wine; he was the priest of God Most High. And he blessed him and said: "Blessed be Abram of God Most High, Possessor of heaven and earth; And blessed be God Most High, Who has delivered your enemies into your hand."*

Genesis 14:18-20 (NKJ)

One of the most powerful things that Melchizedek, King of Jerusalem and Priest of God Most High told Abraham was simply this: "God has delivered your enemies into your hands." This one statement reveals the "high level of spiritual authority" that Abraham was operating in. By this one statement Melchizedek established the fact that Abraham was a "governmental figure within the eternal structure of God's Kingdom." This statement also implies that Abraham was not "waiting on God to rebuke the devourer on his behalf," because God had already given him a "prevailing spiritual position of authority" to rebuke and bind the devourer for himself. What Melchizedek said to Abraham sounds a lot like what Jesus said to His New Testament apostles.

"Look, I have given you authority over all the power of the enemy, and you can walk among snakes and scorpions and crush them. Nothing will injure you."

Luke 10:19

What Jesus told His apprentice apostles is in direct contrast to the teachings of the proponents of the "Malachi 3:8-12 tithing model." The Malachi 3:8-12 tithing model forces God's people to take a position of passivity when dealing with the power of the devil. The Malachi 3:8-12 tithing model teaches people to "wait on God to rebuke the devourer on their behalf." In the passage from Luke 10:19, Jesus clearly shows us that the priestly Order of Melchizedek brings about a "divine militancy" in our regenerated spirits. This divine militancy in our regenerated spirits changes the way we deal with the devil. Jesus told His apprentice apostles that He had already given them the "spiritual authority" to "tread on serpents and scorpions and completely overpower them."

Then Jacob was left alone; and a Man wrestled with him until the breaking of day. Now when He saw that He did not prevail against him, He touched the socket of his hip; and the socket of Jacob's hip was out of joint as He wrestled with him. And He said, "Let Me go, for the day breaks." But he said, "I will not let You go unless You bless me!" So He said to him, "What is your name?" He said, "Jacob." And He said, "Your name shall no longer be called Jacob, but Israel; for you have struggled with God and with men, and have prevailed."

Genesis 32:24-28

We have already established the fact that God's own testimony concerning Abraham was that, "Abraham was able to command his sons after him to obey the ways of the Spirit that God had revealed to him." We know for a fact that Abraham taught his sons about the priestly Order of Melchizedek and how to tithe into it. We also know for a fact that Jacob, Abraham's grandson was aware of the "concept of tithing" according to Genesis 28:11-16. This leads us to the conclusion that Jacob, who later became the father of the nation of Israel, was also an active member of the priestly Order of Melchizedek.

We will now examine Jacob's encounter with God at the river Jabok from the perspective of the benefits of tithing into the priestly Order of Melchizedek. The Bible tells us that Jacob was terrified when he learned that his greatest nemesis, Esau was headed towards him with four hundred trained soldiers. ***Jacob realized that he needed to come into a "prevailing spiritual position of authority" over his elder brother in order to defeat him.*** Jacob was left alone with God and the angel of the Lord in the form of a man wrestled with him "till the breaking of a new day!" During this powerful time of the God encounter, Jacob's name was changed to "Israel." "Israel" means "one who has the power to prevail with God and with man."

Defining the power to prevail

"The Power to prevail is a prevailing spiritual position of favor with God which gives us the spiritual buoyancy to rise above every circumstance and every attack of the enemy, so we can fulfill the original call of God upon our lives."

When we start tithing into the priestly Order of Melchizedek, God will quickly bring us into this prevailing spiritual position of power. God will put the "power to prevail" inside our spirit and mind. We won't have to "wait on God to rebuke the devourer for our sake" because God has invested His almighty power in our born-again spirits. We can activate this awesome power by using Jesus' name.

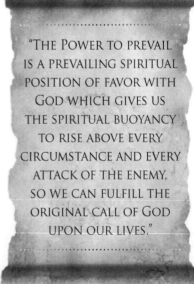

"THE POWER TO PREVAIL IS A PREVAILING SPIRITUAL POSITION OF FAVOR WITH GOD WHICH GIVES US THE SPIRITUAL BUOYANCY TO RISE ABOVE EVERY CIRCUMSTANCE AND EVERY ATTACK OF THE ENEMY, SO WE CAN FULFILL THE ORIGINAL CALL OF GOD UPON OUR LIVES."

"Remember, I have given you authority: so you can trample down snakes and scorpions, indeed, all the Enemy's forces; and you will remain completely unharmed."

Luke 10:19 (CJB)

Delivers us from Generational Curses

"...you shall not bow down to them nor serve them. For I, the LORD your God, am a jealous God, visiting the iniquity of the fathers upon the children to the third and fourth generations of those who hate Me, 6but showing mercy to thousands, to those who love Me and keep My commandments."

Exodus 20:5-6 (NKJV)

Perhaps one of the most powerful spiritual benefits of tithing into the priestly Order of Melchizedek is the "awesome power this priestly Order has over generational curses." We have already discussed the fact that when Adam and Eve sinned, they "introduced sin and its death agencies into the human bloodline." The entrance of sin and death into the human bloodline "corrupted the human gene pool and forced man's genetic code to mutate into something satanic." This "satanic mutation in man's DNA" set him on the pathway of death and made him susceptible to "ongoing demonic influences" through his bloodline.

This means then that the "spiritual weaknesses and evil tendencies" of parents can be "passed on to their children and grandchildren" through bloodline genetics. We can conclude then that if a father struggles with "sexual lust or homosexual tendencies," this inherent genetic disposition in the father can easily be transferred to his sons and grandsons. This also means that if a mother struggles with being "controlling or has low self esteem issues," the chances of her daughters and granddaughters suffering the same fate are very high. This would explain the old adage, "like father like son, like mother like daughter." ***This negative genetic phenomenon is also known as a "Generational Curse."***

Then Abraham took a tenth of all he had captured in battle and gave it to Melchizedek. The name Melchizedek means "king of justice," and king of Salem means "king of peace." There is no record of his father or mother or any of his ancestors—no beginning or end to his life. He remains a priest forever, resembling the Son of God.

Hebrews 7:1-4

Across the nations of the world, deliverance ministers who specialize in teaching on the subject of "breaking generational curses" have mushroomed. I want to go on record and say that I sincerely applaud the efforts of many of these deliverance ministers who are set on helping God's people find freedom from these insidious generational bondages. My only regret however, is that many of these deliverance ministries who are attempting to break generational curses over the lives of God's children have no "clear-cut revelation concerning the priestly Order of Melchizedek." This is why many of these ministers force the people who are looking to them for deliverance to dig heavily into their past. The people looking for deliverance are compelled into digging into their past for all the dirty details that may have happened in their bloodline. This practice is so unnecessary and is based upon a "flawed understanding" of the true spiritual position of New Testament believers under the New Testament Melchizedek priesthood.

Once the global Church rediscovers the priestly Order of Melchizedek, its "spiritual technology for breaking generational curses" will change dramatically. The apostle Paul tells us that the priestly Order of Melchizedek is the only spiritual order known to mankind that has "no earthly genealogy or ancestry." The High Priest (Christ) of this divine priestly order has no earthly "father or mother." He (Christ) has no "beginning or end of days." This is very exciting because all generational curses require that one has either a "father or mother" who is responsible for imparting the "genetic code" of the bloodline in question. Without the presence of the "father and mother's DNA" in the genetic sequence, demons have "no entrance point" for engineering generational curses. This is why "bringing people under the priestly Order of Melchizedek" is the quickest way to "deliver them from generational curses once and for all."

When we start tithing into the priestly Order of Melchizedek with the same level of spiritual consciousness that we had exercised when we were tithing according to Malachi 3:8-12, God will begin to "give us a genetic sequence that is based upon Christ's divine nature," which has "no entrance points for demonic spirits and influences." I really believe that the deliverance ministers of the "future" are going to be extremely "powerful and highly effective." Future deliverance ministries will be based on a "more excellent way" of doing things. I look forward to the breaking of this powerful "day of God!"

ONCE THE GLOBAL CHURCH REDISCOVERS THE PRIESTLY ORDER OF MELCHIZEDEK, ITS "SPIRITUAL TECHNOLOGY FOR BREAKING GENERATIONAL CURSES" WILL CHANGE DRAMATICALLY

Delivers us from
pursuing our own earthly agenda

" There was a famine in the land, besides the first famine that was in the days of Abraham. And Isaac went to Abimelech king of the Philistines, in Gerar. Then the LORD appeared to him and said: "Do not go down to Egypt; live in the land of which I shall tell you. Dwell in this land, and I will be with you and bless you; for to you and your descendants I give all these lands, and I will perform the oath which I swore to Abraham your father. Then Isaac sowed in that land, and reaped in the same year a hundredfold; and the LORD blessed him. The man began to prosper, and continued prospering until he became very prosperous. "

Genesis 26:12-13, 22 (NKJV)

We have already demonstrated how Abraham's decision in his earlier years led him to Egypt during a time of famine. This uninformed decision brought "spiritual chaos" into his life and almost destroyed his marriage to Sarah. We also know that when Abraham came out of Egypt, Pharaoh gave him male and female servants as payment for taking Sarah. One of the female servants the king of Egypt gave to Abraham was a young maid called Hagar. Her entrance into Abraham and Sarah's life produced a "child of the flesh" called Ishmael. The birth of Ishmael has caused so much turmoil for the "sand-seed descendants of Abraham" (Jews) throughout the course of human history. One of the most dangerous things that we all have to be aware of is the "diabolical nature" of our own fleshly agendas. If God in His mercy does not intercept our "inherent propensity to choose our own fleshly agendas," the decisions we make would only serve to strengthen the "technology of death" against us. Tithing into the Order of Melchizedek will deliver us from our inherent propensity to choose our own fleshly agendas.

After Abraham's death there was a similar type of famine which challenged his son, Isaac just like it had challenged Abraham many years earlier. *We must remember that the first heaven which controls "the earth's climate" is in a fallen state.* This means that the first heaven is easily manipulated by "demonic powers" who have a hellish desire to create spiritual chaos and economic troubles here on earth. This is why God's people must never make "spiritual decisions" on the basis of what's happening in their immediate circumstances.

What may seem as our darkest hour may actually be the "breaking of a new day!" Isaac panicked and made the decision to "go down" to Egypt. Since

Isaac was already a member of the Order of Melchizedek, there was an immediate "interception in the course of his life" from this priestly order. I have already shown you that one of the powerful aspects of the priestly Order of Melchizedek lies in its "power of interception." In Genesis 14:18-20 Melchizedek the Priest of God Most High intercepted the course of Abraham's life before the king of Sodom had a chance to sway him off course. *In this instance God "intercepted the course of Isaac's life," when he was standing at the peripherals of making the biggest mistake of his life.* This supernatural intervention of God is one of the spiritual benefits we get from tithing into the priestly Order of Melchizedek.

WE MUST REMEMBER THAT THE FIRST HEAVEN WHICH CONTROLS "THE EARTH'S CLIMATE" IS IN A FALLEN STATE. THIS MEANS THAT THE FIRST HEAVEN IS EASILY MANIPULATED BY "DEMONIC POWERS"

A place of Supernatural Rest and Joy

For this Melchizedek, king of Salem, priest of the Most High God, who met Abraham returning from the slaughter of the kings and blessed him, to whom also Abraham gave a tenth part of all, first being translated "king of righteousness," and then also king of Salem, meaning "king of peace."

Hebrews 7:1-2 (NKJV)

Another very important aspect and benefit of tithing and living under the priestly Order of Melchizedek concerns the whole aspect of *"spiritual rest."* The apostle Paul shows us that Melchizedek, who met Abraham when he was returning from the slaughter of the kings, symbolizes several things. Here is a summary of what Melchizedek symbolizes:

1. The name "Melchizedek" means "King of righteousness." We know that "righteousness" means "right-thinking." Righteousness brings us into a place of "right-standing" with God, man and the devil. Since "righteousness" is based on "right-thinking," it follows that the "spirit of righteousness" deeply affects the "spirit and state of our minds" more than any other part of our being.

2. Melchizedek's title as "King of Salem" (later known as Jerusalem), means "Prince of peace." We know that the word peace comes from the Hebrew word "Shalom" which carries the meaning of, "nothing broken and nothing missing." We also know that "peace" describes an "emotional state of being." This means that the peace of God deeply affects "our emotional state" more than anything else in our life.

Then Jesus said, "Come to me, all of you who are weary and carry heavy burdens, and I will give you rest. Take my yoke upon you. Let me teach you, because I am humble and gentle at heart, and you will find rest for your souls.

Matthew 11:28-29

Under the priestly Order of Melchizedek, the "streams of righteousness and peace" combine to make a lasting and meaningful impact on the people who tithe into this priestly Order. When we tithe into this powerful priestly order, God will begin to "invade our minds with supernatural concepts of right thinking." Once these accurate and righteous thinking patterns begin to "saturate our minds" they will inevitably "infuse peace of God" over our "fragmented emotions." The supernatural superimposition of God's peace over our "fragmented emotions" will bring us into a "place of supernatural rest and unspeakable joy."

"For all who have entered into God's rest have rested from their labors, just as God did after creating the world."

Hebrews 4:10

It is interesting to note what the great apostle to the Church has to say about the ***"true nature of the Kingdom of God."***

"For the kingdom of God is not eating and drinking, but righteousness and peace and joy in the Holy Spirit."

Romans 14:17 (NKJV)

The great apostle to the Church tells us that the Kingdom of God operates on "three spiritual cylinders," namely: "righteousness, peace and joy in the Holy Spirit." What is very striking to me about this passage is that Saint Paul lists these three spiritual cylinders in the order of their importance and then ends with identifying the "spiritual power" behind these spiritual cylinders.

The apostle Paul lists righteousness first because "peace" is the result of the "transformation of the spirit of our minds" when we adopt "the right-thinking patterns of the Kingdom of God." "Joy" on the other hand is the direct result of "the peace of God" being superimposed on our emotions, bringing us into a "place of total tranquility or rest." This means that it's impossible to have "supernatural Joy" without the "peace of God ruling our heart." We also know that it is impossible for the "peace of God" to be superimposed on our emotions without "righteousness."

I am very glad that the apostle Paul did not just end with identifying the three spiritual cylinders that drive the engines of the Kingdom of God. The apostle Paul goes a step further and identifies the "spiritual power" which makes these three spiritual cylinders work together in "perfect divine symmetry." This power is the "person of the Holy Spirit." What's very exciting to

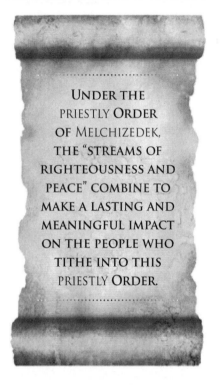

UNDER THE PRIESTLY ORDER OF MELCHIZEDEK, THE "STREAMS OF RIGHTEOUSNESS AND PEACE" COMBINE TO MAKE A LASTING AND MEANINGFUL IMPACT ON THE PEOPLE WHO TITHE INTO THIS PRIESTLY ORDER.

me is that the spiritual elements that the apostle Paul lists as being an integral part of the Kingdom of God are the same ones that we have already identified in Hebrews 7:1-3 as belonging to the priestly Order of Melchizedek.

This simple fact has far-reaching spiritual ramifications on how we view the person of the Holy Spirit. This literally means that the **"Holy Spirit,"** who is the governor of the Kingdom of God here on earth, is also an integral part of the priestly Order of Melchizedek. *He is here on earth to reveal Christ and service every New Testament believer who has been called to serve under the priestly Order of Melchizedek.* Think about this: "the Holy Spirit is of the Order of Melchizedek." Selah! This should come as no surprise if we study the Scriptures. Jesus Christ, who is the High Priest of the priestly Order of Melchizedek, told us what the role of the Holy Spirit on earth would be. The Holy Spirit is in the earth to reveal Jesus Christ and bring lost souls under the priestly Order of Melchizedek by transforming us into a Kingdom of kings and priests unto God. Listen to what Jesus told His apprentice apostles about the mission of the Holy Spirit.

"I still have many things to say to you, but you cannot bear them now. However, when He, the Spirit of truth, has come, He will guide you into all truth; for He will not speak

on His own authority, but whatever He hears He will speak; and He will tell you things to come. He will glorify Me, for He will take of what is Mine and declare it to you."

John 16:12-14

When we consider all the things we have just discovered about the priestly Order of Melchizedek, we can begin to see just how powerful "tithing into this priestly Order" really is. When we use the "Lost Key" which is the "Abrahamic tithing model," we will "unlock the supernatural flow" of righteousness, peace and joy in the Holy Ghost into our lives. The benefits of tithing into the priestly Order of Melchizedek are infinitely superior to those that are listed in Malachi 3:8-12.

Favor to Possess

"When Isaac planted his crops that year, he harvested a hundred times more grain than he planted, for the Lord blessed him. He became a very rich man, and his wealth continued to grow. He acquired so many flocks of sheep and goats, herds of cattle, and servants that the Philistines became jealous of him. So the Philistines filled up all of Isaac's wells with dirt. These were the wells that had been dug by the servants of his father, Abraham."

Genesis 26:12-15

I once heard a dear man of God, Dr Mike Murdock declare, "One day of favor is better than a thousand days of labor." I also heard Bishop T. D Jakes say, "Favor isn't fair and it is better than money." I completely agree with these powerful pronouncements. One of the most powerful "spiritual forces" that God ever gave to mankind is the "force of favor." The question which comes to mind is simply this: "What is favor?" To arrive at the answer to this very important question, I did an exhaustive study of biblical characters who exhibited the force of favor and the difference it made in their lives. I studied and traced the force of favor in the life of Joseph, King David and Queen Esther and I arrived at what I believe is a "reasonable definition" of favor.

My definition of favor

The Favor of God is a special endowment of grace and a spiritual position of privilege that God bestows upon a person or a people for the sake of advancing His Kingdom agenda and accelerating the fulfillment of the God-given destiny.

This special endowment of favor usually comes upon believers who are walking in a spirit of total obedience to God. This special endowment of grace and new spiritual positioning allows God to quickly remove obstacles in our pathway while simultaneously opening spiritual doors of blessings that would otherwise be closed.

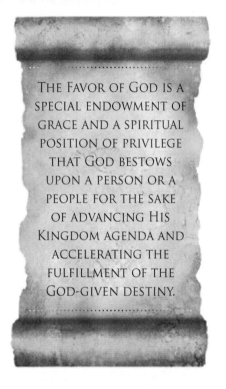

THE FAVOR OF GOD IS A SPECIAL ENDOWMENT OF GRACE AND A SPIRITUAL POSITION OF PRIVILEGE THAT GOD BESTOWS UPON A PERSON OR A PEOPLE FOR THE SAKE OF ADVANCING HIS KINGDOM AGENDA AND ACCELERATING THE FULFILLMENT OF THE GOD-GIVEN DESTINY.

When we begin to tithe into the priestly Order of Melchizedek and bring ourselves under the complete spiritual covering of our Lord Jesus Christ we will "multiply the flow of the favor of God in our life." This is what I believe happened to Isaac when God stopped him from going down to Egypt. God told him to stay in Gerar regardless of the terrible famine which was ravaging the land around him. God then moved on Isaac to do a "ridiculous thing." God told Isaac to "plant his seed" into the dry land and the most "ridiculous miracle" took place. The seed which he had planted in the dry soil produced a "hundredfold harvest" within the same year! How could a seed planted in dry soil during a famine produce such a large crop? The answer is simply this: God held the dry land hostage to the mighty workings of His divine power and forced it to grow crops out of its natural sequence.

"Who has believed our message? To whom has the LORD revealed his powerful arm? 2 My servant grew up in the LORD's presence like a tender green shoot, like a root in dry ground."
Isaiah 53:1-2

In the above passage of Scripture, the prophet Isaiah shows us the "spiritual technology" which God employed to multiply the seed which Isaac had sown in the dry ground. The prophet Isaiah describes Jesus as the servant of the Lord who grew up like a "tender green shoot" out of the dry ground. How can a "tender green shoot" emerge from soil which is completely dry? The answer to this perplexing question is simply this: the "root of the tree was not drawing its resources from the dry ground, but from the presence of the Lord." This is what I believe happened in Isaac's case and caused the Philistines to envy his prosperity.

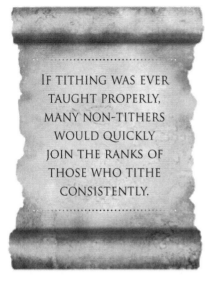

IF TITHING WAS EVER TAUGHT PROPERLY, MANY NON-TITHERS WOULD QUICKLY JOIN THE RANKS OF THOSE WHO TITHE CONSISTENTLY.

The Scriptures contain undeniable evidence that everything in life grows in God's presence, especially seed that is sown in faith.

The Philistines were terrified of the *force of favor* which was flowing in Isaac's life. Out of their own sense of panic they tried to shut down all the wells of water around Isaac, but they failed to "stop the flow of the favor of God in his life." The flow of favor in Isaac's life eventually reached a "tipping point" when it brought him into a "position of great power and prominence" until he became unstoppable. Isaac became more powerful than his enemies. *The favor of God upon his life forced his enemies to establish "peace treaties" with him.*

Abandoning that one, Isaac moved on and dug another well. This time there was no dispute over it, so Isaac named the place Rehoboth (which means "open space"), for he said, "At last the LORD has created enough space for us to prosper in this land."

Genesis 26:22

Coincidentally, this brings us to a very important "difference" between the "Malachi 3:8-12 tithing model" and "the Abrahamic tithing model." Under the Malachi 3:8-12 tithing model, non-tithers were punished by the superimposition of a "curse" as was prescribed by the Mosaic Law. This is because the Levitical priesthood originated from the "Mountain of Law" which permits "blessings and curses, life and death" to flow from the same stream within the cylinder of time. Nevertheless, applying this aspect of the Mountain of Law to the eternal priestly Order of Melchizedek is both dangerous and unbiblical, not to mention "highly confusing" to God's people. *The failure to discern this critical difference by many teachers of the Word has caused them to unwittingly pronounce "the curse of the Law" upon New Testament believers for their failure to tithe.*

The dictates of Malachi 3:8-12 are spiritually dangerous and quite confusing when it is applied to New Testament believers. This is because the "power of life and death" lies in the tongue. Even born-again believers can be affected negatively by pronouncements made from the tongues of anointed men and women of God, even when these words were spoken from a place of ignorance. *This means that even though the lack of tithing does not place a "curse" on New Testament believers, the devil can still use the "idle words" of senior ministers to create a demonically-engineered curse against the saints.*

If senior pastors keep telling their people that they are "cursed" if they do not tithe, they may give entrance to a "demonically-engineered curse" into the lives of the people who are under their "spiritual authority and covering." The teaching that born-again Christians are cursed for not tithing is also unbiblical because in its truest essence, Malachi 3:8-12 was addressed to the Jewish nation who lived under the Mosaic Covenant. It was never addressed to New Testament believers who have been given access to a "better Covenant which is established on infinitely better promises."

The doctrine that New Testament believers are cursed if they fail to pay their tithes also creates a "spirit of confusion" in the spirits and minds of God's children who do not know whether they are "blessed or cursed." This is especially true if they know that they have not been very consistent in their giving of tithe. Under the Malachi 3:8-12 tithing model, God's people go from "being blessed one moment to being cursed in the next" based upon whether they paid their tithes or not. This spirit of confusion has disenfranchised many potential tithers in the global Church.

Many of God's precious people have simply "given up on the whole idea of tithing" and have simply surrendered themselves to the hands of fate. This is quite unfortunate because "tithing is one of God's greatest ideas." *If tithing was ever taught properly, many non-tithers would quickly join the ranks of those who tithe consistently.* Some of the people who have given up on the idea of tithing have said to me, "Dr. Myles, if I am already cursed because I missed a couple of tithes in the past, why even bother remedying the situation?" Some on the other hand have "continued to give their tithes religiously, but without a spirit of joy." For many of these disenfranchised believers, their attitude towards tithing can be likened to a "woman who has been forced to have sex with a man she does not love in an arranged marriage." Many women can still remember the time when most women could not choose the man they married. For many of these precious saints only the revelation of "the Abrahamic tithing model (Genesis 14:18-20)" can truly restore the joy of tithing and remove the "guilt of feeling like they are cursed" because of their past struggles with tithing.

I do not want to be misconstrued as saying that New Testament believers have nothing to fear if they refuse to participate in the covenant of tithing. Please remember that I wrote this book to show the global Church a "more excellent way

NON-TITHERS UNDER THE PRIESTLY ORDER OF MELCHIZEDEK ARE "CHASTISED" WITH A "DIMINISHED CAPACITY FOR MANIFESTING THE FAVOR OF GOD" IN THEIR LIVES.

of exacting the tithe." I did not write this book to give rebellious believers a license to abort the giving of tithes, but to inspire more believers to follow Abraham's example. So here is the million-dollar question: "Are there any spiritual consequences for not tithing under the priestly Order of Melchizedek?" The answer is a resounding yes!

Under the eternal priestly Order of Melchizedek, "non-tithers" are reprimanded by God in the same way that a loving father disciplines a disobedient child. Under the priestly Order of Melchizedek, non-tithers are not punished by the imposition of a "curse" because the Order of Melchizedek is an eternal priesthood and it exists in a perfect state. In this eternal and perfect state there is simply "no room" for any curse to co-exist with the incorruptible life of God. We must also remember that any curse that originates from the eternal realm is also eternally irreversible.

Please remember that in this eternal order, "God is the only light of that City (spiritual Jerusalem, which is the mother of us all.)" There is no Sun or Moon in Heaven because God and His Christ are the light thereof. John the revelator in the book of Revelation tells us that there is no "lie or curse" in this eternal spiritual order, because this realm is home to the throne of God and of the Lamb. This leads us to a very revealing question. "If God was to curse anyone from this eternal spiritual order, where would He find the curse, since there is no curse that exists in this eternal priestly order?"

"No longer will there be a curse upon anything. For the throne of God and of the Lamb will be there, and his servants will worship him. And they will see his face, and his name will be written on their foreheads. And there will be no night there—no need for lamps or sun—for the Lord God will shine on them. And they will reign forever and ever."

Revelation 22:3-5

John the Apostle was shown the state of affairs in this eternal realm that the priestly Order of Melchizedek operates from. Listen carefully to John's testimony: "there is no curse upon anything!" **To the contrary, non-tithers under the priestly Order of Melchizedek are "chastised" with a "diminished** *capacity for manifesting the favor of God" in their lives.* This means that "spiritual doors and blessings" which are ours by divine birthright take "longer to open and manifest" for us because we are failing to give the King of kings His rightful endowment of tithe. This means that every "satanic obstacle" that the devil places in our pathway "may take a lot longer" to remove from our pathway than God ever intended.

The delayed manifestation of God's blessings in our lives may feel like we are "cursed" but this is not the case. Under the priestly Order of Melchizedek, "God may choose to resist us" for refusing to honor Him with His rightful endowment of tithe. But this does not mean that He has cursed us!" Should we choose to "honor Him" with our tithes God will "command His holy angels" to work in our favor. The increased activity of God's holy angels on our behalf will "increase and accelerate" the flow of God's favor in our lives. If the "desire to honor Jesus Christ our great King and direct His favor" towards our life are not "compelling reasons" in themselves to make us want to tithe consistently into the Kingdom of God, then we are already spiritually dead!

Deliverance from False Doctrines

And Melchizedek, the king of Salem and a priest of God Most High, brought Abram some bread and wine. Melchizedek blessed Abram with this blessing: "Blessed be Abram by God Most High, Creator of heaven and earth. And blessed be God Most High, who has defeated your enemies for you." Then Abram gave Melchizedek a tenth of all the goods he had recovered.

Genesis 14:18-20

Perhaps there is nothing that is as "toxic" as the "infiltration of the doctrine of demons" into the spirit and mind of a believer. Jesus said that the only thing that has the power to corrupt a person comes from within and not from without. The apostle Paul wrote to young Timothy and told him that in the last days, there would be an "onslaught of seducing spirits and doctrines of demons" that are designed to deceive the Church of God. Roget's thesaurus defines doctrine as "a principle or body of principles presented for acceptance or belief, as by a religious, political, scientific, or philosophic group; dogma." Said simply, doctrine is the basis of belief. When Melchizedek appeared to Abraham, He gave Abram "heavenly bread and wine," which are the spiritual emblems of this eternal priestly order.

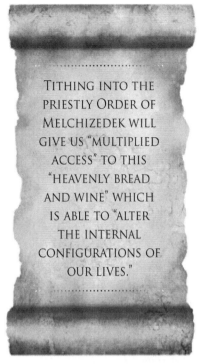

"Give us this day our daily bread. And forgive us our debts, As we forgive our debtors. And do not lead us into temptation, But deliver us from the evil one."
Matthew 6:11-13 (NKJV)

"Bread" represents the "Word or the doctrine of the Kingdom of God," whereas "Wine" represents the "Anointing or the Spirit of the Kingdom of God." The devil came to tempt Jesus during His forty-day fast. The devil tried to seduce Jesus into buying into the "doctrines of demons" but in each instance, Jesus Christ responded by quoting from the "bread of God's Word" under the anointing of the Holy Spirit. In Matthew 6:11-13 Jesus suggests that partaking of the heavenly bread has the power to intercept the flow of evil towards our life and close doors of spiritual temptation.

What Jesus is inferring in this passage of Scripture sounds similar to what Melchizedek did to Abraham thousands of years before. Melchizedek gave Abraham the sacred meal of "Bread and Wine." This sacred meal gave him the "power to withstand" the onslaught of evil that was presented to him by the king of Sodom. The bread and wine that Melchizedek gave to Abraham also gave him the power to "break free from greed."

We are living in the day and age where we keep losing good ministries to illicit lifestyles brought about by feeding on the doctrines of demons that have infiltrated the life stream of the global Church. There are some ministers of the gospel within the global Church who believe that the "amount of money" a person has is a direct reflection of their spiritual position of righteousness in the kingdom of God. The doctrinal mantra of many of these ministers is "show me the money." Some of these men and women of God think that "financial prosperity" is the primary indicator of a man's spirituality. What they forget to mention is that some of the richest men in the world are also some of the world's worst sinners.

Do not get me wrong; I believe that "financial prosperity is an integral part of our stewardship portfolio in the Kingdom of God." But I do not believe that money is an end in itself. ***Tithing into the priestly Order of Melchizedek will give us*** *"multiplied access"* **to this** *"heavenly bread and wine"* **which is able to** *"alter the internal configurations of our lives."* This sacred bread and wine which Melchizedek (Jesus Christ) gives to His blood-washed people has the power to "destroy spiritual darkness and deception" in our spirit and over our mind. This is exactly what happened to the disciples from Emmaus. When Jesus broke bread with them, their "spiritual eyes" were opened and they "saw Him for who He really was."

> *"By this time they were nearing Emmaus and the end of their journey. Jesus acted as if he were going on, but they begged him, "Stay the night with us, since it is getting late." So he went home with them. As they sat down to eat, he took the bread and blessed it. Then he broke it and gave it to them. Suddenly, their eyes were opened, and they recognized him. And at that moment he disappeared!"*
>
> Luke 24:28-31

When we tithe into the priestly Order of Melchizedek, it will be quite difficult for the enemy to "easily deceive us and sway us" from walking on the pathway of life. God will give us the power to sidestep many of these doctrines of demons, especially those of us who live in the developed countries of the West. Many developed nations are increasingly becoming more liberal and loose in their morals. Our Churches are being patronized by a "generation" of young people who have been raised and schooled in these ultraliberal Universities who are becoming "increasingly hostile" to "traditional Judaic-Christian" values. If we do not consciously bring our Churches under the priestly Order of Melchizedek, we are going to lose this second generation to the "doctrine of demons."

Unleashes our Infinite Imagination For Wealth Creation

Then Jacob awoke from his sleep and said, "Surely the Lord is in this place, and I wasn't even aware of it!" But he was also afraid and said, "What an awesome place this is! It is none other than the house of God, the very gateway to heaven!" And this memorial pillar I have set up will become a place for worshiping God, and I will present to God a tenth of everything he gives me."

Genesis 28:16-17, 22

I once heard, Dr N. Cindy Trimm define the imagination as being simply, "an image being projected from another nation." The projecting nation might be the Kingdom of God or the kingdom of darkness. This is why we need to effectively "police" the images that we allow to appear in our minds. As the old adage goes, "A mind is a terrible thing to waste." Unfortunately, one of the greatest tragedies in the Church of the living God is that we simply do not have many Kingdom citizens who "are receiving images of greatness from the Kingdom of God." Many of us just think too small. Many of us have allowed demonic powers to restrict our infinite imagination.

When Jacob was fleeing from his brother Esau, he stopped to rest at a place called Bethel. While he was sleeping, God gave him a supernatural dream about his prophetic calling and spiritual inheritance. The dream was simply mind-boggling. I have sometimes wondered why God loves to visit His people while they are sleeping. I think I now know the answer to this question. God has a deep desire to "unleash His people's infinite imagination" so that we can begin to see with the eyes of our spirit-man rather than with our natural eyes. The vision of our natural eyes is quite limited, when we compare it to the vision of our spirit-man.

When Jacob woke up he was so moved by what he had seen and heard that he entered into a **covenant of tithe with the house of God.** We have already established the fact that the only priesthood Jacob was aware of at this time, was the priestly Order of Melchizedek. I once heard Dr Myles Munroe say, "Eyes that look are common, but eyes that see are rare." When we start tithing into the priestly Order of Melchizedek, God will begin to remove the scales from our spiritual eyes, so we can have clear-cut strategies for wealth creation to advance His Kingdom here on earth.

WHEN WE START EMPLOYING THE ABRAHAMIC TITHING MODEL, GOD WILL BEGIN TO GIVE US SUPERNATURAL "IMAGES FROM HIS KINGDOM NATION" IN ORDER TO GIVE BIRTH TO "PROSPERITY AND GREATNESS" IN OUR REGENERATED SPIRITS

"What wages do you want?" Laban asked again. Jacob replied, "Don't give me anything. Just do this one thing, and I'll continue to tend and watch over your flocks. Let me inspect your flocks today and remove all the sheep and goats that are speckled or spotted, along with all the black sheep. Give these to me as my wages. In the future, when you check on the animals you have given me as my wages, you'll see that I have been honest. If you find in my flock any goats without speckles or spots, or any sheep that are not black, you will know that I have stolen them from you."

Genesis 30:31-33

The first time I read the above passage of Scripture I was reading a powerful book written by the pastor of the world's largest Church, Dr Paul Yongi Cho. This book is titled *The Fourth Dimension*. In this bestselling book, Dr Cho expounds on how he has successfully used this powerful principle of "activating the imagination" by visualizing by faith what he desired to accomplish for the Kingdom of God. Jacob came to his trickster uncle and father-in-law and told him that he would no longer accept a paycheck from his hand. In the place of his wages, Jacob took "one-colored cattle, goats and sheep" and separated them from the rest of the flock. He then gave Laban the most ridiculous business proposal anybody had ever given him. He told his uncle that he would watch over the one-colored cattle, goats and sheep, and should any one of them give birth to "spotted offspring" they would be Jacob's wages. *Anybody who understands the laws of biogenetics knows how impossible it is for a one-colored animal to give birth to offspring who bear more than one color.*

Jacob's business proposal to Laban was like asking a black couple to give birth to a Caucasian baby. This is why Laban wasted no time placing his signature on the dotted line. He was convinced that Jacob had lost his mind. What Laban did not know was that Jacob was a member of the priestly Order of Melchizedek, a priesthood which specializes in revealing mysteries. After Laban agreed to Jacob's proposal, Jacob took fresh tree branches and carved spots on them using his hunting knife. He then placed these spotted branches in front of the animals when they were mating. Suddenly the impossible began to happen. Most of the one-colored cattle, goats and sheep began to give birth to spotted cattle, goats and sheep. God used "Jacob's infinite imagination" to alter the "genetic code" of the single-colored animals that Laban had placed in his care. Jacob ended up with more cattle, goats and sheep than Laban. Talk about genetic engineering! Jacob's case is a classic example of genetic manipulation through the power of God.

My dear friend, Jacob's case is a classic example of the awesome power and benefits of tithing into the priestly Order of Melchizedek. When we start employing the Abrahamic tithing model, *God will begin to give us supernatural "images from His Kingdom nation" in order to give birth to "prosperity and greatness" in our regenerated spirits.* If there is nothing else we can learn from Hollywood, we must at least acknowledge the fact that the Hollywood movie industry has shown us that there are "billions of dollars" to be made in simply using one's imagination. I truly believe that in the future the greatest multimillion dollar blockbuster movies will come from the "infinite imagination" of God's Kingdom citizens. The sudden rise of movie producer Tyler Perry and the amazing success of Christian-made films like "Fireproof" are classic examples of how God is anointing the infinite imagination of His Kingdom citizens to create uncommon wealth for advancing His Kingdom.

Tithing into the priestly Order of Melchizedek as Abraham did will unleash the faculties of the infinite imagination of many of God's people for the sake of Kingdom advancement here on earth. I truly believe that we are going to see "more successful businesses" birthed by God's Kingdom citizens under the priestly Order of Melchizedek than at any time in human history. The rise of many Kingdom-minded businessmen and women is going to completely eliminate lack within the global Church.

The priestly Order of Melchizedek is a "Royal" priestly Order, because our High Priest is both a King and a Priest. In both the New and Old Testaments, kings have always been responsible for "leadership, provision and protection." Under this priestly Order of Melchizedek, we are going to see many believers who are called to the marketplace, take more active leadership roles within the global Church and also become responsible for providing "provision and protection" for God's Kingdom agenda here on earth. I have expounded on this issue in one of my previous books titled, *"The Order of Melchizedek: Rediscovering the Eternal Priesthood of Jesus Christ."*

Delivers us from the Poison of our own Mistakes

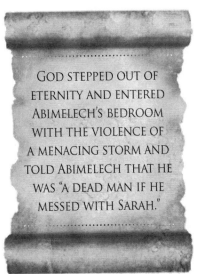

GOD STEPPED OUT OF ETERNITY AND ENTERED ABIMELECH'S BEDROOM WITH THE VIOLENCE OF A MENACING STORM AND TOLD ABIMELECH THAT HE WAS "A DEAD MAN IF HE MESSED WITH SARAH."

Abraham introduced his wife, Sarah, by saying, "She is my sister." So King Abimelech of Gerar sent for Sarah and had her brought to him at his palace. But that night God came to Abimelech in a dream and told him, "You are a dead man, for that woman you have taken is already married!" Now return the woman to her husband, and he will pray for you, for he is a prophet. Then you will live. But if you don't return her to him, you can be sure that you and all your people will die."

Genesis 20:2-3, 7

I have been in ministry for many years and I have also lived long enough to come to terms with the fact that "Even the best of us can make stupid mistakes, because we are all human." The human element even in the most spiritual of us can sometimes override the better judgment of our born-again spirit, which is joined to the Lord. I know that this has been my humble experience. Somebody said that "to make mistakes is human but to forgive is divine." Nevertheless some mistakes can be very costly. Some mistakes can become "serious demonic entry points" into the course of our lives. There is nothing the devil would like more than to "destroy our ministry and testimony" through our own mistakes.

Abraham the man of Covenant and friend of God made a grave mistake that almost cost him his marriage. Abraham's mistake also placed his wife Sarah, in a very compromising position. When Abraham and Sarah got to the border of the country of Gerar, Abraham asked his wife to lie about the true nature of their relationship. He told her to tell the Philistines of Gerar that she was his sister instead of his wife because he was afraid that they would kill him in order to get her. Sarah being the submissive wife that she was, obeyed her husband's voice, which set her on the pathway of death and destruction. Abimelech, king of Gerar, brought Sarah into his bed chamber intending to have sex with her.

It does not take a rocket scientist to figure out the fact that Abraham's decision made out of fear had "opened doors" for demonic spirits who wanted to abort the birth of Isaac through Sarah. Sarah stood petrified in Abimelech's bed chamber like a chicken caught in the rain. She could see the unfeigned lust in the eyes of Abimelech, king of Gerar. She knew that he had not brought her into his bedroom to discuss matters of the State. He wanted to have sexual intercourse with her.

Suddenly, God stepped out of eternity and entered Abimelech's bedroom with the violence of a menacing storm and told Abimelech that he was "a dead man if he messed with Sarah." God told Abimelech that He was going to kill him if he did not restore Sarah back to Abraham. The king of Gerar was scared to death. He pleaded with God and told Him that he did not know that Sarah was married to Abraham. Abimelech restored Sarah back to Abraham in haste and then asked Abraham to leave his country. In most cases, lying to a king during Abraham's era was an offense punishable by death, but the king of Gerar did not even bring this charge against Abraham. He was quite terrified of the God of Abraham and Sarah.

One of the most powerful spiritual benefits of tithing into the priestly Order of Melchizedek is simply this: "*God will not allow all the stupid mistakes we may make while trying to obey His call upon our lives,"* to destroy our ministry. God will defuse some of the "poison" created by many of our mistakes so that the devil does not take advantage of us. Abraham's decision to lie about the true nature of his relationship with Sarah was a major mistake, but nevertheless God did not allow the "devil to fully exploit" this mistake in Abraham's life. This is why I am so excited at the privilege of tithing into the priestly Order of Melchizedek. If we are of the priestly Order of Melchizedek, the last mistake we made must not be allowed to become the "graveyard" of our prophetic call and destiny. We can always bounce back and become wiser the second time around.

Supernatural Interception of the Second Generation

"At sundown he arrived at a good place to set up camp and stopped there for the night. Jacob found a stone to rest his head against and lay down to sleep. As he slept, he dreamed of a stairway that reached from the earth up to heaven. And he saw the angels of God going up and down the stairway. At the top of the stairway stood the Lord, and he said, "I am the Lord, the God of your grandfather Abraham, and the God of your father, Isaac. The ground you are lying on belongs to you. I am giving it to you and your descendants. Your descendants will be as numerous as the dust of the earth! They will spread out in all directions—to the west and the east, to the north and the south. And all the families of the earth will be blessed through you and your descendants. What's more, I am with you, and I will protect you wherever you go. One day I will bring you back to this land. I will not leave you until I have finished giving you everything I have promised you." Then Jacob awoke from his sleep and said, "Surely the Lord is in this place, and I wasn't even aware of it!"

Genesis 28:11-16

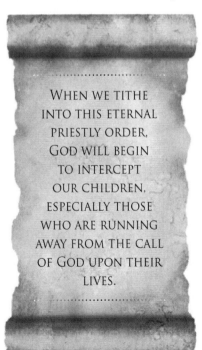

WHEN WE TITHE INTO THIS ETERNAL PRIESTLY ORDER, GOD WILL BEGIN TO INTERCEPT OUR CHILDREN, ESPECIALLY THOSE WHO ARE RUNNING AWAY FROM THE CALL OF GOD UPON THEIR LIVES.

There are no spiritual or natural assets which are as important to God as our children. In the second chapter of Malachi God makes it quite clear that "He hates divorce," especially when it involves born-again believers. This is because God desires to harvest a godly offspring from the marriage between two believers. When two believers get married, God has every intention to bless them with the "fruit of the womb" because He is in search of a "godly offspring."

By taking a closer look at how God deals with His people from one generation to the next, we will begin to see a very powerful prophetic principle at work. We will begin to see that *"God operates on the principle of continuance," which simply means that God loves to work generationally even up to a thousand generations.* This means that God wanted Abraham to take everything that he had touched in God and transfer it to his sons and grandsons. God wanted to make certain that what He had invested in Abraham was not lost on the second generation.

This would explain why Jesus got angry with His disciples when they tried to "send away" the little children, who were coming to Him. The disciples probably thought that they were doing Him a favor by shielding Him from the children. They were completely mistaken. Jesus used this time to showcase the "passion of God" for the second generation. He told them that first and foremost, the Kingdom of God belongs to "little children." He also told them that if they did not humble themselves like "little children" they would never see the Kingdom of God.

On an even more serious note, Jesus made a very startling statement. He said that "it was better for those who molest or offend little children to never have been born!" This statement more than any other, underscores the passion of the heart of God for the second generation. When Jacob went into exile, because he was afraid his brother Esau might kill him, God intercepted him at a place called "Bethel." Even while he was on the "run," Jacob could not escape the "spiritual reach" of the priestly Order of Melchizedek that his father Isaac belonged to.

This is one of the most powerful spiritual benefits of tithing into the priestly Order of Melchizedek. **When we tithe into this eternal priestly order, God will begin to intercept our children, especially those who are running away from the call of God upon their lives.** In the ensuing supernatural interception, God will "superimpose His prophetic purpose and divine destiny" over our children. I truly believe that this benefit alone should be "reason enough" to inspire Christian parents to tithe into the New Testament Order of Melchizedek priesthood of our Lord Jesus Christ.

Access to Powerful Dimensions of Healing

One of the most important aspects and benefits of tithing into the priestly Order of Melchizedek is that this priestly order also gives us access to an unlimited supply of God's healing power. When Adam and Eve sinned, sin and death agencies entered this world's spiritual and natural environment. The driving power behind these death agencies is sin, because sin always leads to death. One of those death agencies which came with the entrance of sin is "disease and sickness."

In 2007 US presidential candidate John Edwards announced on nationwide television that his wife had been diagnosed with treatable but incurable bone cancer. It was a somber moment for the nation, as we all reflected on what it would take to stem the tide of cancer. When I observe the struggles of men with the tyranny of disease and sickness, I am thankful to God that I serve a priestly order which is saturated with "God's healing power and the Spirit of divine health."

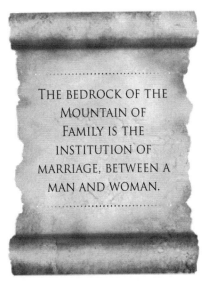

THE BEDROCK OF THE MOUNTAIN OF FAMILY IS THE INSTITUTION OF MARRIAGE, BETWEEN A MAN AND WOMAN.

"Jesus traveled throughout the region of Galilee, teaching in the synagogues and announcing the Good News about the Kingdom. And he healed every kind of disease and illness. News about him spread as far as Syria, and people soon began bringing to him all who were sick. And whatever their sickness or disease, or if they were demon possessed or epileptic or paralyzed—he healed them all."

Matthew 4:23-24

When Jesus arrived on the scene, He began to demonstrate the supremacy of His order of priesthood over the whole demonic sphere of disease and sickness. No other man in the history of the world has ever manifested the same level of dominion over diseases and sicknesses like Jesus did. The people of His era certainly knew that a new order of priesthood had arrived. We now know that this new order of priesthood is the priestly Order of Melchizedek, because the Scriptures identify the Lord Jesus Christ as the High Priest of this eternal priesthood. This simple fact has far-reaching spiritual implications, which affect us deeply.

When we tithe into the priestly Order of Melchizedek we are "storing up reservoirs of healing and health" for our lives. If we are faithful tithers into this New Testament priesthood, we have the right to expect divine intervention in the form of healing from this eternal priestly order. I am not suggesting that tithing buys healing, but it does go a long way in placing us in divine alignment with the Lordship of Jesus Christ. In conclusion, it does not take a rocket scientist to figure out the fact that there are "far more spiritual benefits" offered to us when we tithe into the priestly Order of Melchizedek than there are under the popular Malachi 3:8-12 tithing model.

Supernatural Protection of the Mountain of Family

Abraham introduced his wife, Sarah, by saying, "She is my sister." So King Abimelech of Gerar sent for Sarah and had her brought to him at his palace. But that night God came to Abimelech in a dream and told him, "You are a dead man, for that woman you have taken is already married!" Now return the woman to her husband, and he will pray for you, for he is a prophet. Then you will live. But if you don't return her to him, you can be sure that you and all your people will die."

Genesis 20:2-3, 7

There is nothing which the devil deeply desires to destroy in our society more than the Mountain of Family. This is why there has been such a vicious and ongoing attack of the enemy on families all over the world. The institution of family is rapidly disintegrating across the nations of the world. Popular liberal views on what constitutes a family have not helped the cause of preserving the traditional and biblical structure of the family. The high rate of divorce in our modern societies has slowed down the fight to maintain and preserve the Mountain of Family. Even the Church has about the same rate of divorce as the world we have been called to reach.

"Therefore shall a man leave his father and mother, and shall cleave unto his wife; and they shall be one flesh. And they were both naked, the man and his wife, and were not ashamed."

Genesis 2:24-25 (NKJV)

The bedrock of the Mountain of Family is the institution of marriage, between a man and woman. The vicious global gay agenda to redefine the traditional and biblical view of marriage as a covenant union between a man and a woman is destroying the divine structure of the Mountain of Family. The institution of marriage between husband and wife is the birthplace of the Mountain of Family. This is why you cannot marry Adam and Steve or Susie and Sally and throw children in the mix and then call them a family. What you end up

•305•

having is not a family unit as God intended. According to God, who is the creator of all humans, the Mountain of Family always begins with marriage between a man and a woman. This is why preserving the sanctity of the institution of marriage from demonic manipulations is crucial to preserving the sanctity of the Mountain of Family.

One of the most powerful benefits of tithing into the priestly Order of Melchizedek lies in the supernatural power which is released to preserve the sanctity of the institution of marriage, which in turn protects and preserves the Mountain of Family. When Abraham lied to Abimelech, king of Gerar about the true nature of his relationship with Sarah, the devil moved in for the kill. Within hours Sarah found herself in the bedchamber of the king of Gerar, about to be raped. The devil wanted to destroy the sanctity of Abraham's marriage by planting his own diabolical seed and spirit into Sarah's womb, through the unholy sexual union that was about to happen between Sarah and the king of Gerar.

Without warning, God Almighty made a grand entrance into Abimelech's bedchamber and nearly scared him to death. God told him in a dream to restore Sarah to Abraham or be killed instantly. The king of Gerar repented and pleaded for God's forgiveness. The king of Gerar quickly restored Sarah to Abraham and asked Abraham to leave his country. When we start tithing into the priestly Order of Melchizedek, we must expect God to show Himself strong on our behalf. If the Mountain of Family in our lives is under demonic onslaught, God will defend and protect our family heritage. In view of all of these incredible spiritual benefits that accompany tithing in the priestly Order of Melchizedek, why would any God-fearing Christian fail to actively participate in the "covenant of tithing?" I rest my case.

The prophet Malachi gave us six benefits of tithing into the priestly Order of Aaron. It does not take a stroke of genius to notice that there are more spiritual benefits for tithing into the priestly Order of Melchizedek than there are under the Malachi 3:8-12 tithing model. It is my prayer that you will upgrade the technology of tithing in your life and embrace this more excellent way of tithing.

LIFE APPLICATION SECTION

Point to Ponder:

Tithing into the priestly Order of Melchizedek will increase our "spiritual awareness" that we are citizens of the heavenly kingdom, even though we are still living here on earth. By far there are more spiritual benefits for tithing into the priestly Order of Melchizedek than under the Malachi 3:8-12 pattern of tithing.

Verse to Remember:

"By this time they were nearing Emmaus and the end of their journey. Jesus acted as if he were going on, but they begged him, 'Stay the night with us, since it is getting late.' So he went home with them. As they sat down to eat,[b] he took the bread and blessed it. Then he broke it and gave it to them. Suddenly, their eyes were opened, and they recognized him. And at that moment he disappeared!'"

Luke 24:28-31

Questions to Consider:

• How does tithing into the priestly Order of Melchizedek protect us from the poison of our own mistakes?

_____
_____
_____
_____
_____

• What are some of the benefits of tithing into the priestly Order of Melchizedek?

_____
_____
_____
_____
_____

Journal Your Thoughts

THE BLESSING OF ABRAHAM

W e started this book by reminding ourselves of the fact that God's Word commands us to look to Abraham. The apostle Paul also lets us know that the main reason why Jesus went through the painful and shameful death of the cross was so that the *"blessing of Abraham"* could come upon the Gentiles. One of the God-given methods that we can employ to activate the flow of the blessing of Abraham into our life is to start tithing into the Kingdom of God as Abraham did. Abraham tithed into the royal priesthood of Melchizedek. Simply put, Abraham gave tithes to a "King." Since every "king" has a "kingdom," it is safe to assume that Abraham's tithes were used to support a kingdom. This means then that the "Abrahamic tithing model" is a "Kingdom-driven and Kingdom-minded tithing model." This is why it is the highest form and level of tithing mentioned in the Scriptures. Under the Levitical priesthood, "tithes" were given to "support the priesthood," whereas under the Order of Melchizedek, tithes are used to "support" the advancement of God's Kingdom here on earth. *Abraham's prophetic tithing model is therefore a "strategic key" which unleashes the blessing of Abraham upon Kingdom citizens.*

> *"But Christ has rescued us from the curse pronounced by the law. When he was hung on the cross, he took upon himself the curse for our wrongdoing. For it is written in the Scriptures, 'Cursed is everyone who is hung on a tree.' Through Christ Jesus, God has blessed the Gentiles with the same blessing he promised to Abraham, so that we who are believers might receive the promised Holy Spirit through faith."*

> Galatians 3:13-14

Since our Lord Jesus Christ went through tremendous sufferings to bring us into the blessing of Abraham, it behooves us to understand what is meant by the term "the blessing of Abraham." The billion-dollar question therefore is as follows: "What is the Blessing of Abraham?" The answer to this very important question is four-fold.

The Blessing of Abraham is...

1. The Governing Influence of His mighty hand over our lives.
2. An Anointing to Prosper in every situation.
3. The Power for Total Obedience to God in every situation.
4. The Power to Manifest Christ-likeness in our human life.

The Power of His Mighty Hand

Then Melchizedek king of Salem brought out bread and wine; he was the priest of God Most High. And he blessed him and said: "Blessed be Abram of God Most High, Possessor of heaven and earth; And blessed be God Most High, Who has delivered your enemies into your hand."

Genesis 14:18-20 NKJV

One of the most important aspects of the blessing of Abraham is *"the governing influence of the hand of the LORD over our lives."* The invisible element that made Abraham unstoppable and unbeatable was the inner workings of God's sovereign hand in all of Abraham's affairs. Even though Abraham had made a grave mistake in telling the king of Egypt that Sarah was his sister instead of his wife, God stopped the Egyptian king from killing Abraham once his deception was discovered. This is what happens when the hand of God is over our life. Lying to Pharaoh, who was considered to be a god by many in Egypt, was an offense punishable by death, but Abraham was spared from this sentence and in fact was allowed to keep the gold and silver, livestock and servants that Pharaoh had given him, and was granted safe passage out of Egypt.

ABRAHAM GAVE TITHES TO A "KING." SINCE EVERY "KING" HAS A "KINGDOM," IT IS SAFE TO ASSUME THAT ABRAHAM'S TITHES WERE USED TO SUPPORT A KINGDOM.

By all practical means, Abraham should have been killed for bringing embarrassment to the Egyptian Crown. But God's intervention had scared the living daylights out of the king of Egypt. Pharaoh was so afraid of the hand of God that he refused to institute the normal protocol for punishing those who had insulted the crown. Abraham and Sarah came out of Egypt unharmed and their material possessions were not confiscated. The governing influence of the power of God's hand over Abraham's life had placed a "restraining order" on demonic powers and stopped them from destroying this marriage. My dear friend, this is what I call the blessing of Abraham.

"The victorious invaders then plundered Sodom and Gomorrah and headed for home, taking with them all the spoils of war and the food supplies. They also captured Lot— Abram's nephew who lived in Sodom—and carried off everything he owned. But one of Lot's men escaped and reported everything to Abram the Hebrew, who was living near the oak grove belonging to Mamre the Amorite. Mamre and his relatives, Eshcol and Aner, were Abram's allies."

Genesis 14:11-13

When the man who had escaped the invasion of the country of Sodom, came to Abraham the Hebrew who lived in the plains of Mamre, he told him that the foreign invaders had kidnapped his nephew Lot and his entire family. When Abraham heard this, he took an army of 318 men who were trained in his own house and went after the foreign invaders. When he found them, Abraham ambushed them in the night and completely destroyed this formidable invading horde, which had previously destroyed five other nations. Abraham rescued Lot and everybody else who had been captured with him. Abraham also recovered all the treasures of gold and silver which the invading horde had taken from the country of Sodom. *How could a man with an army of only 318 men destroy foreign armies who had hundreds of thousands of trained soldiers?*

" Then Melchizedek king of Salem brought out bread and wine; he was the priest of God Most High. And he blessed him and said: 'Blessed be Abram of God Most High, Possessor of heaven and earth; And blessed be God Most High, Who has delivered your enemies into your hand.'"

Genesis 14:18-20 NKJV

Melchizedek the Priest of God Most High tells us why Abraham was able to defeat such a large army with only a handful of men. Melchizedek (the King-priest) hinted to Abraham that *God's invisible hand had been working mightily behind the scenes while Abraham and his men fought on the battlefield.* The foreign armies saw

Abraham and his men, but in the realm of the spirit they were fighting against the Lord of hosts. We must count ourselves among the favored ones of God, whenever the Lord chooses to place His mighty hand over the affairs of our lives.

The governing influence of the hand of the LORD over our lives not only aids us in battle, but it also helps to form and fashion us in a manner that is pleasing to the Lord. Dr. Jonathan David likes to say that God can only trust and use a man whose life His own hands have formed and fashioned. When God knows that He is the one who has formed and fashioned our life, nothing can stop us from entering into our spiritual inheritance. This is the blessing of Abraham which we must desire to come upon our life.

The Anointing to Prosper

"So Abram left Egypt and traveled north into the Negev, along with his wife and Lot and all that they owned. (Abram was very rich in livestock, silver, and gold."

Genesis 13:1-2

One of the most common fears that plagues many people of faith is the fear of success. God wants His people to live in abundance, especially in the area of

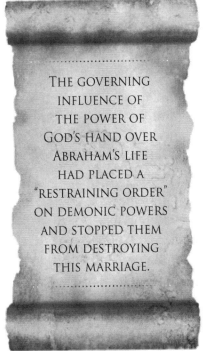

THE GOVERNING INFLUENCE OF THE POWER OF GOD'S HAND OVER ABRAHAM'S LIFE HAD PLACED A "RESTRAINING ORDER" ON DEMONIC POWERS AND STOPPED THEM FROM DESTROYING THIS MARRIAGE.

finances. I have met many Christians who are terrified of financial prosperity, because they are convinced that money is the root of all evil, even though the Scriptures are clear that *"the love of money and not money itself is the root of all evil."* Many Christians in the United States and in the global Church have been repulsed and disgusted by the excessive self-indulgence of some self-appointed prosperity teachers and also by the apparent lack of financial integrity by some in the prosperity camp. This has caused some critics to feel like a Christian should not have a lot of money.

This sense of disappointment over the excesses of some prosperity preachers has caused many in the Body of Christ to conclude that the prosperity message is not of God. Whereas I would not consider myself as a typical prosperity teacher, I know that physical and financial prosperity are an integral part of the blessing of Abraham. This would explain why the Scriptures go to the extent of uncovering the fact that Abraham was not a poor man. On the contrary, Abraham would be considered to be a multibillionaire in today's economy. This means that the blessing of Abraham comes with a supernatural anointing to prosper financially.

> *"When Isaac planted his crops that year, he harvested a hundred times more grain than he planted, for the Lord blessed him. He became a very rich man, and his wealth continued to grow. He acquired so many flocks of sheep and goats, herds of cattle, and servants that the Philistines became jealous of him."*
>
> Genesis 26:12-14

After the death of Abraham, the blessing of Abraham was transferred to his son, Isaac. Almost immediately we begin to see the same grace for prosperity in Isaac's life. Demonic powers manipulated the climate and a demonically-engineered famine dried up the flow of water in the area where Isaac was living. Isaac almost made the greatest mistake of his life when he decided to go down to Egypt to shield himself from the famine. *There was an immediate interception from the priestly Order of Melchizedek when God suddenly appeared to Isaac and warned him against going down to Egypt.* God instructed him to remain in the famished land.

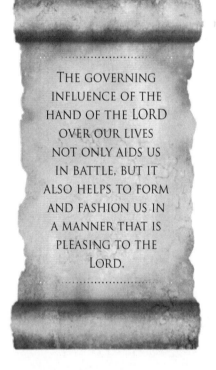

THE GOVERNING INFLUENCE OF THE HAND OF THE LORD OVER OUR LIVES NOT ONLY AIDS US IN BATTLE, BUT IT ALSO HELPS TO FORM AND FASHION US IN A MANNER THAT IS PLEASING TO THE LORD.

After this time of the God encounter, Isaac did something that made no natural sense. He decided to plant seed in the dry land. What happened next underscores what really happens once the blessing of Abraham becomes fully operational in our life. Isaac reaped a harvest of a hundred fold within the same year. ***The anointing (or grace) to prosper which comes with the blessing of Abraham had changed the nature of the soil and quickened the planted seed in a very powerful way.*** The grace to prosper which comes with the blessing of Abraham caused Isaac to become rich in gold, silver, material possessions and in male and female servants. Isaac became so wealthy that his prosperity attracted the envy of the Philistines. When is the last time your neighbors envied you because you were so blessed financially?

To refuse to believe in financial and material prosperity in the light of these passages of Scripture is to operate on the peripherals of spiritual ignorance. I truly believe that there is a place of true biblical prosperity which operates outside the confines of mere human greed. I also believe that this place of true biblical prosperity is found by adhering to the apostolic admonishment of the apostle John.

"Beloved, I pray that you may prosper in all things and be in health, just as your soul prospers."

3 John 1:2

The Power of Total Obedience

And Abraham picked up the knife to kill his son as a sacrifice. At that moment the angel of the Lord called to him from heaven, "Abraham! Abraham!" "Yes," Abraham replied. "Here I am!" "Don't lay a hand on the boy!" the angel said. "Do not hurt him in any way, for now I know that you truly fear God. You have not withheld from me even your son, your only son."

Genesis 22:10-12

One of the most critical aspects of the blessing of Abraham is "the power for total obedience to God which accompanies this blessing." We are living in an age where the moral and spiritual decline of the world we live in and even that of the Church has reached alarming proportions. We are currently dealing with the emergence of a hip-hop generation within the global Church which has never known the place of total obedience to God. Many pastors are ministering to a generation of Christians who want to drink from the cup of the blessing but refuse to drink from the cup of Obedience. Many Christians in the global Church have lost the power for total obedience to God which was displayed in Abraham's life. This is why we need to lay hold of the blessing of Abraham, which is enhanced by tithing into the priestly Order of Melchizedek and as well as walking by faith.

When God gave Abraham a difficult and ridiculous instruction to sacrifice Isaac, the son of his old age, Abraham did not even hesitate. Never mind that Sarah his beloved wife would have killed him first before allowing him to lay his hands on their son. I really believe that had Abraham told her what God had told him to do, she would have resisted him profusely. How many fathers do you know of who would have done what God asked Abraham to do? Not very many, I dare say. What God told Abraham to do required extreme obedience to God. This is why Abraham is the only man in human history who is truly qualified to be called the father of faith.

ONE OF THE MOST CRITICAL ASPECTS OF THE BLESSING OF ABRAHAM IS "THE POWER FOR TOTAL OBEDIENCE TO GOD WHICH ACCOMPANIES THIS BLESSING."

The lack of obedience to God is destroying many ministries and diminishing the impact of the Kingdom of God on the affairs of nations. The greatest need of the global Church is to find this place of total obedience to God. The blessing of Abraham is not limited to financial prosperity. In its highest form, the blessing of Abraham is revealed by this *"supernatural ability to obey God without question."* This mentality of total obedience to God is the spiritual mindset that we must all fight for zealously.

The Manifestation of Christ-likeness in Our Life

"And I will put enmity, Between you and the woman, And between your seed and her Seed; He shall bruise your head, And you shall bruise His heel."

Genesis 3:15 NKJV

The epicenter of the manifestation of the blessing of Abraham is the manifestation of Christ-likeness in the lives of ordinary men and women. When Adam and Eve disobeyed God's command and ate of the tree of the knowledge of good and evil, they lost their Kingdom authority and dominion. Their kingly authority over the earth was transferred to an "unemployed Cherub called Lucifer." Sin and death agencies entered the world. Since then mankind has been ravaged by sin and terrorized by an inherent fear of death.

In the midst of the spiritual chaos which was created by Adam and Eve's rebellion to God's divine authority God released a prophecy of redemption and recovery through the coming of a violent Messianic-Seed through the loins of the woman. God promised the devil that this Messianic-Seed shall crush his head and restore mankind to their God-given destiny and spiritual inheritance. After about four thousand years of recorded human history outside the gates of Eden, God sent forth His Son, born of a woman, under the Law to destroy the works of the devil. The apostle Paul lets us know that our Lord Jesus Christ was the Messianic-Seed that God had promised to give to Abraham thousands of years earlier.

Now to Abraham and his Seed were the promises made. He does not say, "And to seeds," as of many, but as of one, "And to your Seed," who is Christ.

Galatians 3:16, NKJV

God had promised Abraham that through this promised Messianic-Seed, He would bless all the nations and make Abraham the father of many

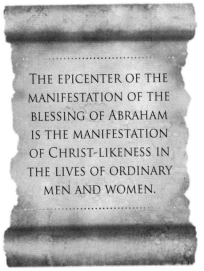

THE EPICENTER OF THE MANIFESTATION OF THE BLESSING OF ABRAHAM IS THE MANIFESTATION OF CHRIST-LIKENESS IN THE LIVES OF ORDINARY MEN AND WOMEN.

nations. The most fascinating aspect of the life of the Lord Jesus Christ lies in the fact that He was both the "Sand-seed and Star-seed" of Abraham. Jesus Christ is the Seed of David who was and is destined to rule the nations with a rod of Iron. The Scriptures declare that whosoever believes on this Messianic-Seed of Abraham is forgiven of their sin and passes from death to life. This Messianic-Seed of Abraham is also the one who made provision for the free gift of divine salvation to the Jew first and then to the Gentile also. When men and women from all the nations of the world respond to the preaching of the gospel, they instantly become children of Abraham through the power of the Holy Spirit. Henceforth it's through the Messianic-Seed that Abraham truly becomes the father of many nations.

A New Way of Living

"And so, dear brothers and sisters, we can boldly enter heaven's Most Holy Place because of the blood of Jesus. By his death, Jesus opened a new and life-giving way

through the curtain into the Most Holy Place. And since we have a great High Priest who rules over God's house."

Hebrews 10:19-21

It is my deepest prayer that your prayerful reading of this book has opened up new pathways in the realms of the Spirit for a new way of living. The priestly Order of Melchizedek is the most powerful spiritual order and priesthood that God ever gave to His Kingdom citizens. I sincerely hope that you now realize that as a New Testament believer, you are under the eternal priestly Order of Melchizedek and not under the Levitical priesthood. As we have observed, the priestly Order of Melchizedek comes with great power and innumerable blessings. *Welcome to a new way of living and a more excellent way of tithing.*

It is my heartfelt prayer that reading this book has shifted your technology of tithing from the Malachi 3:8-12 tithing model to the Genesis 14:18-20 tithing model. I trust that from now on your tithe will be in accordance with the priestly Order of Melchizedek and not patterned after the Levitical priesthood. I trust that you now realize that the "Lost Key" which opens up the whole priestly Order of Melchizedek *is the tithing model that is based upon the prophetic pattern of tithing that was set by Abraham when he met Melchizedek in the Valley of the Kings.*

I am confident that after reading this book, you will make a mental migration from the attitude of **"paying your tithes"** to the attitude of **"giving your tithes."** *I believe that under this new way of living you will never give your tithes to God because you are afraid of being cursed. To the contrary, I want to challenge you to give your tithes because you cannot afford not to give the King of the heavenly Jerusalem, His proper endowment of tithe.* I trust that you will give your tithes out of a deep love and deep-seated desire to honor the Lord Jesus Christ (Priest of God Most High).

" So Jacob served seven years for Rachel, and they seemed only a few days to him because of the love he had for her."

Genesis 29:20

Please remember that Jacob worked for Laban for fourteen years in order to earn the right to marry Rachel, the love of his life. Those fourteen years seemed like fourteen days! How can fourteen years of hard labor seem like fourteen days? The answer is stunningly simple, but deeply profound. Jacob was in love and love makes you do crazy things. A mother's love for her child can compel her to fight a hungry lion, just to protect her child. Such is the power of love. I trust that your

•317•

tithing experience will be greatly enhanced by changing your primary motivation for tithing from one of fear and self centeredness to one of a lover stricken by the magic of love. I once heard Pastor Mike Bickle of Kansas City say that, "a lover can outwork a servant any day!" I could not agree more. I trust that under this new way of living, tithing will now become one of your "greatest joys and the least of your struggles." If this is the spiritual position which this book has placed or positioned you in, then welcome to a new way of living in God's Kingdom.

LIFE APPLICATION SECTION

Point to Ponder:

The most fascinating aspect of the life of the Lord Jesus Christ lies in the fact that He was both the "sand seed and star seed" of Abraham, who was destined to rule the nations with a rod of Iron. The blessing of Abraham is not limited to financial prosperity; it also includes the supernatural ability to obey God without question.

Verse to Remember:

And Abraham picked up the knife to kill his son as a sacrifice. At that moment the angel of the LORD called to him from heaven, "Abraham! Abraham!" "Yes," Abraham replied. "Here I am!" "Don't lay a hand on the boy!" the angel said. "Do not hurt him in any way, for now I know that you truly fear God. You have not withheld from me even your son, your only son."

Genesis 22:10-12

Questions to Consider:

• What is the blessing of Abraham?

• Is there an anointing to prosper?

• How does Jesus Christ make Abraham the father of many nations?

JOURNAL YOUR THOUGHTS

SUGGESTED TITHING PRAYER:

"Heavenly Father, thank you that I am the New Creation and that I am a member of the Order of Melchizedek under the headship of the Lord Jesus Christ. You have called me to be a King and a Priest in the earth. I come boldly before your Throne of Grace to offer sacrifices of praise and adoration. You are the King of the Universe and my creator and as such you are worthy of my adoration and honor. I bring my "tithes of honor" to your throne room in a spirit of heartfelt humility and honor.

I am tithing not because I am afraid that you might Curse me if I do not tithe. I am already blessed with every spiritual blessing in Christ Jesus (Ephesians 1:3). I am tithing to acknowledge your Lordship over my life and property. I tithe to excite the supernatural release of the heavenly bread and wine that I need to achieve my destiny. I tithe because I know that my tithes shall be used to advance your Kingdom in the earth and I love your Kingdom. I tithe to activate the technology of divine interception in my life. I tithe to shut down the engines of Greed in my life and ministry. I tithe to demonstrate that I am a faithful steward of the mysteries of God. I tithe to overturn and overthrow the train of the king of Sodom that is headed my way. I tithe to sanctify all the channels of wealth creation in my life. I tithe to confirm the covenant of faith that God made with my father Abraham. I tithe to activate my God-given, infinite imagination for multimillion-dollar business ideas and witty inventions. In Jesus name I pray. Amen.

Made in the USA
San Bernardino, CA
07 November 2013